MW00916081

Game On!
Sensible Answers about Video Games and Media Violence

Courtney Plante, PhD
Craig A. Anderson, PhD
Johnie J. Allen, MSc
Christopher L. Groves, PhD
Douglas A. Gentile, PhD

ZenGen LLC

Ames, Iowa
© 2020

The authors wish to thank Tracie-Lynn Lamoreux and Paula Rotger González for their help hunting typos.

Table of Contents

Introduction:

Six Critical Questions to Begin this Book

1 - How do I use this book?

The Short Answer:

This book is organized into a series of questions, each divided into a short, simple answer and a long, more nuanced answer. We recommend using this book in one of three ways, depending on what you want from the book. One way is to read through only the short answers, giving you just a brief overview of the media violence research – enough to help you make an informed decision, win an argument or answer a nagging question! Another way is to treat this book like a reference manual, the way you would a textbook or encyclopedia: Start by reading the question you're interested in and jump around from topic to topic as you wish. The third way is to read the book cover-to-cover, from start to finish. This method is the most thorough and is designed to ease you into the heart of the media violence research in the most logical way possible. It also gives you an explanation for each answer, as well as references to relevant academic papers so that skeptics can check out the research and make up their minds for themselves!

The Long Answer:

Different readers will be interested in what this book has to say for very different reasons. Parents will want to find out if they should worry about what their child is watching. Gamers will read the book skeptically, ready to challenge the ridiculous things they've heard in the news about what media violence research "proves." Students will borrow the book from the school library to help them write a research paper for class, or it may be assigned to them as part of a class on psychology. Politicians and policy-makers may find the book helpful when trying to summarize vast amounts of research on media violence into a handful of talking points.

To cater to such a broad audience, we have designed the book around a series of frequently asked questions, each of which has a short answer and a long answer. Depending on which of these answers you read, and the order in which you read the questions, you should be able to get exactly what you're looking for out of this book.

This book can be read in several different ways, depending on your interests, needs, and timeframe. For parents, or really anyone just needing a quick answer to a practical question, just read the *Short Answers*: They skip all of the unnecessary detail and give you the straightforward answer you're looking for.[a] In

---

[a] Think of them as the kind of answers you *wish* your politician would give!

fact, you could read all of these short answers in about an hour, allowing you to get a fairly good overview of the research. You don't even need to check it out of the library or buy it from the store![b]

But wait, there's more! This book can *also* be treated as a reference, the same way you'd treat a dictionary, textbook, or Wikipedia. Kept on the shelf (or tablet, since this *is* the 21st century!), this book serves as a handy go-to when you have a specific question. In this way, we suggest you read the *Long Answer* sections, which give you a fuller explanation of the topic in which you are interested, complete with all the nerdy scientific evidence to back it up! These deeper explanations are useful for students (e.g., a handy source of references for any research paper), gamers (e.g., back up your position and win internet arguments!), and parents (e.g., explaining the reasons for the policies by organizations like the American Academy of Pediatrics). Parents may also find these answers helpful when discussing with their children the reasons for household rules about media use.

Another key feature of the book's structure is that each section is designed to stand on its own, but also directs the reader to other sections with related information, in the same way an encyclopedia does. Unlike other reference books, however, this one can also be read cover-to-cover to provide the most comprehensive look at the research (good luck trying to read an encyclopedia cover-to-cover!)

As you read this book, it's important to keep in mind three caveats. First: like a dictionary or an encyclopedia, this book is intentionally *very* self-referential, meaning we frequently direct interested readers to jump ahead or back in the book to learn more about related topics. For example, in Question #52, we answer a question we get a lot from concerned parents: "If my child has problems with aggressive behavior, should I take their violent media away?" Within this question, we reference Questions #46 and #47, both of which discuss the effectiveness of different strategies for limiting children's media use. Like a dictionary or encyclopedia, the answer to Question #52 is written so that you don't *have* to read any other questions to get a good answer to the question. Nevertheless, you might find your interest piqued and *want* to know more about other topics while reading (anyone who's searched for an answer on Wikipedia and found themselves spending the entire afternoon hopping from page to page knows how interesting it can be to follow your curiosity!) As you read this book, we encourage you to dog-ear the heck out of the pages (literally or digitally), jump back and forth between topics, and let your curiosity get the better of you!

The second important caveat is that this book should be considered an *introduction* to media violence research, not the final word on the subject. The information in this book is presented in a very condensed, summarized form – we've taken the liberty of streamlining tens of thousands of pages of research into one convenient, easy-to-carry book! We also realize that most people don't have a

---

[b] That said, we'd appreciate it if you considered buying it anyway! =)

3

degree in psychology, so we've stripped away the boring technical discussions researchers have about the subtleties of experimental, correlational, and longitudinal designs and statistics. The result of our efforts is that the research is quite easy-to-digest. But beware! This streamlining might lead you to the false impression that social scientists don't spend a lot of time discussing technical matters like sampling issues, statistical limitations, or alternative explanations. In actuality, a considerable portion of the published studies, review papers, handbooks, and encyclopedia articles that we cite are devoted to these very topics!

In a similar vein, we want to be crystal clear that it's *impossible* to learn everything there is to know about media violence research from an afternoon of reading or from a single book. Think of it like learning a language: Reading the dictionary cover-to-cover won't make you a fluent English-speaker – ultimately it's a *skill* that needs years of practice to master. Similarly, reading this will not, by itself, turn you into a skilled social psychologist. The skills involved in designing, analyzing, and critiquing studies takes *years* of focused study on statistics, psychology, and research methodology – none of which this book can give you. What it *can* do, however, is give you a good summary of what media violence researchers have found after decades of study. It also will make you a better consumer of scientific research – one who challenges the claims of laypersons, journalists, and politicians about media violence research, rather than simply taking them at their word.

The final caveat (we promise!) is that media violence research is still very much an active field. As new evidence becomes available, some of the answers in this book may be overturned or modified. This is less likely to happen for the answers based on dozens or even hundreds of studies, and is more likely to happen for research areas that are still very new. For example, decades of research have shown that there's a causal relationship between violent media and aggression (see Question #11), so this conclusion isn't about to change. However, newer research, like questions about whether realistic violent media content is more or less harmful than cartoonish violent media, (Question #18), questions about media addiction (Question #42), and questions about the effects of media on attention (Question #37) may still surprise us and change dramatically in the upcoming decade. While it's more likely than not that future research will tend to support the current answers, a good scientist must remain open to the possibility that new studies may change our understanding of how the world works. In short, treat the conclusions in this book as a summary of what we know *today*, not as the infallible word of God, Allah, Jehovah, Google, or your preferred deity/ies.

2 - Who are you?

The Short Answer:

"We" are Courtney Plante, PhD, Craig A. Anderson, PhD, Johnie J. Allen, MSc, Christopher Groves, PhD, and Douglas A. Gentile, PhD, and we're all social or developmental psychologists. Or, to put it another way, we're scientists who specialize in designing studies that test how screen media (TV shows, movies, video games) affect the way people think, feel, and behave. Dr. Plante has been studying video game violence for five years, starting with research that he did for his doctoral dissertation. Dr. Anderson has been conducting research on media and aggression for more than thirty years and is renowned as one of the world's foremost experts on the subject. Johnie J. Allen and Chris Groves are current and former graduate students (respectively) of Dr. Anderson, specializing in researching media effects on aggression, prosocial behavior, well-being, and gaming addiction. Dr. Gentile has conducted research on both positive and negative effects of media on children and adolescents, including media violence, prosocial media, and video game addiction for more than 20 years, and is known as one of the world's top experts on these topics.

The Long Answer:

We – the authors of this book – are all experimental psychologists who specialize in the field of social or developmental psychology. Collectively, we also have expertise in personality development and cognitive psychology. Like true academics, we just gave you a mouthful of words that probably mean very little to you. To help, let's break that job description down into its basic parts. First and foremost, we're psychologists. This means that it's our job to study behavior scientifically: What causes people to behave a certain way, and why? As it turns out, there are a lot of different ways you can study behavior. For example, you can sit in an armchair and speculate about all the things that might cause someone to act a certain way. Alternatively, you can find people who are doing a particular behavior and find out what they all have in common. Another way is to observe people trying to change their behavior and watch to see what does and doesn't work. All of these are just some of the many ways you *could* study behavior. It just so happens that our preferred way to study behavior, as hinted at in the job title "experimental psychologist," is to conduct experiments on people. In other words, we study behavior and its causes by running experiments on people and seeing how they behave under different conditions. And, when it's unethical or impractical to use an experiment to study a research question, we use *other* scientifically valid methods like correlational studies. For more information about these types of scientific studies, see Question #9.

We conduct experiments on people to learn about behavior. But what makes us "social" psychologists? Is it because we're particularly *friendly* and *likable* psychologists? (*We* certainly like to think we are!) Nope. The word "social" in our job title can be thought of as meaning "environmental" or "situational." We're psychologists who study how our surroundings influence the way we think, feel, and behave. When you think about it, a *lot* of things around us affect our behavior. These things include other people *directly* (e.g., my behavior changes when my boss is looking over my shoulder), other people *indirectly* (e.g., I'm less likely to litter because I know that society would disapprove), and even non-human things (e.g., I'm more likely to wear shorts when the temperature outside is very hot). As social psychologists, we specialize in understanding how these situational factors influence our behavior. This is somewhat different from other psychologists, like cognitive or clinical psychologists, who study how the things going on *inside* your head affect your behavior.[a]

Okay, so we're a group of experimental social psychologists, which means we've spent years learning how to design and critique experiments to test how things in our environment affect the way we think, feel, and behave. But there are a *lot* of "things in our environment" – far too many for any one person to be an expert in all of them! Even a behavior as simple as reading this book is affected by hundreds, even thousands, of short- and long-term environmental influences: Your history of learning how to read, your educational background, whether other people are around, the level of noise in the room, the last time you ate, whether you've got kids or are studying for a class – to name just a few! To make the study of environmental factors more manageable, we, like all researchers, focus our attention on specific environmental factors that interest us. In our case, it happens to be screen media, which refers to any entertainment or information sources that involve looking at evideo screens (e.g., television shows, films, video games, the internet, mobile devices). Together, the five of us share a common interest in studying how screen media affects the way people think, feel, and behave. And, as experimental psychologists, we agree that the best way to study media effects is to carefully design experiments (and other types of scientifically valid data-based studies) to test hypotheses about these effects, rather than speculating from an armchair, asking friends for anecdotes, or relying on what our gut tells us is true.

---

[a] Just because we specialize in studying the effects of situations on behavior doesn't mean that we *ignore* what's going on inside our head! In fact, most psychologists recognize that you can't get a complete picture of human behavior without understanding who a person is, what's going in their head, and the situation around them. We just happen to focus on the last of these factors more than other psychologists do.

Our conclusions about what's true or false are based on scientific evidence-based data collection, not opinion, values, or preconceived notion.[b]

Even though we all share an interest in understanding how media affect us, the five of us *do* differ when it comes to which questions we think are the most interesting. Courtney (Dr. Plante), for example, is interested in the role of immersion in media effects. His studies test whether viewers *need* to feel immersed in a piece of media to be affected by it (see Question #26 for more discussion about immersion in media). For example, if a violent television show is playing in the same room that you're in, but you're not paying attention to it because you're talking with a friend, that media may have less of an effect on you than it would if you were giving the show your uninterrupted attention. In a related vein, Courtney also studies what it takes to make and break immersion in a piece of media (e.g., a cell phone in a movie theatre likely angers us because it *breaks* our immersion into the film!) Courtney has been doing this work since his graduate school days at the University of Waterloo. He is currently Assistant Professor at Bishops University in Quebec, after spending two years working with Craig (Dr. Anderson) as a postdoctoral fellow funded by the Social Sciences and Humanities Research Council of Canada and two years as an instructor at MacEwan University.

Craig's initial interest in media effects came from two very different sources. First, beginning in the 1980s, he and his graduate students were developing a general model to explain when, why, and how people behave aggressively or violently toward one another (see Questions #7 and #8 for more on aggression). While working on this model and reviewing existing theories of aggression, he realized that any model claiming to explain *all* interpersonal aggression *needed* to be able to explain the many studies up to that point showing that TV and movie violence increase aggression in viewers. Second, Craig was a gamer himself (one might call him an "old-school" gamer, though not when he's within earshot!). He started playing video games at their origin in the late 1970s, during the final years of his PhD at Stanford University (1980). These two factors – his professional interest in aggressive behavior and his personal interest in video games – led him to do some of the earliest (and simplest) studies on the effects of violent video game on players' thoughts, feelings and behaviors. In recent years, Craig's research interests have expanded to include *positive* effects of prosocial video games (see Question #41) and the positive and negative effects of fast-paced media on attention skills and attention problems (see Question #37). Furthermore, Craig has been recognized by leading scientific societies for his contributions to and expertise in social and personality psychology. For instance, he has been recognized as a Fellow of the Association for Psychological Science (1988), Fellow of the American Psychological Association (1990), President of the

---

[b] Which isn't to say we don't *have* opinions, values, or preconceived notions! But we've learned, through years of schooling, how to set them aside and let the data do the driving!

International Society for Research on Aggression (2010-2012), and an Eminent Psychologist of the Modern Era (2014). More recently he received the Society for the Psychological Study of Social Issues *Kurt Lewin Award* in 2017 (their top award for research with impact on society), and the Society of Personality and Social Psychology *Distinguished Scholar Award* (2018).

Johnie's interest in media research currently focuses on how media (especially video games) affect our sense of morality and morally relevant behavior (e.g., helping others in need). He also studies how identifying with fictional characters in stories might cause the effects of media on us to be stronger (see Question #26). Some of his work includes studies where players make immoral decisions in video games (e.g., killing innocent people) and then report whether or not they feel guilt afterward, particularly for those who identify more strongly with the character doing the immoral deeds. More recently, Johnie has begun to explore how video games (and the way we play them) can affect our well-being and which players may develop problems with gaming if video games become their only source of satisfaction (see Question #42 for more on the topic of video game addiction). Johnie is currently conducting this research as Craig's doctoral student.

Christopher Groves' interests in the field are fairly broad. Chris studies the effects of violent media use on aggression (see Questions #11 and #12), but also studies prosocial media effects, gaming addiction (see Question #42), and the effects of media use on attention problems. His recent work has focused on better understanding the challenges of doing experiments on media effects: Many people (including researchers!) underestimate how difficult it is to conduct a well-designed media effects experiment (see Question #16). As such, he is working to better understand how researchers in this field can improve the quality of their studies (and how studies are interpreted!) He recently graduated as Craig's PhD student and is currently an assistant professor at University of Wisconsin Oshkosh.

Douglas Gentile's training was as a child developmental psychologist (although much of his work fits in with social psychology as well). As such, he is most interested in what contributes to healthy child development. Given how much time children and adolescents spend with screen media, he became interested in which uses were healthy and which might pose risks. He put a lot of quarters into *Space Invaders* and *Asteroids*, but really got interested in media effects when he became a game coder for an early multiplayer online game (which he still helps to run). He noticed that the behavior that occurred in the game was real human social behavior, even though it was "just" a game. For example, when someone flirted with you in a game, you would react humanly despite knowing you were looking at pixels on a screen. This realization sparked an interest in studying how media influence us, both intentionally (e.g., advertising) and unintentionally (e.g., media violence). He has studied multiple media (e.g., TV, video games, music, movies, social networks), and a wide range of issues, such as how prosocial media influence empathy and helping behavior, media violence and aggression, parental monitoring of media, the value of media ratings systems, and is one of the top researchers in the world on the topic of video game addiction. Douglas has been recognized by leading scientific societies for his contributions to and expertise in media psychology. For instance, he has been recognized as a Fellow of the Association for Psychological Science (2017), Fellow of the American Psychological Association (2016), and was awarded for Distinguished Scientific Contributions to Media Psychology by the American Psychological Association (2010).

Douglas has been highly involved in media creation as well as studying media effects. He has a nationally-syndicated comedy music radio show (The Tom and Doug Show), he has a television show that airs regionally, he has had films shown in juried film festivals, he has coded his own video games and done voice-acting for other video games. He was the Director of Research for the National Institute on Media and the Family for 11 years, and has been a professor of psychology at Iowa State University since 2003.

It is important to note that although all of our primary expertise is in social or developmental psychology, our research skills were not developed in a vacuum. Over time, researchers develop some familiarity with concepts and methodologies from other areas (e.g., a cardiologist may specialize in heart disease, but they've likely learned a thing or two about the lungs along the way!) As such, we have also collaborated with researchers from other areas of psychology, including cognitive psychology (the study of mental processes such as attention), personality psychology (the study of what makes people different from one another), developmental psychology, (the study of how people grow and change over time), and cognitive neuroscience (the study of how the brain functions while its user is doing various tasks). In fact, when studying media violence effects, researchers from different backgrounds frequently interact to better understand the topic from all sides (see Question #10 for more information about the various disciplines who study the effects of media on consumers). Over the years, we have had the great fortune to work with many experts from around the world who have helped to broaden our understanding of different techniques and perspectives on media violence effects.

Figure 2.1 illustrates eight psychological specialties that contribute to our understanding of media effects. We have used all of the approaches in our various studies.

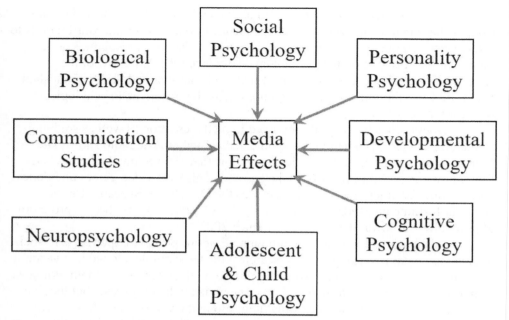

Figure 2.1. Who Studies Media Effects?

In sum – the authors of this book are all psychologists whose research interests involve, in one fashion or another, understanding the ways that media influence us. Our academic background informs our theoretical understanding of media effects, the evidence we use to support our claims, and the studies we conduct to gather that evidence. As we discuss in Question #3, this background makes us ideally suited to answer questions about the effects of violent media using scientific evidence, something that politicians, gamers, and parents – who normally rely on opinion, anecdote, or intuition – typically don't do.

3 - Why should I trust what you say about media violence?

The Short Answer:

Social psychologists have a specialized set of skills which makes them *ideally* qualified to answer scientific questions about media violence and behavior. As scientists, our goal is to discover truths about the world, whatever they might be. A scientist's conclusions are not based on intuition, wishful thinking, religious belief, political ideology, or their own anecdotal experience. The same cannot be said of most people who weigh in on the subject of media violence. Our conclusions are based on more than a thousand studies from the past 60 years conducted by *hundreds* of scientists worldwide, all with the common goal of better understanding truths about human behavior. Ultimately, the question of whether media violence affects us is a social psychological one, and is best informed by experts in social psychology and closely related fields. The idea of turning to relevant experts when answering a question is the reason why we turn to a physician for questions about physical health, a mechanic for engine problems, or a lawyer for legal advice.

The Long Answer:

What would you do if you suddenly woke up in the middle of the night experiencing a shortness of breath and chest pains? You could respond in many ways – including doing nothing at all – but we imagine *most* people would make seeing a physician a very high priority. But let's ask a somewhat silly, if important question: *Why* would you seek out the advice of a physician? Why not ask a lawyer or an auto mechanic for *their* advice? After all, lawyers are professionals with university degrees from prestigious institutions of learning, and it's likely your mechanic has specialized training and years of experience fixing broken machines. And chances are good that if you asked a lawyer or a mechanic for *their* opinion about your shortness of breath and chest pain, they could probably offer you some reasonable-sounding advice, perhaps based on their own experience, things they've seen on television, a gut feeling, or just good-old common sense. But, in that frantic moment at 3am, with your life on the line, would you trust what your lawyer or your mechanic had to say? Why or why not?

We're fairly confident that most readers would side with the physician over the lawyer or the mechanic. We're also fairly confident we know the reason why: It's a matter of expertise. You probably recognize that neither a lawyer's nor or a mechanic's skills and expertise qualify them to make important medical decisions. Of course, this doesn't mean that lawyers and mechanics are unskilled –

11

far from it! Our lawyer would be the first person we would call for legal advice, and who better than a mechanic to fix the weird noises coming from under the hood of our car? But you chose the physician for your health problem because you realize that having expertise in *one* domain doesn't make you an expert in *all* domains. Most of us understand that decisions about our physical health are best left to physicians, who have developed skills and knowledge through focused studying of the accumulated efforts of thousands of medical researchers. Even the best lawyer or mechanic in their field lacks the relevant expertise that makes the physician the most qualified of the three to address a medical issue.

With this same principle in mind, we can ask which experts are best-suited to answer questions about the effects of media on behavior. The question is, at its core, a social psychological one: It asks about the influence of an environmental factor (media) on behavior, the focal point of the field of psychology (see Question #2 for more on the definition of social psychology). As a social psychological question, those who have spent years conducting research on the topic, publishing in relevant scientific journals, and who have been recognized by the top scientific societies as the leading experts on the subject are the most ideally qualified to answer it.

Of course, plenty of other people have something to say about media violence. In fact, when it comes to media violence, most people have at least *some* opinion about it: Concerned parents, gamers, politicians, game developers, media lobbyists, and political activists all routinely give their two cents on the matter. What sets social psychologists apart from these other groups, however, is the same thing that sets a lawyer or a mechanic apart from a layperson: They have knowledge and experience that gives them an evidence-based understanding of the subject. Most people who have an opinion about media violence effects tend to base their opinions on intuition, wishful thinking, anecdotes, political values, or emotion. It can be tempting to trust these opinions, especially if they seem common-sense or if they are expressed with supreme confidence. But it simply doesn't make sense to favor an opinion over the conclusions of expert researchers who have come to their position through a review of the existing scientific research. It would be like trusting a layperson to perform your heart surgery, defend you in court, or install after-market pistons in your Chevy 350 small block.

To be fair, *some* politicians, activists, or concerned parents attempt to become knowledgeable by reading some scientific studies on their own (and such efforts should be commended!). The problem arises, however, when people who have read a small amount of research conclude that they are just as informed as experts. In reality, this is almost never the case. Remember, researchers base their conclusions on a thorough and systematic analysis of dozens, or even hundreds of studies, and spend years learning how to understand, interpret, and critique research on the subject. In short, it's not enough to pick up a copy of a scientific journal and skip ahead to its conclusions: Researchers have to understand the statistics involved, how to properly sample a population, the intricacies of study design, and all of the underlying theory upon which those studies are grounded before they can reasonably assess the strengths and weaknesses of a study (something which becomes apparent in any undergraduate research methods class!). Learning to do science properly is a skill that requires years to hone, just as there's a difference between a skilled surgeon and a person who's thumbed through an anatomy textbook. No matter how well-intentioned you may be, and regardless of how skilled you may be in other areas, there's just no substitute for years of focused study and intensive practice.

At this point, we should probably mention that social psychologists are certainly not the *only* scientific experts on the subject of media violence. There are plenty of examples of experts in other fields who, through considerable time and devoted study, have similarly become experts in media violence effects with different theoretical approaches to the topic. These experts come from the medical sciences (e.g., Dr. Victor Strasburger), developmental psychology (e.g., Dr. Rowell Huesmann, Dr. Paul Boxer), and communications studies (e.g., Dr. Joanne Cantor, Dr. Edward Donnerstein, Dr. Brad Bushman, Dr. Erica Scharrer), and are referenced throughout this book. Despite coming from different backgrounds, these experts all have one thing in common: They approach the study of media violence with at least *some* expertise in social psychological techniques and skills, and employ many of the same methods, theories, and statistical techniques that social psychologists do.

It's also worth noting that even social psychologists who spend *years* studying media effects can reasonably disagree when it comes to the best way to conduct research or how to interpret findings, as you will see in Question #17. At first glance, such disagreements can lead laypersons to believe that experts have no idea what they're talking about, or worse, that their conclusions are just opinions, and are therefore no more valid than anyone else's nonexpert opinion. However, disputes and disagreements are very common across all fields of science. In fact, disagreements between scientists is one of the ways our knowledge improves – by rooting out which of the two competing hypotheses is better supported by the data! Over time, researchers typically reach a consensus, often when enough data have been collected which point to a single conclusion (this point has almost certainly been reached in the media violence literature, as we discuss in Question #11). As a final point, we'd like to make one thing perfectly clear: We're *not* saying that anyone with an appropriate advanced degree or who claims to be an expert should be blindly trusted, nor are we saying that experts cannot be biased or make mistakes. History is *full* of cases of "experts" who have made mistakes or let their personal biases cloud their judgment. Although experts possess knowledge and skills which allow them to make informed decisions about a topic, they aren't *immune* to flaws, fallacies, and human motivation. This is precisely why it's so important to remember that science is never a single expert's opinion about a subject: It's a peer-reviewed, self-correcting process, where the work of every researcher is checked by other experts and where no one's conclusions are totally above criticism.

In this spirt, we, the authors of this book, do not claim to be immune to error or impervious to fault. For this reason, we provide references to back up the claims we make in this book to "show our work," so to speak. In doing so, we invite others to review the information which led us to our conclusions to see whether you reach the same conclusions. We also hope that providing these references will make it clear that our conclusions are not "mere opinion" or wishful thinking, but instead are the result of the collective work of hundreds of scientists.

To summarize: You can trust the conclusions presented in this book, not because we are infallible or immune to mistakes, but because we show that the conclusions are grounded in the same sort of expertise that leads you to trust your physician, but not your mechanic or your lawyer, about that pain in your chest.

4 - Do you just hate violent media and want to ruin it for everyone else?

The Short Answer:

Not at all! It's a popular misconception that researchers studying media violence hate violent media themselves and want it to be banned. Even if this *were* the case, it wouldn't change the fact that research consistently finds that violent media are a risk factor for aggression. That said, most researchers – including the authors of this book – *are* fans of television, films, and video games (*including* violent ones!) Social scientists tend to research topics they find interesting, personally relevant, or have experience with. In other words, it's *better* for a researcher to be a fan themselves: It gives them a first-hand look at the mindset of players/viewers, knowledge about which games/films are popular, and insight into the most relevant questions to consumers. And, fans or not, researchers are ultimately driven by a desire to learn what's true, not a need to dictate what others should or shouldn't watch or do.

The Long Answer:

Critics often assume that media violence researchers are against violent content in principle. As an illustrative example, one of the authors of this book, Craig, has been described by online writers as an "anti-violent video game professor[1]," suggesting that Craig's professional career is devoted solely to stopping violent video games. This particular belief stems from the fact that Craig's own research has found that there is a relationship between playing violent video games and player aggression. The commenter *assumed* that the results of Craig's studies reflect Craig's own feelings about violent media: If his studies found evidence of violent media effects, it *must* mean that Craig wants violent media to be banned! Because of this, laypersons often assume that media violence researchers are on a crusade to ban violent media, and that this leads to biased research being conducted to justify policies, programs, or laws to censor violent media.

Needless to say, these claims make a *lot* of assumptions. Let's break them down one at a time and see whether they hold any water.

To start, it's easy to understand *why* people might assume that media researchers dislike violent media. The field of social psychology is famous for studying societal ills such as war, discrimination, injustice, and apathy. Usually, these topics are studied in the hopes of better understanding them so we can ultimately find a way to put an end to them. The argument makes a lot of sense: Prejudice researchers think prejudice is bad and want to study prejudice so that we, as a society, can learn how to put a stop to it. So doesn't it make sense that media violence researchers study violent media so they can put a stop to aggression by banning violent media?

The argument seems to make sense at first glance, but closer inspection reveals that it has several flaws. First, let's assume for a moment that it's absolutely true that *every* violent media researcher secretly hates violent media and wants to have it banned. Even *if* this were the case, simply *hating* violent media wouldn't be enough to make media violence effects appear out of thin air. As anyone who has tried to reason with a two-year old can tell you, reality does not bend to one's whims. Hundreds of studies conducted by hundreds of different researchers around the world for more than half a century have found that there is a link between violent media and aggression (see Question #11). This is compelling evidence that the link between violent media and aggression is something real that scientists routinely observe – it's not simply something that embittered media violence researchers *wish* were true.

Of course, you *could* argue that the effect isn't real at all, that media researchers simply conduct biased studies and cherry-pick their data to find results that agree with their violent-media-hating beliefs. But if *that* were true, it would mean that hundreds of independent researchers worldwide have been faking or selectively interpreting their results for decades – an international, cross-generational conspiracy! What's more, for this to be the case, every peer-reviewed psychological journal responsible for *publishing* these articles would themselves have had to turn a blind eye to this blatant disregard for proper scientific practice!

Put simply, researchers' actual attitudes toward violent media matter very little in the grand scheme of things. By now, so much research on the subject of violent media has been done that, if there really were no effects, the data would have overwhelmingly shown this to be the case after more than a thousand studies. A researcher wishing the world were flat is not enough to actually make the world flat: Eventually, the evidence accumulates and the truth is revealed. That's the beauty of science!

Returning to the original argument, we can see that it breaks down on other levels as well. For one thing, the effects reported by media researchers are fairly modest in scale – nothing warranting country-wide panic or a state of emergency. Now, let's imagine for a moment that you *were* out to get violent media banned from store shelves. Wouldn't you want to scare people by telling them that violent media plays a *huge* role in aggression and causes untold amounts of violence without any redeeming features? That'd be a sure-fire way to make every parent, politician, and policy-maker take you seriously and try to ban or censor games for the good of society.

But is this how researchers *actually* talk about violent media? Let's have a look at the actual conclusions of a fairly typical media violence paper:

"The influence of violent mass media is best viewed as one of *many* potential factors that influence the risk for violence"[2].

Well, it's not *quite* a moral panic. Perhaps a different one will sound the alarm:

"Clearly, media violence is not the sole cause of aggression. But it is likely that it is one of several causes leading to it. Children with high levels of hostility are more likely to be involved in fights than low-hostile children. If they expose themselves to more video game violence, their odds of being involved in fights increase even more."[3]

When you put it *that* way, the threat of violent media sounds less like a national emergency and more the side effects on an aspirin bottle. If violent media researchers *are* trying to get violent media banned, they're doing a pretty lousy job of it by describing these effects as modest and describing them as just one of *many* risk factors (see Question #14 for more on this). Similarly, many of these same researchers also publish studies showing that media – including violent media – can also have *positive* effect on consumers[4,5] (for more on this, see Question #41). These don't sound like the actions of someone crusading to ban violent media; they sound like boring scientific progress toward a nuanced understanding of violent media effects.[a]

This leads to yet another reason why the argument that researchers are trying to ban violent media is so flawed: Researchers' jobs are that of methodical fact-finders, not legislators, activists, or politicians. We discuss this issue in greater detail in Question #56, but for now it's enough to say that most media researchers chose a career where their job would be to test whether and how media affects consumers. It was not to dictate how consumers *ought* to behave, or what society *ought* to do about violent media. Sure, researchers have their own opinions about what they think is appropriate, and some avoid violent media themselves or limit the amount their children consume. But as a group, researchers typically have little interest in forcing others to do their bidding – that's a politician's job! This isn't unique to media researchers either: Medical researchers recognize that junk food is bad for one's health, but almost none of them are demanding that congress pass laws banning fast food and chocolate! Researchers ultimately want people to be aware when modest risks exist and to make informed decisions. None of the researchers we know, and we know almost all of them, have ever advocated for censorship. The idea of a "moral panic" seems, therefore, to be a false one.

To see why, let's return one last time to the original argument, which assumed that *all* media violence researchers hate violent media. As it turns out, many media violence researchers use violent media themselves and attribute their interest in media research to their own enjoyment of this media. Using ourselves as examples, all of the authors of this book consider ourselves to be fans of video games, including violent ones. Courtney, the lead author, is an avid gamer whose favorite games include violence (*Fallout: New Vegas, Doom 2016, XCom: Enemy*

---

[a] As it turns out, most science is a slow, repetitive, methodical grind toward truth, unlike its portrayal in television shows like *Mythbusters* and *Bill Nye the Science Guy*!

Unknown, and *Shadowrun Returns.*) Seeking to ban violent games would be directly undercutting his favorite hobby! In fact, it was this very hobby that drew Courtney to video game research in the first place, since it let him merge his hobby with his passion for studying human behavior. Being a gamer lets him keep up with what games are popular and advances in gaming technology and allows him to design laboratory studies of video game play that feel more natural for gamers. What's more, being a gamer also gives him the technical skills to modify games for his experiments – skills that a non-gamer might otherwise lack.

And, as noted in Question #3, Courtney is not the only video game player on the team. Both Johnie and Chris are avid gamers who use many of their favorite games in their own research. And as for Craig, he was playing video games (including violent ones) before many readers of this book were even born![b] Douglas has written and voice-acted for games. Craig and Douglas both have been video game enthusiasts for decades and their children grew up playing video games (mostly nonviolent, because of concerns that emerged from the research). Both of them have advocated for the use of video game technology in positive ways for children and adolescents for decades. Neither have ever advocated for the banning or censorship of violent media of any type.

Readers may find themselves asking whether it's hypocritical for media violence researchers to also watch violent media. We would argue "no," for the same reason that a dietician can occasionally eat junk food or a hepatologist (liver doctor) can enjoy a glass of wine with dinner: Acknowledging that an activity has risks is *not* the same thing as calling for it to be banned or judging those who engage in it as bad. In the end, media researchers just want to know the truth about how violent media affects us so that people – themselves included – can make informed decisions about whether they're willing to accept those risks. They want nothing more than to report their findings and leave it to people to decide for themselves whether they want to play violent video games or let their children watch violent media, fully informed about the risks and the ways they can reduce those risks (see Question #51).

References

1. Masnick, M. (2011). Supreme Court says anti-violent video game law violates the first amendment. techdirt. Retrieved from https://www.techdirt.com/articles/20110627/11000414873/supreme-court-says-anti-violent-video-game-law-violates-first-amendment.shtml
2. Huesmann, L. R. & Taylor, L. D. (2006). The role of media violence in violent behavior. *Annual Review of Public Health, 27,* 394.
3. Gentile, D. A., Lynch, P. J., Linder, J. R., & Walsh, D. A. (2004). The effects of violent video game habits on adolescent hostility, aggressive behaviors, and school performance. *Journal of Adolescence, 27,* 5-22.

---

[b] He killed his first Klingons (with a photon torpedo) back in 1978.

4. Ewoldsen, D. R., Eno, C. A., Okdie, B. M., Velez, J. A., Guadagno, R. E., & DeCoster, J. (2012). Effect of playing violent video games cooperatively or competitively on subsequent cooperative behavior. *Cyberpsychology, Behavior, and Social Networking, 15*(5), 277-280.
5. Greitemeyer, T., Traut-Mattausch, E., & Osswald, S. (2012). How to ameliorate negative effects of violent games on cooperation: Play it cooperatively in a team. *Computers in Human Behavior, 28*(4), 1465-1470.

5 - Why are you writing a book about violent media?

The Short Answer:

For four main reasons. First, we wanted to write a book that thoroughly reviews all of the nooks and crannies of media violence research, one that's simple and accessible for all audiences. If you read just the *Short Answers*, you'll get a fairly good overview of the topic in about an hour. Other books on the subject tend to be targeted toward academics (read: boring and complex), can be overly simplistic (e.g., only focus on video games, only scratch the surface of the research), or inaccurately represent the state of scientific research on the subject. The second reason is that we want to counteract the misinformation about media violence that always seems be circulating. As science reporting in both reputable news outlets and online have become increasingly inaccurate (imagine that, people on the internet are often wrong!), there is greater need for scientists to speak up and set the record straight. Third, we'd like our research to reach beyond the "Ivory Tower" of academia. Researchers frequently discuss their findings with other researchers, but rarely make their findings accessible to the average person. We believe that we have a moral obligation to make this research publicly available, since much of it is publicly-funded (we're surprised taxpayers don't demand this of scientists more often!) Lastly, we're frequently contacted by people – students, parents, reporters, and gamers – who want answers to the very questions we address in this book. It'd be nice (and time-saving!) to provide them with all the answers to their questions in one place that gives them both an answer to their question and the option to dive deeper into the research upon which that answer is based.

The Long Answer:

We've got a confession to make: We're *not* the first researchers to write a book about media violence (gasp!) Heck, for some of us, this isn't even our first *book* on the subject: Craig and Douglas wrote books about media violence more than a decade ago! So why go to the effort of writing a book at all if others have already done it?

We did it because we believe that there's a gap needing to be filled when it comes to mainstream books on media violence. To be sure, books such as Steven Kirsh's *Children, Adolescents, and Media Violence: A Critical Look at the Research*[1] offer an incredibly thorough review of the research on media violence and books such as Anderson, Gentile, & Buckley's *Violent Video Game Effects on Children and Adolescents: Theory, Research and Public Policy*[2] do a terrific job of walking the reader through the nitty-gritty details of video game violence research from start to finish. But these books tend to be fairly detail-heavy and theory-oriented – certainly not the sort of thing you read before bed or on a bus in ten-minute bursts. This is mostly because their target audience is people who *already* know a thing or two about media violence research (e.g., college students, media scholars, and public policy wonks.) Most people simply don't have the experience to make heads or tails of books filled with academic gobbledygook.

Which isn't to say that there aren't excellent books intended to be read by concerned parents and lay audiences (in fact, we list several in Table 5.1.) But even *these* books require considerable time and effort to find the answers people are looking for. What's worse, there are other books out there which, while trying to be easy to read, end up painting an overly simplistic or outright inaccurate picture of the research. Some of these take an overly alarmist stance (e.g., violent video games will turn your children into murderers!) while others outright deny what decades of research says (e.g., violent media have no effects, except when it comes to good ones!). As researchers, we refuse to sacrifice accuracy for readability. But we also don't believe that you *have* to give up one to have the other![a]

Table 5.1. Recommended Books on Media Violence

1. Anderson, C. A., Gentile, D.A., & Buckley, K.E. (2007). *Violent Video Game Effects on Children and Adolescents: Theory, Research, and Public Policy.* New York: Oxford University Press. *This was our first book on media violence. It was written for a general audience, but has sufficient detail for use by media violence scholars and as a textbook.*
2. DeGaetano, Gloria (2004). *Parenting well in a media age: Keeping our kids human.* Fawnskin, Calif.: Personhood Press. *This book is targeted towards parents. It addresses many issues concerning media use by children, not just violence.*
3. Dill-Shackleford, Karen E. (2016). *How Fantasy Becomes Reality: Information and Entertainment Media in Everyday Life.* New York: Oxford University Press. *This general audience book explores a host of issues concerning entertainment media, including violence, but also stereotyping, fandom, and politics.*
4. Gentile, Douglas (Editor). (2014). *Media violence and children: A Complete Guide for Parents and Professionals, 2nd Edition.* Oxford, England: Praeger. *This collection of excellent chapters covers a wide array of media violence issues by leading scholars.*
5. Kirsh, Steven J. (2012). *Children, Adolescents, and Media Violence: A Critical Look at the Research, 2nd Edition.* Los Angeles: Sage Publications. *This book reviews the vast research literature on media violence, from the*

---

[a] Case in point, we could have phrased this sentence "the two are not mutually exclusive". It would mean the exact same thing and let us show off fancy words, but what's the point if we can just use plain language that everyone understands?

view of a developmental psychologist.

6. Strasburger, Victor. (2019). *The Death of Childhood: Reinventing the Joy of Growing Up.* Newcastle upon Tyne, UK: Cambridge Scholars Publishing. *This book is timely, easy to read, and well-researched. It will greatly benefit parents and grandparents who read it and children in the care of such people.*
7. Strasburger, Victor C., Wilson, Barbara J., & Jordan, Amy B. (2013). *Children, Adolescents, and the Media, 3nd Edition.* Thousand Oaks, CA: Sage. *This highly acclaimed book, now in its third edition, presents tons of information in an accessible and entertaining way.*
8. Warburton, Wayne A., & Braunstein, Danya. [Eds.]. (2012). *Growing Up Fast and Furious: Reviewing the Impact of Violent and Sexualised Media on Children.* Sydney: The Federation Press. *This collection of chapters addresses two major media issues, the impact of violent media and of sexualized media on children, both of which are growing problems for children and their parents.*

That's where we see this book fitting in: An up-to-date, middle-ground approach between the thoroughness of a textbook and accessibility of a book targeted toward people who don't have time to slog through hundreds of pages of media research jargon. On top of that, the book also has a unique format, presenting topics as short, easily-digestible question-and-answer segments (for more on this and how to use this book, see Question #1). We know they're the questions that people want to know about, because they're the ones we get asked by reporters, concerned parents, students, and gamers.

Okay, so this book has a unique structure and fills a void left by other media violence books. But *why* do books about media violence exist at all? Don't researchers argue about this stuff with themselves, figure out the answers, and then the findings trickle their way into public knowledge? In theory, yes. In practice, not so much. There has been a growing gap between what researchers learn about media violence and what the public (*especially* the American public) knows about this research. Illustrating this point: You may believe that media violence research is a new and hotly debated topic for researchers. In reality, the subject is hardly new: Media violence research has been going on for more than *half a century*. Nor are the basic findings still "up in the air": The U.S. Surgeon General came to a conclusion on the subject back in 1972, a conclusion which has since been agreed upon by every major scientific body that has ever examined the topic.[b]

---

[b] Access to over a dozen such reports can be found at the following web page:
http://www.craiganderson.org/wp-content/uploads/caa/StatementsonMediaViolence.html

But how can this be, since video games are still fairly new, and video game technology is coming out with new advances all the time? Well, it's because modern discussions about media violence tend to focus on video game effects as if the subject is completely new, but psychologists have been studying different types of media violence – including television, comic books, and music – since at least the 1950s[5]. In fact, by the time researchers started looking at violence in video games in the late 1970s and early 1980s[6], the basic question of whether media violence increases the risk of aggression had been answered pretty conclusively: Violent media effects, regardless of the medium itself, were well-studied and accepted as fact by the Surgeon General's Scientific Advisory Committee on Television and Social Behavior *and* the National Institute of Mental Health.[7,8] We discuss this research in much greater detail in Questions #9, #11, and #15.

Despite this consensus among major scientific and public health organizations, and the fact that three decades of additional research since then has provided additional supporting evidence, the general public is increasingly being told something *very* different[9]. This is somewhat like the mistaken belief that climate scientists are still debating the existence of climate change (they aren't[10]), or that scientists cannot show a clear link between cigarettes and lung cancer (tobacco companies themselves have known about this link since the 1950s[11]). To be fair, there are some researchers who question the size of, or outright deny the existence of media violence effects, but this position is the minority one, and goes against mountains of psychological research and theory (we discuss this in greater detail in Question #17). Unfortunately, as is often the case in news outlets and online, vocal minority opinions become amplified and gain credibility when media outlets describe the field as "contentious"[12] or even worse, describe media effects as a "myth"[13]. The result is a population confused about the research on media violence, just as they were for decades about the effects of cigarettes and continue to be about climate change. This book aims to counteract this misleading narrative about media violence by going straight to the research itself, bypassing the filter of commercial media entirely.

This book also addresses a related problem: Researchers often find themselves in an academic bubble, completely isolated from the general public. In the course of their day, researchers discuss their work with other researchers, collaborate with one another on future studies, critique existing studies by other researchers, and publish their work in scientific journals so other researchers can read about it. Nowhere in this routine do they find time or get an opportunity to speak to the public about their work, nor are they even encouraged to. What makes this even worse is the fact that researchers have a *moral* obligation (in our view) to inform the public about their findings, since much of this research is funded by taxpayer dollars. To clarify, publicly-funded research is incredibly important – that's not the problem. The problem is that, very often, this research gets funded, conducted, and then published in academic journals outside the reach of the public.[c] To be fair, some researchers do try to share their findings with the general public through "Ted Talks," YouTube videos, public radio, and other outlets. Even so, researchers are so used to speaking in the jargon-filled language of academia that their attempts to convey their findings to the general public leave most people totally confused.

The authors of this book take our moral responsibility to inform the public about research seriously. That's why we believe that it's important to not only talk about the research with anyone who wants to know about it, but to do so in plain, practical language that everyone understands. We've been encouraged to see how motivated people are to look things up themselves and to try to read through scientific journal articles to get knowledge straight from the source! But even *with* a degree in psychology it's easy to get lost in a sea of jargon and statistics. For this reason, we've tried to make this book as approachable, pain-free, and interesting as possible without watering down the research or treating the average person in an insultingly simplistic way.

Another reason we've written this book is because it allows us to speak about *all* of the media violence research in one fell swoop. Often, people learn about research in bits and pieces, hearing about a single study here or there in brief news reports or stories. Parents, journalists, and politicians don't have hundreds of hours to read *thousands* of papers on the subject, and so they often take the results of a single study and base their opinions on it (e.g., a scientist ran a study and found no effects – I guess that answers the question for me!) Researchers, on the other hand, are taught not to draw conclusions from a single study or a single paper. Instead, they're trained to think about how new studies combine with dozens or even hundreds of other studies to form a nuanced answer to a question. In short: Scientists *rarely* rely on a single study to answer a question. In this same spirit, we provide the reader with as broad a picture of the research as possible, not just the results based on a single study. Of course, we occasionally use a single study as an *example* to help illustrate a more general point, but our emphasis is always on what has been found again and again across many studies. This, we hope, will help you better understand that the field's conclusions are based on a huge body of research, rather than on what the latest study suggests.

Up to this point, we've painted ourselves in a pretty positive light, writing this book to improve academic outreach, to improve societal understanding, and even for moral reasons! But, if we're being completely honest, we need to admit that there's also a practical, somewhat selfish reason we're writing this book too. Over the years, we've been contacted, through e-mail and in-person, by concerned parents, journalists, colleagues, friends, fellow gamers, and countless others who all want simple, straightforward answers to their questions about violent media. We're always happy to answer these questions. After all, we're scientists: We love

---

[c] Most academic journals have a subscription fee and require people to pay for access to research articles – sometimes as much as $30-$40 for a single article.

the things we study and we're excited whenever someone else takes an interest in it! Plus, it gives us hope when people turn to scientific evidence to support their opinions rather than relying solely on intuition, rumors, or anecdotes. But after repeatedly responding to questions on this subject for years, three issues have become apparent:

1. It almost always takes us longer than we expect to write a response because there's just so much research out there to condense. We want to be as thorough and accurate as possible in our responses, but it can take up to an hour to respond to a single email question!

2. People are thirsty for knowledge, but often don't know where to get it! When they turn to us, it's often because they don't know where else to find the answers, leaving them to rely on their intuition, misinformation in the media, well-intentioned but misinformed parenting books, or the internet.[d]

3. We get questions from a wide array of parents, politicians, gamers, and journalists, but all of them seem to be interested in the same set of questions about violent media.

To put it simply, we wrote this book to tackle all three of these issues at once. We truly hope, as we write this book, that it will function as the e-mail we *want* to send to every person who has a question about media violence. In the end, that's our biggest reason for writing this book: We believe that we can contribute positively to the world by providing clear, scientifically-based answers to parents, care-givers, politicians, policy-makers, students, and gamers which enables them to make healthy, informed decisions about their media diet.

References
1. Kirsh, S. J. (2006). *Children, Adolescents, and Media Violence: A Critical Look at the Research* (pp. 4-8). Thousand Oaks, California: Sage Publications.
2. Anderson, C. A., Gentile, D. A., & Buckley, K. E. (2007). *Violent Video Game Effects on Children and Adolescents: Theory, Research, and Public Policy*. New York, NY: Oxford University Press.
3. Siegel, A. E. (1958). The Influence of Violence in the Mass Media Upon Children's Role Expectations. *Child Development, 29*(1), 35-56.

---

[d] Yes, even (or especially) *Wikipedia*, which can be edited by pretty much anyone, often includes serious mistakes (look no further than the long line of celebrities who Wikipedia has erroneously declared dead despite their being very much alive at the time, including Ted Kennedy and Miley Cyrus!)

4. Anderson, C. A., & Ford, C. M. (1986). Affect of the game player: Short term effects of highly and mildly aggressive video games. *Personality and Social Psychology Bulletin, 12,* 390-402.

5. Murray, J. P. (1973). Television and violence: Implications of the Surgeon General's research program. *American Psychologist, 28,* 472-478.

6. National Institute of Mental Health. (1982). Television and Behavior: Ten Years of Scientific Progress and Implications for the Eighties, Vol. 1. Rockville, MD: U.S. Department of Health and Human Services.

7. Bushman, B. J., & Anderson, C. A. (2001). Media violence and the American public: Scientific facts versus media misinformation. *American Psychologist, 56,* 477-489.

8. Cook, J., Nuccitelli, D., Green, S. A., Richardson, M., Winkler, B., Painting, R., Way, R., Jacobs, P., & Skuce, A. (2013). Quantifying the consensus on anthropogenic global warming in the scientific literature. *Environmental Research Letters, 8,* 1-7.

9. Cummings, K. M., Brown, A., & O'Connor, R. (2007). The Cigarette Controversy. *Cancer Epidemiology, Biomarkers & Prevention, 16,* 1070-1076.

10. Fox News Technology. (2014, March 25). *Do violent video games boost aggression? Study adds fire to debate.* Retrieved from http://www.foxnews.com/tech/2014/03/25/do-violent-games-boost-aggression.html

11. Gallagher, M. D. (2010, May 10). Video Games Don't Cause Children to be Violent. *U. S. News.* Retrieved from http://www.usnews.com/opinion/articles/2010/05/10/video-games-dont-cause-children-to-be-violent

6 - Why should I care about media violence effects?

The Short Answer:

We *all* should care about the effects of media violence, whether as consumers of media, as parents of children who consume media, or as a society interested in reducing inappropriate aggression and violence. Although the harmful effects of violent media are often small and short-lived in the minutes following exposure, other harmful effects accumulate slowly over time and lead to bigger, long-term changes in the way we think, feel, and behave. In a way, you can compare it to smoking or eating junk food: You won't get cancer from a single cigarette, nor will you develop heart disease from a single cheeseburger. Regular smoking *does*, however, increase your risk of lung cancer, just as a diet of unhealthy food increases your risk of heart disease. In the same way, understanding media violence effects involves understanding both the effects of a single exposure as well as the long-term effects of accumulated exposure. It's important to understand how these effects have an impact on us, but as parents this knowledge can also help us to make informed decisions about how best to raise our children. And, as members of a society that regularly consumes violent media, we really *should* care about its effects because, despite their relatively modest size, small effects can have a big impact when applied to millions of people.

The Long Answer:

For the sake of argument, let's begin this section with a simple assumption: Let's assume it's *true* that violent media exposure represents one fairly modest risk factor (among dozens) that contribute to a person's likelihood of behaving aggressively. In other words, we'll assume that when a person consumes violent media, their chance of engaging in aggressive behavior later on goes up *ever-so-slightly*. For now, we won't debate this point – we review the evidence for[1] and against it in later chapters (e.g., Questions #11, #13, #15, and #17). Right now, we'll simply consider what it *actually* means if it's true that a person's risk of aggression increases with each exposure to violent media. Is this small increase in risk even worth worrying about?

Let's start with some examples of what this small increase in risk looks like. In laboratory studies, the effects seem pretty mundane. For example, studies show that playing a violent video game makes a person more likely to fill in partial words (e.g., c h _ _ e) to make violent words (e.g., "choke")[2]. They're also more likely to punish strangers with painful blasts of noise[3] or to force people who hate spicy food to eat hot sauce[4]. Other studies show that violent media causes people to have less of a physical reaction (e.g., heart rate, sweating) to the sight of real violence[5] and makes people feel more hostile and irritable[6]. Typically, these effects last for about 10 minutes after playing the game[4] before fading away (although they can sometimes last much longer.) "So what?" you might be thinking. Completing word puzzles with "violent" words and giving hot sauce to someone is a far cry from fistfights and gunshots. Besides, we just said that these fairly tame effects only last for a few minutes anyway. What's the big deal?

We address this issue more fully in Questions #7, #8, and #9, but for now we should mention that researchers only study hot sauce and noise blasts in the lab because we *can't* study more extreme aggression for the sake of participant safety. In a nutshell, it would be highly unethical to run a study where we put two people in a room, get them riled up, and let them hit each other with baseball bats (it would also be illegal *and* we'd find ourselves with a shortage of willing volunteers!) For the record, we're not the only researchers with a soft spot for our participants' well-being: *All* researchers have an ethical obligation to avoid doing any real harm to their participants. This puts us in the difficult position of trying to design studies that measure aggression without actually letting people get harmed.

Fortunately for researchers, theories of aggression state that, when you get right down to it, aggression is aggression: Whether it's someone blasting another person with noise, saying mean things to them, or attacking them with a knife, the risk factors and underlying mental processes are the same[7]. To a psychologist, blasting your little brother with noise or force-feeding him hot sauce is based on the same causes and uses the same psychological and neurological mechanisms as punching or insulting him (and at this point, Courtney wishes to offer his heartfelt apologies to his little brother for years of picking on him.) What does this mean from a practical standpoint? If behaviors like fighting and making threats are important to you, then you *should* care when researchers find that violent media increases mundane measures of aggression in the laboratory, because the same processes are at play for more extreme forms of aggression in the real world.

Okay, so maybe it's worth caring about violent media for a *few minutes* immediately after consuming violent media. But why get worked up over such a small window of time? For most of us, our last exposure to violent media was hours, perhaps even days ago. If we just asked people to sit around and relax for a few minutes after playing a violent game or watching a violent movie, there'd be no problem at all, right?

If the problem were limited to only those few troublesome minutes after exposure, we would probably agree. Unfortunately, each exposure to violent media carries with it more than just its immediate effect on mood and behavior: It leaves behind a very small, lasting impact on the mind of the viewer. In the short term, these effects may be too small to notice, but they accumulate over time. For a related example, imagine learning a new language. Each time a student sits down to practice for 15 minutes, the improvement on their overall ability to speak the language will be so small that you probably won't even notice. After each given session, they may know a few new words, but their overall ability to speak the language will seem virtually unchanged. And yet, day after day of repeated practice will start to have a noticeable effect: they'll start to speak more quickly, with fewer mistakes, until the entire process is second nature to them. A similar process occurs with violent media: The effects of repeated exposure are slow and gradual, but they do accumulate and become more noticeable if you know how to look for them.

We're talking about violent media exposure as a repetitive process, and that's because for many of us, it is. It's rare for gamers to pick up a game and play it only once. Likewise, people rarely watch a single episode of a television show and then never watch it again. Players put hundreds of hours into their favorite video games over years of play, and many of us binge-watch entire seasons of our favorite television shows on streaming services like Netflix and watch dozens of movies every year. Furthermore, because so many shows, movies, and games include violence as a feature, we will see similar acts and scripts even when watching different media. As a result, most of us could probably be described as repeat consumers of violent media.[a]

So, what does the research say about the long-term effects of repeated exposure to violent media? To put it simply, long-term exposure changes the way we think, feel, and behave[7], in many of the same ways that short-term exposure does. For example, violent media make people more likely to have aggressive thoughts and beliefs in the minutes following, which makes them more likely to behave aggressively as well[8]. In one experimental study with children, researchers found that playing a children's violent video game for 20 minutes (that is, a game in which cartoonish characters killed other characters but did so without blood, gore, or screams of pain) increased attempts to harm another child by 47%[8]. Repeated exposure to violent media has a similar effect, making a person more likely to believe that the world is a hostile place[9] and to have more aggressive thoughts even when they *haven't* been exposed to violent media in the past hour[8]. And, just like short-term effects, these long-term changes in beliefs and thoughts can translate into increased odds of physical aggression ranging from fighting at school to abusing one's spouse or engaging in violent criminal behavior[10].

So why should we care about media violence effects? Because seemingly trivial short-term effects can accumulate over time and lead to far more significant long-term outcomes for ourselves and for our kids.

But let's keep things in perspective: Even when we're talking about long-term effects of accumulated exposure, we're still talking about fairly modest effects for individual people. Most of us don't commit violent crimes or engage in violent behavior, and there doesn't seem to be an epidemic of murders (for more on these particular criticisms, see Questions #28, #29, and #30). So is there *really* any reason to treat media violence as an issue that society as a whole should be concerned about?

---

[a] The authors are not too proud to admit that they recently got together and re-watched all of the *Tremors* films – a series one would be hard-pressed to describe as anything *but* violent!

We would argue yes, because relatively minor effects for individuals can become a much more significant problem when applied to all of society. Let's do a simple thought experiment to demonstrate what we mean. Imagine that, in the last year, you called in to work sick twice when you weren't actually sick (we're not judging you – most people have done it!) The effect of this action may be fairly minimal to you: In terms of your annual income, it's not likely to be more than a 1% difference. But imagine if you're a company with 10,000 employees, each of whom did the same thing you did in the last year. Together, the combined actions of these employees represent 160,000 hours of lost productivity – a number which is certainly not trivial (think of all the things you could do with 160,000 people-hours of productivity, especially considering a typical house can be built with around 2,000 person-hours of work!) Returning to the issue of media violence and aggression, one study suggests that violent media may increase a child's one-year likelihood of getting into a fight at school from 28% to 50%[8]. For a typical child, this might be the difference between getting into no fights versus getting into a single fight in a given school year. But take that number and apply it to a school with a thousand students. We're *now* talking about dozens or even hundreds of additional fights per year! And applied to an entire city or, indeed, the entire country, the numbers run easily into the thousands!

What does this mean for you, who may *never* encounter anything more than minor forms of day-to-day aggression? Well, first of all, wouldn't it be nice to be exposed to less day-to-day aggression and fewer unpleasant or unkind people? Furthermore, when we consider that there are *millions* of other people, and that rare and more extreme events do happen, and that such events *do* affect everything from crime rates to the cost of health care and policing to policies which influence how we travel, work, and raise our children, then even small effects of media violence become societally important. And, of course, this is all ignoring the fact that you're also more likely to be personally victimized – even if the likelihood is still relatively rare.

Ultimately, what we are talking about is changing the odds that you might be involved in some aggressive encounter. It could be verbal aggression, road rage, relational aggression, physical aggression, or any of several other subtypes of aggression. The odds go up a little, but even a little aggression is usually more than anyone wants. In short, the effects of media violence are worth paying attention to, even if the effects may be small and may not seem to affect us at first glance.

At this point, it may be helpful to point out that the issue of small effects having a large impact when applied to millions of people is *not* unique to media violence. We can turn to the field of medicine and the case of aspirin for an interesting comparison.

You may have heard that people who are at risk for a heart attack can be given small, daily doses of aspirin to reduce this risk (and if you didn't know, now you do!) Ask your physician and they will likely tell you this, since it's explicitly stated in no uncertain terms by the American Heart Association: "Aspirin can help prevent heart attack"[11]. To understand where this recommendation comes from, we turn to a study which found that aspirin's effect of reducing death from heart attack was big enough that it was considered unethical to continue running the "no-aspirin" (or "placebo") condition in the study![11]

When we put it that way, it sounds like aspirin must have a *huge* effect on the rate of fatal heart attacks. So, what *did* the data from the study show? The study looked at nearly 22,000 people, of which 293 had a heart attack[12,13]. Some were randomly assigned to be in the "aspirin" condition, while others were in the placebo ("sugar pill") condition for comparison. At the end of the study, 104 people in the aspirin condition had a heart attack, almost half as many as in the placebo condition (see Figure 6.1). While this seems like a big difference, practically speaking, it's a difference of 85 heart attacks in a sample of more than 22,000 people – or the difference between the two sliver-thin bars in the figure.

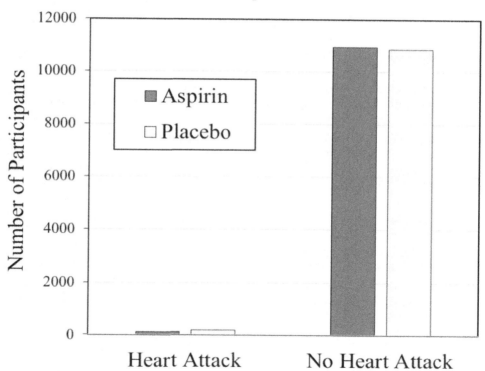

Figure 6.1. A significant practical effect of aspirin on preventing heart attacks.

If you *only* looked at the number of people who didn't have a heart attack, you might ask "Since most people don't have a heart attack anyway, why make a big deal about these findings – the 85 saved people are just a drop in the bucket!"

But if you're the family of one of those 85 people, it would certainly make a difference to you! And if you had a choice in the matter, which condition would *you* prefer to be in, the aspirin condition or the placebo condition?

Also keep in mind that this study looked at 85 heart attacks in a sample of 22,000 people. Now, imagine we extended these findings to include the approximately 735,000 Americans who have a heart attack every year[14]. Suddenly, this very "small" effect for 85 people translates to the potential to save thousands of lives per year! Is it any wonder the American Heart Association recommends aspirin so strongly?

Of course, it's important to maintain a sense of perspective: Aspirin and heart attacks aren't the same thing as violent media and aggression, and we don't intend to say that the consequences of violent media should be considered as lethal as heart attacks. Heart attacks are life-or-death affairs, while the effects of violent media exposure are *far* more likely to involve increases in minor, day-to-day forms aggression, like shouting, threatening, or shoving. But when you compare the size of the *effect* of media violence on aggression to the effect of aspirin on heart attacks, the media violence effects *are* considerably larger[15]. What does this mean? Well, when we think about media effects, we need to think about them not just at an individual level, but also on a societal level. To use just one example: Elementary school boys who watched a lot of violent TV shows were, 15 years later, *3 times more likely* to be convicted of a crime than those who watched few such shows as children[10]. While your own chances of being a criminal or a victim of crime are quite low, how many *extra* crimes does this increased risk represent in a population of millions? How many additional assaults, cases of spousal abuse, and instances of schoolyard bullying are we talking about? Media violence may just be a drop in the proverbial bucket, but every drop matters when we're talking about 325 million "buckets" in the United States, into which media violence drips every day.

References
1. Anderson, C. A., Shibuya, A., Ihori, N., Swing, E. L., Bushman, B. J., Sakamoto, A., Rothstein, H. R., & Saleem, M. (2010). Violent video game effects on aggression, empathy, and prosocial behavior in eastern and western countries: a meta-analytic review. *Psychological Bulletin, 136*(2), 151-173.
2. Anderson, C. A., Carnagey, N. L., Flanagan, M., Benjamin, A. J. Jr., Eubanks, J., & Valentine, J. C. (2004). Violent Video Games: Specific Effects of Violent Content on Aggressive Thoughts and Behavior. *Advances in Experimental Social Psychology, 36*, 199-249.
3. Anderson, C. A., & Dill, K. E. (2000). Video Games and Aggressive Thoughts, feelings, and Behavior in the Laboratory and in Life. *Journal of Personality and Social Psychology, 78*(4), 772-790.

4. Barlett, C., Branch, O., Rodeheffer, C., & Harris, R. (2009). How long to do the short-term violent video game effects last? *Aggressive Behavior, 35*(3), 225-236.

5. Carnagey, N. L., Anderson, C. A., & Bushman, B. J. (2007). The effect of video game violence on physiological desensitization to real-life violence. *Journal of Experimental Social Psychology, 43,* 489-496.

6. Carnagey, N. L., & Anderson, C. A. (2005). The Effects of Reward and Punishment in Violent Video Games on Aggressive Affect, Cognition, and Behavior. *Psychological Science, 16*(11), 882-889.

7. Anderson, C. A., & Bushman, B. J. (2002). Human Aggression. *Annual Review of Psychology, 53,* 27-51.

8. Anderson, C. A., Gentile, D. A., & Buckley, K. E. (2007). *Violent Video Game Effects on Children and Adolescents: Theory, Research, and Public Policy.* New York, NY: Oxford University Press.

9. Gentile, D. A., Li, D., Khoo, A., Prot, S., & Anderson, C. A. (2014). Practice, Thinking, and Action: Mediators and Moderators of Long-term Violent Video Game Effects on Aggressive Behavior. *JAMA Pediatrics*, Published online March 24, 2014.

10. Huesmann, L. R., Moise, J., Podolski, C. P., & Eron, L. D. (2003). Longitudinal relations between childhood exposure to media violence and adult aggression and violence: 1977-1992. *Developmental Psychology, 39*(2), 201-221.

11. American Heart Association. (2015, August 31). *Aspirin and Heart Disease.* Retrieved from http://www.heart.org/HEARTORG/Conditions/HeartAttack/PreventionTreatmentofHeartAttack/Aspirin-and-Heart-Disease_UCM_321714_Article.jsp#.VirDWGt0pTU

12. Steering Committee of the Physician's Health Study Research Group. (1988). Preliminary report: Findings from the aspirin component of the ongoing physicians' health study. *The New England Journal of Medicine, 318,* 262-264.

13. Rosenthal, R. (1990). How are we doing in soft psychology? *American Psychologist, 45*(6), 775-777.

14. Centers for Disease Control and Prevention. (2015, August 10). *Heart Disease Facts*. Retrieved from http://www.cdc.gov/heartdisease/facts.htm

15. Anderson, C. A., Berkowitz, L., Donnerstein, E., Huesmann, L. R., Johnson, J. D., Linz, D., Malamuth, N. M., & Wartella, E. (2003). The Influence of Media Violence on Youth. *Psychological Science in the Public Interest, 4*(3), 81-110.

Chapter 1

Aggression 101: The Basics of Media Violence Research

7 - Are violence and aggression the same thing?

The Short Answer:

Not quite. *Aggression* is a broad category that includes any behavior intended to harm another person who doesn't want to be harmed. *Violence* refers specifically to aggressive behavior where the goal is to cause *severe* physical harm (e.g., injury or death). This means that all violence is aggression, but not all aggression is violence. This distinction becomes more obvious when you think about less-severe physical aggression (e.g., shoving), verbal aggression (e.g., threats, insults), or relational aggression (e.g., excluding someone from an activity, spreading rumors about someone): None of these would be considered violent, but all of these would be considered forms of aggression. This distinction is an important one, because when psychologists are talking about the effects of violent media, they're usually talking about the effects on a person's risk for *aggression*, not *violence*. That said, most aggression and violence researchers agree that the same psychological processes underlie aggression and violence. In other words, the difference is in how *extreme* they are, not in what causes them.

The Long Answer:

Aggression is defined by psychologists as any behavior that is *intended* to inflict harm on someone who does not wish to be harmed[1,2].[a] In other words, aggression is all about *intentions*, not about outcomes. Let's walk through a few examples to illustrate what we mean.

1. Johnie reaches out to grab his coat off the hanger just as Chris walks by. Johnie's elbow accidentally catches Chris in the face. Would psychologists consider Johnie's actions to be aggressive? No: Even though Johnie's actions have inflicted harm on Chris, Johnie didn't *intend* to do so, so there was no aggression. Of course, Chris might *misinterpret* Johnie's behavior as

---

[a] The last part about "who does not wish to be harmed" exists to account for masochists – people who enjoy the experience of pain. In other words, if a masochist were to ask you to spank them and you granted them their wish, you *wouldn't* be committing an act of aggression, according to psychologists. And yes, these are the sorts of deep, philosophical conundrums that keep psychologists up at night!

intentional, motivating Chris to punch Johnie in retaliation.[b] This time, Chris' punch would be considered aggression, because it *was* intended to cause harm.

2. Annie is a surgeon. Her patient has a gangrenous foot. Annie realizes that she needs to amputate the patient's foot to save their life. In this case, Annie is *intentionally* cutting the patient's foot off, but it would again not be considered aggression. Although Annie's actions *are* intentional (she didn't "accidentally" cut off the foot), she's doing them to *help* her patient, not harm them. Remember, aggression is not determined by the behavior itself (using a knife on someone) or the outcome (the patient losing their foot), but by the intended goal of the person doing the action.

3. Jeff decides he's had enough of Doug's sass, and angrily takes a swing at Doug. However, Jeff trips over his own feet and the punch misses Doug entirely. Unlike the other two examples, this *would* be considered aggression, because Jeff *wanted* to hurt Doug. It would also be aggression if, instead of trying to physically harm Doug, Jeff started spreading rumors around the office that Doug was stealing office supplies so that Doug would be fired. It doesn't matter whether harm was *actually* done, or even what sort of harm Jeff was trying to inflict: Jeff did something with the intent of harming Doug, which, according to psychologists, makes his actions aggressive.

Hopefully these examples show just how tricky it can be for scientists to define aggression, since "aggression" includes a *lot* of different behaviors. At first glance, most people would think the definition of aggression is pretty straightforward, since the first things to come to mind are obvious examples of physical aggression (e.g., one person punching another). And it's within this category of physical aggression that we find the related concept of "violence" – aggression intended to inflict *severe* physical harm on another person[1,3].

So what's the difference between the two? It helps to imagine the difference between slapping someone across the face and shooting them in the face. In both cases, the culprit is engaged in physical aggression – they're inflicting physical harm on someone. In the case of the slap, the culprit likely intends to cause pain to the victim, but they likely aren't intending to cause any lasting physical injury. In contrast, when the culprit shoots the other person in the face, they're probably reasonably sure that their actions are going to cause severe injury or even death.

So let's imagine slapping and shooting as being on opposite ends of a physical aggression scale (see Figure 7.1). On the "low" end of the scale, we have

---

[b] In fact, as we discuss in Question #12, Chris is more likely to make such an error if he frequently consumes media violence or has consumed media violence recently.

less severe, day-to-day forms of physical aggression – the kind you might see between two fighting siblings or in a heated argument. On the "high" end, we have very extreme, very rare forms of physical aggression. As you get toward the higher end of the scale, the actions become more and more violent. Where you decide to draw the line between "violent" and "non-violent" will differ from person to person, and researchers themselves do not always agree on where, precisely, to put this line. But we can say that while not all of these examples of physical aggression will meet the threshold for "violence," all of these actions fall somewhere on this aggression scale. Another way to state this is to say that all violence is, by definition, aggression, but not all aggression is necessarily violent.

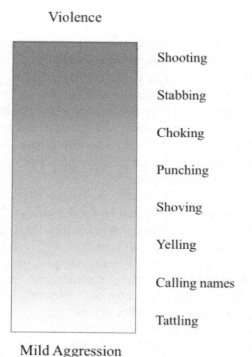

Violence

Shooting

Stabbing

Choking

Punching

Shoving

Yelling

Calling names

Tattling

Mild Aggression

Figure 7.1. Aggressive behaviors of increasing severity.

People are remarkably creative when it comes to finding ways to harm one another. Aggression researchers have yet to come up with a perfect way to organize all of these different ways of aggressing and, as such, researchers often disagree about the "right" categorization scheme[4]. Let's shine a bit of light on why the task is so hard. First, recall from our earlier examples that not all harm is physical: People can insult one another (verbal aggression) or find elaborate ways to sabotage another person's social status (relational aggression)[1]. Second, consider how aggression can be active – directly harming another person – or passive – allowing harm to befall another person (e.g., choosing not to warn someone they're about to step on broken glass).

If all of that weren't confusing enough, these aggressive behaviors have to be differentiated from anti-social behavior, which is any behavior that goes against what people consider to be *acceptable* in our society[5,6]. By this definition, aggression seems like it would always be anti-social, since there are laws against violent crimes. Then again, there are times when aggression is perfectly acceptable (e.g., a boxing match).

Aggression also needs to be separated from *assertiveness*, which is when a person stands up for themselves in a way that still shows respect to others[8,9]. If a bully cuts in front of you in the lunch line, the *assertive* response would be to tell the bully that they're being inconsiderate to others and insisting that they move to the back of the line. The *aggressive* response is to shove the bully to the back of the line or insult them. So we see that assertiveness can sometimes involve aggression, but not always.

These distinctions don't even begin to cover all the different ways people use the term "aggression" to describe behavior that psychologists wouldn't call aggressive. For example, an *aggressive* salesperson probably isn't intending to harm their customer when they try to persuade them to buy a car! They are being stubborn, or perhaps rude, but certainly not aggressive as psychologists would define it.

By this point, you may find yourself feeling a bit overwhelmed by what should have been a very simple definition. Don't feel bad! Researchers who've spent their lives studying aggression often find themselves in the same boat, disagreeing and debating about what should count as aggression or whether it makes sense to distinguish between "direct" and "indirect" aggression. You might even find yourself asking "who cares?" After all, does it *really* matter whether insulting someone or punching them are considered to be the same *kind* of aggression, or whether we distinguish "violence" from more common types of physical aggression?

We recognize that these kinds of quibbles often seem trivial. As it turns out, however, these sorts of distinctions turn out to be *incredibly* important to aggression researchers, in part because precise language helps them to be clear about the claims they're making in their studies. In fact, it's precisely because non-experts do *not* make these distinctions that there is so much confusion in the news and in the general public's understanding about what, exactly, media violence research has shown (see Questions #29 and #35 for two popular beliefs people have based on these misunderstandings).

To illustrate how imprecise language leads to misunderstandings, consider this: Media violence researchers typically claim that being repeatedly exposed to violent media increases your likelihood of engaging in aggression[9]. If you know that "aggression" refers to everything from day-to-day spats to insults to gossip at work, this claim seems fairly reasonable and tame. Is it really so hard to believe that people who spend hours consuming violent media might be a bit more likely to insult someone, shove them, spread rumors about them, or react with violence if provoked? However, if you misunderstand what "aggression" means and assume that "aggression" means "violence," the reasonable claim suddenly sounds ridiculous, especially if you don't know what researchers mean when they talk about an "increased likelihood". For example, you might read the statement as "playing violent video games causes normal people to become mass murderers." The statement itself is absurd, and none of the media researchers we know (and we know almost all of the top ones) would make such a ridiculous claim.

And yet, these claims are put into the mouths of media violence researchers by others! For example: "Ask anyone who's ever played *Grand Theft*

Auto IV and not killed a pimp in real life: We say videogames don't lead to violent behavior. But many studies, written by people who have more degrees than me, suggest they do."[10]

This quote perfectly demonstrates how treating violence and aggression as the same thing leads people to completely misunderstand what media violence research says! The original article is entitled "Yet more proof that violent videogames don't cause aggression," yet the author's example *only* talks about violence and not more mundane forms of aggression, like insulting someone over a headset while playing a video game.[c] The nuance and subtlety of the researchers' position is replaced with a straw man that can be easily torn down, letting gamers dismiss researchers as out-of-touch kooks.

As an analogy to this absurdity, imagine a cardiology researcher said "Our research shows that a diet full of junk food increases your risk for heart disease." Now, imagine if, in response to this very reasonable statement, the news reported the researcher's words like this: "Doctors say junk food kills everyone who eats it." What started as a modest position is absurd when important concepts ("risk of heart disease") become oversimplified ("kills everyone"). And in case you think we're exaggerating, we encourage you to Google the responses of gamers, pundits, and critics and see how their portrayals of media violence research positions match up with what researchers *actually* say in any of the articles we reference in this book!

To be clear, it's not only gamers and skeptics who misunderstand or overstate what researchers say. Well-intentioned parents, child-advocacy groups, and public policy folks sometimes come to the same exaggerated conclusions ("violent video games turn normal children into mass killers") and respond in ways that *seem* reasonable when based on those extreme conclusions, but are completely unwarranted based on what researchers *actually* say.

In the rest of this chapter we try to make it crystal clear exactly what media researchers say about media violence based on what decades of studies have shown (Question #11). We also explore how researchers gather this evidence so that you can better understand how to make sense of the research for yourself. This includes a discussion about how researchers measure aggression (Question #8), how they design studies to test their hypotheses (Question #9), and theories they base their hypotheses on (Question #12). We promise that when you understand the terminology and methods that researchers use, their claims really do become reasonable and the absurdity of the many public misconceptions become obvious.

---

[c] Two of the authors readily admit that they've stopped playing online games *precisely* because of how commonly this sort of toxicity occurs in online multiplayer shooter games.

References

1. Bushman, B. J., & Huesmann, L. R. (2010). Aggression. In *Handbook of Social Psychology* (5th ed., Vol 2., pp. 833-863). Hoboken, NJ: John Wiley & Sons Inc.

2. DeWall, C. N., Anderson, C. A., & Bushman, B. J. (2012). Aggression. In H. Tennen, J. Suls, & I. B. Weiner, (Eds.), *Handbook of Psychology* (2nd ed., Vol 5, pp. 449-466). Hoboken, NJ: John Wiley & Sons Inc.

3. Anderson, C. A., & Bushman, B. J. (2002). Human aggression. *Annual Review of Psychology, 53,* 27-51.

4. Parrott, D. J., & Giancola, P. R. (2007). Addressing "The criterion problem" in the assessment of aggressive behavior: Development of a new taxonomic system. *Aggression and Violent Behavior, 12*(3), 280-299.

5. DeWall, C. N., Anderson, C. A. (2011). The general aggression model. In *Human aggression and violence: Causes, manifestations, and consequences* (pp. 15-33). Washington, DC: American Psychological Association.

6. Krahé, B. (2013). *The social psychology of aggression* (2nd ed.). New York, NY: Psychology Press.

7. Parham, J. B., Lewis, C. C., Fretwell, C. E., Irwin, J. G., & Schrimsher, M. R. (2015). Influences on assertiveness: Gender, national culture, and ethnicity. *Journal of Management Development, 34*(4), 421-439.

8. Warland, J., McKellar, L., & Diaz, M. (2014). Assertiveness training for undergraduate midwifery students. *Nurse Education in Practice, 14*(6), 752-756.

9. Anderson, C. A., Shibuya, A., Ihori, N., Swing, E. L., Bushman, B. J., Sakamoto, A., Rothstein, H. R., & Saleem, M. (2010). Violent video game effects on aggression, empathy, and prosocial behavior in eastern and western countries: a meta-analytic review. *Psychological Bulletin,* 136(2), 151-173.

10. Pinchefsky, C. (2013, May 8). Yet More Proof That Violent Videogames Don't Cause Aggression. *Forbes.* Retrieved from http://www.forbes.com/sites/carolpinchefsky/2013/05/08/yet-more-proof-that-violent-videogames-dont-cause-aggression/

8 - How do you measure aggression?

The Short Answer:

There's no one "right" way to measure aggression, partly because there are so many ways to be aggressive. That said, psychologists *have* devised numerous creative ways to measure aggressive thoughts, feelings, and behaviors. We can measure aggressive behavior as the frequency or intensity of specific aggressive acts (e.g., fights) by asking people about their own behavior or, if we're worried about participants being dishonest, by asking their friends, teachers, parents, or even studying their police records. In the laboratory, aggressive behavior can be measured by giving participants the chance to harm another person (usually in a very mild way, or in a way that's rigged so that no harm actually occurs.) Aggressive thoughts and feelings can be measured by seeing how participants respond on puzzle-like "fill-in-the-blank" tasks, with sophisticated computer programs and medical devices, or by simply asking participants how angry they feel. It's important to note that *none* of these measures are perfect. Then again, there *are* no perfect measures of anything! Researchers overcome the imperfections of specific measures by using a combination of different measures to see if, despite their different limitations, they all point to the same pattern of results.

The Long Answer:

If you plan to do good research on human aggression, you've got a pretty tough job ahead of you. Part of this difficulty stems from getting everyone to agree on the definition of aggression (see Question #7 for more on this). Let's assume, for the moment, that we're able to do this. The next tricky part is figuring out what type of aggression you're interested in (e.g., verbal, relational, physical; impulsive or planned), what part of the aggression process you're interested in (e.g., thoughts, feelings, behavior), and how to measure it. At first glance, it might seem pretty simple. After all, humans are an inventive bunch, and we've come up with some pretty clever ways to measure all sorts of things in the world around us.[a] So what's the problem?

Well, when we think about measuring something, what usually comes to mind is something tangible, a physical thing in our environment. For example, you might be thinking about how to measure Jane's height. It seems so straightforward

---

[a] For one very clever example, the Greek mathematician Eratosthenes was able to estimate the circumference of the Earth more than 2,000 years ago by measuring the angle of a shadow cast by a vertical object at noon on a sunny day and some basic geometry!

that asking how to measure Jane's height almost seems like a trick question, doesn't it? Chances are, you'd ask Jane to stand up straight, grab a tape measure, put one end on the floor, extend the other end upward along Jane until you get to the top of her head. From there, you simply read the number on the tape closest to where Jane's head is, converting Jane's height into a single number representing the number of inches or centimeters (depending on where you're from) tall that she is. Piece of cake, right? Not only is it easy to do, but you'll get fairly consistent results if you try it again, or if different people try it. Heck, Jane's height will be the same whether she's being measured in Berlin, Osaka, or Chicago, and chances are pretty good that she'll be about the same height tomorrow as she is today. You can also assume that her height will be about the same if we measure it with a tape measure, a yardstick, or even a series of smaller rulers taped together!

Okay, so we all agree that it is laughably easy to measure Jane's height. But let's think for a moment about *why* it's so easy to do:

1. We all agree on what "height" is. We might quibble over whether to use inches or centimeters, but we're able to convert between those systems and we can all agree that both measure the exact same thing.

2. We have standardized measures of height. An "inch" refers to the same amount of height no matter where you are or what you're measuring. Jane's "65 inches tall" is the same height as Muniba's "65 inches tall."

3. Jane's height is a physical feature that we see with our senses: We can see how tall she is, just as we can see her hair color and what she's wearing. If Jane is 65 inches tall and Rowell is 62 inches call, we can confirm with our own eyes that Jane is taller than Rowell.

4. Jane's height is fairly stable: It may change slightly over the course of her adult life, but it does so very gradually and predictably. It would be very unusual for Jane's height to increase and decrease by two feet over the course of a day.

Now, let us give you a second task: Measure Jane's aggression. How would *you* try to measure it? It's informative to stop reading for a moment and take a moment to challenge yourself to come up with a way before reading ahead. Don't worry, we'll wait!

So, what did you come up with? Maybe you decided to measure Jane's aggression by simply counting the number of times Jane did something aggressive. This seems like a pretty common-sense way to measure aggression. But is it really that easy? What makes something count as aggressive behavior, and how would you put numbers to it exactly? If Jane tries to shoot a policeman, is that really equal to that time she tripped her brother when she was five?

Is it really practical to count up *all* of the aggressive things Jane ever did? Surely Jane can't be expected to remember *every* time she acted aggressively? And even if she did, can we trust Jane to be honest? Maybe Jane will "conveniently forget" to mention the fight she started in high school because it makes her look like a bully. We *could* ask Jane's parents, teachers, or friends, who might give us a more honest answer, but that would leave out any aggressive things Jane did that nobody found out about.

But the problem becomes even messier! What if Jane was a very aggressive person when she was a child, but has mellowed out as an adult – is *that* equal to a person who has consistently done a few aggressive things throughout their life? And what about cultural differences in aggression: Does Jane wrestling with her brother mean the same thing in the inner-city as it does in a well-off suburb? Would it mean the same thing if Jane was a boy instead of a girl? What if Jane grew up in South Africa, Japan, Saudi Arabia, Denmark, or Canada – would her wrestling be considered equally aggressive in all of these cultures?

Think about the measure you came up with, and ask yourself if some of these problems apply to your own measure. Chances are, you found the task of measuring Jane's aggression to be a *lot* harder and messier than the task of measuring her height. Don't feel bad, you're not alone! Researchers similarly struggle with the task of measuring aggression. This is because, unlike Jane's height, which is relatively easy to measure, Jane's aggression has several characteristics that make it hard to measure:

1. People disagree about what, exactly, is being measured. Even if we have a general definition of what aggression is, your threshold for what counts as aggressive behavior may differ from mine. If we're working from different theories, or come from different backgrounds, we may have different definitions of what "counts" as aggressive, or what actions count as more aggressive.

2. There is no standardized unit of measurement for aggression.[b] This makes it hard to "compare apples to apples" when discussing aggression. We might all agree that punches and insults count as aggression, but how do we turn these into meaningful numbers? How do we compare physical aggression to verbal aggression? Is a punch worth 2.5 insults? Is starting a vicious rumor worth more or less than threatening to beat someone up, and if so, by how much?

---

[b] We think it would make research far more interesting if we could describe aggression in terms of "millifights," "centihurts," or "megaharms"!

3. Aggression is not a physical, tangible thing that we can pick up, see, taste, or touch. We can observe Jane's height with our own eyes, agree that Jane is taller than Rowell, and can even pull out a ruler to say by how much. We can't, however, pop open Jane's head and use a ruler to measure Jane's aggression because Jane's aggression is not a physical thing. We can observe the products of Jane's aggression, like the frequency and intensity of specific behaviors (e.g., hitting others). But behavior is the result of aggression, which is a person's intent to inflict harm on others. "Intent" isn't something we can pick up, hold, and measure. Instead, we either have to guess what Jane's intentions are based on her behavior or ask Jane herself. We might be able to make very good guesses by observing Jane, and she may be very in touch with herself and know exactly what her intentions were. Even so, we're still relying on indirect and imperfect ways to measure something that doesn't physically exist.

4. Aggressive behavior is usually caused, at least in part, by the situation a person finds themselves in[1] (see more about this in Questions #12 and #14). This means that a person who shows no aggression at one point in time may act aggressively only minutes later. For example, Jane may show no signs of aggression as she walks to school. But imagine Jane bumps into her jerk ex-roommate who "accidentally" spills hot coffee on her and laughs at Jane's ruined sweater. Jane may suddenly lash out, insulting her ex-roommate, threatening her, or even physically attacking her. Walking away, Jane would probably calm down and go about the rest of her day, showing no more signs of aggression at school. Later on, however, she may lash out at her partner for accidentally throwing out her yearbook while cleaning. As we can see, in the span of just a few hours, Jane's aggression has spiked and fallen several times, sometimes changing in a matter of seconds. This fluctuation makes it hard to know how we should measure Jane's aggression: Continuously throughout the day? At the end of the day? Collect the highest and lowest points throughout the day? Take one sample at the same time every day? How we measure Jane's aggression will depend on whether we're interested in the question "How aggressive is Jane in general?" or the question "How aggressive is Jane when provoked?" This is very different from Jane's height, where wouldn't make sense to ask whether Jane is "generally tall" or "tall in certain situations."

For these reasons, as well as many others, researchers have not, and never will, come up with a single perfect, universally agreed-upon way to measure aggression. This doesn't mean it's impossible to measure aggression, of course! Researchers are both persistent and clever. Over decades, they've come up with many creative ways to measure aggression, as shown in Table 8.1. We'll divide these into two categories: "real-world measures" and "laboratory measures."

Let's start with real-world measures of aggression. These are probably very similar to the sorts of measures that came to your mind when you were trying to think of ways to measure Jane's aggression. They involve measuring aggression in Jane's day-to-day life. This includes figuring out how often people get into arguments or physical fights, insult or harass others, or deliberately sabotage others' relationships or reputation. One of the benefits of these measures is that they look at the type of aggression that most of us think about and deal with in the real world. Many researchers have studied aggression this way by asking people how often they have said nasty things about someone[2], how often they hit or threaten others[3,4], or how often they carry a weapon to school[5].

Despite the common-sense appeal of these measures, there are two common weaknesses with these *self-report* measures: Sometimes people lie, and sometimes people just can't remember. It's pretty obvious why someone might lie about their aggressive behavior. Practically speaking, most *violent* behavior is illegal (e.g., assault), and participants may worry that admitting this behavior to researchers could land them in legal trouble. But even when it comes to smaller, day-to-day aggression, people may still feel compelled to lie. After all, aggression is typically frowned upon in society, and most of us want to paint ourselves in a positive light[6]. For these reasons, we can expect participants to under-report their aggression to researchers. This is a real problem if our goal is to get an accurate measure of aggression as it occurs in the real world.

But even if we *did* find a group of participants that was freakishly honest about their past aggression, we would still need to be concerned about bias creeping into the measure in other ways. As a simple example, people often can't report accurately, even when they want to, because they simply don't remember. Can *you* remember how many mean things you said to other kids between third and sixth grade? Participants will also differ in the way they interpret the questions or their own behaviors. One participant might include the insult "you are smelly" because they believe it counts as "saying something mean," while another participant might consider that statement to be too minor to even bother counting as "mean".

We don't want readers at this point to come away with the message that all self-report measures are bad. As we've already mentioned, there are plenty of reasons to use self-report measures of aggression, including the fact that they're simple, straightforward, and pretty common-sense. In general, self-report measures usually work well and correlate well with other more "objective" measures of aggression. Instead, the message is that researchers need to consider the drawbacks of self-report measures when designing, conducting, and interpreting the results of studies that use them. As you'll see, this same advice should be applied to *any* measure used in a study.

Table 8.1. Some Common Measures of Aggressive Behavior.

Real-World Aggression	Laboratory Aggression
Self-report	Physical (shock, noise, pain)
Other-Report	Verbal (insults, ratings)
Archives	Subtract rewards (money, points)
Trained Coders	Interfere with others' goals

To get around these problems with self-report measures, researchers have come up with other ways to measure aggression. One of the simplest workarounds is to just ask *other* people about the participant's behavior, assuming that they won't have the same reason to lie to the researchers. For example, researchers might ask parents or teachers to rate how often a child fights with or bullies other students[7]. Or they may ask spouses or close friends to report how frequently the participant calls them names, gets angry at them, or slaps them[8]. Of course, relying on others has its own limitations. Parents may under-report their child's aggressiveness for fear that it reflects poorly on their parenting. A person might not feel safe reporting on their partner's aggressive or abusive behavior for fear of repercussions from their partner. And of course, the reality is that other people may simply be unaware of all the aggressive behavior someone else gets up to.

Because of these limitations, some researchers have decided to do away with asking people altogether. Instead, they try to find undisputable evidence of aggressive behavior in public records, archives, and other official data sources, like arrest records or criminal convictions[8]. One strength of these measures is that they're fairly objective: If a person was charged with assault, chances are it's because they committed an assault. As long as the definition of assault or the way assaults are reported hasn't changed dramatically over time, you should be able to compare assault data across time (e.g., an assault in 1975 is probably similar to an assault in 2005). Of course, even these measures have their own limitations. One major drawback is that they only measure extreme behavior (e.g., criminal violence). No one keeps public records about the number of times you insult someone or start a rumor at work. As a result, these measures are typically only useful for studies looking specifically at violent or extreme forms of aggression, not more typical day-to-day forms of aggression. Additionally, it can be very difficult for researchers to get permission to access some types of records. And, even when researchers *are* able to access records, they may often be incomplete (e.g., lost files), or useless if the criteria for collecting and reporting data have changed over time (e.g., reporting policies for crimes such as rape have changed in recent decades in many police departments).

A final common way to assess aggression in the real world involves having trained coders observe the target person's behavior and record the types and/or frequency of aggressive behaviors. For example, coders might observe children on a playground, and record how often specific children hit, push, yell at, and exclude other children. Sometimes the targets are video and audio recorded, so that coders can use the recordings to perform their task. An obvious advantage of such measures is that they assess behavior in natural settings. Potential problems with such measures include difficulty in perceiving, counting and categorizing aggressive behaviors accurately, and the fact that people often behave differently if they know that they are being observed or recorded. And, there are ethical issues involved with recording people without their knowledge.

As it turns out, it's harder than one might expect to measure aggression in the "real world." Because of this, some researchers have tried to "bottle" aggression in the laboratory (we discuss some of these methods, as well as their limitations, in greater detail in Questions #15 & #16). These laboratory measures tend to focus on measuring aggression in the short-term, at one point in time, rather than trying to measure a person's general tendency to be aggressive in any situation. To do this, researchers create situations which give people the chance to behave aggressively (e.g., the chance to get revenge on someone who insulted them by giving them electric shocks or forcing them to eat hot sauce.) Researchers then measure the frequency or intensity of the participant's aggressive responses.

Laboratory measures have numerous benefits, the biggest of which is the control they give researchers over the laboratory environment. Every participant goes through the same situation, allowing researchers to eliminate most of the "messiness" that comes with real-world violence. For example, if you and I are put in an identical provoking situation and *I* respond aggressively while *you* do not, researchers can meaningfully compare our responses and conclude that *my* behavior was more aggressive. These measures are often fairly objective as well because the controlled laboratory setting allows researchers to carefully observe and record *exactly* what participants did. How many times did they shock someone? How long did they hold down the "shock" lever? What, precisely, did they say to the other person? Rather than relying on the flawed memories, biased reports, or the word of others, researchers can measure behaviors directly. But all of this increased control comes at a cost: ethical restrictions and artificiality.

Ethics boards play an important role in monitoring researchers' studies to protect participants from harm. Put simply, ethics boards limit what researchers can and can't do to participants in their studies. It's easy to assume that researchers hate ethics boards for stopping them from doing the "really interesting" studies. In reality, researchers recognize the importance of ethics boards to the field. After all, if an evil scientist were harming participants in their study, it would not only harm the field's reputation as a whole, but it would make it pretty hard for us to recruit participants into our own studies!

Ethics boards ensure that researchers design studies with participant well-being in mind. This means that any measure of aggression used in the lab *must not* significantly harm participants. Trying to study aggression – intent to do harm – without allowing any harm to happen, can be tricky! After all, if we didn't care about participant well-being, all we'd have to do is make two participants angry at each other, give them both baseball bats, and watch the sparks fly. Because we care about the ethical treatment of participants, researchers instead have to craft situations where participants *think* they're doing harm to another person when, in reality, there is no potential for serious harm.

To see just how tricky designing this sort of measure can be, take another moment to pause and think about how *you* might design an ethical measure of aggression in the lab (this is a long answer – you deserve another break!) Remember, your measure has to be designed so that observers agree "yes, the participant is *definitely* trying to harm someone else," but it also has to ensure that there is *no* way anyone in the study can actually be harmed (at least, not significantly).

Now, keep your own measure in mind as we look at one example of how researchers tried to solve the same problem. The task is a *very* commonly used measure of aggression called the "competitive reaction time task"[9,10,11,12]. Imagine that you, as part of a study, are brought by the researcher into a room with a computer and a pair of headphones. You're told that this is a test of your reaction time, and that it will involve another participant, who will be competing against you. You're told that your opponent is sitting at an identical computer in another room. Even though you can't see them or hear them, you will be competing against them to see who is faster. You're then shown the task, which is very simple. A box in the middle of a computer screen will change color from red to yellow to green. Your job is to click on the box the moment it turns green. If you click the box *before* your opponent does, you win. If you're slower than your opponent, you lose.

Seems simple enough, but what's with the headphones you're wearing? That's when you learn that this task has stakes – there's a punishment for losing. Each time you lose, the headphones will emit a loud blast of screeching, static-y, wailing noise.[c] Each time you win, you not only avoid hearing a noise blast, but you get to *inflict* it on your opponent. In fact, you get to choose how *long* and how *loud* to make the noise by moving a pair of sliders on a scale from "0" to "10." If you're feeling friendly, you can make the blast short and quiet – half a second long and about the volume of a normal conversation, or even turn it off entirely. You *could* do that. *Or* you could make the noise blast ten times longer and 32 times louder (about as loud as a jackhammer, but below levels that could cause permanent hearing damage). After each blast, the task resets and you play it again, usually about 25 times.

---

[c] It's really hard to describe the sound to someone who hasn't heard it. All we can say is that it's about as fun to listen to as fingernails on a chalkboard.

There's a trick to this task, a piece of information the researchers don't give to you: There is no opponent. You *do* get blasted with very real noise after each "loss," of course. But when you win, your noise blasts are falling on deaf ears, so to speak. Instead of another player, you're actually playing against a computer program, one rigged to make you randomly "win" and "lose" about half of the time. Every participant experiences the same number of "losses," the same number of provoking noise blasts, and the same opportunities to blast their "opponent" with noise.

But what do noise blasts have to do with how aggressive someone is? Well, researchers treat the noise blasts that you "give" to your opponent as a measure of your aggression: When you give your opponent long, loud blasts of noise that you *know* are unpleasant to listen to, you're doing something to them that you *know* they don't want. True, you're trying to win so you can avoid getting blasted with noise yourself. But, once you've won and avoided the noise blast, there's no real reason to give your opponent a loud, long blast of noise instead of a short, quiet one, or no noise at all. At that point, the only reason you're giving a loud blast is because you want to inflict something unpleasant on them – the very definition of aggression. And if you think that noise blasts are too "soft" to count as "real" aggression, the original measure (and a few recent studies) used painful (but safe) electric shocks instead of "noise blasts," and found virtually the same effects.[13,14]

In other studies, researchers have done away with noise blasts and electric shocks entirely, choosing instead to measure aggression on a different sense: taste. The measure is sometimes called the "hot sauce paradigm,"[d] and it's another way to measure aggression safely in the laboratory[15,16,17]. It typically goes something like this: You're told that you'll be completing a series of short, unrelated studies today. The first one involves reading a short essay written by a person in another room. The researchers have rigged the experiment so that you always read an essay that's *very* critical of your own political beliefs. As a result, you're probably not fond of this unseen other participant. Later, you're told that part of the study is about taste preferences. You read the taste profile of the same unseen participant and discover that, among other things, they *hate* spicy food. The researcher then instructs you to create a sample sauce for the other participant to rate. When you taste one of the ingredients for yourself, you discover that it is *incredibly, even painfully,* spicy. You get to decide how much of it to put into the cup for the other participant: You can put in as much or as little as you would like. The researchers later measure how much of the spicy sauce you put into the cup and use this as a way of measuring your aggression. Since you know that the other person hates spicy food, giving them a lot of spicy sauce is a way of inflicting something

---

[d] The creators of this measure were inspired in part by a scene from the film *Mrs. Doubtfire*, where Robin Williams' character sneaks into the kitchen at a restaurant and spikes his romantic rival's meal with excessive amounts of cayenne pepper.[16]

undesired upon them – aggression. Of course, like with the noise blast studies, no one is actually harmed because there is no "other participant," once again fulfilling researchers' ethical obligation to protect participants from harm.

The noise competitive reaction time task and the hot sauce task are far from the only two ways scientists have devised to measure in-lab aggression. Other creative measures involve sabotaging another person's work on a puzzle, forcing another person to view unpleasant videos, or forcing them to hold their hand in very cold water. These tasks have all been approved by various ethics boards, and are generally considered to be ethical measures of aggression. However, in making the measures ethical, critics have raised two important questions: Are these procedures *believable* to participants, and are they comparable to *real-world* aggression?

Put yourself back in the shoes of the participant in the competitive reaction time task. You're told that you're playing against another participant in the other room, and many participants believe that this is the case. But do you ever actually *see* the other participant? Do they react to you increasing or decreasing the volume of the noise blasts you give *them*? Or what about the hot sauce paradigm: Would it seem a bit *too* much of a coincidence that, shortly after being insulted by someone you can't see in another room, you're given the perfect chance to retaliate against them? Although most participants in these studies do not report feeling suspicious when talking with researchers afterward, it is worth considering how believable these procedures are to participants and whether their aggressive responses represent their true intentions to harm or are simply them testing their suspicions about what is and isn't real in the study.

The second critique, that these measures are not comparable to real-world aggression, seems to make a lot of sense. In the real world, if you get angry at your little brother, your first instinct might be to shove him or yell at him, not blast him with loud noise or make him eat something unpleasant.[e] And if you're competing with someone in a real world competition, you *often* have the opportunity to confront that person face-to-face. While researchers try their best to create situations in the laboratory that *feel* natural and believable, sometimes there's just no substitute for the real thing. In the end, it's hard to escape the fact that most measures conducted in a laboratory setting will be somewhat artificial. Because of this, critics are right to challenge whether a person's reaction to a fake situation in the lab tells us anything about how they would *actually* act in the real world (this issue is discussed in depth in Question #16). It seems that laboratory measures of aggression, like real-world measures of aggression, are not perfect, and bring with them a unique set of limitations.

---

[e] Douglas remembers that when he was young, he would indeed try to force his younger brothers to eat very bad-tasting food. He called it a game at the time, but we now know that it was a form of aggression (He knew too…but wasn't willing to admit it).

Unfortunately, the challenge of measuring aggression goes far beyond just measuring aggressive *behavior*. True, aggression researchers are *ultimately* interested in understanding, predicting, and reducing aggressive behavior. But psychologists also know that a person's thoughts, feelings, and even what their body is doing (e.g., heart rate) can *lead* to aggressive behavior. Put another way, if a person is thinking aggressive thoughts, believes that aggression is acceptable, feels angry, and has a racing heart, they're *far* more likely to behave aggressively (for more on this, see Question #12).

For this reason, some researchers try to get around the problem of measuring aggressive behavior altogether by measuring aggressive thoughts, feelings, beliefs, and physical arousal instead. Researchers know that thoughts, feelings, beliefs, and physical arousal are not aggression in and of themselves, but they *are* factors which lead to aggressive behavior. As such, if a researcher learns that doing X will make a person angry or activate aggressive thoughts in their mind, they can fairly safely assume that they would also find an increased likelihood of aggressive behavior if they measured it. As an added bonus, studying aggression-related thoughts, feelings, beliefs, and bodily responses also helps researchers testing scientific theories about how or why certain factors (like media violence, being provoked, or frustration) make people more likely to behave aggressively and how or why other factors (like taking a calming breath or playing a prosocial video game) make people less likely to behave aggressively. We could write an entire book just on the countless ways that researchers have measured aggressive thoughts, feelings, beliefs, and physiological arousal. For now, we'll stick to just a handful of examples to show the range of different measurement tools available to researchers.

When it comes to measuring aggressive feelings and beliefs, researchers often ask participants to report their responses to questions by picking a number from a scale (e.g., 1 to 7) and often include "distraction items" – questions that ask about other feelings, to make it less obvious what the researchers are measuring.[f] For example, researchers measure aggressive feelings like anger or hostility by asking participants how much they agree with statements like "I feel like yelling at somebody" or "I feel like banging on a table"[18,19]. In other studies, researchers measure participants' beliefs about how appropriate aggression is with items such as "It's okay for a boy, Tom, to hit a girl, Julie, if Julie hits Tom first.").[20]

Measures of aggressive thoughts are among the most creative measures used in aggression studies. These measures are designed to tap into whether a

---

[f] This is done to avoid two phenomena called "demand characteristics" and "reactance". Demand characteristics are when participants think they know what the study is about, and try to behave in the way they think the researchers want them to behave. Reactance is just the opposite: When participants intentionally respond in the opposite way from what they think the researchers expect to prove that their behavior cannot be predicted.

person has aggression on their mind – whether they realize it or not.[g] Aggression-related thoughts include – but are not limited to – how easily aggression-related words, images, and concepts come to their mind. One way that researchers measure these aggressive thoughts is by asking participants to "fill in the blanks" of incomplete words[19]. Researchers deliberately choose combinations of letters and blanks that can be completed as aggressive words *or* non-aggressive words. For example, the combination "k i _ _" can be completed as "kiss" or "kind," two words that are *not* aggressive. Alternatively, you could complete the same task with the word "kill," a word with a *clearly* aggressive meaning.

So how does filling in one word or another tell us something about whether a person is having aggressive thoughts? The logic is that if a person is having violent or aggressive thoughts, aggression-related words should come to mind faster and easier than if they were not having aggressive thoughts – this is a concept known to psychologists as "psychological priming." Other studies take this principle one step further, going beyond completing individual words and asking participants to complete an entire story[22]:

"Todd was on his way home from work one evening when he had to brake quickly for a yellow light. The person in the car behind him must have thought Todd was going to run the light because he crashed into the back of Todd's car, causing a lot of damage to both vehicles. Todd got out of his car and surveyed the damage. He then walked over to the other car. What happens next?"

The logic is the same as with the word completion task: If a person has a lot of aggression-related thoughts on their mind, they're more likely to complete the story in an aggressive manner (e.g., "Todd yelled at the other man, 'Hey jackass, are you blind or something?'"), whereas participants who don't have a lot of aggression on their mind will create less aggressive story completions (e.g., "Todd asked the other man if he was okay").

As you've probably guessed, these measures of aggressive thoughts, beliefs, and feelings are not without their own limitations. Unlike measures of aggressive behavior, which are usually fairly straightforward (e.g., number of fights a person has been in), measures of aggressive thoughts frequently involve assumptions about what is being measured. If a person fills in the word "kill" instead of "kiss," does this *really* mean aggression is on their mind, or is it the case that the word "kill" occurs more commonly in writing than the word "kiss"? Measures like these are often more open to debate among researchers when it comes to interpreting their meaning. Researchers almost always have solid theoretical reasons for why these measures are measuring the thing they claim to, but *intuitively* the measures themselves can feel quite removed from what they're actually measuring.

---

[g] Stop and take a moment to realize the implications of designing a measure to tap into something in a person's mind that they, themselves, are unaware of! How would *you* do it?

Up to this point, you've seen many ways researchers measure aggression and aggression-related concepts. It's probably occurred to you that there were potential concerns with every single one of the measures we talked about: ethical restrictions, biased responding, artificiality, problems with interpretation – and these are only *some* of the problems that arise when researchers debate the quality of these measures. The whole thing can leave you wondering if there are *any* measures of aggression that don't have problems. The answer, surprisingly, is a resounding "no": There are no *perfect* measures of aggression. Every single measure of aggression ever conceived carries with it a list of limitations, strengths, and potential problems. This may lead the skeptical reader to ask a very important question: If scientists use flawed measures, how can we learn *anything* about aggression?

Well, let's start by revisiting the original task of measuring Jane's height. Remember how *simple* it seemed, compared to how muddy and complex the issue of measuring aggression has gotten? But let's take another look at the measures used in the task. Are a tape measure or a ruler *really* a perfect way to measure her height? Scientists know, for example, that metal expands when it's heated and contracts when it's cooled. This means that if you measure Jane's height using a metal ruler, it will actually *differ* depending on the temperature of the room. You can't get around the problem by using a non-metal ruler either: Humidity can affect the flexibility and elasticity of a fabric-based tape measure, and wooden or plastic rulers can become warped or bent. And none of these problems even *consider* the possibility of manufacturing defects!

The more you think about it, the more you start to realize that even measuring devices as straightforward as a ruler are, at some level, flawed instruments. For this reason, it may seem impossible to get a "perfect" measure of Jane's height. It's enough to make someone throw up their hands and give up on the whole endeavor of measuring *anything*.

Don't despair, noble reader, because we'll let you in on a secret: Science isn't built on perfection, it's built on a whole lot of "good enoughs." We don't need perfect measures – just measures that are good enough to fulfill our needs. For example, you may never have thought about the flaws of rulers and tape measures because, when it comes to picking out appropriately-sized clothes for yourself or identifying someone in a crowd, you didn't need perfect measures of height. Depending on the size of the thing being measured, some devices are more appropriate than others (e.g., try measuring the height of a mountain or the diameter of a molecule with a ruler), but there will always be *some* "error" in the measurement! The point is to choose the right measurement tool for the job, the one that will give you a "good enough" answer.

With all this in mind, let's return to our imperfect measures of aggression one last time, and ask ourselves if we can compare Jane's aggression to her friend Rowell. Jane admits that she has been in a couple of fights at school; Rowell says that he has never been in a fight. Jane's parents and teachers both agree that Jane sometimes bullies the other students; Rowell's parents and teachers can't recall ever seeing Rowell be mean to others. In the laboratory, Jane strongly agrees that she feels like banging her hands on a table and yelling at others; Rowell only somewhat agrees with these statements. When filling in words, Jane completes "k i _ _" and "c o f f _ _" with "kill" and "coffin"; Rowell completes the same words with "kiss" and "coffee." Finally, Jane blasts her opponents with long, intense bursts of noise in the competitive reaction time task; Rowell, on the other hand, gives shorter blasts of quiet noise.

Given everything you've just heard about Jane and Rowell, what can you conclude about their levels of aggression? Even though every single one of the measures of aggression are flawed, you probably have an idea of whether Jane or Rowell is more aggressive. You can probably predict very accurately, based on the results provided by these imperfect measures, which of the two is more likely to lash out at a younger sibling, yell at a teacher, or wind up in a juvenile delinquency center.

This trick of using many different procedures to overcome the weaknesses of each individual procedure[23,24] is called "converging evidence". Converging evidence is *very* important to scientists, which is one of the major reasons why there are so many different ways of measuring *aggression*. Researchers know that each measure is uniquely flawed, and so they design new measures to overcome the flaws of the existing measures. Having all of these different measures allows researchers to carry out their work and be confident in their conclusions despite working with imperfect measures. If we didn't, we could continually fall into the trap of not doing *any* research and not believing *any* study that came out simply because it used an imperfect measure. Ultimately, the flaws that exist in each of our measures are overcome by the strengths of other measures.[h]

In later questions (e.g., Question #17), we discuss how media violence researchers use the principle of converging evidence to respond to criticisms of the field. For now, we'll say that it's not enough for a critic to point out that a study uses an imperfect measure, because if we were to dismiss *every* study that used an imperfect measure, we would have no evidence for anything! To be fair: it *is* important to consider all of the limitations of a measure, especially in cases where two different measures come to two different conclusions. For example, if Jane hit others more than Rowell, but Rowell yelled at others more than Jane, we need to ask ourselves *why* the differences exist: Are Jane and Rowell aggressive in different ways? Is one measure more sensitive than the other? Is Jane's aggression more extreme than Rowell's? If we included several more measures and found that most of them pointed to the conclusion that Jane was more aggressive than

---

[h] This isn't a quirk of psychology, either. *Every* scientific field uses imprecise measurement tools. To be sure, many have tools with a greater degree of precision or fewer sources of measurement error, but no scientific discipline can claim to have *perfect* measures. Ultimately, scientists from across all disciplines rely on converging evidence across multiple measures and a variety of studies to reach their conclusions.

Rowell, we, as researchers, can be fairly confident in this conclusion, even if it does raise new questions about why some measures don't show this difference.

To summarize, it's important to understand how researchers conceptualize and measure aggression if you want to understand and critique media violence research. Knowing that there are no perfect measures of aggression helps us understand why researchers use so many different measures of aggression: self-reported fighting, teacher and parent reports, archival data, and laboratory measures of aggressive thoughts, feelings, and behaviors. Researchers are okay with the fact that there are no perfect measures, because the principle of converging evidence allows us to remain confident in our findings. Understanding the principles of measurement and converging evidence also plays an important role in how researchers design and interpret studies, as Question #9 will show.

References

1. Anderson, C. A., & Bushman, B. J. (2002). Human aggression. *Annual Review of Psychology, 53*, 27-51.
2. Krahé, B., & Möller, I. (2010). Longitudinal effects of media violence on aggression and empathy among German adolescents. *Journal of Applied Developmental Psychology, 31*, 401-409.
3. Elliot, D. S., Huizinga, D., & Ageton, S. (1985). *Explaining delinquency and drug use.* Beverly Hills, CA: Sage Publications.
4. Anderson, C. A., & Dill, K. E. (2000). Video Games and Aggressive Thoughts, Feelings, and Behavior in the Laboratory and in Life. *Journal of Personality and Social Psychology, 78*(4), 772-790.
5. Ybarra, M. L., Huesmann, L. R., Korchmaros, J. D., & Reisner, S. L. (2014). Cross-Sectional Associations Between Playing Video and computer Game Playing and Weapon Carrying in a National Cohort of Children. *Aggressive Behavior, 40*, 345-358.
6. Baumeister, R. F., & Hutton, D. G. (1987). Self-Presentation Theory: Self-Construction and Audience Pleasing. In B. Mullen & G. R. Goethals (Eds.), *Theories of Group Behavior.* New York, NY: Springer-Verlag.
7. Boxer, P., Huesmann, L. R., Bushman, B. J., O'Brien, M., & Moceri, D. (2009). The role of violent media preference in cumulative developmental risk for violence and general aggression. *Journal of Youth and Adolescence, 38*(3), 417-428.
8. Huesmann, L. R., Moise-Titus, J., Podolski, C-L., & Eron, L. D. (2003). Longitudinal Relations Between Children's Exposure to TV Violence and Their Aggressive and Violent Behavior in Young Adulthood: 1977-1992.
9. Giancola, P. R. & Chermack, S. T. (1998). Construct validity of laboratory aggression paradigms: A response to Tedeschi and Quigley (1996). *Aggression and Violent Behavior, 3*(3), 237-253.

10. Anderson, C. A., & Murphy, C. R. (2003). Violent Video Games and Aggressive Behavior in Young Women. *Aggressive Behavior, 29*, 423-429.

11. Anderson, C. A., Shibuya, A., Ihori, N., Swing, E. L., Bushman, B. J., Sakamoto, A., Rothstein, H. R., & Saleem, M. (2010). Violent video game effects on aggression, empathy, and prosocial behavior in eastern and western countries: a meta-analytic review. *Psychological Bulletin,* 136(2), 151-173.

12. Warburton, W. A., & Bushman, B. J. (2019). The Competitive Reaction Time Task: The development and scientific utility of a flexible laboratory aggression paradigm. *Aggressive Behavior*, 45, 389-396.

13. Taylor, S. (1967). Aggressive behavior and physiological arousal as a function of provocation and the tendency to inhibit aggression. *Journal of Personality, 35*(2), 297-310.

14. Giancola, P. R., & Parrott, D. J. (2008). Further evidence for the validity of the Taylor Aggression Paradigm. *Aggressive Behavior, 34*(2), 214-229.

15. Barlett, C., Branch, O., Rodeheffer, C., & Harris, R. (2009). How Long do the Short-Term Violent Video Game Effects Last? *Aggressive behavior, 35*, 225-236.

16. Lieberman, J. D., Solomon, S., Greenberg, J., & McGregor, H. A. (1999). A hot new way to measure aggression: Hot sauce allocation. *Aggressive Behavior, 25,* 331-348.

17. Warburton, W. A., Williams, K. D., & Cairns, D. R. (2006). When ostracism leads to aggression: The moderating effects of control deprivation. *Journal of Experimental Social Psychology, 42,* 213-220.

18. Anderson, C. A., Deuser, W. E., & DeNeve, K. (1995). Hot temperatures, hostile affect, hostile cognition, and arousal: Tests of a general model of affective aggression. *Personality and Social Psychology Bulletin, 21,* 434-448.

19. Anderson, C. A., & Carnagey, N. L. (2009). Causal effects of violent sports video games on aggression: is it competitiveness or violent content? *Journal of Experimental Social Psychology, 45,* 731-739.

20. Huesmann, L. R., & Guerra, N. G. (1997). Children's Normative Beliefs About Aggression and Aggressive Behavior. *Journal of Personality and Social Psychology, 72*(2), 408-419.

21. Anderson, C. A., Carnagey, N. L., & Eubanks, J. (2003). Exposure to violent media: The effects of songs with violent lyrics on aggressive thoughts and feelings. *Journal of Personality and Social Psychology, 84,* 960-971.

22. Bushman, B. J., & Anderson, C. A. (2002). Violent video games and hostile expectations: A test of the general aggression model. *Personality and Social Psychology Bulletin, 28,* 1679-1686.

23. Warburton, W. A., & Anderson, C. A. (2015). Social psychological study of aggression. In J. Wright [Ed.], *International encyclopaedia of social and behavioral sciences* [2nd Edition] (pp. 295-299). Oxford, UK: Elsevier.

24. Warburton, W. A., & Anderson, C. A. (2018). Aggression. In T. K. Shackleford & P. Zeigler-Hill [Eds.], *The SAGE handbook of personality and individual differences: Vol. 3 Applications of personality and individual differences* (pp. 183-211). Thousand Oaks CA: Sage.

9 - How do you study whether media violence causes aggression?

The Short Answer:

When testing whether media violence affects viewers, good researchers are quite different from laypersons: They don't base their conclusions on anecdotes or intuition. Instead, they conduct scientific studies designed to test hypotheses and base their conclusions on the results of many different types of studies. These different types of study include one-time surveys, long-term studies of changes over time, and experiments that usually take place in a laboratory but are occasionally conducted in natural settings (e.g., school playgrounds, shopping malls). No study design is perfect. Each should be thought of as a tool, designed to be useful for some purposes, but limited and imperfect for others. The combined strengths and weaknesses of different study types overlap with one another, allowing media researchers to get conclusive answers about media violence effects even with imperfect studies.

The Long Answer:

A common theme throughout Chapter 1 is that laypersons and psychologists differ in how they think about violent media and aggression. In Question #8, we showed that laypersons tend to assume that measuring aggression is as simple as counting the number of violent acts a person commits, whereas psychologists have many ways of understanding measurement and rely on a variety of overlapping and imperfect ways to measure aggression. In this question, we'll use similar logic to show that psychologists draw conclusions about the relationship between media violence and aggression in much the same way: By using a combination of imperfect, but overlapping studies with different designs.

To start, let's imagine that your friend wants the two of you to eat at a restaurant, and they ask you what you think about it. How would *you* go about answering the question? If you're like most people, you might start by recalling your own experience with the restaurant – perhaps you remember that time your meal took forever to arrive and, when it did, it was cold and tasted awful.

Of course, if your friend is skeptical, your story might not be enough to convince them to avoid the restaurant. They tell you, "Okay, but that's just *one* bad experience. That's probably not *normal* for the restaurant!"

What now? You *could* agree to give it another shot, but what if you're *sure* that this place is horrible? Maybe you try to bolster your case by thinking about what other people have told you about it. In fact, now that you think about it, you remember that about a month ago your parents *also* complained about this restaurant. And you remember hearing about a friend of a friend who said that they wouldn't be coming back to the restaurant. Together, that's *three* anecdotes from three *different* people who *all* seem to be telling the same awful story about this place. Put yourself in your friend's shoes: Would *you* be convinced to avoid the restaurant based on this evidence?

The example above illustrates how laypersons typically try to use data to answer questions and make arguments. Is this any different from what researchers do? After all, when you boil it down, isn't doing a study just collecting opinions from people?

An easy way to see the difference is to look at how researchers and laypersons would address the original question: "Should we eat at this restaurant?" To start with, a good, skeptical researcher would, like your friend, probably not be persuaded by your story alone. No matter how disgusting you said the food was and how much profanity you used in your story, a researcher would recognize that this is a single point of data.

But what about the experience of your parents and your family? Heck, maybe your dad is a chef himself, and thus an *expert* in all things culinary! *His* opinion should count for a lot more, right? Well, actually, no – your dad's experience, just like yours, is only one point of data. In total, you've based your conclusion on three data points – hardly a compelling case for a researcher!

So what *would* a researcher do? Well, one of the first things would be to find the average rating of *hundreds* of customers: Perhaps they would give out a survey that asked people to rate their favorite places to eat in the city or find a website like Yelp which lets users rate their experience at a restaurant. This body of information contains the collective experience of many diners, all with different tastes, backgrounds, and expectations, and would mean more to our researcher than your experience or the experience of a single critic. Why? Because this data tells us about the experience of the *average* person at this restaurant. This rules out the possibility that their ratings were the result of an unlucky coincidence, a single "bad day," or someone with unusually picky tastes.[a]

Taking what we've just learned, let's look at the question of media violence. Whether we take the layperson's approach of looking at a handful of anecdotes or the researcher's approach of doing studies on many participants, both are simply trying to answer the same question: Is it true that violent media increase a person's risk of aggression? We can see what these approaches might look like and what sorts of conclusions they might lead to through two imaginary

---

[a] Of course, taking the average doesn't *guarantee* that we've solved all of these problems! After all, it's more likely that a person will go online to comment on a very good or a very bad dining experience rather than to comment about a very *average* experience. The result may be an average that's biased toward really good or really bad scores. This is a problem known as *sampling* bias, and it's one of many that researchers have to consider when designing studies!

people: Sean, a high school student and avid gamer, and Amanda, a media researcher.

Sean might try to answer the question by thinking about his *own* experience, asking "can I think of a time when I acted aggressively *because* of video games?" He might remember the time he was playing a video game with his roommate and angrily smacked him for his in-game behavior (e.g., taunting Sean, being a bad teammate.) If he thinks really hard about it, Sean might be able to come up with a handful of such incidents. He'll also be able to think about times when he was aggressive *without* video games, like that time he got into a fistfight at school. When Sean thinks about these anecdotes together, he's probably going to conclude that:

a)   There are lots of times when I'm aggressive, but haven't been playing video games.

b)   Most of the time when I play video games I don't do anything crazy like smacking my roommate.

c)   It therefore seems unlikely that violent games are causing me to be aggressive.

If Sean was feeling *particularly* thorough that day, he might also look to his friends and family for more examples: his friend Jamal rarely plays video games, and he's one of the kindest people Sean knows. Sean's boss Stanley, on the other hand, plays first-person shooter games in his spare time, and is always yelling and insulting people. Sean's favorite professional gamer spends hours a day playing violent video games and seems pretty laid-back and kind. And a recent school shooter in the news supposedly had a bunch of psychological problems and didn't play many video games.

In the end, no matter how thorough Sean tries to be, his conclusion about media violence effects will come down to a handful of anecdotes interpreted through his own beliefs about media violence. For example, let's say Sean believes that violent video games *do* increase one's risk of aggression. If this were the case, Sean might focus on his own hand-slapping behavior, his friend Jamal, and his boss Stanley as evidence for this. They all seem to prove Sean's point: The people who play more violent games are more aggressive, while the people who play fewer violent games are less aggressive. If, however, Sean believes that violent video games have *no* effect on players, he might focus instead on all the times when he did *not* act aggressively after playing video games, on the professional gamer, and on the school shooter as evidence. These examples seem to show that people can be aggressive even without video games, and show that some people who play a lot of video games aren't aggressive (for more on these issues, see Questions #14 and #29).

61

Regardless of which position he believed, Sean could build a convincing case from his anecdotes. But our scientist, Amanda, would not be convinced by Sean's evidence, for at least four reasons.

First, Sean's conclusions are based on a very small amount of data. The original question was whether violent media increase people's risk of aggression, not whether it increases the risk of aggression in Sean, the people Sean knows, or the people Sean has heard about in the news. The question is asking about children, adults, people from all cultures, people from different economic backgrounds, and people with different levels of aggression. In fact, the question isn't even asking about a particular *type* of violent media or a certain *type* of aggression: The question is broad enough to include violent music, television, movies, video games, and books, and includes physical, verbal, and relational aggression (see Question #7 for more on this). Because this question is so broad, any scientific answer will need to include all sorts of media users, all types of media, and look for lots of different types of aggression. Any answer that doesn't include these will fail to persuade our scientist Amanda, since the answer will only be addressing part of the question.

The second reason Amanda would not be convinced by Sean's evidence is because Sean's evidence was collected in a *non-systematic* way. This just means there was no rhyme or reason to how Sean gathered his data: His examples were simply "whatever comes to mind". And, "what comes to Sean's mind" is biased by many factors, including his expectations, his desired "answer," what he's been doing recently, and even the temperature of the room he's in. Likewise, his examples of "aggression" were all over the place and included everything from a mild slap to mass murder. Should we *really* be comparing the murderous rampage of a mass shooter to Sean smacking his roommate? Is the amount of game-playing Sean's boss does comparable in any way to the professional gamer? There's no way to *meaningfully* compare or combine Sean's anecdotes or the people in them, because they're a disorganized mess of people of all ages, backgrounds, personalities, and histories, none of which is taken into account. Because of this, it's hard to know what we can take away from Sean's "whatever comes to mind" examples.

A third reason Amanda would not find Sean's evidence convincing is because Sean himself may be motivated, consciously or unconsciously, to reach a particular conclusion.[b] If Sean is an avid player of violent games, he might feel threatened by the possibility that his favorite activity could be harmful to him or

---

[b] This is not to say that researchers are magical beings who are immune to bias or motivation to be proven correct! It could be argued that nearly all researchers want to find evidence that their particular theory is correct. The big difference, however, is that researchers have to "show their work" to other researchers and have it reviewed and checked for such biases *before* it can be published. This doesn't *completely* eliminate the problem, but it does a pretty good job!

that he might be forced (by parents, societal pressure, even laws) to stop playing his favorite games. The easiest way to eliminate this threat is to conclude that violent games do not cause any harm and then selectively look for anecdotes which prove this point. Psychologists have known for decades that this kind of thinking leads to biased remembering of information, usually without people even knowing that they're doing it![c]

A fourth and final reason why Amanda would take Sean's evidence with a grain of salt was mentioned in Question #7 and was often pointed out by the famous television character Dr. Gregory House: People lie. They lie to others, and sometimes they lie to themselves. Indeed, recent research has found that avid gamers will lie about how aggressive they are when participating in a study that they believe is testing the violent games-aggression hypothesis.[1] As such, given that Sean is an avid gamer, there is reason to believe that some of his anecdotes cannot be taken at face value.

Okay, we've spent a lot of time ripping on Sean's method of gathering data. So what is it that scientists like Amanda do that Sean isn't doing that makes *their* results so much more compelling? The answer is that they conduct "scientific studies." Scientists follow the scientific method and run studies specifically-designed to test the hypothesis that violent media and aggression are associated. These studies are designed to produce organized and meaningful data that either directly support or oppose the hypothesis. The results of these studies – not just one, but dozens or even hundreds – are what scientists draw their conclusions from. If there is no link between violent media and aggression, repeated studies should show that this is the case. If there *is* a link, well-designed studies which find evidence for this link will start to pile up.

We could, at this point, write an entire book just on the subject of how to design good scientific studies (and, indeed, dozens of such books exist[2]). We'll avoid boring you with a textbook-length discussion of the subject by limiting ourselves to a *very* brief overview of some of the types of studies media violence researchers run. We'll discuss three categories of studies in particular: cross-sectional studies, longitudinal studies, and experimental studies.[d] Each type of study allows researchers to test the link between media violence and aggression in different ways. Like our discussion of aggression measures, each design has its own set of strengths and weaknesses.[3]

---

[c] One of us is old enough to remember the public debate about whether smoking cigarettes caused lung cancer. Many smokers showed this type of biased remembering by recalling people who smoked and lived long lives, all to avoid thinking about what it would mean for them if what scientists were saying about smoking and lung cancer was true.

[d] If you get nothing else out of this book, let it be learning what these impressive-sounding terms mean so you can throw them around and impress your friends with your science literacy!

Cross-sectional media violence studies are designed to answer the question "are rates of violent media use related to rates of aggression?" Or, to put it another way, they ask whether people who consume a *lot* of violent media are more aggressive on average than people who consume *less* violent media. They involve gathering a sample of the population of interest (e.g., American undergraduates, Japanese children, *World of Warcraft* players), which determines who the study's conclusions will apply to. Samples can be as ethnically, financially, and politically narrow or broad as the researchers wish. As just one example, we'll look at a study from 2004 that tested the relationship between computer game violence exposure and aggressive behavior in a sample of over 600 Grade 8 and 9 Midwestern U.S. students[4].

Once researchers gather their sample, all participants are given the same set of questions, either through in-person interviews or, more commonly, surveys. The questions asked differ from study to study, but usually include at least one measure about the amount of violent media participants consume and at least one measure about their aggression. More thorough studies will include multiple measures of violent media use and aggression and will also include other variables such as personality, socioeconomic status, and parental involvement. By measuring these other variables, researchers can statistically test for, and rule out, the possibility that a relationship between violent media and aggression is due to some other variable (this issue described in more detail in Question #14).

In our example study, the researchers asked participants to name their three favorite video games, indicate how much they played each, and indicate how much violence was in each game. These questions allowed the construction of a measure of the relative amount of violent video game exposure for each participant. For example, a participant who played no games at all and one who played lots of games but did not have any violent games among their favorites would be considered "low" in violent game exposure. On the other end of the scale, a participant who listed two or three violent games among their favorites and who spent lots of time playing each week would score higher in violent game exposure. The researchers also asked about getting into fights at school, and measured how hostile their personality was.

After collecting data from all of these participants, the researchers then conducted a series of statistical analyses. To avoid turning this book into a stats textbook, the techniques can be thought of like this: The researchers tested whether there was a pattern in the data and, if there was, how strong the pattern was. The analysis generates a number, called a *correlation coefficient*, that tells researchers the direction of the pattern in the data and how strongly the data tend follow that pattern. In this case, the pattern being tested was whether the students who use a lot of violent media were also the same students who scored the highest on measures of aggression. This study happened to find that participants who spent more time playing violent video games were the most likely to get into fights at school.

If the amount of violent media people use can reliably tell us something about how aggressive they are, scientists conclude that there is a significant correlation between these two variables (i.e., there is a link between them). If the amount of violent media people use is *unrelated* to how aggressive they are, scientists conclude that there is *no* correlation. In our example study, the researchers found that those students who were exposed to more violent media were also more likely to score higher on the measure of aggression than those who were exposed to less violent media. This type of cross-sectional study uses the same design as studies that examine the effects of smoking cigarettes on one's likelihood of getting lung cancer (i.e., do the people who smoke the most have the highest risk of lung cancer?)

One important feature of these studies is that researchers are looking at *average* tendencies across all of the participants in the study. If on average people who use lots of violent media are more aggressive than people who use less violent media, it doesn't matter if there are some exceptions to this pattern. In other words, there are probably some low violent media users who are more aggressive than some high violent media users, and vice-versa. The existence of some exceptions to the rule does not change the fact that the relationship is present for *most* people. Remember: Researchers are answering questions about the effects of violent media on the average person, not about whether there are some people who seem to go against this rule (see Question #19 for more on this topic). Again, we can compare this to the example of smoking and lung cancer: Some smokers do not die of lung cancer, and some nonsmokers do die of lung cancer. The existence of these somewhat unusual cases doesn't change the fact that, on average, smokers are more likely to die of lung cancer than are non-smokers.

So, cross-sectional studies can tell us whether a link exists between violent media use and aggression in the real world. However, critical readers might notice that there's a problem with such results: A correlation between media violence and aggression doesn't prove that media violence *causes* aggression. After all, the data in our example study can't tell us which came first, the violent video games or the aggression. Because of this, the study can only conclude that it's equally possible that playing lots of violent video games *causes* students to become more aggressive and that already-aggressive students choose to play more violent video games. This *causal order* question is one of the biggest drawbacks to cross-sectional studies: They can tell us whether two variables are related but not the causal direction of this relationship. A second difficult question posed by cross-sectional studies is the possibility that some *third variable* may be the true underlying cause of the relation between media violence and aggression. For example, maybe attention deficit hyperactivity disorder (ADHD) causes children to like playing video games *and* causes high aggression. We'll discuss these issues in greater detail below and in Questions #13 and #15.[e]

For now, let's turn our attention away from cross-sectional studies and look at another type of study that researchers commonly conduct: the longitudinal study. Longitudinal studies are specifically designed to answer a different type of question. Whereas cross-sectional studies ask if people who consume more violent media are more aggressive than people who consume less violent media, longitudinal studies ask whether people who consume lots of violent media *become* more aggressive over time than people who consume less violent media. The two questions seem very similar at first glance, but longitudinal studies ask participants the same questions at multiple points in time, which allows them to better test which came first: The aggression or the violent media.

Longitudinal studies can be run the same way as cross-sectional studies. Both involve gathering data from a sample of people about their violent media consumption and their aggression. The big difference is in how *many* times participants complete the study. In cross-sectional studies, the researchers collect data from participants only once, giving then a snapshot of the participants at a single moment in time. In a longitudinal study, the researchers ask the same participants questions again in the future. "The future" can be several months away (e.g., at the start and end of a school semester) or much longer (e.g., in early childhood and again in adulthood). Longitudinal studies can also involve more than two points in time (e.g., the same survey at the start of each school year for every year of high school).

As an example of a longitudinal study, we'll refer to a 2008 study of German teenagers[5]. In this study, the researchers surveyed 653 Grade 5 to Grade 7 students from a half-dozen different schools in 1999. They asked participants how often they played different video games and watched different films (each answer was rated by researchers as "violent" or "non-violent"). The researchers also asked participants whether they had engaged in aggressive behavior (e.g., "I have taken part in a fight," "I have beaten up somebody badly). Two years later, the researchers were able to track down and survey 314 of the original participants and asked them the same questions as before.

---

[e] Unfortunately, this same "reverse causality" argument was used by the tobacco industry to argue that there was no evidence *proving* that cigarettes caused lung cancer. As we shall see later, there *are* ways to compare these alternative explanations, as we'll describe in Question #13. It's also the case that researchers can use a series of well-designed cross-sectional studies to test and rule out many of these alternative explanations, leaving media violence (or cigarette smoking) standing as the most reasonable explanation across the whole set of studies.

You'll notice that the sample size of the second wave of the survey was less than *half* of what it was in the first wave. This illustrates an important drawback to longitudinal studies: It's hard enough to do a survey of hundreds of people, but it's even *harder* to track down the same people years later! But the extra effort is definitely worth it. Why? Because the second wave of data lets scientists measure how participants have changed over time. Did they become more aggressive? Did they consume more violent media? And, most importantly, did participants who used lots of violent media become *more* aggressive over time (or vice-versa)? Researchers use complex statistical techniques to test which of these patterns of results are supported by the data. In our example of the German students, the researchers found evidence that two distinct effects were happening: Aggressive students used *more* violent media over time (see Figure 9.1, Path A) *and* students who used more violent media became *more* aggressive over time (see Figure 9.1, Path B.)

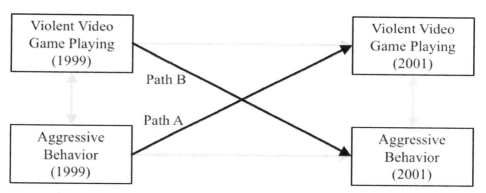

Figure 9.1. Simplified Results of a Longitudinal Media Violence Study.

This last finding is particularly relevant to our question of whether violent media increase one's risk of aggression. As we'll discuss in Question #13, critics sometimes argue that the link between media violence and aggression operates in the opposite direction: That more aggressive people are drawn to consume more violent media. This particular study is informative because it shows that both hypotheses can be true without negating the other – both were supported by the data!ᶠ In other words, just because one direction is true doesn't mean that the other one necessarily has to be false. Such situations are called *bidirectional* effects, and they can lead to increasing or decreasing "spirals". In this case, aggressive people may be drawn to violent video games which, in turn, increase their risk for

---

ᶠ We should point out that even though this particular study found evidence that the effect occurred in *both* directions, many other longitudinal studies only find evidence that violent media increases the risk of aggression, not the other way. When both effects *are* found, the "violent media increases aggressiveness" effect is usually the stronger of the two.

aggression, something that may lead them to seek out even *more* violent media in the future. This sort of bidirectional effect isn't unique to media violence: A similar effect can be found between alcohol abuse and depression, where one leads to the other in a continuous cycle.[6]

As these findings suggest, longitudinal studies are particularly useful at helping researchers test *causal order* questions. In the case of media violence research, it can help test whether the media violence-aggression link is due to highly aggressive people preferring violent media or due to violent media increasing consumers' risk of aggression.

Longitudinal studies are not without their own limitations. They're very expensive to run, because researchers have to track down the original participants months or even years later. They also take a considerable amount time for the results to come in (i.e., years.) And, although longitudinal studies let scientists test a host of alternative explanations of the violent media-aggression link, it is difficult for such studies to rule out *all possible* alternatives. In other words, a well-conducted longitudinal study allows stronger causal conclusions than a well-conducted cross-sectional study precisely because it allows tests of causal order and related alternative explanations. Even so, complex versions of the "third variable problem" can exist in longitudinal studies (we'll address these more in Questions #13 and #15.)

One solution is to conduct additional studies that measure these potential third variables so that scientists can statistically rule them out. Another is to conduct studies where the third variable in question cannot possibly play a role. For example, a testosterone alternative explanation is ruled out by studies showing that a similar relationship between media violence and aggression exists in samples of young children (before puberty kicks in) and in samples of girls. In both of these populations, testosterone levels are relatively low and stable, ruling out testosterone as an explanation for the link between media violence and aggression.

Where does that leave us? So far we've described two ways researchers study media violence and aggression in the "real world" – that is, they measure how much people consume violent media and engage in aggressive behavior when left to their own devices. But, as we've seen, these studies have several limitations, owing, at least in part, to the fact that the real world is a messy, complex place. The final type of study –experiments – reduces these problems by creating an artificial situation which lets researchers experimentally control how much exposure people have to violent media and then measure peoples' aggression afterward.[g]

---

[g] To clarify, experimental studies *often* take place in a carefully-controlled laboratory setting, but they don't always *have* to! Sometimes both media violence exposure and the measurement of aggression takes place in a fairly natural setting, like in an elementary school classroom or on a playground. These types of studies are a *lot* more work and are fairly uncommon, however!

Like cross-sectional and longitudinal studies, experiments aim to answer a unique flavor of the media violence question: Does media violence exposure increase the risk of aggressive behavior above and beyond every other factor (e.g., history of violence, testosterone, or poverty)? Experiments can answer questions about *causal direction* and *why* violent media may increase the risk of aggression (e.g., by changing the way consumers think, by increasing their heart rate.)

In a typical media violence experiment, participants arrive at the lab and are exposed to some form of media. As an example, we'll use a 2013 study of 77 French college students[7]. Unbeknownst to participants, they were *randomly* assigned (e.g., via coin-flip) to a violent media condition or a non-violent media condition. In this study, half of the participants played a violent first-person shooter game (either *Call of Duty 4* or *Condemned 2*), while half played a non-violent racing game (either *Dirt 2* or *SBK 09 Superbike*). After exposure to the media – in this case, 20 minutes of playing their assigned game– participants were then put into a situation where they had the chance to behave aggressively. In this study, the aggression involved blasting an opponent with unpleasant noise (see Question #8 for more information about this task, called the competitive reaction time task). Researchers then compare how aggressively participants from the two conditions responded. In this study, the participants who played the violent game gave blasts of noise that were about 25% *longer* and *louder* than participants who played the racing game. We can therefore conclude that the violent game *caused an increase* in the player's aggression relative to the nonviolent game.

The logic of the experiment is actually quite simple and elegant. By assigning participants to the "violent" and "non-violent" game conditions *at random*, the researchers effectively make these two groups of participants statistically equal in every way *except* for the type of media that they're exposed to. We'll avoid all the statistical gobbledygook and simplify it by stating that if you divide people into two groups in a *completely* random way (e.g., a coin flip), there is no reason why one group should have significantly more men, older people, skilled people, or inherently aggressive people than the other. In the eyes of statisticians, the groups are about as equal as you can make them, especially as the experimental groups get larger and larger. In short, when you randomly assign participants to groups, we can treat them as equal on *everything* except for whatever we are doing differently to the two groups – which scientists call an *independent* or *experimental* or *manipulated* variable.

Why is it so important that the groups are equivalent at the start of the study? Because when researchers compare the average aggression scores of the two groups at the end of the study, any differences can *only* be due to whatever we manipulated between the groups. It's the same logic used by medical researchers to test the effectiveness of a new treatment. Sick participants are randomly assigned to a "treatment" and a "no treatment" condition. If the patients in the "treatment" condition recover significantly faster than those in the "no treatment" condition, the difference must be caused by whatever the participants in the "treatment" condition got that those in the "no treatment" condition did not. It can't be because people in the "treatment" condition just happened to be healthier at the start of the study, because random assignment makes this possibility extremely unlikely. This ability to rule out alternative explanations and directly test whether X *causes* Y to change is the reason why experiments are the "gold standard" among researchers for testing causation (we describe this in greater detail in Questions #13 and #15.)

Of course, even experiments have limitations! As we mention in Question #8, the artificial nature of laboratory studies increases the likelihood that participants' observed behavior isn't the same as real-world behavior, a topic we discuss in Question #16. A second limitation of experiments is that it's impossible to know with absolute certainty that your groups are equal on all possible variables at the start of the study. Random assignment gives us a pretty good chance of this being the case, but scientists *always* recognize the potential for statistical anomalies. After all, winning the lottery is a statistical anomaly, but with enough players and enough time, people do win![h] Scientists are well aware of this problem, and this is why they expect experimental studies to vary somewhat when it comes to their results: Due to random chance alone, two identically-run studies will differ somewhat in their results. This is why scientists are always wary of being overly confident in the results of a single study.

To avoid diving too deep into this topic and extending an already-long answer even further, let's finish up this conversation about experiments by saying that:

1. Many studies show that laboratory measures of aggression can tell us a lot about real-world aggression despite seeming somewhat artificial.

2. Some experimental studies *are* conducted in real world settings, and they tend to show the same sorts of media violence effects as laboratory studies.

3. Media violence experiments tend to yield fairly consistent results showing that violent media does increase a person's risk for aggression.

4. The limitations of experimental studies are worth keeping in mind, especially if you want to critique the quality of any given experiment.

Let's review what we've learned in this response: Researchers commonly use three different types of studies to test whether violent media increases the risk of aggression in consumers. Cross-sectional studies test whether media violence exposure is *correlated* with aggression in the real world by testing whether high

---

[h] If this example hadn't made it clear, statisticians have a fairly pessimistic view of the lottery, which should tell you something if you're a regular buyer of lottery tickets!

consumers of media violence are more aggressive than low consumers of media violence. Longitudinal studies allow researchers to measure violent media and aggression across several points in time to see if the correlation is due to media violence *increasing* the risk of aggression over time (or vice-versa, or both). Experimental studies are the best tool researchers have for testing whether violent media exposure, and not something else, *causes* an increase in aggression; they do so by randomly assigning people to "violent" and "non-violent" media conditions and measuring differences in aggression between the two groups after exposure.

We began this answer by discussing the limitations of anecdotal evidence: It's non-systematic, often riddled with bias, and typically involves very small sample sizes. We showed a number of common study designs scientists use with the hope of showing that there is a better way to answer questions about media violence effects. But we acknowledge that these studies, while much better than anecdotal evidence, are not perfect. Not only do they all rely on imperfect measures of aggression (as we discussed in Question #8), but they are each limited in their ability to fully test whether violent media increase the risk of aggression.

Scientists can still draw important conclusions from sets of studies despite the fact that any one is imperfect. The best researchers are keenly aware of these limitations and are trained to recognize them. They are also trained to know that studies have unique strengths which can overcome the weaknesses of other study designs. For example, cross-sectional and longitudinal studies focus on real-world aggression, something that experimental studies typically can't do for ethical reasons.[i] But cross-sectional studies are *weak* at showing causal direction, and although longitudinal studies provide *good* evidence for causal order they still are somewhat susceptible to complex third variable alternative explanations. Experiments, on the other hand, are *specially designed* to answer questions about causality and to rule out third variable alternative explanations. The best researchers rely on the overlapping strengths of different study types, in conjunction with how well their results mesh with other well-established theories and psychological principles, to draw scientifically valid conclusions about media violence effects. If all three types of studies show the same general result, this is strong evidence for the effect because the strengths of one type of study compensate for the weaknesses of other types.

This is why it's so important to base your conclusions on the results of more than a single study. A layperson asks "what does this study prove?" but a researcher asks "what does this study add to the hundreds of studies that came before it?" It's also why researchers can accept a flawed and imperfect study, warts and all, and still see its value in contributing to our knowledge. We realize that if we were to throw out every study that was imperfect, we would be left with nothing at all upon which to build our understanding of the world. *This is true of*

---

[i] For example, we can't randomly assign 6-year olds to play a violent or nonviolent video game in a classroom and then give them baseball bats to see who inflicts more carnage on the playground.

all sciences, not just behavioral science! Instead, good researchers design new studies with these trade-offs and limitations in mind and use them to overcome the limitations of other prior studies, ultimately advancing the entire field's knowledge one step at a time. In other words: No one study is enough to definitively *prove* or *disprove* media violence effects – despite what the media or internet posters might tell you.[j] This is why one or two studies that show no effects of media violence on aggression do not negate the hundreds of studies showing that there is an effect.

It should be clear to you now that laypersons and researchers take dramatically different approaches when it comes to answering questions about violent media and aggression. Researchers take a systematic approach, using specifically-designed studies and considering what they have to say as part of a larger body of evidence. For a layperson, it often seems like it's enough to come up with a handful of personal experiences to defend their position. When a layperson reads the scientific literature, she or he may be content to look at a single study, not realizing how little a single study means without considering the broader research context. Ultimately, scientists answer questions in a slow, rigorous, and systematic way, which is why they often spend decades trying to find a clear answer to a single question. It's this devotion to rigor and detail that differentiates the scientific study of media violence from merely having an opinion about it.

References

1. Bender, J., Rothmund, T., & Gollwitzer, M. (2013). Biased estimation of violent video game effects on aggression: Contributing factors and boundary conditions. *Societies, 3*(4), 383-398.
2. Goodreads.com. *Popular Research Methods Books.* Retrieved September 15, 2016 from https://www.goodreads.com/shelf/show/research-methods
3. Prot, S., & Anderson, C. A. (2013). Research methods, design, and statistics in media psychology. Chapter in K. Dill (Ed.) *The Oxford Handbook of Media Psychology* (109-136). New York: Oxford University Press.
4. Gentile, D. A., Lynch, P. J., Linder, J. R., Ruh, J., & Walsh, D. A. (2004). The effects of violent video game habits on adolescent hostility, aggressive behaviors, and school performance. *Journal of Adolescence, 27,* 5-22.

---

[j] As an analogy, think about scientists as carpenters. It would be foolish for a carpenter to try to do their job with *only* a hammer. While a hammer is certainly a useful tool for driving in nails, it's not so good at removing screws or measuring a length of drywall. The best carpenters carry a variety of tools and use the most appropriate tool for the job. Likewise, the best researchers use the most appropriate study design for the task at hand and use a variety of different studies with overlapping strengths.

5. Hopf, W. H., Huber, G. L., & Weiß, R. H. (2008). Media violence and youth violence: A 2-year longitudinal study. *Journal of Media Psychology, 20*(3), 79-96.

6. Pacek, L. R., Martins, S. S., & Crum, R. M. (2013). The bidirectional relationships between alcohol, cannabis, co-occurring alcohol and cannabis use disorders with major depressive disorder: Results from a national sample. *Journal of Affective Disorders, 148*(2-3), 188-195.

7. Hasan, Y., Bègue, L., & Bushman, B. J. (2013). Violent video games stress people out and make them more aggressive. *Aggressive Behavior, 39*, 64-70.

10 - Why do psychologists study media violence?

The Short Answer:

Researchers have been interested in the effects of exposure to violent media for decades – and for many good reasons! In the 1960s, psychologists studied how people learned by watching others, including children learning and imitating behavior they saw on a TV screen. Later researchers studied media violence to better understand how things that we learn in one setting can be applied to other settings. Some researchers are not interested in media violence specifically, but study it as part of a broader interest in how technology affects the way we think, feel, and behave. Yet another group of media researchers are mainly interested in the social problem of aggressive behavior, and have been working backwards from this problem to understand its numerous causes. Researchers with overlapping interests from different disciplines have studied media violence for decades, bringing with them unique theories, perspectives, and methodologies that, when combined, help us come to a more thorough understanding of the topic.

The Long Answer:

Science rarely proceeds in a straight line. It meanders, branches off, doubles back on itself, and frequently runs into dead ends. It's also rarely as organized as nonscientists imagine it to be. We often treat sciences like psychology and biology as being entirely separate "boxes" when, in reality, researchers from different disciplines often find themselves tackling the same questions and finding similar answers. For example, calculus was independently developed by two scholars with *very* different backgrounds: Gottfried Leibniz, a German philosopher, and Issac Newton, an English physicist. Likewise, electrical current was discovered by both Thomas Edison, a telegraph operator and entrepreneur, and Nikola Tesla, a physicist and an engineer. And, if you're thinking this only happens in fields like physics, we should point out that the history of psychology is *full* of researchers from different fields who had an interest in human behavior. In fact, two of the most famous names in psychology, Ivan Pavlov[a] and Sigmund Freud, had a *huge* impact on the field despite neither one being formally trained in psychology (Pavlov was a physiologist who studied, and won a Nobel Prize for, his work on digestion[1], while Freud was a physiologist who studied brain anatomy[2]).

The point of this little history lesson is to show you that there are many reasons for a scientist to study a given question. Pavlov, best known for making

---

[a] Hopefully that name "rings a bell!"

dogs salivate at the ring of a bell, laid the foundation for psychological theories of learning. But he never *intended* to study learning! Pavlov was *trying* to study digestion in dogs, but was frustrated by the fact that his dogs were salivating *before* the food was even in their mouths[3]. An entire field of psychology owes its existence to a physiologist trying to track down and eliminate a nuisance in his digestion studies! Ultimately, the reasons for Pavlov's research are not as important as what psychologists learned from it.

With this idea fresh in our minds, let's think about the issue of media violence research and who would want to study it. As it turns out, researchers from many theoretical backgrounds have been studying the topic for decades. The reasons for their interest range from testing if people can learn by watching others to wanting to understand the basic processes that make our mind work. They include researchers wanting to know how technology affects brains that evolved before the invention of electricity and researchers simply wanting to know what causes aggression and how they might reduce it. In the following section, we'll review some of these different approaches and how they influenced the methods we use to study media violence (see Question #9 for more on these methods) and the types of questions media violence researchers have been interested in (see Question #12, and Chapter 2 for discussions of these questions.)

Some of the first researchers to study media violence did so using a theory called social learning theory[4]. In a nutshell, social learning theory hypothesized that people are able to learn vicariously from one another – that is, they can learn by watching what happens to others[5,6]. While this might seem pretty obvious now, it was an important step forward for psychology during a time when researchers thought that people could only learn from things which happened to them *directly*.

To illustrate what this theory entails, let's use an example. Imagine that you stuck a fork into an electrical outlet. Your behavior would have a consequence: One heck of an electric shock! According to classic learning theory, this negative experience would discourage you from sticking a fork into an electrical socket again. Pretty advanced stuff so far, right?[b]

Now let's imagine that *you* weren't the one who stuck the fork in outlet. Instead, you watched *me* do it.[c] As a result of my behavior, *I* receive an electric shock, but *nothing* happens to you. According to classical learning theory, something happening to me should have no effect on what you've learned, meaning there should be nothing stopping you from following in my footsteps and doing the exact same stupid thing that I just did.[d]

Obviously, this isn't what happens in the real world. Clearly, if you see me getting electrocuted from sticking the fork in the outlet, you're going to think twice about doing it yourself, meaning *you've* learned something from *my* experience. This is the heart of social learning theory: We learn things not just

---

[b] Hopefully nothing about this is *shocking* to you.

[c] And you did nothing to stop me – you monster!

[d] Okay, now we're even!

from our own experience, but also by watching what happens to others. It's the "social" part that really makes social learning theory so important!

So what do forks and power outlets have to do with violent media? Well, to test social learning theory, psychologist Albert Bandura and his colleagues conducted a famous set of experiments in the early 1960s which we refer to today as the "Bobo doll" studies.[7,8] A Bobo doll is a 3-foot tall, inflatable vinyl toy with a weight at the bottom, which causes the doll to return to an upright position after being tipped or pushed over. In these studies, young children were randomly assigned to watch an adult playing in a room in one of two ways. Some of the children watched the adult beat up the Bobo doll (e.g., jumping on it, punching it in the nose, throwing it around the room). Children in the *other* condition watched the same adult quietly and calmly playing with other toys in the room.

After watching the adult, the children were taken to another room. Here, the researchers made the children frustrated: They showed the children a bunch of really cool toys before quickly telling the children that these toys were the best ones and would be given to *other* children in the study. The researchers then ushered the children into a different room, without any of the cool toys. If you've ever babysat young children, you know *exactly* how mad this would have made them. So now the children are angry and left alone in a room with a bunch of less-interesting toys, including the Bobo doll. The question: What would they do?

The researchers' findings were clear: The children who watched the adults playing aggressively played more aggressively themselves compared to the children who watched the adults play in a non-aggressive way. Children often imitated the behavior of the aggressive adults – saying similar things, jumping on the Bobo doll, hitting it in the face, and trying to throw it.[e] Bandura and his colleagues concluded that people, including children, learned behaviors – including aggression – by watching the behavior of others. Later studies would go on to show that children weren't just mindlessly mimicking the adult's aggression: When aggressive adults were *punished* for being aggressive, children were *less* aggressive later on during the play session, but when they saw adults being *praised* for their aggression, the children became *more* aggressive[9].[f]

The Bobo doll studies provide compelling evidence that people learn by watching others. But the studies raised important new questions. Does the person being observed have to be physically present for people to learn from them? Can people learn aggression by watching a *film* of someone being aggressive? Does the observed person even have to be *human*? Bandura and his colleagues tested these

---

[e] It's not hard to find video footage of this study online, and we highly encourage you to look it up. It's both amusing and a bit surprising to see it for yourself.

[f] The behavior in the Bobo Doll studies would not technically be considered true aggression by our modern definition because there is no intent to harm another "person." For this reason, modern reviews of media violence studies typically don't include these studies.

questions and found that children who saw aggression being modeled, either in-person or on film, were more aggressive than children who had not seen the aggressive behavior[7]. This increase in aggression was found even for children who watched a video of a *cartoon cat* modeling the aggression. Bandura concluded that people can and do learn by watching what others are doing, regardless of whether those others are in front of us, on film, or not even human!

More than fifty years later the influence of social learning theory can still be found on media violence research. Scientists continue to study how and what people learn from what they see in violent media. Technology has vastly improved since the 60s, allowing us to test whether the same hypotheses hold true when using video games instead of black-and-white films. These same advancements have inspired new questions as well. For example, researchers have tested whether identifying with a violent video game character (e.g., the character you're playing as) increases aggressive behavior after playing the game (the answer, turns out, is "yes".)[10] Despite these advances in technology, however, modern media violence studies still follow the same basic design logic of the original social learning studies: Compare the aggression of participants after they're exposed to either violent or non-violent media[11].

Social learning theorists have had a major impact on the way we study media violence today. But they're not the only ones to study media violence. Many social psychologists are interested in understanding how the mind works, a field known as social cognition. They study the human mind as a sort of computer that takes in information about others, interprets it, forms judgments about them, stores and retrieves this information from memory, and uses this information to respond in day-to-day life[12]. Social cognition researchers seek to understand how the brain's "mental software" works, in the hope of using this knowledge to understand and predict social behavior better. This perspective includes several key concepts from social learning theory and has been *very* influential on modern media violence research. This influence is most obviously seen as researchers shift away from the question, "*does* violent media increase one's risk of aggression" toward a new question, "*how* does violent media increase the risk of aggression?"

To illustrate why social cognitive researchers are interested in the topic of media violence, let's look at two important cognitive psychology concepts: "schemas" and "scripts" (we will explain in greater detail how these processes relate to media violence in Question #12). Schemas refer to the way information is organized in the brain. When you see the word "knife" written on a page, somewhere in your brain a particular set of neurons becomes activated – we'll call these your "knife" neurons. As your "knife" neurons become activated, they activate other neurons which fire in response to concepts *related* to knives: What knives look like (e.g., pocket knives, bowie knives, daggers), what they can be used for (e.g., cooking tool, decoration, weapon), and features of knives (e.g., sharp, dangerous, pointy). The pattern of concepts that become active in your mind when you see or hear the word "knife" is an example of a schema – in this case, your "knife" schema.

So why do researchers care so much about our schemas? It's because the content of our schemas plays an important role in our attitudes, beliefs, and behavior. To illustrate, use your imagination for a moment and think about the mental image that comes to your mind when I say, "Anthony is holding a knife." Even though I've given you very limited information, you've already put together a basic mental picture of the scene. But *your* mental picture and *my* mental picture will differ depending on the content of our "knife" schemas. Our knife schemas will differ greatly if we've had very different life experiences with knives.[13] Even though we started with the same information, we may end up with *completely* different scenes, which could dramatically change what we think about Anthony or how we would behave if we were in this scene.

Let's say that the concept you most strongly associate with "knife" is "food preparation tool." If that's true, you might be picturing "Chef Anthony" chopping vegetables for a soup. If, however, your "knife" schema includes strong associations with the concepts "stabbing," "murder," and "weapon," you might be picturing "Anthony the knife-wielding murderer" chasing his next victim. The dramatic difference in these two interpretations illustrates how the content of our schemas can affect the way we think, feel, and behave in response to information about the world. Social cognitive psychologists are interested in how violent media may, over time, change the content of our schemas and, by extension, change the way we behave.

Scripts are a concept closely-related to schemas, and are also important to social cognitive researchers. Script theory proposes that much of our behavior is organized into patterns that we learn and refine with experience. These patterns operate much like scripts for a play or film: As actors, we follow the content of our scripts.

To see a script in action, think about your behavior in a restaurant. Chances are, you've got a script for how to behave in a restaurant and you follow it, even if you're not aware that you're doing it. When you enter a restaurant that you've never been to before, you probably have an expectation about how you and others will behave. You expect to sit down somewhere and be shown a menu. You'll probably decide what you want to drink first because you expect a server to come by and take your drink order *before* they take your food order. Without being told or having to think about it, you expect your food to arrive later. After you're done eating you also expect, without having to be told, that you will have to pay for your meal before you leave. These are all things you expect even though you've never been to this restaurant before – these are behavioral scripts.[g]

We develop behavioral scripts through a combination of our own experiences, the media we consume, and watching and interacting with other people. Young children must learn these behavioral scripts, which becomes

---

[g] To understand why we use behavioral scripts, imagine what life would be like if, every time you went to a new restaurant or met a new person you had to re-learn every single behavior from scratch!

apparent when they seem oblivious to concepts such as "sit down and patiently wait for your meal," "don't yell and throw things," and "no, you can't order canned ravioli." We can also marvel at the fact that, over time, we've not only learned a "restaurant" script, but several variations of that script which include the "fast-food restaurant" script, the "cafeteria" script, and the "sit-down dinner" script.[h]

Some researchers interested in script theory are drawn to media violence research to study how media influence the behavioral scripts that we develop. To illustrate how this might be the case, imagine that you're standing in a crowded bar holding your drink. Someone walks by you and roughly bumps your shoulder. The impact causes you to spill your drink and stain your new shirt. How do you respond? In situations like these where you have a split-second to make a decision, well-practiced behavioral scripts tend to take over and prevent us from just standing there, dumbfounded. In other words, your automatic (some would say – incorrectly – your "instinctive") response will be based on whatever behavioral script best fits this situation.

Now, let's consider how your history of media exposure might affect which behavioral script you activate in this situation. Maybe you watch a lot of comedy, where it's common for people to look silly, get embarrassed, and laugh it off when something like this happens. All of this slapstick humor might cause you to develop an "accidents happen, and they can be funny" script, where you interpret the bump as an accident and you dispel the tension by laughing it off.

But imagine if you consumed a lot of media where people shove one another to challenge them to a fight. This could lead you to form a "defend yourself when provoked" script that leads you to automatically (that is, without conscious thought) assume the other person shoved you on purpose and prepare yourself for a fight.

The difference in the learned scripts and their influence on behavior is why some researchers study media violence: For the potential role it plays in the development of these scripts and as a possible explanation for the link between media violence and aggressive personality.[14]

Like with social learning theory, the impact of the social cognition perspective on media violence research is most evident in the methods used by researchers from this perspective. As we discuss in Question #8, researchers have developed many ways to measure aggressive behavior and aggression-related concepts. The social cognition perspective offers numerous ways to measure aggressive thoughts and the activation of aggressive schemas and scripts, including word completion, story-writing, reaction time comparison and decision-making under time pressure. The prominence of these measures in modern media

---

[h] If you've ever eaten in an authentic restaurant from another culture, or even an extremely expensive restaurant, you might, like at least one of the authors, have had the uncomfortable experience of not having an appropriate script (e.g., "which fork am I supposed to use?")

research illustrates the impact that researchers from the social cognitive perspective have had on the field.

Although many media violence researchers put the emphasis on "violence," others are less interested in violent content itself. Instead, they're interested in how people use and react to interactive media (e.g., video games.) Part of this interest stems from the fact that our brains evolved to survive in a world that was very different from the world we know today. Evolution is a slow process that involves gradual changes in a population over many generations. In contrast, screen media are a very recent development, going back only a few generations. The result? We're forced to react to screen media with brains that didn't evolve in an environment where we can see and hear people who aren't real or who aren't behaving in the real world.

To illustrate what we mean, think about the saddest film you've ever seen.[i] Now, ask yourself: *Why* does the film make you cry? After all, the characters in the film aren't real: They're paid actors (or in many cases, computer-animated animals or objects!) The story itself is also typically fictional, portraying events that didn't and probably couldn't actually occur.[j] And yet we respond to these films as *though* they were real. We *know* they're not, but it's as if some part of our brain didn't get the message. And why should we expect it to – it evolved in a time when, if we saw something sad, it's because something sad was *actually* happening in front of us! For this reason, even when we tell ourselves "it's only a movie" many of our mental processes are unable to make this same distinction. Film directors capitalize on this to make sad scenes elicit sad responses and scary scenes elicit fear responses.

This ability of media to blur the lines between fantasy and reality and influence our thoughts, feelings, and behaviors is another reason media psychologists study media. As we've seen, these questions aren't limited to violent content. The same principles used to study violent media can be used to study other media effects as well. For example, as we'll discuss in greater detail (Question #41), media with positive messages can inspire helping and sharing behavior.[k] In fact, many media researchers may not be all that interested in violence, but find themselves studying violent media because it just happens to be the topic that people are most interested in.

We can see the impact of this broader interest in *all* media effects by looking at the growing number of studies about non-aggression effects, many of

---

[i] For one of the authors, the answer is, hands-down, *The Green Mile*, which makes him sob every time he sees it!

[j] And even when the story *is* inspired by real events, the film you're seeing is likely not footage of the original event.

[k] In fact, two of the research teams behind the most widely-cited modern theory of violent video game effects (Dr. Anderson's and Dr. Gentile's teams) were *also* the teams who published some of the first studies showing *positive* effects of prosocial video games!

which use the same theories, concepts, and study designs as media violence researchers.[11,15,16] Many of these same researchers are also looking beyond the content itself and are instead asking questions about *how* people consume media: Do they become immersed, do they identify with characters in the story, where are they consuming the media, and do any of these factors change how they are affected by it?

The last, and perhaps most obvious group of researchers studying media violence is aggression researchers. These are social scientists who seek to understand the causes of aggression and violence and use it to reduce aggression and violence in the real world. Aggression researchers are primarily interested in media effects as a way to further their understanding of what drives aggression. In fact, one of us perfectly fits this description, having begun studying media violence as a way to test key hypotheses about a model of aggression called the General Aggression Model (for more on this model, see Question # 12)![17,18]

Because their goal is to reduce societal aggression and violence, some aggression researchers use the knowledge they gain from media violence research to develop ways to break the link between media violence and aggression (e.g., school programs, campaigns to inform parents) or, at the very least, to reduce the number of people who are exposed to excessively high levels of violent media. Their contribution to the field of media violence research includes aggression-reducing intervention studies and solid measures of real-world aggression.

We'll summarize this answer by returning to a point we made in Question #8 – there are no perfect measures of aggression – and the point we made in Question #9 – there's no such thing as a perfect study. This same theme can be applied to our current discussion of the different perspectives of media violence researchers: No one perspective is the "correct" one. There are strengths and weaknesses to all of the approaches we discussed, and our understanding of media violence benefits from this range of researchers, disciplines, and perspectives.

To an outsider, all of these perspectives might give the impression that the field is disorganized or fragmented. However, as Question #11 discusses, there is a remarkable amount of consistency in researchers' conclusions about media violence effects across these different perspectives. This converging evidence is what allows us to have considerable confidence in these conclusions.

References
1. Auterhoff, H. (1967). *Nobel Lectures, Physiology or Medicine 1901-1921, Including Presentation Speeches and Laureates' Biographies*. New York, NY: Elsevier Publishing Company.
2. Sheehy, N. (2004). *Fifty key thinkers in psychology*. London: Routledge.
3. Tarpy, R. M. (1975). *Basic Principles of Learning*. Glenview, IL: Scott, Foresman and Company.

4. Sparks, G. G., Sparks, E. A., & Sparks, C. W. (2008). Media Violence. In J. Bryant & M. B. Oliver (Eds.), *Media Effects: Advances in Theory and Research* (3rd ed.) New York, NY: Routledge.
5. Bandura, A. (1963). *Social learning and personality development.* New York, NY: Holt, Rinehart, and Winson.
6. Bandura, A. (1977). *Social learning theory.* Oxford, England: Prentice-Hall.
7. Bandura, A., Ross, D., & Ross, S. A. (1961). Transmission of aggression through the imitation of aggressive models. *Journal of Abnormal and Social Psychology, 63*(3), 575-582.
8. Bandura, A., Ross, D., & Ross, S. A. (1963). Imitation of film-mediated aggressive models. *Journal of abnormal and Social Psychology, 66*(1), 3-11.
9. Bandura, A. (1965). Influence of models' reinforcement contingencies on the acquisition of imitative responses. *Journal of Personality and Social Psychology, 1*(6), 589.
10. Konijn, E. A., Bijvank, M. N., & Bushman, B. J. (2007). I wish I were a warrior: the role of wishful identification in the effects of violent video games on aggression in adolescent boys. *Developmental Psychology, 43*(4), 1038-1044.
11. Anderson, C. A., Shibuya, A., Ihori, N., Swing, E. L., Bushman, B. J., Sakamoto, A., Rothstein, H. R., & Saleem, M. (2010). Violent video game effects on aggression, empathy, and prosocial behavior in eastern and western countries: a meta-analytic review. *Psychological Bulletin, 136*(2), 151-173.
12. Fiske, S. T., & Taylor, S. E. (2013). *Social Cognition: from brains to culture* (2nd ed.). Los Angeles, CA: SAGE Publications Ltd.
13. Bartholow, B.D., Anderson, C. A., Carnagey, N.L., & Benjamin, A.J. (2005). Interactive effects of life experience and situational cues on aggression: The weapons priming effect in hunters and nonhunters. *Journal of Experimental Social Psychology, 41,* 48-60.
14. Huesmann, L. R. (1986). Psychological processes promoting the relation between exposure to media violence and aggressive behavior by the viewer. *Journal of Social Issues, 42,* 125-139.
15. Saleem, M., Anderson, C. A., & Gentile, D. A. (2012). Effects of prosocial, neutral, and violent video games on children's helpful and hurtful behaviors. *Aggressive Behavior, 38,* 281-287.
16. Gentile, D. A., Anderson, C. A., Yukawa, S., Ihori, N., Saleem, M., Ming, L. K., Shibuya, A., Liau, A. K., Khoo, A., Bushman, B. J., Huesmann, L. R. & Sakamoto, A. (2009). The effects of prosocial video games on prosocial behaviors: International evidence from correlational, experimental, and longitudinal studies. *Personality and Social Psychology Bulletin, 35,* 752-763.
17. Anderson, C.A., & Bushman, B.J. (2002). Human aggression. *Annual Review of Psychology, 53,* 27-51.

18. Boxer, P., Huesmann, L. R., Bushman, B. J., O'Brien, M., & Moceri, D. (2009). The role of violent media preference in cumulative developmental risk for violence and general aggression. *Journal of Youth and Adolescence, 38,* 417-428.

11 - Is there a link between violent media and aggression?

The Short Answer:

Yes. More than six decades of research on media violence have shown fairly consistently that violent media – whether television, film, music, or video games – is a risk factor for increased aggressive thoughts, feelings, and behaviors. The effect is fairly modest in size, and has been found in different samples of people using different methodologies by different researchers. Importantly, these conclusions are *not* based on the results of a single study, but rather the combined results of hundreds of separate studies over the years. This means that the effect is unlikely to be a simple coincidence, an anomaly, or a statistical fluke. The evidence supporting this link is as strong as the link between cigarette smoking and lung cancer or a high fat diet and heart disease.[a]

The Long Answer:

To answer this question, we need to be crystal-clear about what it means when scientists say there is a link between violent media and aggression. In Question #9 we briefly explained what a correlation is: A pattern between two variables (e.g., "violent media use" and "aggression") where scores on one of the variables are related to scores on the other variable. Or, to put it another way: A correlation between violent media and aggression means that knowing how much violent media a person consumes should let us predict how aggressive that person is more accurately than if we were to guess how aggressive they were *at random*.

This probably seems like an overly roundabout way to talk about a link between media violence and aggression.[b] Why not simply say "violent media

---

[a] We are *not* saying that the magnitude of *media violence-to-aggression* link is the same size as the *cigarette smoking-to-lung cancer* link. In fact, the latter effect size is larger. What we are saying is that the evidence that these links are real and causal is equally strong, because they both are based on extensive research designs that adequately address competing or alternative hypotheses. In terms of relative size of effect, the *media violence-to-aggression* effect size is more like the *second-hand-smoke-to-lung cancer* effect.

[b] Indeed, scientists are somewhat infamous for their tendency to take a seemingly simple question and make it far more complicated than most of us would prefer. As a famous example of this, breakfast-eaters have lamented for *years* about how scientists couldn't seem to give them a simple answer about whether eggs are bad or good for them!

cause violence" and leave it at that? Well, as we outlined in Question #7, when people use overly-simplistic, imprecise language like this without understanding the nuances of research, it leads to misunderstandings about researchers' *actual* conclusions. This is why it's important to understand *exactly* what we mean when we're talking about a "correlation" between variables.

So, what *do* researchers mean when they say that media violence and aggression are related? To start, it's important to know that a correlation only means that a relationship or pattern exists: It doesn't have to be a "perfect" pattern. Let's start with an example of what a perfect correlation would look like. Imagine that for every 100 hours of violent media you consumed, you would get into *exactly* 1 fist fight every year. If *every* participant in our study followed this *exact* rule (e.g., 100 hours = 1 fist fight, 200 hours = 2 fist fights, etc…), we would be able to *perfectly* predict a participant's number of fist fights based on the amount of violent media they consumed. So if one participant watched 400 hours of violent media per year, we could correctly predict that they get into exactly 4 fistfights every year (see Figure 11.1).

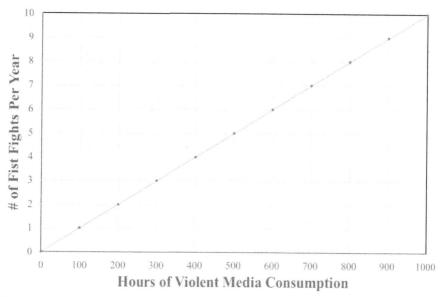

Figure 11.1. A hypothetical perfect correlation between fist fights and violent media consumption.

Unfortunately, reality is a messy place where perfect correlations are pretty much non-existent. Our world is full of all sorts of extra variables (e.g., statistical "noise") and our measures of them are all imperfect (see Question #8 for more on this topic.) For example, think about *all* the different factors that could affect how many fist fights a person gets into: Whether they live in a rough neighborhood, their age, alcohol consumption, criminal behavior, changes in their

85

financial situation – just to name a few! Our perfect correlation is possible only if violent media were the *only* thing that influences a person's fist fighting. Because other factors also matter (see Question #14) and different people will have different amounts of each factor, we're going to wind up with imperfect correlation.

To see just how easy it is to break a perfect correlation, let's imagine that there's a *single* participant who doesn't follow our "100 hours = 1 fist fight" rule. They consumed 100 hours of violent media, but they got into 4 fist fights because they live in a fairly rough neighborhood. We can no longer claim that there is a *perfect* correlation between media violence and aggression, because there is some "noise" in our data that prevents us from *perfectly* predicting someone's fist fighting based on their media consumption.

Laypersons often employ this tactic to try to "disprove" the existence of a correlation: They believe that if they can find a single example of a person who doesn't *perfectly* match the described pattern between two variables, the correlation cannot exist (for more on this argument, see Question #29). This argument is faulty however, because it assumes that if a correlation isn't perfect, there's no correlation at all. You can see for yourself why it's faulty by looking at Figure 11.2, which shows an imaginary, imperfect correlation between a particular drug and lifespan. As you can see, taking more of the drug seems to be associated with a shorter lifespan. But the correlation isn't a perfect one: There are several cases of people who don't take the drug who nevertheless don't live very long (Person A), and there are examples of people who take the drug and live quite long (Person B). But if it were *your* life on the line, would you prefer to be a person taking the drug 5 times per day or not taking the drug at all? If you chose "not taking the drug at all," then congratulations, you understand the concept of an imperfect correlation! In most of scientific psychology, we are talking about one thing changing the odds or likelihood of another in a predictable manner.

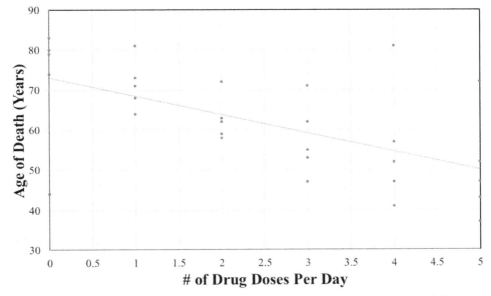

Figure 11.2. A more typical imperfect correlation between a hypothetical drug and age of death.

When predicting things as complex as life expectancy or human behavior, there are virtually no examples of studies with perfect correlations, where a scientist can *perfectly* predict a person's outcome from a single variable (or even from two, ten, or *one hundred* variables!) The problem isn't unique to psychology, the social sciences, or even "physical" sciences like physics or chemistry[c]. A lack of perfect correlations doesn't make the goal of trying to understand the world around us pointless. After all, even if we can't *perfectly* predict something as complex as human behavior, it's still impressive to be able to predict an outcome with *some* accuracy, especially if we're only using one variable to predict it! A scientist may not be able to *perfectly* predict a person's aggressive behavior based on the amount of violent content they consume, but if they can predict how aggressive they are 5% better than if we just guessed their aggression randomly, that's *still* an improvement in our understanding of aggression!

Now that we have a basic understanding of correlations, let's look at what the research on media violence *actually* shows. The answer is pretty consistent, and it has been for decades. Media violence is a significant *risk factor* for aggressive (and even violent) behavior. Basically, knowing how much media

---

[c] Some correlations in physics and chemistry are *far* closer to perfect than we find in psychology, in part because they have fewer "noise" variables to deal with. Imagine how much messier these fields would be if atoms or gravity had a mind of their own and could *choose* what they wanted to do!

violence a person consumes *does* allow us to predict their aggression better than chance: Those who consume more violent media *tend* to be more aggressive than those who consume less. This doesn't mean media violence is the *biggest* risk factor a person can have for aggression (joining a violent gang, for instance, is one of the biggest risk factors for youth violence). But it can tell us *something* about a person's aggression. This also doesn't mean that there aren't people who play *lots* of violent media and don't behave aggressively (we address this in-depth in Question #29). But, just like our drug example above – just because some exceptions exist doesn't mean there isn't an important relation!

In other parts of this book, we discuss some of the important considerations and limitations of our conclusion that violent media are a risk factor for aggression. In Question #17 we talk about studies which sometimes fail to find this relation[1,2] and what they mean. In Question #21 we look at whether these effects are the same for males and females[3], or for people with mental illnesses[4] (Question #34).

Of course, if you look at only one study at a time or focus on whether the effects differ for different people, it's easy to throw your hands up and say "who knows, it's too confusing and nobody agrees!" As we point out in Questions #8 and #9, science is a messy process, and it's easy to find yourself "unable to see the forest for the trees." But it *is* possible to get a clearer answer by looking at evidence from dozens, even hundreds of studies at once – a way to step back a bit from the trees so we can see the *entire* forest.

Statisticians have come up with techniques for doing exactly this in a mathematical way – a process called meta-analysis. To avoid getting *too* much into geeky stats territory, we can describe meta-analysis simply as putting together data from *many* studies to test whether all of the data *combined* show a correlation between two variables.

So what happens when you look at the media violence literature with a meta-analysis? Well, a clear picture emerges. Since 1977, scientists have done more than a *dozen* different meta-analyses of the media violence literature[5-16]. Some of these are fairly small, looking at two dozen studies with a combined sample of a few thousand participants. Others are massive, including more than 100 studies with more than 100,000 participants.

Two of the smaller meta-analyses (which some have argued were somewhat biased in their choice of studies) concluded there was either no relationship[14] or a mixed[11] relationship between media violence and aggression. Nearly all of the other meta-analyses, including the largest ones, have reached the opposite conclusion, that there is a modest correlation between media violence and aggression. The largest of these meta-analysis[6] included *all* of the relevant studies from the two smaller meta-analyses, as well as many, many more. The authors concluded that violent media exposure *was* associated with an increased risk for aggressive thoughts, feelings, and behavior regardless of whether researchers used a cross-sectional, longitudinal, or experimental study (see Question #9 for more on these designs). The researchers also found media violence effects regardless of the country where the study was conducted or the sex of the participants in the study.

In short, the evidence from these meta-analyses is quite clear: The evidence for a link between media violence and aggression isn't due to a flaw in one study or the use of a bad measure or "cherry-picking" one's favorite study. Of course, critics *could* go through each of the separate studies in each meta-analysis and find that each has its own weaknesses and limitations. But, as we've pointed out, there are no perfect measures and there are no perfect studies.[d] Pointing out that each of these studies is flawed does not change the fact that, despite their differing strengths and weaknesses, they tend to point to the same conclusion. In the end, researchers must ask which scenario is more likely:

1. There is, in reality, no link between violent media and aggression, even though numerous important psychological theories state that there *should* be a link (see Question #12), and even though there are hundreds of different studies by hundreds of different researchers around the world which *have* found the association, all of these studies had mistakes and coincidentally just *happened* to point to a link between media violence and aggression where there is none.

    OR

2. There really *is* a link between violent media and aggression as theory would predict, and all of these studies – which, admittedly, aren't perfect – seem to be finding evidence of this link.

To conclude, the association between media violence and aggression is a modest one, an imperfect one. Because it's not *huge* in size, and because media violence is not the *biggest* risk factor for aggression[17], it might be tempting to assume it doesn't exist and to ignore evidence that it might exist. If we only look at one study at a time and focus on their weaknesses, we may find ourselves wondering how strong the evidence for the link between media violence and aggression is. But if we look at the research as a whole and what hundreds of separate studies collectively tell us, the data clearly show that exposure to media violence is related, in a small but significant way, to aggression. We are hardly the first to make this point: Every major science organization that has conducted a thorough review of the research since 1972 has come to this same conclusion. You can read these reports for yourself online at http://www.craiganderson.org/wp-content/uploads/caa/StatementsonMediaViolence.html

---

[d] This includes those same critics' *own* studies!

References

1. Ferguson, C. J., & Meehan, D. C. (2010). Saturday night's alright for fighting: Antisocial traits, fighting, and weapons carrying in a large sample of youth. *Psychiatric Quarterly, 81,* 293-302.
2. Manning, S. A., & Taylor, D. A. (1975). Effects of viewed violence and aggression: Stimulation and catharsis. *Journal of Personality and Social Psychology, 31*(1), 180-188.
3. Polman, H., Orobio de Castro, B., & Van Aken, M. A. G. (2008). Experimental study on the differential effects of playing versus watching video games on children's aggressive behavior. *Aggressive Behavior, 34,* 256-264.
4. Talkington, L. W., & Altman, R. (1978). Effects of Film-Mediated Aggressive and Affectual Models on Behavior. *American Journal of Mental Deficiency, 77*(4), 420-425.
5. Anderson, C. A., Carnagey, N. L., Flanagan, M., Benjamin, A. J., Eubanks, J., & Valentine, J. C. (2004). Violent video games: Specific effects of violent content on aggressive thoughts and behavior. *Advances in Experimental Social Psychology, 36,* 199-249.
6. Anderson, C. A., Shibuya, A., Ihori, N., Swing, E. L., Bushman, B. J., Sakamoto, A., Rothstein, H. R., & Saleem, M. (2010). Violent video game effects on aggression, empathy, and prosocial behavior in Eastern and Western countries. *Psychological Bulletin, 136,* 151-173.
7. Andison, F. S. (1977). TV Violence and Viewer Aggression: A Cumulation of Study Results 1956-1976. *Public Opinion Quarterly, 41,* 314-331.
8. Hearold, S. (1986). A synthesis of 1043 effects of television on social behavior. In G. Comstock (Ed.), *Public Communication and Behavior, 1,* 65-133. New York: Academic Press.
9. Wood, W., Wong, F., & Cachere, J. (1991). Effects of media violence on viewers' aggression in unconstrained social interaction. *Psychological Bulletin, 109*(3), 371-383.
10. Hogben, M. (1998). Factors moderating the effect of television aggression on viewer behavior. *Communication Research, 25,* 220-247.
11. Savage, J., & Yancey, C. (2008). The effects of media violence exposure on criminal aggression: A meta-analysis. *Criminal Justice and Behavior, 35,* 772-791.
12. Paik, H., & Comstock, G. (1994). The effects of television violence on antisocial behavior: A meta-analysis. *Communication Research, 21*(4), 516-546.
13. Sherry, J. (2001). The effects of violent video games on aggression: A meta-analysis. *Human Communication Research, 27,* 409-431.

14. Ferguson, C. J. (2015). Do angry birds make for angry children? A meta-analysis of video game influences on children's and adolescents' aggression, mental health, prosocial behavior, and academic performance. *Perspectives on Psychological Science, 10*(5), 646-666.
15. Ferguson, C. J. (2007). Evidence for publication bias in video game violence effects literature: A meta-analytic review. *Aggression and Violent Behavior, 12,* 470-482.
16. Greitemeyer, T., & Mügge, D. O. (2014). Video games do affect social outcomes: A meta-analytic review of the effects of violent and prosocial video game play. *Personality and Social Psychology Bulletin, 40*(5), 578-589.
17. Anderson, C. A., Suzuki, K., Swing, E. L., Groves, C. L., Gentile, D. A., Prot, S., Lam, C. P., Sakamoto, A., Horiuchi, Y., Krahé, B., Jelic, M., Liuqing, W., Toma, R., Warburton, W. A., Zhang, X., Tajima, S., Qing, F., & Petrescu, P. (2017). Media violence and other aggression risk factors in seven nations. *Personality and Social Psychology Bulletin, 43,* 986-998. DOI: https://doi.org/10.1177/0146167217703064

12 - How does violent media exposure make people more aggressive?

The Short Answer:

People often believe that violent media only affect people who can't tell the difference between what's real versus what's on the screen. In fact, the relationship between media violence and aggression is far more complex. It involves many short-term effects, including making us feel positive about aggression, leading us to believe aggression is useful, causing us to interpret the world as a hostile place, and desensitizing us to the negative consequences of aggression – at least in the minutes following exposure. But the effects of media violence aren't just short-term. Repeated exposure can create long-term changes in our beliefs and the way we think and feel about aggression, which can shift the odds to increase our risk of aggressive behavior long after we've turned the screen off. No one factor is solely responsible for the link between media violence and aggression: The combination of *all* of these subtle changes is what increases a person's likelihood to respond aggressively in any given situation, whether or not media are present at the time.

The Long Answer:

We're often approached by moviegoers or gamers with questions about media violence. When we tell them that media violence is a risk factor for aggression, their usual response is to deny this, claiming that violent media hasn't affected *them*.[a] We imagine that many readers may find themselves in the same boat: You've probably watched a few violent movies or played a few violent games, and yet, here you are, (presumably) not in prison for a violent crime. This belief is based on flawed logic, however: Many people believe that violent media haven't affected them because they don't understand *how* violent media affects people. The argument goes something like this:

"I watch violent movies all the time, but I *know* that the movie isn't the real world. I *know better* than to act that way in real life! Therefore, these films haven't affected me at all!"

Although it might make a certain amount of sense at first, the argument assumes that media violence *only* affects people if they can't tell fantasy from

---

[a] For now, we'll ignore the fact that, even if this claim were true, it wouldn't change the fact that a correlation can *still* exist between media violence and aggression, a point we discuss at length in Question #11.

reality.[b] We'll discuss the flaws in this particular argument in greater detail in Question #33, but for now let's think about the small kernels of truth in the argument.

For starters, most people *can* tell fantasy and reality apart. In fact, most children can do this within the first few years of their life[1,2], and by the time they reach adolescence, only a very small fraction of people have *any* problem with this.[3,4] So it's *true* that most people who play video games or watch movies know that what they're seeing isn't real. Knowing they're fake does not, however, keep them from having effects. All adults know that advertisements are not real, but ads still work on them.

There's also a second kernel of truth: When people engage in aggression, they *rarely* justify it by saying "I did it because it was okay to do in a video game" or "I saw this in a movie once, so I figured it was okay to do in real life!" Combined with the first kernel of truth, this all seems pretty obvious. This is why media researchers often seem pretty foolish to people who think all there is to media violence effects is struggling to tell fantasy from reality. If that's all there was to it, media researchers would seem like the ones who were out of touch with reality!

But the fantasy/reality argument falls apart if you look at the explanations media researchers *actually* give for why media violence is a risk factor for aggression. As it turns out, no credible researcher believes consumers simply can't tell fantasy and reality apart. When gamers, the entertainment industry, or critics argue "Most people can tell fantasy and reality apart, meaning violent media *can't* cause aggression," they're arguing against a position that *no one* is making.[c]

To see how absurd this argument seems to a media researcher, imagine someone said "Junk food can't be bad for your health because junk food doesn't contain cyanide!" Yes, it's true that junk food doesn't contain cyanide, but the argument overlooks the fact *nobody* is claiming that cyanide is the link between junk food and poor health. The point is, if you're going to challenge whether media violence is a risk factor for aggression – and some researchers do (see Question #17) – you have to first understand *what* researchers claim is causing the effect and *then* provide evidence that it can't be true.[d]

---

[b] True, being unable to tell fantasy and reality may explain certain instances of violence, particularly in young children or in adults with a serious mental illness. These are very rare cases, however!

[c] This is what's known as a "straw man" – when you set up an overly-simplistic, easily-defeated version of someone's position so you can make them look foolish and knock them down easily.

[d] Another nail in the coffin for the fantasy/reality argument is the fact that many studies show that adults, like children *do* behave more aggressively after playing a violent video game or watching a violent film, despite being able to tell fantasy from reality!

So how *do* researchers explain the causes of aggressive behavior? Well, there's actually no single, agreed-upon model. We could write an *entire* book explaining all of the different theories of aggression.[e] It's probably safe to assume you *don't* want to read hundreds of pages of psychological theory, so we'll spare you the time and effort and focus on one of the best-known and commonly-used modern theories of aggression: the General Aggression Model (GAM)[5].

To keep it simple, the GAM says that there's no *one* cause of *all* aggressive behavior. Instead, aggression is caused by a combination of who you are and the situation you find yourself in. In other words, aggression is rarely caused solely by who you are or the situation you're in: It's usually a combination of both! You probably recognize this for yourself: You probably know some people who are more likely to be aggressive than others (e.g., teenage boys compared to elderly women), but they're *more* likely to be aggressive in some situations (e.g., after being insulted) than in others (e.g., during a relaxing day at the beach). Even so, it's *very* possible for a low-risk person to behave aggressively if they're put in a high-risk situation (e.g., an old lady fighting for her life). To make matters even *more* complicated, in *any* of these cases a person's initial impulse to act aggressively might be "overridden" if they have the time (e.g., a minute to think things over), mental capacity (e.g., not drunk or distracted) and motivation to do so (e.g., "I shouldn't punch my boss because I need this job!")

According to the GAM, the situations we find ourselves in contribute a *lot* to our risk of behaving aggressively at any given moment. Take a moment to think about a situation that might make *you* behave aggressively. What is it about that specific situation that would make aggression more likely?

Scientists know that aggression-provoking situations tend to have a lot of things in common. For starters, they often involve someone's hostile behavior or something which provokes you, which can make you *feel* angry[6], and make your body respond with increased arousal (e.g., feeling "pumped up," your heart racing)[7]. These same situations also activate aggressive thoughts and scripts in peoples' minds[8]: You may find yourself *thinking* aggressive thoughts that you wouldn't normally think. All of these things make you more likely to respond aggressively in that situation[5].

In <u>Question #10</u>, we mentioned that our brains evolved in a world without screen media. This means that some key parts of our brains have no reason to think that what we're seeing on the screen isn't really happening (this is why we cry at sad movies or experience fear at horror movies). So is it any wonder that our brains respond to violent media as though they were *real* hostile situations? Even though the conscious part of *you* knows it's not real, some parts of your brain don't get the message, and as a result, you temporarily experience an increase in aggressive feelings, aggressive thought patterns, and physical arousal – all of

---

[e] Writing this book seems to be giving us a *lot* of ideas for other books we could write!

which can make you more likely to behave aggressively – at least while you're exposed to the violent media and for a few minutes afterward[9].[f]

At this point, you may have come to an important realization: People don't spend every waking moment of their lives glued to a TV screen or a monitor (although studies have suggested that teenagers spend up to one third of their day in front of some form of media![10]) Because many of these short-term effects only last for about 5 or 10 minutes after exposure[9], you might be thinking to yourself "What's the big deal if the effects just wear off once you stop watching?" After all, if smoking a cigarette only affected your lungs for a few minutes afterward and then they returned to normal, smoking probably wouldn't be a big deal. It's true that violent media effects probably wouldn't be a big deal if short-term effects were the *only* effects violent media had. But, just as only some of the immediate effects of smoking one cigarette dissipate quickly, only some of the immediate effects of watching or playing violent media dissipate quickly.

That's where the second part of the GAM kicks in. Remember, aggression is a combination of both the situation and the *person* in the situation. Violent media are the *situation*, and that comes and goes. But people bring their personalities with them from situation to situation, and what they learn in various situations can change their personalities over time. Whether you're extroverted, organized, or aggressive, you bring that personality with you. People with an aggressive personality are more likely to behave aggressively than people with less aggressive personalities, *regardless* of what situation they find themselves in. So what goes into an aggressive personality? According to the GAM, it's a combination of factors including, but not limited to[5]:

1. Believing that aggression is a useful and appropriate response to problems

2. Having a positive attitude toward aggression and aggressive people

3. Seeing the world as a mean and hostile place

4. Interpreting others' behavior as intentional, provoking, or aggressive

5. Becoming desensitized to, and less bothered by, violence and its consequences

6. Having well-practiced, easily-accessible scripts for aggressive behavior.

---

[f] To see examples of this, you can look online for videos of gamers losing their temper, throwing controllers, and shouting obscenities when their character is killed in a violent video game. One of the authors admits to having broken a controller this way (the game was *Dark Souls*, for any readers who are fans of the game and know just how unfair the Bed of Chaos fight is!)

So that's what goes into an aggressive personality. But can violent media *create* these aggressive personalities?

In the short term, no. It's unlikely that one violent movie or an hour of playing a violent video game is going to change your personality.[g] Watching Quentin Tarantino's violence-fest *Kill Bill* isn't going to *dramatically and permanently* change your beliefs about how appropriate aggression is, your perception of the world as a hostile place, or your interpretation of your partner's behavior as provoking. Similarly, seeing the multiplication fact that 6 x 7 = 42 one time won't measurably change your (or your child's) multiplication skill.

The story changes, however, with repeated exposure. *Repeatedly* seeing aggression rewarded on-screen, feeling positive feelings (e.g., excitement, fun) when violence is happening on-screen, and seeing strangers constantly portrayed as threatening or violent *does* have long-term effects, in the same way that years of chain-smoking does cause long-term biological changes in your body, or the way that repeated practice of multiplication tables improves your skill at multiplying numbers. Studies show that the more violent media people see over time, the more likely they are to have pro-violence attitudes and beliefs[12], to see aggression in others' behavior[13], and to become desensitized to violence[14].

When you put the pieces together, it becomes apparent just how complex and multi-faceted the puzzle of media violence effects really is (see Figure 12.1). In the short-term, violent media create situations that increase a person's risk for aggressive behavior. In the long run, repeated exposure to violent media changes the way we see, think about, and react physically to aggression. As you can see, the real story of media violence effects is *far* more complex than simply "Can you tell if it's real or not?"

---

[g] Unless, of course, it's so disturbing that it creates Post-Traumatic Stress Disorder or a similarly extreme reaction, which *can* happen with some children.[11]

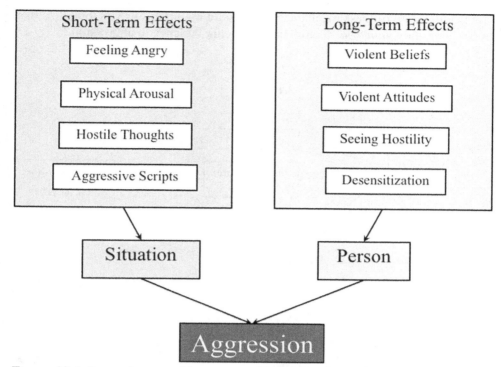

Figure 12.1. Some short- and long-term effects of media violence on one's risk of aggression.

Because media violence effects are subtle, complex, and often affect non-conscious parts of the brain, their influence can be impossible for you to notice in yourself (see Question #29 for more on this). It seems to go against common sense or our own intuition, since we don't *feel* like violent media has affected us.[h] In the end, however, it doesn't matter whether we *think* we're affected by media: Unlike Tinkerbell, the existence of media effects is not based on whether we believe in them. This is why it's dangerous to rely on opinions, intuition, personal experience, or wishful thinking to determine whether the media we consume affects us.

Before we finish this topic, we should also point out we've only described *some* of the mechanisms underlying media violence effects for simplicity's sake.[5, 15] In reality, the GAM is *far* more complex than what's summarized in Figure 12.1. Recent review articles on violent media research show that there are multiple well-established ways that violent media increase aggression and at least two additional ways that are supported by some new studies but are in need of further

---

[h] Most of us say the same thing about advertising, and yet *billions* of dollars are spent advertising to us every year. Companies *must* be getting something out of it!

investigation.[16] Figure 12.2 illustrates these pathways. Instead of bombarding you with details on all of these mechanisms, it's more important for you to realize that researchers study *numerous* factors linking media violence to aggression.

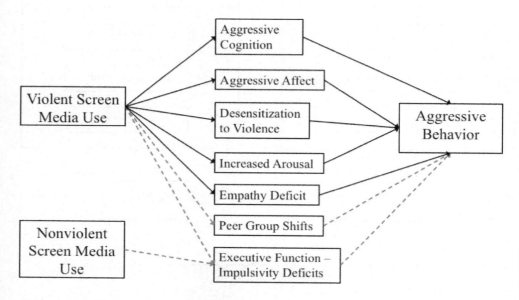

Solid lines indicate well-established effects.
Dashed lines indicate effects that could use additional evaluation.
Figure 12.2. Media Violence Paths to Increased Aggression.

If nothing else, we hope we've convinced you that researchers' arguments are too nuanced and complex to be shot down by the simple claim that "I can tell fantasy and reality apart, so media doesn't affect me!"

References

1. Smith, P. K. (2010). *Children and play.* West Sussex, England: Wiley-Blackwell

2. Woolley, J. D., & Wellman, H. M. (1990). Young children's understanding of realities, nonrealities, and appearance. *Child Development, 61*(4), 946-961.

3. Lynn, S. J., & Rhue, J. W. (1988). Fantasy proneness: Hypothesis, developmental antecedents, and psychopathology. *American Psychologist, 43*(1), 35-44.

4. Wilson, S. C., & Barber, T. X. (1983). The fantasy-prone personality. Implications for understanding imagery, hypnosis, and parapsychological phenomena. *PSI Research, 1*(3), 94-116.

5. Anderson, C. A. & Bushman, B. J. (2002). Human Aggression. *Annual Review of Psychology, 53,* 27-51.

6. Anderson, C. A., Carnagey, N. L., & Eubanks, J. (2003). Exposure to violent media: The effects of songs with violent lyrics on aggressive thoughts and feelings. *Journal of Personality and Social Psychology, 84,* 960-971.
7. Jeong, E. J., Biocca, F. A., & Bohil, C. J. (2012). Sensory realism and mediated aggression in video games. *Computers in Human Behavior, 28,* 1840-1848.
8. Bushman, B. J. (1998). Priming effects of media violence on the accessibility of aggressive constructs in memory. *Personality and Social Psychology Bulletin, 24*(5), 537-545.
9. Barlett, C., Branch, O., Rodeheffer, C., & Harris, R. (2009). How long do the short-term violent video game effects last? *Aggressive Behavior, 35,* 225-236.
10. Rideout, V. J., Foehr, U. G. & Roberts, D. F. (2010). *Generation M2: Media in the lives of 8-18 year olds.* Merlo Park CA: Henry J Kaiser Foundation.
11. Cantor, J. (1998). "Mommy, I'm scared": How TV and movies frighten children and what we can do to protect them. San Diego, CA: Harvest/Harcourt.
12. Funk, J. B., Baldacci, H. B., Pasold, T., & Baumgardner, J. (2004). Violence exposure in real-life, video games, television, movies, and the internet: Is there desensitization? *Journal of Adolescence, 27,* 23-39.
13. Möller, I., & Krahé, B. (2009). Exposure to violent video games and aggression in German adolescents: A longitudinal analysis. *Aggressive Behavior, 35*(1), 75-89.
14. Bartholow, B. D., Bushman, B. J., & Sestir, M. A. (2006). Chronic violent video game exposure and desensitization to violence: Behavioral and event-related brain potential data. *Journal of Experimental Social Psychology, 42,* 532-539.
15. Anderson, C.A., Berkowitz, L., Donnerstein, E., Huesmann, L.R., Johnson, J., Linz, D., Malamuth, N., & Wartella, E. (2003). The influence of media violence on youth. *Psychological Science in the Public Interest, 4,* 81-110.
16. Anderson, C. A., & Bushman, B. J. (2018). Media violence and the General Aggression Model. *Journal of Social Issues, 74,* 386-413. doi: 10.1111/josi.12275

13 - Couldn't it be the other way around, that aggressive people prefer violent media?

The Short Answer:

Yes and no. There is *some* evidence showing that aggressive people *do* prefer to consume violent media more than non-aggressive people do. But it's *also* true that violent media consumption is a risk factor for aggressive behavior and leads to the development of more aggressive personalities. The effect seems to go both ways, though the "violent media increases the risk of later aggression" effect is found more consistently than the "aggressive behavior causes people to later prefer violent media" effect. Also note that even if aggressive people prefer violent media, this does not *disprove* the fact that violent media consumption *also* increases aggression. What's more, converging evidence from many different studies finds evidence for violent media effects *even after* statistically controlling for the possibility that aggressive people may prefer to consume violent media.

The Long Answer:

In Question #11 we noted that researchers consistently find that aggression and violent media consumption are correlated with one another: People high in one of these variables also tend to be high on the other (or at least higher than we would expect if scores on the two variables were completely random and unrelated to one another.)

But critics of media violence effects research, as well as reasonably skeptical or critical readers of this book, may have come to an important realization: Just because two things are *related* doesn't mean that one necessarily *caused* the other to occur. In fact, it would be a mistake to simply *assume* that violent media are the *cause* and aggression is the *effect* without any evidence. This concern is commonly used by gamers and skeptics to discredit media violence research, and it can be a perfectly valid concern in certain circumstances! If researchers conduct a cross-sectional study (see Question #9) and show that media violence and aggression are correlated with one another, they technically cannot claim that one of these variables *causes* the other to happen, certainly not on that basis alone. Correlations *by themselves* do not provide strong evidence of causation.

We hope to show, by the end of this question, that you are not alone in thinking about this issue! Media violence researchers are well aware of it and take this criticism very seriously. In fact, they design studies (e.g., cross-sectional, longitudinal, experimental) *specifically* aimed at addressing these very concerns![a]

But before we discuss some of those studies, let's first make sure we *actually* know what it means to say "correlation does not equal causation." We can start by considering a comparable, non-media example: cigarette smoking and drinking.

Studies show that alcohol consumption and cigarette smoking are correlated with one another[1]. Specifically, high-frequency smokers also tend to be high-frequency drinkers, while low-frequency smokers tend to be low-frequency drinkers.[b] All these data can tell us, however, is that smoking and drinking are somehow positively related to one another. We have no information about the *causal direction* of this relationship. In cross-sectional studies, where researchers might ask participants how frequently they smoke and drink, the researchers are asking about both of these at the *same point in time*. This means there's no way to know how these two variables are causally related. Three possibilities exist:

1. Smoking *causes* drinking to happen. Maybe smoking cigarettes makes people thirsty, which makes them more likely to consume alcoholic beverages to quench that thirst.

2. Drinking *causes* smoking to happen. Maybe drinking alcohol lowers people's inhibitions, making them more likely to take up smoking or less able to resist the craving to smoke.

3. Something else causes *both* drinking and smoking to occur. Maybe being highly stressed increases the likelihood that people will *both* drink and smoke. If this is the case, drinking and smoking may not cause one another, but are related only because they are *both* caused by stress.

All three explanations for the link between drinking and smoking are plausible if we don't have any additional evidence suggesting otherwise. Of course, some explanations are more plausible than others. For example, one *could*

---

[a] It's funny to us how little credit people sometimes give to scientists! Chances are pretty good that if a layperson or casual observer realizes something important about a topic, a scientist who has devoted their entire life to studying that topic has probably realized it too!

[b] For the nerds out there, what we're describing is actually called a *positive correlation*: As one variable goes up, the other goes up as well. But this isn't the *only* type of correlation! There is another type of correlation, called a *negative correlation*, where one variable going up is related to another variable going down. You can see example of a negative correlation in a car's mileage and its resale value: As the car's mileage goes up, its resale value goes down.

claim that Martians have mind-control powers over some humans and are using those powers to increase both alcohol and tobacco consumption in these people. This claim, however, is not plausible, given the lack of evidence for both mind control and the existence of Martians. As such, while this claim is certainly *possible*, its implausibility makes it unworthy of scientific investigation. Our Martian explanation aside, we can't rule out any of the three *plausible* possibilities. We can debate about which explanation makes more sense until the end of time, but it will get us nowhere without additional studies that appropriately test these various plausible alternative explanations (see also Question #9).

Let's return to the topic of media violence research. When laypersons or reporters talk about violent media, they often claim that sure, scientists have shown that violent media and aggression are *associated* with one another, but they can't *prove* which comes first. Because it's possible that the association can be explained by aggressive people preferring violent media, some critics believe (or hope) that they can write off media violence effects altogether. Let's ignore, for a moment, the fact that one causal direction being true does not eliminate the possibility that the other direction is also true. The argument is flawed for a far bigger reason: It's *completely* inaccurate to say that researchers can show *only* correlation and have no evidence about the causal direction of these effects.

In fact, researchers have been conducting both longitudinal and experimental studies for decades, both of which can answer the question of causal direction. Longitudinal studies involve asking the same questions to the same people at multiple points in time. This allows researchers to test *both* causal directions: Media violence increasing later aggression *and* aggression leading to later consumption of media violence. Statistical techniques allow researchers to test *both* directions at the same time, which lets them test whether one, both, or neither causal direction is true.

Experimental studies also let researchers establish causal direction. In fact, well-conducted experimental studies are universally accepted among scientists as the most convincing way to demonstrate causality (or a lack of causality) between two variables. Experimental studies involve randomly assigning people to two or more groups that are virtually identical with one exception — a variable the researcher manipulates between the groups (e.g., gives to one group, but not the other.)[c] If differences are observed between the two groups later in the study (differences that were not there at the start of the study), the researchers can assume that the differences were *caused* by whatever they manipulated at the start of the study. For example, if the one difference between the groups is that one group played a violent game and the other played a non-violent game, the researchers can reasonably conclude that the type of game played caused the

---

[c] In some fields, what psychologists call *experiments* are called *randomized controlled design studies*.

differences observed later in the study, because the gameplay came *before* the difference occurred and was the only major difference between the groups.[d]

With this review of basic research methods in mind, what does it mean when people claim that media researchers can't prove the direction of causation between violent media and aggression? Well, they are implying that researchers have *never* conducted longitudinal or experimental studies. To be fair, cross-sectional studies are among the most popular media violence studies conducted by researchers. Such studies have been used to show that violent video media are associated with hostile beliefs about the world[2], hostile personality[3], anger[4], aggressive behavior[5], and a host of other aggression-relevant variables.

But researchers regularly *do* conduct studies that can determine causal direction! For example, playing more violent games at one point in time predicts, at a later point in time, having less empathy for the suffering of others[6], having increased aggressive thoughts[7], and having increased aggressive behavior.[8,9] They also regularly conduct experimental studies. To name just a few, laboratory experiments have shown that exposing participants to violent media (compared to non-violent media) increases their feelings of hostility[10], desensitizes them to subsequent violence[11], increases their aggressive thoughts[12,13], increases estimates of the frequency of violence in the real world[14], and increases their aggressive behavior[15,16,17,18]. In short, claiming that media researchers don't have the data to make causal claims about media violence and aggression is blatantly ignoring the existence of decades of longitudinal and experimental studies.

Because longitudinal and experimental studies are so important to establishing causal direction, it does raise an important question: Why are so many cross-sectional studies conducted and why do respectable journals publish them if they can't prove causation? The answer is quite simple: Single cross-sectional studies can't prove causal direction by themselves, but well-conducted cross-sectional studies (in medicine, behavioral science, and even domains such as astronomy) *can* rule out some alternative explanations. There are several fairly complex reasons for this, mostly having to do with the sort of boring philosophy of science discussions that make one's eyes glaze over.[19] The simple version is that cross-sectional studies often measure more than just media violence exposure and aggression, which lets researchers statistically control for some alternative explanations.

A simple example can help illustrate our point. A plausible alternative explanation for the correlation between media violence consumption and

---

[d] Of course, for some scientific questions a true experiment cannot be conducted. Sometimes this is for practical reasons (we can't randomly assign a star to a new location in space and test its gravitational effects). Other times it's for ethical reasons (we refuse to randomly assign infants to grow up in smoking versus nonsmoking households to test long-term effects of 2nd hand smoke). In such cases, scientists rely on cross-sectional and longitudinal studies, as well as on whatever theoretically-relevant experimental studies *can* be reasonably done.

aggressive behavior is that a third variable, called "amount of time spent in solitary activities," might cause both. Some have suggested (quite reasonably so) that kids who consume a *lot* of violent media are also more aggressive because spending time on TV, films, and video games – solitary activities – gives them little time to learn how to get along with other kids. This alternative explanation suggests that it's not the violent content *per se* that causes the association between media violence and aggression, but rather the amount of time spent on solitary activities, regardless of whether they involve violent media or not.

Fortunately, researchers can test this alternative hypothesis! They do this by measuring and statistically controlling for the amount of time participants spend in solitary activities and then, after doing so, testing whether violent media *still* correlates with aggression. If it does, this means that solitary activities can't fully account for the relationship between media violence and aggression. In fact, studies have found this to be the case: Violent media exposure is correlated with aggression even *after* controlling for solitary time spent on *all* types of screen media. As it turns out, nonviolent media exposure rarely (if ever) is correlated positively with aggression and, if anything, may even correlate positively with *helping* behavior.[20]

As we outlined in Question #9, there are no perfect studies, and this includes longitudinal and experimental studies. Experiments *do* provide powerful evidence for causation, but they're limited by the fact that, for ethical reasons, researchers cannot create conditions that risk real harm to participants or to others. Researchers avoid this problem by using mild forms of aggression that allow participants to *think* they're harming others without actually doing so.

But there is another type of experimental study that can ethically manipulate exposure to media violence and measure *real life* aggression and violence. These are called intervention studies. They involve randomly assigning participants to either a "treatment" condition that *reduces* exposure to media violence over a period of time (e.g., 5 weeks) or to a "no-treatment" condition, where they consume media as they usually would.[e] Later in time (e.g., months or years later), researchers can measure the amount of real world aggression participants in both conditions engaged in to see whether reducing violent media consumption led to a reduction in real world aggression. Such studies are rare, given that they are incredibly resource-intensive, but several high-quality ones *have* been conducted. These studies tend to find that when the treatment condition *actually* succeeds in reducing media violence use,[f] there is a significant reduction in real-life aggression.[21, 22]

As we point out in Question #11, it's not enough to look at the results of a single study or a single *type* of study if you want to get a complete picture. The

---

[e] This design is built around the fact that, left to their own devices, most people consume a pretty large amount of media violence to begin with.

[f] As it turns out, it's a lot easier said than done!

strengths of each study can overcome weaknesses of other studies. Laypersons who look only at cross-sectional studies and claim that there is no evidence for causation are ignoring the fact that cross-sectional, experimental, and longitudinal studies all point, in their own unique – if incomplete – ways, to the conclusion that violent media increases the risk of aggression.[g] The data we've discussed here, along with the meta-analyses reviewed in Question #11 show that violent media are not only *associated* with aggression, but that they play a *causal* role as a risk factor for aggression.

Let's remember something we said way back at the start of this section though: Evidence for *one* causal direction does *not* mean that there isn't evidence for other causal directions. It seems like common sense that aggressive people should *prefer* playing aggressive games more than non-aggressive people. After all, if a person hates violence, why would they spend their time watching violent television or playing violent games? And there is some truth to this idea: Some studies show that aggressive people *are* more likely than non-aggressive people to be drawn to violent media[23, 24]. But the fact that this may be true is *not* evidence that violent media cannot therefore be a risk factor for aggression. People often want to see the world in a simple, black-and-white, one-or-the-other way. But, as we know, reality is usually messy and complex.

Researchers recognize that both causal directions can be true, and even have a name for it: A bidirectional effect. These bidirectional effects can be a cause for concern, as they may lead to what are called *positive feedback systems*. Imagine if violent media increases the user's aggression, which in turn leads to a greater preference for violent media, which then increases the user's aggression. This can create a cycle that continues to escalate until some sort of breaking point. To date, no study that we know of has directly tested this positive feedback system for media violence over multiple-year periods (although there are some shorter ones), but all of the elements for such a system may be present, making it an important topic for future research.

To summarize: If you look at media violence research as a whole, there is strong evidence that violent media exposure increases the user's risk of aggression – an effect that occurs whether or not it's true that aggressive people also tend to prefer violent media. Critics often focus only on cross-sectional studies, claiming that researchers can't prove causal direction from these studies. They may also argue that longitudinal and experimental studies are imperfect, meaning they can't be used as evidence for causal direction. Ultimately, there is no "silver bullet" study that can single-handedly prove, once and for all, that media violence *causes* aggression, for the same reason that no single study can ever conclusively "prove" that smoking *causes* cancer (for more on this comparison, see Question #53). Instead, scientists rely on converging evidence from multiple studies with

---

[g] As Richard Cardinal Cushing said when asked if it was right to call Fidel Castro a communist, "When I see a bird that walks like a duck and swims like a duck and quacks like a duck, I call that bird a duck."

overlapping strengths and weaknesses to draw their conclusions about causal direction. And the combined results of these studies show us that media violence is a causal risk factor for later aggression. There is also some (but much weaker) evidence that aggressive behavior might be a causal risk factor for later media violence exposure.

Now that you've had an introduction to the idea of causation, there is far more to be said on the subject. In several other questions (e.g., #14, #15, #27, #29), we build on this discussion to help you appreciate the sophisticated approach scientists take when describing causal relationships between two variables like media violence and aggression.

References

1. Pohjanpää, A. K. J., Rimpelä, A. H., Rimpelä, M., & Karvonen, J. S. (1997). Is the strong positive correlation between smoking and use of alcohol consistent over time? A study of Finnish adolescents from 1977 to 1993. *Health Education Research, 12*(1), 25-36.

2. Anderson, C. A., & Dill, K. E. Video games and aggressive thoughts, feelings, and behavior in the laboratory and in life. *Journal of Personality and Social Psychology, 78*(4), 772-790.

3. Bartholow, B. D., Sestir, M. A., & Davis, E. B. (2005). Correlates and consequences of exposure to video game violence: Hostile personality, empathy, and aggressive behavior. *Personality and Social Psychology Bulletin, 31*(11), 1573-1586.

4. Bailey, K., West, R., & Anderson, C. A. (2011). The association between chronic exposure to video game violence and affective processing: An ERP study. *Cognitive, Affective & Behavioral Neuroscience, 2*(11), 259-276.

5. Leiner, M., Peinado, J., Villanos, M. T., Alvarado, L. A., Singh, N., & Dwivedi, A. (2014). Psychosocial profile of Mexican American youths who play aggressive video games. *Hispanic Journal of Behavioral Sciences, 36*(3), 301-315.

6. Prot, S., Gentile, D. A., Anderson, C. A., Suzuki, K., Swing, E., Lim, K. M., Horiuchi, Y., Jelic, M., Krahé, B., Liuqing, W., Liau, A., Khoo, A., Petrescu, P. D., Sakamoto, A., Tajima, S., Toma, R. A., Warburton, W. A., Zhang, X., & Lam, C. P. (2014). Long-term relations between prosocial media use, empathy and prosocial behavior. *Psychological Science, 25*, 358-368.

7. Gentile, D. A., Li, D., Khoo, A., Prot, S., & Anderson, C. A. (2014). Practice, thinking, and action: Mediators and moderators of long-term violent video game effects on aggressive behavior. JAMA Pediatrics, Published online March 24, 2014.

8. Anderson, C. A., Gentile, D. A., & Buckley, K. (2007). *Violent video game effects on children and adolescents.* Oxford University Press: Oxford.

9. Möller, I., & Krahé, B. (2009). Exposure to violent video games and aggression in German adolescents: A longitudinal analysis. *Aggressive Behavior, 35*(1), 75-89.

10. Anderson, C. A., Carnagey, N. L., & Eubanks, J. (2003). Exposure to violent media: The effects of songs with violent lyrics on aggressive thoughts and feelings. *Journal of Personality and Social Psychology, 84*, 960-971.

11. Carnagey, N. L., Anderson. C. A., & Bushman, B. J. (2007). The effect of video game violence on physiological desensitization to real life violence. *Journal of Experimental Social Psychology, 43*, 489-496.

12. Anderson, C. A., Carnagey, N. L., Flanagan, M., Benjamin, A. J., Eubanks, J., & Valentine, J. C. (2004). Violent video games: Specific effects of violent content on aggressive thoughts and behavior. *Advances in Experimental Social Psychology, 36*, 200–251.

13. Barlett, C. P., & Rodeheffer, C. (2009). Effects of realism on extended violent and nonviolent video game play on aggressive thoughts, feelings, and physiological arousal. *Aggressive Behavior, 35*(3), 213–224.

14. Green, M. C., & Brock, T. C. (2000). The role of transportation in the persuasiveness of public narratives. *Journal of Personality and Social Psychology, 79*(5), 701-721.

15. Katori, T. (2001). Bouryokuteki bideogemu no kougeki sokushin kouka to sougosayousei [The effects of violent video games and interactivity on aggression]. *Proceedings of the 42nd convention of the Japanese Society of Social Science*, pp. 602-603.

16. Engelhardt, C. R., Bartholow, B. D., & Saults, S. J. (2011). Violent and nonviolent video games differentially affect physical aggression for individuals high vs. low in dispositional anger. *Aggressive Behavior 37*, 539-546.

17. Silvern, S. B. & Williamson, P. A. (1987). The effects of video game play on young children's aggression, fantasy, and prosocial behavior. *Journal of Applied Developmental Psychology, 8*(4), 453-462.

18. Ballard, M. E., & Lineberger, R. (1999). Video game violence and confederate gender: Effects on reward and punishment given by college males. *Sex Roles, 41*, 541-558.

19. Prot, S., & Anderson, C. A. (2013). Research methods, design, and statistics in media psychology. Chapter in K. Dill (Ed.) *The Oxford Handbook of Media Psychology* (109-136). New York: Oxford University Press.

20. Anderson, C. A., Gentile, D. A., & Dill, K. E. (2012). Prosocial, antisocial, and other effects of recreational video games. Chapter in D. G. Singer, & J. L. Singer (Eds), *Handbook of Children and the Media, 2nd Edition,* (pp. 249-272). Thousand Oaks, CA: Sage.

21. Krahé, B., & Busching, R. (2015). Breaking the vicious cycle of media violence use and aggression: A test of intervention effects over 30 months. *Psychology of Violence, 5*(2), 217-226.

22. Huesmann, L. R., Eron, L. D., Klein, R., Brice, P., & Fischer, P. (1983). Mitigating the imitation of aggressive behaviors by changing children's attitudes about media violence. *Journal of Personality and Social Psychology, 44*, 899-910.

23. Greitemeyer, T. (2015). Everyday sadism predicts violent video game preferences. *Personality and Individual Differences, 75*, 19-23.

24. Breuer, J., Vogelgesang, J., Quandt, T., & Festl, R. (2015). Violent video games and physical aggression: Evidence for a selection effect among adolescents. *Psychology of Popular Media Culture, 4*(4), 305-328.

14 - Don't other things cause aggression, like personality, abuse, etc...?

The Short Answer:

Absolutely! Aggressive behavior doesn't have one single cause, or even a handful of causes. *Many* factors contribute to a person's risk of aggression, including both short- and long-term factors and a combination of biological, psychological, and environmental factors. *Who a person is* and *the situation they find themselves in* play roles in this risk, with some factors increasing the risk and others decreasing it. Media violence is just one factor among many that happens to increase the risk that a person's aggressive impulses will "spill over" into *actual* aggressive behavior. Although it's not the biggest risk factor, it's like adding a thimble full of water to a glass: It *does* add to how full the glass is and increases its chances of overflowing. Just because other, bigger risk factors for aggression exist (e.g., bigger thimbles) doesn't mean that media violence doesn't *also* contribute to this risk.

The Long Answer:

In Question #11 we explained that psychologists have shown that there is a modest link between media violence and aggression. In Question #12 we outlined several of the reasons *why* this link exists and showed that this link is consistent with what psychologists know about aggression in general. In Question #13 we explained that violent media does, indeed, cause an increased risk of aggression, instead of it simply being the case that "aggressive people seek out violent media."

With these three points in mind, let's look at what it means to say that something "causes" something else. Can we *really* say that media violence is the cause of aggression when *other* factors seem more obvious, like being provoked, having a history of abuse, or just being an aggressive person?

To start, let's ask what we actually mean when we talk about "causes" in our day-to-day life. We never really stop to think about it because it's one of those things that seems so obvious that it's actually kind of hard to answer. What *caused* my breakfast to happen this morning? Well, *I* caused it. I was the one who put the toast in the toaster, after all. But what caused the bread to become toasted? Electricity, which passed through a resistor in the toaster, creating the heat that toasted the bread. What caused the electricity that heated the bread? Probably the burning of fossil fuel at a power plant nearby.[a] Here we have three neat-and-tidy

---

[a] Or, for one of the authors, the solar panels on the roof!

examples of a simple outcome with a simple, obvious cause. Why can't everything in life be so simple?

Now let's look at human behavior, something that's a *lot* more complex than toasted bread. Unlike the effects of heat on bread or the movement of electrical current, human behavior is a *lot* less predictable and has a *lot* more causes. Let's demonstrate this by imagining a fellow named Jorge, who happens to be a terrific runner.

What *caused* Jorge to be a terrific runner? We *could* argue that Jorge gets a lot of practice – he often runs with his friends, all of whom are skilled runners. Jorge also lives in a town that has a number of beautiful, safe running paths that make it easy for Jorge to go running. But it also might have something to do with Jorge's biology: He doesn't have asthma, he's got great lung capacity, and he's always had a "runner's physique." It *could* also be because Jorge is very competitive, striving to beat his personal best time and refusing to give up when his body feels tired.

Let's assume that *all* of these statements about Jorge are true. So which one of these would you say *caused* Jorge's running prowess? Is it his running friends and the availability of running paths in his town (environmental factors)? Is it his lungs or physique (biological factors)? Is it his competitive and determined mindset (psychological factors)?

Does it seem silly to say that *only* one of these things "caused" Jorge's running skill? After all, many of us have friends who run, but that doesn't guarantee that we're going to become a good runner ourselves. Likewise, we'd be wrong to assume that our asthma-free readers are all superb runners. And it takes a lot more than just being competitive and having willpower to be a terrific runner. None of these factors by themselves can *cause* you to be a good runner.

In fact, none of the factors mentioned are even *necessary* to be a good runner. It's possible for a person with asthma to become a terrific runner, as can a person who doesn't have running friends or a person who isn't particularly competitive. We would describe these factors as neither *sufficient* nor *necessary* to cause good running ability. But even though none of these factors are necessary or sufficient to be a good runner, we *can* agree that each of these factors *does* improve Jorge's odds of being a terrific runner. Someone who has none of the advantages that Jorge has can still become a terrific runner, but it seems like it would be a lot less likely to happen. Or, to put it another way, we can say that each of these factors –social, biological, and psychological – increases the *likelihood* that someone will become a terrific runner. The more of these factors they have, the more likely it is that they'll become a terrific runner.

This is very similar to how modern scientists think about causation: Not in terms of "what one thing causes X to happen," but "which of these things increases the likelihood that X will happen?"[b] Aggressive behavior isn't thought of as having a single cause, but many causes. Social scientists seek to understand all of the different risk factors that make aggressive behavior more or less likely to happen[1,2]. Along the way, they learn which biological, psychological, and environmental factors represent the biggest risks.[c]

Okay, so there's no *one* cause of aggression. So what *are* the different risk factors? The General Aggression Model, which we introduced in Question #12, is a good place to start looking. The GAM distinguishes between short-term factors and long-term factors. Short-term factors, sometimes called "episodic" or "proximal" factors, answer the question "what caused the person to be aggressive *in this particular situation?*" These can include biological, psychological, and environmental factors.

Short-term biological factors often involve physical arousal[3]: People are more likely to be aggressive if they have an elevated heart rate or if their adrenaline is high. Psychological risk factors include the activation of aggressive thoughts in a person's mind. Seeing a gun[4] (or even just a picture of a weapon[5]) can be enough to activate aggressive thoughts and scripts in a person's mind, making them more likely to interpret their situation as hostile and respond with aggression. Environmental factors can also increase the risk of aggression. Psychologists have shown, for example, that people are more likely to be aggressive when they're uncomfortably hot or when they encounter a foul-smelling odor[6,7,8]. If you've ever been trapped in a hot car with someone who could really use a shower, you probably know the feeling.

Long-term or "distal" risk factors are more subtle factors that also increase a person's risk of aggression. They don't necessarily tell us why a person was aggressive in this situation specifically, but they can tell us why *some* people are more likely to act aggressively than others in many situations. In other words, distal risk factors can be said to increase the level of aggression in someone's personality.

Some of these distal factors are biological: People with generally higher levels of testosterone are at a greater risk for aggression than those with lower

---

[b] Warning – Boring technobabble alert! We call this modern way of thinking about causality "probabilistic." To say that something is a causal factor is to say that it increases or decreases the probability of something occurring (after statistically controlling for other plausible causal factors.) If the occurrence is something negative (e.g., a heart attack, violent behavior), a causal factor that *increases* its likelihood is called a "causal *risk* factor," whereas a causal factor that *decreases* its likelihood is called a "causal *protective* factor." Eating junk food would therefore be a causal *risk* factor for heart attacks, while eating salad is a causal *protective* factor.

[c] Similarly, smoking tobacco products is neither a necessary nor sufficient cause of getting lung cancer. It's one of several known causal risk factors.

levels[9].[d] Other long-term risk factors are psychological: Those who grow up in cultures that value defending one's honor[10] or who have learned to expect others to be hostile[11] are at a greater risk for behaving aggressively. Environmental factors that have been repeated or are pervasive are among the biggest risk factors for aggression, as are more extreme factors. Witnessing aggression first-hand[12] and being a victim of aggression in the past[13] *sharply* increases a person's risk of later aggression. Likewise, factors such as poverty[14] may be tied to aggression because they increase the likelihood that someone lives in a "rougher neighborhood" where they're more likely to be exposed to violence and to provocations[15]. The United States Surgeon General's report on youth violence documents approximately 100 scientifically-known risk factors for aggression (including media violence).[16]

By now, we've shown that a combination of short- and long-term biological, psychological, and environmental factors *all* contribute to your risk of aggression. So where does violent media fit among these variables? In Question #12 we discussed how violent media affects many of these other risk factors, including increasing physiological arousal, developing and activating aggressive thoughts and scripts, and altering a person's beliefs about aggression[17]. Long-term risk factors often involve learning, and violent electronic media are an excellent, attention-grabbing way to repeatedly learn that violence is common, should be expected, and is often rewarded when done by the right people or for the right reasons.

Of course, it would be silly to think that media violence is the *only* risk factor for aggression. In many situations, other factors likely play a much *bigger* role in a person's chances of being aggressive. This leads to a valid challenge put forth by some critics of media violence: If there are bigger risk factors, why care about media violence at all?

To answer this question, let's think about a person's "aggression risk" as a glass of water. The higher the level of water in the glass, the more likely a person is to engage in increasingly extreme aggressive behavior. A person's "water level" is determined by combining *all* of the relevant risk factors, with each risk factor adding to the amount of water in the glass. Likewise, protective factors drain off some of the water in the glass.

A person with a *lot* of risk factors walks around in the world with a glass that's always pretty full: They've got a fairly high risk of behaving aggressively regardless of the situation they find themselves in, and it wouldn't take much – just a mildly provoking situation – to overflow their glass. And with the water level being so high, when they *do* become aggressive, it's more likely to be extreme. For such high-risk cases, one could argue that media violence matters a lot, because even if you're only adding a small thimble of water to the glass, it may well be enough to overflow it.

---

[d] This difference likely explains, at least in part, why males on average tend to be more violent than females.

But this isn't the only reason to care about media violence effects. After all, most of us don't walk around with a "full glass of aggressive water," so to speak. For most people, media violence isn't likely to drive them to extreme aggression (an issue brought up in greater detail in Questions #28 and #35). But that doesn't mean violent media can't still affect them! Remember, as the glass becomes fuller, the type of aggressive behavior that results is more likely to be extreme. But that doesn't mean that you can't get aggressive behavior even at "low water levels". Here, instead of being violent, the type of aggression we're likely to see is mundane, "day-to-day" aggression (e.g., more name-calling, insults, starting rumors, shoving).

So it's true that, for most people, a thimble of water won't overflow their glass. Playing a lot of violent video games won't turn a normal, well-adjusted teen (with few risk factors) into a school shooter. Nonetheless, repeated exposure to violent media *does* raises the water level in their glass. Just because other risk factors might raise this water more than violent media can doesn't change the fact that violent media *does* increase the water level, and this *can and does* have measurable effects. To put it another way, even if it's a very modest risk factor, media violence does affect the sorts of aggression that most of us are likely to encounter in our lives: Saying hurtful things to others[17] or doing things to hurt someone's reputation[18] or getting into fights at school.[19] Media violence effects don't have to involve murders or criminal assaults to still be relevant to us.

But there's another reason to care about media violence: Its effect size, while not huge, is also not trivial. It's not the smallest thimble of water among known causal risk factors for aggression. Indeed, in some contexts its effects can be just as large as other important risk factors.[20,21] For example, in one study of juvenile delinquents (who have a lot of risk factors), video game violence measures were *better* predictors of violent behavior than sex, age, race, and age of first juvenile court contact, even *after* controlling for other factors (e.g., psychopathic traits.)[22]

In another recent study, this time with adolescents and adults in the general population of six different countries, media violence exposure was a substantial risk factor for more common forms of aggression, even compared to other known risk factors such as growing up in a crime-ridden neighborhood. Figure 14.1 illustrates this finding.[21]

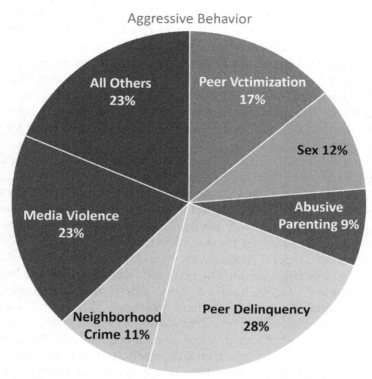

Figure 14.1. Percentages of variance in aggressive behavior accounted for by six risk factors estimated using relative weights analysis.

Also keep in mind that although there *are* other, bigger risk factors for aggression out there (e.g., having delinquent peers), media violence is worth looking at because it's one of the few risk factors that we have a fair amount of control over. Consider other important risk factors: testosterone, experienced childhood abuse, living in a culture that values aggression. These are all risk factors that are outside of our ability to easily change: It's not easy to reduce the amount of testosterone in someone's system without medical procedures and we can't go back in time and prevent someone from experiencing abuse. In contrast, we *can* make a conscious effort to play fewer violent games or cut back on the amount of violent television we watch. More importantly, parents and caregivers play an important role in how much violent media their children are exposed to (for more on this, see <u>Question #46</u>).

Focusing on the factors we *can* control isn't unique to the issue of media violence. For example, genetic factors are an important risk factor for coronary heart disease. Unfortunately, there's little we can do to change our genetics. What we *can* do, however, is eat healthy, exercise, and avoid smoking to reduce our risk for heart disease, *especially* if we know we've got a genetic risk for it! In fact, even if the impact of these other activities is small compared to the risk that one's genes poses, most of us still recognize that it's a good idea to reduce the risk wherever possible, even if it's just by a few percent.

To summarize: media violence researchers recognize that aggression is the result of many different risk factors – short- and long-term, biological, psychological, and environmental[1,2]. Some of these risk factors are stronger than media violence, but that doesn't mean that media violence is *not* a risk factor. It also doesn't mean that we should simply ignore media violence as a risk factor, especially since it's one of the few that we *actually* have control over. Some of the ways we can exert this control are discussed in Chapters 5 and 6.

References

1. Exelmans, L., Custers, K., & Van den Bulck, J. (2015). Violent video games and delinquent behavior in adolescents: A risk factor perspective. *Aggressive Behavior, 41*, 267-279.
2. Gentile, D., A. & Bushman, B. J. (2012). Reassessing media violence effects using a risk and resilience approach to understanding aggression. *Psychology of Popular Media Culture, 1*(3), 138-151.
3. Zillmann, D. (1988). Cognition-excitation interdependencies in aggressive behavior. *Aggressive Behavior, 14*, 51-64.
4. Berkowitz, L., & LePage, A. (1967). Weapons as aggression-eliciting stimuli. *Journal of Personality and Social Psychology, 7*, 202-207.
5. Anderson, C. A., Benjamin, A. J., & Bartholow, B. D. (1998). Does the gun pull the trigger? Automatic priming effects of weapon pictures and weapon names. *Psychological Science, 9*, 308-314.
6. Berkowitz, L. (1993). Pain and aggression: some findings and implications. *Motivation and Emotion, 17*(3), 277-293.
7. Anderson, C. A., Anderson, K. B., Dorr, N., DeNeve, K. M., & Flanagan, M. (2000). Temperature and aggression. *Advances in Experimental Psychology, 32*, 63-133.
8. Rotton, J., Frey, J., Barry, T., Milligan, M., & Fitzpatrick, M. (2006). The air pollution experience and physical aggression. *Journal of Applied Social Psychology, 9*, 397-412.
9. Book, A. S., Starzyk, K. B., & Quinsey, V. L. The relationship between testosterone and aggression: A meta-analysis. *Aggression and Violent Behavior, 6*(6), 579-599.
10. Nisbett, R. E., & Cohen, D. (1996). *Culture of Honor: The Psychology of Violence in the South.* Boulder, CO: Westview.
11. Orobio De Dastro, B., Veerman, J. W., Koops, W., Bosch, J. D., & Monshouwer, H. J. (2002). Hostile attribution of intent and aggressive behavior: A meta-analysis. *Child Development, 73*(3), 916-934.

12. Ferguson, C. J. (2011). Love is a battlefield: Risk factors and gender disparities for domestic violence among Mexican Americans. *Journal of Aggression, Maltreatment & Trauma, 20*(2), 227-236.
13. Malinosky-Rummell, R. & Hansen, D. J. (1993). Long-term consequences of childhood physical abuse. *Psychological Bulletin, 114*(1), 68-79.
14. Spencer, M. B., Dobbs, B., & Swanson, D. P. (1988). African American adolescents: Adaptational processes and socioeconomic diversity in behavioral outcomes. *Journal of Adolescence, 11*(2), 117-137.
15. Eron, L. D., Guerra, N., & Huesmann, L. R. (1997). Poverty and violence. In S. Feshbach, J. Zagrodzka, (Eds.), *Aggression: Biological, developmental, and social perspectives* (pp. 139-154.). New York: Plenum.
16. Satcher, D. (2001). *Youth violence: A report of the Surgeon General.* Retrieved April 9, 2008 from http://www.surgeongeneral.gov/library/youthviolence/report.html#message
17. Anderson, C. A. & Bushman, B. J. (2002). Human Aggression. *Annual Review of Psychology, 53,* 27-51.
18. Anderson, C. A., Carnagey, N. L., Flanagan, M., Benjamin, A. J., Eubanks, J., & Valentine, J. C. (2004). Violent video games: Specific effects of violent content on aggressive thoughts and behavior. *Advances in Experimental Social Psychology, 36,* 200–251.
19. Anderson, C. A., Gentile, D.A., & Buckley, K.E. (2007). *Violent Video Game Effects on Children and Adolescents: Theory, Research, and Public Policy.* New York: Oxford University Press.
20. Coyne, S. M., Nelson, D. A., Lawton, F., Haslam, S., Rooney, L., Titterington, L., Trainor, H., Remnant, J., & Ogunlaja, L. (2008). The effects of viewing physical and relational aggression in the media: Evidence for a cross-over effect. *Journal of Experimental Social Psychology, 44,* 1551-1554.
21. Escobar-Chaves, S.L., & Anderson, C.A. (2008). Media and risky behaviors. *Future of Children, 18,* 147-180.
22. Anderson, C. A., Suzuki, K., Swing, E. L., et al., (2017). Media violence and other aggression risk factors in seven nations. *Personality and Social Psychology Bulletin, 43,* 986-998.
23. DeLisi, M., Vaughn, M. G., Gentile, D. A., Anderson, C. A., & Shook, J. (2013). Violent video games, delinquency, and youth violence: New evidence. *Youth Violence and Juvenile Justice, 11,* 132-142.

15 - Can you *prove* that violent media cause aggression?

The Short Answer:

It depends on what you mean by *prove*. Technically speaking, it's virtually impossible to conduct the perfect, "silver bullet" studies that would be needed to definitively *prove* unquestionably that violent media increases the risk of aggression while ruling out *every* possible alternative explanation. Of course, the same can be said about other known causal risk factors for aggression (e.g., provocation, child abuse) and, indeed, to many other scientific findings (e.g., cigarettes and lung cancer). But if you're talking about proof as the word is used by scientists (a word that scientists hate to use) or proof beyond a reasonable doubt, then the answer is a clear "yes." Scientists have built a very strong case for violent media as a causal risk factor using a combination of longitudinal, cross-sectional, and experimental studies over decades. Don't just take our word for it – this is the conclusion of most of the world's top public health organizations, such as the American Medical Association, the American Academy of Pediatrics, the National Institutes of Health, and two U. S. Surgeons General. The bottom line: If you trust that science has *proven* cigarettes are a causal risk factor for cancer or that an unhealthy diet is a causal risk factor for heart disease, then you have every reason to trust that the same scientific process has *proven* that media violence exposure is a causal risk factor for aggressive behavior.

The Long Answer:

For decades, cigarette companies flat-out denied that there was any causal link between smoking cigarettes and lung cancer. Their argument was simple enough: Scientists could not point to a single study that, by itself, definitively and unquestionably *proved* that smoking cigarettes caused lung cancer without *any* other possible alternative explanation. But despite this lack of a definitive, "silver bullet" study proving the link beyond a shadow of a doubt, people now accept that cigarettes are a risk factor for lung cancer. Why do doctors, scientists, and the general public now believe that this causal link exists, despite the fact that no one study has ever ruled out every possible alternative explanation for the link?

We delve into the nitty-gritty details of this comparison between media violence and cigarette smoking in Question #53. But for now, let's ask ourselves what counts as *definitive* proof that something causes something else to happen. Many of the individual points we're about to cover have been discussed at length in Questions #9, #13, and #14. Here's where we put everything together.

In order to say that A causes B, scientists must show compelling evidence that three facts are true about A and B:

1. A and B must be related to one another either directly or indirectly– that is, a person's score on A must somehow be related to their score on B. They do not have to be *perfectly* correlated, but there must be at least *some* relationship between the two. If there's not, it's impossible for one to *cause* a change in the other.[a] This does not mean that A must be directly related to B. For example, rapid global climate change (A) is causing large populations to attempt to migrate to other countries (M_1), which in turn is causing political, racial, and ethnic conflicts (M_2), which is causing increased intergroup violence (B).[1]

2. A must happen *before* B. If A comes *after* B, it's impossible for A to have *caused* B.[b]

3. There can be no *plausible* alternative explanations for the relationship between A and B. If a third variable, C, causes *both* A and B to happen, then A cannot be said to have *caused* B to happen.[c]

    Note that the key word here is *plausible*. There are *always* implausible alternative explanations for every single scientific fact. Maybe the fossil record is a false trail laid down by a mischievous god-like entity. Maybe our socks go missing because tiny imps employed by sock companies sneak into our rooms and steal individual socks, forcing us to go out and buy more. Maybe cigarettes don't *really* cause lung cancer – it just seems that way because a higher power is punishing those who happen to smoke. The point is, if we force ourselves to consider every single alternative explanation, no matter how supernatural, silly, or implausible it is, before we can call something scientifically *proven*, then nothing can be proven and all scientists should simply give up and do something else with their lives. Of course, this would mean giving up the same enterprise that provided us with modern medicine, automobiles, electricity and, yes, violent video games![d]

---

[a] As an example: Your car's color cannot be said to "cause" your car to go fast if your car's color is completely unrelated to how fast it is. This should be obvious because you can paint your car without changing its performance!

[b] As an example: We can't say that getting a cast put on your leg *caused* your leg to become broken if the cast was put on your leg *after* it was broken.

[c] As an example: If people are more likely to drink *and* smoke, we cannot say that drinking *causes* smoking to happen if there's a possibility that something else – stress – is causing both to occur.

[d] Warning – Boring philosophy babble alert! Deciding what makes an alternative explanation scientifically plausible is a tough question. It's easy to

In previous questions, we've discussed how media researchers have found evidence for points 1 and 2 with respect to violent media effects. Speaking to point number 1, we showed in <u>Question #11</u> that *hundreds* of cross-sectional studies have converged on the fact that people who consume more violent media also score higher on measures of aggression than people who consume less violent media. Speaking to point #2, in <u>Question #13</u> we introduced the concept of longitudinal studies, which show not only that violent media and aggression are related, but that exposure to media violence at an earlier point in time predicts increases in aggression at a later point in time.

But what about point #3, ruling out plausible alternative explanations? It might be a bit tricky to see the problem, so let's use an example. Let's imagine we ran a study and found that the amount of violent TV a person watched was related to how aggressive they were. This *might* seem like compelling evidence that violent television is a risk factor for aggression. But a critic could interpret our data quite differently. They might point out that *other* studies find a link between poverty and increased aggression[2] and that poorer people spend *more* time watching television[3]. For this reason, the critic claims that there is an alternative explanation for the relationship we've found between violent TV and aggression in our study. Maybe violent media aren't *causing* aggression. Instead, being poor might be causing *both* an increase in television-watching *and* an increase in aggression. If the critic is correct, *poverty* would be the "cause" of the aggression we're seeing, *not* violent media. This is a *plausible* alternative explanation.

Let's also imagine that we never thought to collect information about income in our study of violent TV use and aggression. Because we didn't measure it, there's no way for us to rule it out as a possibility. This doesn't mean, of course, that the alternative explanation *must* therefore be correct. But we scientists are a skeptical bunch: Until we have evidence to rule out this alternative explanation, we must accept that there are now two scientifically plausible explanations for our findings.

So how do we figure out which explanation is "correct"? We'll need to pit the two explanations against each other in another cross-sectional or (better yet) longitudinal study, this time making sure to include a measure of income. By

---

provide *examples* of plausible and implausible explanations, but it's a lot harder to define what makes them so. Minds far greater than ours have written at length about this question, and we won't embarrass ourselves by trying to come up with a definition of our own. What we *can* do is mention two important features of plausible alternative explanations. First, they must be testable: If we can't measure or manipulate some part of it to see if it's true, it's not worth considering (this is why supernatural explanations are deemed implausible.) Second, they need to fit with at least *some* other scientifically known phenomenon. If it comes out of nowhere and doesn't jive with anything else scientists know about the world, it's probably not an alternative explanation worth considering.

measuring income, we can now use statistical techniques to "control" for this alternative explanation. After taking it into account statistically, we can test whether there is *still* evidence for a relationship between TV violence and aggression. If so, then poverty can no longer be said to be a plausible alternative explanation.

But there's another problem: Poverty isn't the *only* alternative explanation. In fact, if you were very creative, well-read on the subject of aggression, and had plenty of time, you could probably come up with *dozens* of possible alternative explanations. Some of these alternatives would be more plausible than others, of course. But as good, skeptical scientists, we cannot rule out a plausible alternative explanation until we've collected data on it and controlled for it.

One possible solution is to just run *dozens* of studies – each one designed to rule out a different plausible alternative explanation. As you might imagine, this is pretty impractical: Studies can take *months or years* to run, and they aren't cheap (e.g., research assistants, money to pay participants, finding willing participants). Although it would certainly get the job done, this solution is simply not practical.

Another solution is to design better studies that can rule out *multiple* alternative explanations at once. Researchers could just measure all of the plausible alternative explanations in a single study and be done with it!^e Although this idea sounds great in theory, its impracticality becomes apparent when you actually try to run such a study. The longer a survey is, the less likely people are to fill it out. After all, would *you* be lining up to participate in a two-hour study that was nothing but filling out questionnaires? Even if we *could* find willing participants, people do get bored or annoyed as a questionnaire drags on. The *last* thing you want when you're trying to measure a person's aggression is for your questionnaire itself to be frustrating, thereby making all of your participants aggressive and uncooperative!

Okay, so we can't rule out all of our alternative explanations in a single study either. What do scientists do? Well, often they try to find a solution somewhere between the two extremes: They run cross-sectional studies that test several of the most plausible-sounding alternative explanations. This avoids the need to run an obnoxious number of studies or to have any one study be obnoxiously long.

---

^e Researchers sometimes call these studies "kitchen sink" studies, because ambitious young researchers will often try to cram "everything but the kitchen sink" into a single study.

Even still, it will *always* be possible for critics to think of alternative explanations that weren't measured.[f] In fact, this *science denial* technique is one of the ways cigarette companies were able to deny the link between smoking and cancer for as long as they did. Companies could simply argue that any link found between smoking cigarettes and cancer *could* have been due to an alternative explanation that the researchers simply hadn't measured. As long as plausible alternative explanations existed, companies could hide behind them and claim that there simply wasn't enough evidence to lay the blame on cigarettes as the "smoking gun," so to speak.

Given enough time, most of the fairly *plausible* alternative explanations can be tested. However, even in the best case scenario that all plausible alternative explanations have been tested and ruled out, it is still risky to draw causal conclusions solely from cross-sectional data. Sometimes it's necessary to do so because other scientific study designs are impossible, impractical, or unethical. But it would be nice, when possible to do so, to run studies that can efficiently rule out alternative explanations and satisfy the three criteria needed to show causation.

That's where the experiment enters the scene. They're not perfect, of course: They're often resource- and time-intensive and they often take place in an artificial laboratory setting (see more on this in Questions #9 and #16). But experiments do one thing *very* well: They rule out alternative explanations. By *randomly* assigning participants to an experimental condition (e.g., media violence) or a control condition (e.g., no media violence), researchers can assume, based on statistical laws, that the two groups should be similar in *every* regard. This means there's no reason for younger people, poorer people, or less-educated people to be more likely to have been randomly assigned to be in the violent media condition than in the non-violent media condition.

Why is random assignment so important? If, at the end of the study, the people in the violent media condition *are* more aggressive than the people in the non-violent media condition, this difference is most likely to be caused by our experimental manipulation. Because the groups can be considered statistically equal on all other factors – including aggression – beforehand, none of these alternative explanations is plausible.[g]

---

[f] After all, it only takes a couple of minutes to think up an alternative explanation, but *months or years* to test it! It's simply not possible to keep up with critics this way, especially the highly motivated critics who play by a different set of rules (none) than do scientists!

[g] You might be thinking "hold on now, it *is* possible that, by sheer dumb luck, all of the highly aggressive people were randomly assigned to the violent video game condition!" And you'd be right! It's also *possible* that you can flip a coin 100 times and get heads every single time. "Possible" does not mean "probable," however. The chances of something like this happening are *very* unlikely, and this

Consider a series of three experiments in which participants were randomly assigned to play one of three versions of the same race-car video game: (a) a version in which all violence was rewarded, (b) a version in which all violence was punished, and (c) a nonviolent version. [4] The researchers used the video game *Carmageddon*, a racing game in which players race their cars through streets and are rewarded for running over pedestrians. This was the game played by participants in the violent condition. The researcher reprogrammed the game for the other two conditions. In the punishment condition, players lost points if they hit a pedestrian. In the nonviolent condition, all pedestrians were removed from the game so that no violent in-game action was possible. Because of random assignment and fairly large samples, it is likely that the three groups in each study were evenly distributed in terms of existing aggressive tendencies prior to playing their assigned game.

After playing the game for about 20 minutes, participants did tasks that measured aggressive feelings (e.g., anger), aggressive thoughts, or aggressive behavior. As shown in Figure 15.1, participants randomly assigned to play the violent game experienced greater aggressive affect, had more aggressive thoughts, and behaved more aggressively. And because the only difference between the three groups was the amount of violent content they were exposed to, the studies provide excellent evidence that violent game content was the cause of the brief changes in aggressive affect, cognition, and behavior observed in participants.

---

likelihood gets *smaller* as the sample size of your study gets larger. Likewise, the chances of this happening repeatedly across many large experiments becomes so infinitesimally small that we can treat it as essentially zero.

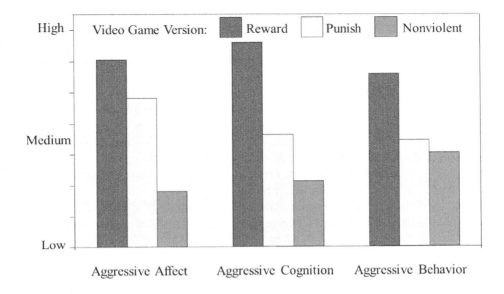

Figure 15.1. Effects of three versions of Carmageddon on aggressive affect, aggressive cognition, and aggressive behavior.

Experiments like the one above suggest that experiments, with their random assignment of participants to conditions, are the *perfect* solution to the causality issue! All we need to do is conduct experiments so that we can always rule out any alternative explanations, right?

This *would* be true, except for two new problems that arise. First, an experiment is only as good as its manipulation. Experiments let us conclude that our manipulation caused the difference between the two groups. But what, exactly, *did* we manipulate? For example, let's say we had participants in a "violent media" condition watch an action-thriller movie, while participants in a "non-violent media" condition watch a video of paint drying. It's true that we manipulated violent content: The action thriller has violence in it, while the paint-drying film does not. But we also accidentally manipulated a *lot* of other things. For instance, the action film is *also* more *exciting* than the paint-drying film. Because of this, the difference we see in aggression between the two groups might not be because of violent content, but rather excitement. The action film also has actors in it, while the paint-drying video has none. So it's also possible that the difference in aggression was caused by seeing other people, not necessarily violence.

As it turns out, it's almost impossible to manipulate *only* the variable you want to manipulate. Try as they might, researchers end up manipulating other variables along the way, something scientists call a "confound." So while experiments *can* eliminate most alternative explanations, they're not perfect because they almost always contain the possibility of a confound. Clever researchers will design manipulations that avoid confounds that also happen to be plausible alternative explanations. For example, since we know that excitement can influence aggression, a good experimental manipulation of media violence should involve violent and nonviolent video games that are *equally* exciting. This was true of the *Carmageddon* studies, which used the *same* video game (slightly modified) to ensure that this was the case. That way, if participants in the violent game condition behave more aggressively, we know that it wasn't caused by differences in excitement or difficulty of the game controls.

The second major limitation of experiments is that they usually take place in an artificial context, usually in a laboratory setting over a relatively short period of time. In a typical violent media experiment, we might bring participants into the lab to watch half an hour of television. This half-hour of TV-watching in a sterile laboratory setting is likely *very* different from how *you* watch TV in the real world. In the real world, people binge-watch TV for hours, change channels mid-show, watch with others, and watch in strange conditions, like sitting in their boxers at 3am[h] or while eating dinner. Additionally, aggression is *far* more complex in the real world than in a laboratory: People rage during the hour-long drive to work, have long-standing feuds with that jerk from the office, shout obscenities at the telemarketer who has called for the fifth time this week… A scientist simply can't capture all of this context for aggression within the sterile settings of a laboratory.

With all of this in mind, let's return now to the issue of critics and their demand for a "silver-bullet" study – that is, a single study that perfectly shows the causal link between violent media and aggression beyond a shadow of a doubt. What would this "perfect" study look like? Ideally, it would be a study that can rule out alternative explanations – an experiment – while also studying media violence and aggression as it exists in the real world – something most experiments just can't do, unless it were a long-term experiment. To do such an experiment properly, we would first have to take a large sample of children who had *never* been exposed to media before. Half of these children would randomly be assigned to consume lots of violent media for a significant period of time – say 15 years – while the other half would never be allowed to consume anything resembling violent media for 15 years. Then, we would wait around for those 15 years and see whether participants in the "violent media" group were more likely than participants in the "non-violent media" group to grow up to be bigger jerks, call other people nasty names, get into physical fights, and be arrested for a violent crime.[i]

_____

[h] None of the authors wish to admit whether this occurs for them with some regularity…

[i] Do we have any volunteers?

Of course, a study like this would be absurd. But it's useful for demonstrating just how *impractical* it would be to run the sort of study that some critics seem to demand. Not *only* would it take years to run such a study, but it would be *impossible* to force people to consume only the media we tell them to consume. In fact, the difficulty in doing exactly this *has* been shown in a study which lasted just a week: Psychologists had trouble getting people who agreed to be in the study to watch only what the researchers told them to watch.[5]

And even if we *could* guarantee that participants watched *exactly* what we told them to watch for 15 years,[j] conducting such a study would be clearly unethical. Not only would it be unethical to restrict participants' freedom for such a prolonged period of time, but remember that researchers have a responsibility to avoid anything that could cause serious harm to their participants. If we hypothesize that a *lifetime* of violent media will significantly affect someone's personality and increase their risk for aggressive behavior, it wouldn't be ethical to subject anyone to the study!

Nevertheless, it sometimes seems like nothing short of this sort of absurd study would convince critics, some of whom will *always* argue that anything less than this sort of study is too flawed to tell us anything. It's analogous to demanding that doctors randomly assign people to smoke for 30 years or not, and then see which of them develop lung cancer. If the sample size were sufficiently large, such a study would probably provide critics with the compelling evidence they need to admit that cigarettes are a causal risk factor for lung cancer, but such a study would be completely unethical.

Despite the inability to conduct these "silver bullet" studies, scientists *have* been able to make a compelling case for the link between cigarette smoking and lung cancer. One way they've done so is by relying on converging evidence from multiple studies. As we've stated, it's nearly impossible to design an experiment without confounds. But imagine if we conducted multiple studies that each used different manipulations of violent media. One study may use equally exciting violent and non-violent games (e.g., a shooter game vs. a racing game[6]), ruling out the possibility of "excitement" as a confound. Another study may use the exact same game in both conditions, but modify whether aggressive content is present in the game or not (e.g., a racing game with pedestrians to run over either present or absent in the game[4]). Still another study might compare sports video games (e.g., American football) that are equally competitive but that differ in violent content. This latter study found that playing an excessively violent sport video game increased aggression by 75%, compared to a same-sport game that was equally competitive but not excessively violent.[7] Other studies could use multiple different violent and non-violent games to rule out the possibility that the

---

[j] Which sounds more and more like a page out of Orwell's *1984* the longer we talk about it!

quirks of a single game led to differences between the "violent" and "non-violent" condition.[8]

As it turns out, the results of all of these different studies have consistently shown that participants in the "violent media" condition are more aggressive than participants in the "non-violent" media condition. This means that one of two things are true. One possibility is that all of these differences just happen to be caused by different confounds in each study that *all* happen to make the "violent game" condition more aggressive than the "non-violent game" condition. The other possibility? Violent media exposure is truly a causal risk factor for aggression.

Of course, critics may argue that laboratory experiments are not a valid way to test the real-world effects of media violence at all. We'll address this point directly in Question #16. For now, however, we'll conclude by saying that media researchers have found – in experiments, longitudinal studies, and cross-sectional studies – evidence that consistently points to the fact that violent media cause an increase in a person's risk for aggression. We may never have a silver bullet study to definitively prove that this is the case. However, most experts are convinced (see Question #11) by this converging evidence and acknowledge the existence of media violence effects, just as experts have now determined that it's been proven that cigarette smoking causes an increase in the risk of lung cancer.

Finally, when scientists study a potential risk factor for a specific bad outcome, they are not just interested in studies that test the association between that risk factor and the bad outcome. They are intensely interested in the underlying mechanisms or processes. How does smoking lead to lung cancer? How does a very high fat diet lead to heart attacks? How does repeated exposure to media violence lead to inappropriate aggression? Studies on these "how" questions are very important in leading to an understanding of basic principles underlying the risk factor-bad outcome link. They also provide additional converging evidence for the "causal" case itself. If we can show that brief exposure to violent media increases aggressive thinking, and we already know from other studies of aggression that aggressive thinking causes increases in aggressive behavior, then we have a better understanding of media violence effects on aggression (see Question #12).

References

1. Miles-Novelo, A., & Anderson, C. A. (2019). Climate change and psychology: Effects of rapid global warming on violence and aggression. *Current Climate Change Reports, 5*, 36-46.
2. Spencer, M. B., Dobbs, B., & Swanson, D. P. (1988). African American adolescents: Adaptational processes and socioeconomic diversity in behavioral outcomes. *Journal of Adolescence, 11*(2), 117-137.

3. Owens, J., Maxim, R., McGuinn, M., Nobile, C., Msall, M., & Alario, A. (1999). Television-viewing habits and sleep disturbance in school children. *Pediatrics, 104*(3), 1-8.
4. Carnagey, N. L., & Anderson, C. A. (2005). The effects of reward and punishment in violent video games on aggressive affect, cognition, and behavior. *Psychological Science, 16,* 882-889.
5. Gorney, R., Loye, D., & Steele, G. (1977). Impact of dramatized television entertainment on adult males. *American Journal of Psychiatry, 132*(2), 170-174.
6. Hasan, Y., Bègue, L., Scharkow, M., & Bushman, B. J. (2013). The more you play, the more aggressive you become: A long-term experimental study of cumulative video game effects on hostile expectations and aggressive behavior. *Journal of Experimental Social Psychology, 49,* 224-227.
7. Anderson, C. A., & Carnagey, N. L. (2009). Causal effects of violent sports video games on aggression: Is it competitiveness or violent content? *Journal of Experimental Social Psychology, 45,* 731-739.
8. Bushman, B. J., & Anderson, C. A. (2009). Comfortably numb: Desensitizing effects of violent media on helping others. *Psychological Science, 20*(3), 273-277.

16 - Can laboratory studies tell us anything about real-world aggression?

The Short Answer:

Yes, in three ways. First, even though in-lab studies can't *perfectly* mimic the real-world conditions in which aggression occurs, laboratory measures of aggression *do* relate to measures of real-world aggression. In other words, people who score high on laboratory measures of aggression *also* score high on measures of real-world aggression. As such, short-term lab studies about media effects on aggression can tell us about short-term media effects on real-world aggressive behavior. Second, lab studies allow us to examine *how* media violence influences aggression. For example, laboratory experiments have shown that brief media violence exposure increases aggressive thoughts and feelings, both of which increase aggressive behavior. Third, because it's impossible (for both ethical and practical reasons) to run laboratory studies of real-world aggression, scientists compare the results of laboratory studies to studies of real-world media use to see how well their results converge. Both lead to the same conclusion, that media violence does increase one's risk of aggression.

The Long Answer:

There are several good reasons for researchers to conduct their studies in laboratories. For one thing, researchers can use samples or procedures that are more pure or uncontaminated than what you could find in the real world (e.g., isolating a *specific* bacterial strain from among thousands for testing, or using pure chemicals rather than handfuls of dirt). Another reason involves costs, both time and money. It's much more efficient to test the effect of different amounts of a chemical (e.g., a weed killer) on an outcome (e.g., weeds growing) in a laboratory than to it is to try to find naturally-occurring concentrations of that chemical in the real world and measure its effects. A third reason is that some studies simply can't be carried out ethically in the real world. For example, we wouldn't want scientists to dump radioactive waste onto a commercial farm to see whether the effects are harmful to the plants (and the people who eat them). As a final reason, sometimes the kinds of measurement tools we need to use simply won't work in the field (e.g., trying to drag a large gas chromatograph into a field to conduct analyses.) For these reasons, some of the best (from the standpoint of establishing what causes what) and most efficient (from a cost/benefit standpoint) studies are conducted by researchers in highly-controlled laboratory settings (some of which are actually outdoors, in real fields, or caves, or at the South Pole).

In a similar way, psychologists have their own reasons for wanting to conduct laboratory-based studies. If, for example, we want to know whether brief exposure to media violence increases aggressive behavior, we *could* randomly assign children at a daycare to watch a violent children's show (e.g., *Mighty Morphin' Power Rangers*) or an equally interesting and exciting nonviolent children's show (e.g., *The Magic School Bus*) and then give them martial arts weapons and observe the carnage during recess. Obvious ethical issues make such a study impossible, of course. Furthermore, if we simply tried to find a real-world daycare where children just happened to be randomly assigned by the staff to watch violent or nonviolent shows, we would be searching for a long, long time. To put it simply, laboratory-based experiments are necessary to make such tests possible.

This example illustrates a point that we've made elsewhere (Question #8, #15). Scientists are unable to (and certainly prefer not to) use measures of aggression that involve participants actually harming others. Letting participants get harmed – whether physically or psychologically – is not only unethical, but ultimately hurts the research, because all research on the same topic would be shut down. Because of this, measuring any kind of "real world" aggression in a laboratory study is out of the question. This leaves aggression researchers with two ways to study aggression:

1. Study real-world aggression using *existing* data (e.g., records of incarceration for violent crime[1]) or by asking participants to self-report past aggression (e.g., "how often do you get into fights?"[2]) These studies are almost always correlational or longitudinal in nature.

2. Study aggression in the laboratory using carefully-crafted aggression measures that don't *actually* involve anyone being seriously hurt.

Researchers going the first route use measures of aggression that are pretty common sense: How many fights a person gets into seems like a fairly straightforward way to measure their aggression. But what about those going the second route, where people don't *actually* get hurt? In Question #8 we introduced some of the ethical ways that scientists have measured aggression-related variables in the laboratory, which include:

- How much hot sauce you force another person who doesn't like spicy food to eat[3,4]
- The intensity / duration of an electric shock[5] / blast of noise[6,7] you give someone
- How long you wait before you stop two people from fighting[8]
- Deliberately sabotaging someone's chances of winning a prize[9] or getting a promotion[10]

- How long you force someone to hold their hand in painfully cold water[11]
- Forcing someone to watch unpleasant video clips[12]

These measures are designed so that no one is seriously harmed while convincing participants that they *are* harming someone. For example, in one study, children were told that the loudest blasts of noise they could give may cause permanent hearing damage. None of the participants expressed suspicion or doubt about this fact.[6] As far as the participants were concerned, they could really inflict harm on another person (of course, no one actually heard such blasts).[a]

As the initial question suggests, however, critics have raised concerns about whether these measures are *actually* measuring aggression. If a participant in a study blasts an opponent with what they think is a deafeningly loud noise, is this *really* the same as verbally abusing or physically striking someone in the real world? Critics point out that when people are in the laboratory, they *know* that their actions are being monitored by the researchers and that the situation itself is artificial. Because of this, critics claim, participants' behaviors in the laboratory can't be considered true aggression.

Let's consider the critics' position for a moment, and imagine what it means if a participant blasts an opponent with noise. It might be, as researchers claim, because they're genuinely trying to harm the other person. But it could also be that the participant *knows* a researcher is watching them, so they feel the need to prove just how unpredictable they can be.[b] It could also be that they're doing what they think the researchers *want* them to do. After all, why would the researchers give them a "blast the opponent with noise" button if they didn't want them to use it?[c] Yet *another* possibility is that participants aren't being *aggressive*, they're being *competitive*, saying "bring it on!" to the other person. Finally, since participants know that they're in an artificial situation where they probably can't do any real harm, they might simply be testing the boundaries of it to see what they're allowed to get away with. Each of these alternative explanations is potentially a valid criticism of in-lab aggression measures, and does raise concerns about what laboratory measures of aggression are *actually* measuring.

Fortunately, these concerns aren't new to aggression researchers. Nor are they unique to aggression research. Any time researchers study something in the laboratory, they have to worry about whether reactance, demand characteristics,

---

[a] In aggression experiments, it's fairly common for the target of the aggression to not really exist, making the act victimless – although the participant doesn't know this! In some studies, however, there *is* a real target who actually *does* endure the aggressive behavior. In such cases, the aggression levels are *carefully* controlled to be mild to avoid any potential for long term harm.

[b] This concept is known as psychological reactance.

[c] This concept is known as demand characteristics.

and the artificial setting prevent them from measuring their variable as it exists in the real world. But rather than throwing the baby away with the bathwater and giving up on laboratory studies altogether, researchers instead face these criticisms head-on. How? By testing whether what they measure in the laboratory *is* related to the same behavior in the real world.

Let's see what this looks like with some examples of how researchers have done this with laboratory measures of aggression.

One way that researchers test whether laboratory measures of aggression are internally valid[d] is by measuring aggression using lab measures and seeing if they relate to other measures that, themselves, are related to real-world measures of aggression. Studies testing this have found that scores on lab measures of aggression correlate fairly well with real-world measures of aggression.[13,14,15] For example, in one study, participants who gave louder blasts of noise *also* scored higher on a self-report measure that included items asking about their willingness to assault someone in the real life[16]. This same scale, called the Buss-Durkee Hostility Inventory, has, in other studies, been found to be associated with acts of real-world aggression, including criminal violence[17]. In other words, people who engaged in criminal violence were *also* more likely to score higher on the Buss-Durkee, and participants who scored higher on the Buss-Durkee were more likely to give louder blasts of noise in the laboratory (see Figure 16.1). So while, on the surface, giving noise blasts in the laboratory might not *look* like real world aggression, it *is* related to the sorts of attitudes and intentions that *are* associated with real-world aggression!

---

[d] *Internal validity* refers to whether a measure actually measures the thing it claims to measure (try saying *that* three times fast!)

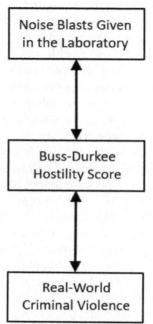

Figure 16.1. Relationship between lab measures of aggression, hostile personality, and real-world violence.

Another way that media violence researchers test the validity of laboratory measures of aggression involves what's called converging evidence. Elsewhere, we've discussed how the limitations of any one study can be overcome with evidence from other studies that don't have the same limitations (Questions #8, #9, #11, #13) – this is called converging evidence.[18,19] Using this same logic, researchers argue that their laboratory measures of aggression are, in fact, measuring the same thing as real-world measures of aggression. For example, the meta-analyses discussed in Question #11 found that exposure to violent media tends to increase in-lab aggression *regardless* of how that aggression is measured. So what do *all* of these laboratory measures have in common if it's *not* aggression?

If it's true that *none* of these measures actually measures aggression, then the doubters have to explain each and every one of these effects separately. Why does violent media cause people to give more hot sauce to others? Why does it cause people to force others to listen to painfully loud noises? Why does it cause people to want to expose others to stressful films? Why do violent criminals give more electric shocks than nonviolent criminals? In the end, it comes down to a question of which is more likely: That violent media affects aggression, or that violent media have a weirdly specific effect on our desire to give people hot sauce, make them listen to loud noises, and watch undesirable films? We then have to also explain why violent media *also* reduces people's willingness to cooperate[20] and their willingness to help others[21,22], two more findings that make sense if our measures are *actually* measuring aggression, but makes a lot *less* sense if they're all measuring random, non-aggression things.

To summarize: Researchers have long acknowledged the limitations of laboratory measures of aggression and have, for decades, provided evidence that their measures are not only ethical, but are useful proxy measures for real-world aggression. Laboratory measures generally correspond to real-world measures, and since laboratory studies seems to arrive at conclusions similar to those from studies of real-world aggression, researchers are confident in their conclusions. This isn't to say, of course, that there aren't valid criticisms of all of these measures – no measure is perfect after all. But it's important to think critically about what a measure can and can't tell us, and just as important to have realistic expectations about the measures we use. It's not worth dismissing all laboratory measures of aggression out of hand just because they don't always *seem* like they're measuring real-world aggression.

References

1. Kruttschnitt, C., Heath, L., & Ward, D. (1986). Family violence, television viewing habits, and other adolescent experiences related to violent criminal behavior. *Criminology, 243*, 235-267.
2. Escobar, S. L., Kelder, S., & Orpinas, P. (2002). The relationship between violent video games, acculturation, and aggression among Latino adolescents. *Biomedica, 22*, 398-406.
3. Hollingdale, J., & Greitemeyer, T. (2014). The effect of online violent video games on levels of aggression. *PLoS ONE, 9*(11), e111790.
4. Warburton, W. A., Williams, K. D., & Cairns, D. R. (2006). When ostracism leads to aggression: The moderating effects of control deprivation. *Journal of Experimental Social Psychology, 42*, 213-220.
5. Berkowitz, L., & Alioto, J. T. (1973). The meaning of an observed event as a determinant of its aggressive consequences. *Journal of Personality and Social Psychology, 28*(2), 206-217.
6. Konijn, E. A., Bijvank, M. N., & Bushman, B. J. (2007). I wish I were a warrior: The role of wishful identification in the effects of violent video games on aggression in adolescent boys. *Developmental Psychology, 43*(4), 1038-1044.
7. Warburton, W. A., & Bushman, B. J. (2019). The Competitive Reaction Time Task: The development and scientific utility of a flexible laboratory aggression paradigm. *Aggressive Behavior*, 45, 389-396.
8. Molitor, F., & Hirsch, K. W. (1994). Children's toleration of real-life aggression after exposure to media violence: A replication of the Drabman and Thomas studies. *Child Study Journal, 3*(24), 191-207.

9. Sprafkin, J., & Gadow, K. D. (1988). The immediate impact of aggressive cartoons on emotionally disturbed and learning disabled children. *Journal of Genetic Psychology, 149*(1), 35-44.

10. Coyne, S. M., Nelson, D. A., Lawton, F., Haslam, S., Rooney, L., Titterington, L., Trainor, H., Remnant, J., & Ogunlaja, L. (2008). The effects of viewing physical and relational aggression in the media: Evidence for a cross-over effect. *Journal of Experimental Social Psychology, 44,* 1551-1554.

11. Ballard, M. E., & Lineberger, R. (1999). Video game violence and confederate gender: Effects on reward and punishment given by college males. *Sex Roles, 41*(7-8), 541-557.

12. Barongan, C., & Hall, G. C. N. (1995). The influence of misogynous rap music on sexual aggression against women. *Psychology of Women Quarterly, 19,* 195-207.

13. Anderson, C. A., Lindsay, J. J., & Bushman, B. J. (1999). Research in the psychological laboratory: Truth or triviality? *Current Directions in Psychological Science, 8,* 3-9.

14. Carlson, M., Marcus-Newhall, A., & Miller, N. (1989). Evidence for a general construct of aggression. *Personality and Social Psychology Bulletin, 15,* 377-389.

15. Giancola, P. R. & Chermack, S. T. (1998). Construct validity of laboratory aggression paradigms: A response to Tedeschi and Quigley (1996). *Aggression and Violent Behavior 3,* 237-253.

16. Hammock, S., & Richardson, D. (1992). Predictors of aggressive behavior. *Aggressive Behavior, 18,* 219-229.

17. Selby, M. J. (1984). Assessment of violence potential using measures of anger, hostility, and social desirability. *Journal of Personality Assessment, 48,* 531-544.

18. Warburton, W. A., & Anderson, C. A. (2015). Social psychological study of aggression. In J. Wright [Ed.], *International encyclopaedia of social and behavioral sciences* [2nd Edition](pp. 295-299). Oxford, UK: Elsevier.

19. Warburton, W. A., & Anderson, C. A. (2018). Aggression. In T. K. Shackleford & P. Zeigler-Hill [Eds.], *The SAGE handbook of personality and individual differences: Vol. 3 Applications of personality and individual differences* (pp. 183-211). Thousand Oaks CA: Sage.

20. Sheese, B. E. & Graziano, W. G. (2005). Deciding to Defect: The effects of video game violence on cooperative behavior. *Psychological Science, 16*(5), 354-357.

21. Bushman, B. J. & Anderson, C. A. (2009). Comfortably Numb: Desensitizing effects of violent media on helping others. *Psychological Science, 20*(3), 273-277.

22. Saleem, M., Anderson, C. A., & Barlett, C. P. (2015). Assessing helping and hurting behaviors through the Tangram help/hurt task. *Personality and Social Psychology Bulletin, 41,* 1345-1362.

17 - Aren't there studies that find no effects of violent media on aggression?

The Short Answer:

Yes – there are a number of studies which have found no or only weak evidence of a relation between media violence and aggression. This is true in any science, including studies of dietary habits and heart disease. Whenever dealing with a complicated scientific problem, researchers expect a certain percentage of studies to fail to find statistically significant effects. It's difficult to know how to interpret such findings, however, as one can fail to find evidence of an effect for many reasons. One possible reason is that there really is no effect – this is the interpretation that many critics use. But there are other reasons a study can find no evidence of an effect. For instance, the study may be poorly designed, may have too few participants, or it may use an insensitive measure of aggression. Although the results of a single study can be illuminating, it's always important to look beyond the results of a single study and ask what all available research on the subject says. Also, although the field as a whole strongly supports the existence of a modest media violence effect, critics play a valuable role by forcing researchers to think carefully about how they design and interpret their studies and by ensuring that researchers are doing science properly.

The Long Answer:

Non-scientists often assume that science progresses any time a new study comes along and either "proves" something we didn't know or "disproves" something we thought we knew. News media often encourage this sort of thinking, in part because it generates catchy headlines like "Study proves that X causes cancer" or "Study proves that everything we knew about Y is wrong."[a] As interesting as such stories are, however, the reality is that scientific understanding is *rarely* overthrown with a single study.[b]

A single study should be thought of as a point of data amidst dozens, or even hundreds of other points. Since individual studies are imperfect, each one makes a fairly modest contribution to our knowledge about a topic, especially in fields with hundreds of prior studies. A particular study may add specific details to

---

[a] Admit it, these sorts of headlines are enticing. *We'd* certainly want to read a story with a headline like that!

[b] Science is less about mind-blowing revelations about the truths of the world and more about slow, repetitive, nitty-gritty chipping away at the truth.

135

our understanding about a topic, and if it's an entirely novel topic, it may well have a fairly big impact on a field. But one study rarely overturns our understanding of a subject – especially if there are already hundreds of other studies on the topic.

Nonetheless, although individual studies have a fairly small impact, however, they do pile up over time. Eventually, those individual points of data start to converge and give us a clearer picture of how something in the world works. Studies that support our hypotheses are exciting and help us feel more confident in our theories, while studies that fail to support our hypotheses force us to reconsider our theories. But regardless of how a study comes out, it's important to maintain a sense of perspective: What does this study's results tell us in the context of existing theory and all the other research which came before it? This context is far easier for scientists to consider than for laypersons, because scientists spend their careers reading and contributing to this literature. In contrast, a layperson may only ever read one or two studies on a subject. This is why laypeople often base their opinions on what a single study has to say. Worse yet, they might base it on a news article about a study.

Another common mistake that laypersons (and some scientists) make when reading about a study is to interpret the findings in an "all or nothing" fashion. One of the authors has recently seen this for himself when looking for research on the long-term effects of different diets. When he looked at the scientific literature, the researchers would discuss the strengths and weaknesses of different diets, recognizing that there were benefits and drawbacks to many of them. There were very few simple, clear-cut answers. But when he looked at how the same studies were reported in the media, they were described in very all-or-nothing, black-or-white language:

- "Scientists prove that diet X causes diabetes!"
- "Why everyone should be eating diet Y!"
- "Diet Z is a scary experiment!"

The same thing happens whenever news outlets or laypersons discuss the findings of media violence research: Every study is treated as either providing definitive proof that violent media *do* have an effect or that they absolutely *do not* have an effect, with no room for a middle-ground interpretation. In reality, researchers in this field spend less time arguing about whether effects exist or not and more time trying to understand the underlying processes (i.e., how the effect works; Question #12), or gauging *how* big or small the effect of media violence is. Many media violence researchers believe that the effect, while modest in size, is large enough to be worth discussion by parents and policy makers, while critics typically argue that the effect is too small to care about. As such, the top media violence researchers conduct studies designed to understand the various ways that media violence affects consumers. Occasionally some of them summarize the existing studies to get an overall estimate of the size of the effects. Only then do they judge whether it more strongly supports the "big enough to care" conclusion or the "too small to care" conclusion. It's a very different approach than news and web-based debate over the untenable "media violence turns people into serial killers" position versus the equally untenable "violent media have no effect whatsoever" position that's popular in mainstream discussions.

Warning: Boring (but important) statistics ahead! Don't worry – we won't wade *too* far into the sea of statistics, since this isn't a stats textbook. But a bit of statistics understanding can go a *long* way to understanding how researchers discuss and interpret study results!

Let's start by talking about what we mean when we're talking about an "effect size". The strength of a relationship between any two variables (e.g., a correlation – see Question #9 for an introduction to correlations) is called its effect size. Any two variables (e.g., media violence and aggression) will have an effect size that falls somewhere between the values of -1 and +1.[c] A value of "+1" means that media violence is *perfectly* related with aggression: For each hour of media violence people consume, there is an *exact* amount that their likelihood of aggression will increase (see Figure 17.1, top). A value of "-1" means the *opposite* direction is true: For each hour of media violence someone consumes, there is an exact amount that their likelihood of aggression will *decrease* (see Figure 17.1, middle). A value of 0, which falls right in the middle of those two extremes, means that there is absolutely *no* relationship between media violence and aggression: How much violent media you consume is unrelated to how aggressive you are (see Figure 17.1, bottom).

---

[c] Actually, there are several different measures of "effect size" commonly used. Just like the temperature measures Fahrenheit, Celsius, and Kelvin, they can be translated into each other. We use the coefficient *r* version for simplicity. Keep in mind that this effect size measure *r* is used for true experiments as well as correlational studies.

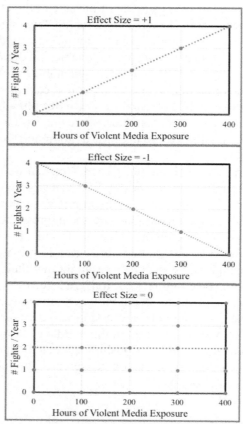

Figure 17.1. Various effect sizes of the relationship between media violence and aggression.

By thinking about effect sizes in this way, we can turn researchers' hypotheses about media violence effects into estimates about how big the effect size is. Researcher A, who believes that there is a *small* effect of violent media on aggression, might predict that the effect has a value of, say, 0.20: bigger than no effect (0), but nowhere near a perfect relationship (+1). In contrast, Researcher B, who believes that there is virtually no effect of violent media on aggression might predict that the effect size is 0.

So now we have two competing hypotheses: Researcher A says the effect size will be closer to 0.2, while Researcher B says that the effect size will be closer to 0. Now, let's imagine that they worked together to run a media violence study. The study produces an estimate of how big the effect size is. If that estimate is closer to 0 than to 0.20, the researchers would probably conclude that the evidence more strongly favors Researcher B's hypothesis – Not that Researcher B is *undeniably* correct or that this is undisputable evidence of *no* effect – just that the evidence more strongly favors one hypothesis over another. And if the estimate is closer to 0.20 than to 0, they would probably conclude that the evidence more strongly favors Researcher A. And an effect of 0.10? Well, that's a matter for debate (or another study!)

Now, imagine Researcher A and B decided it would be best to conduct a *bunch* of different studies of media violence, and take the average of *all* of those effect sizes to get a good overall estimate of what the true effect size is. Of course, if we ran all these studies, we wouldn't expect each one to give the exact same estimate. Why? Because there's *always* going to be some random "noise" in the results, even if each study was conducted in *exactly* the same way. Different participants doing the study at different times will yield somewhat different results. This would be similar to doing a study where you flip a coin 10 times, and then do it again and again and again. Sometimes it'll come up heads 7 times, other times 3 times. But, the more times that you do the study, the more it will become clear that (assuming it's a fair coin), heads will come up about half of the time. Likewise, the more we run and re-run media violence studies, the closer we should get to homing in on the "true" effect size.

As we discussed in other questions (e.g., Questions #8 and #9), we could run all sorts of studies (e.g., cross-sectional, longitudinal, and experimental), all using different measures of aggression (e.g., self-report, parent report, archival), to help us get an even better estimate. In fact, we might even conduct the studies in different locations, using participants of different ages, and mix up the types of media used, letting us get the estimate of all violent media effects across all contexts using all sorts of people. With all of these different modifications to the studies, we're bound to get a variety of different estimates, some of which will probably overestimate the true effect size and others which will underestimate the true effect size.

Let's imagine, for the sake of argument, that the "true" effect size was 0.15. If we conduct enough well-designed studies, over time they should average out to an overall estimate of 0.15. Some of the studies might estimate effect sizes as high as 0.5 or as low as -0.3. This is *precisely* why we should never rely on a single study to draw conclusions about an effect. If we grabbed one study out of the pile and found that its estimate was -0.2, we might wrongly conclude "Hey, it turns out media violence actually *reduces* aggression!" But when we look at all the findings *together*, the studies suggest otherwise: In this particular pile of studies, some will be closer to Researcher B's hypothesis of 0, and some will fall closer to Researcher A's hypothesis of 0.2. But by looking at the *average* estimate, we can get a sense of which hypothesis is better supported by the data.[d]

---

[d] For context, the average effect size, based on the meta-analyses discussed in Question #11, have been estimated at: 0.06[1], 0.13[2], 0.15[3,4], 0.18[5,6], and 0.19[7,8]).

With this framework in mind, it should be clear that researchers aren't out to "prove" or "disprove" a theory so much as they are to get the most accurate estimate of how big a particular effect size is. For this reason, it's important for them to know what causes some studies to *underestimate* the true effect size and what causes some studies to *overestimate* the true effect size.

When it comes to underestimating an effect size, it often comes down to how well the study and its measures are designed. It's surprisingly easy to create a poorly-designed study that finds no relationship (an effect of 0). To see *how* easy it is, let's imagine running an experiment where participants randomly play one game or another. After playing one of the games, we measure their aggression to see if there are any differences between the two groups. Now let's imagine that we had never actually played either of the two games before, and so we didn't know that both games contained high levels of media violence (e.g., In one game, players jump on top of enemies to kill them while in another players shoot enemies). We *could* argue that the "shooting" game is technically more violent than the "jumping" game, and therefore we're testing a "high" and "low" violence condition. Because both games clearly involve killing lots of enemies, however, there will probably be *very* little difference in how much they affect the aggression of participants in the two conditions (an effect size of near 0).

We *could* interpret these results as evidence that the amount of violent content in a video game has no effect on players' aggression. However, it's more likely that the lack of difference between these two groups has more to do with the poor choice of a "nonviolent" game rather than there being no relationship between violent media and aggression. In short, if the researcher does not choose an appropriate violent and nonviolent control condition, it can lead to an underestimation of the true effect of media violence on aggression. Unfortunately, studies with this obvious flaw in design do exist, and have been claimed to "prove" that media violence has no effect on aggression.

For another example of how bad study design can lead to an underestimation of the effect of media violence, imagine a study where participants in one condition got to play a violent game while participants in another condition were told that there was a technical problem with the game and, because of this, they had to sit there and watch *another* person play a violent game. At the end of the study, the data might show that participants in both conditions were equally aggressive, leading the researchers to conclude that playing a violent game has no effect on aggression, since "players" were no more aggressive than "watchers."

Can you think of another way to interpret these findings? How would you feel if you were a "watcher" in this study – told that you were going to get to play

---

The meta-analyses which have been based on the *most* studies tend to yield the largest estimates, while meta-analyses with smaller estimates tend to be based on smaller samples of studies.

a video game, but then forced to watch someone else have fun instead? Do you think that might make you a bit annoyed, or frustrated? Perhaps a bit angry? Further imagine that the participants were 12-year old boys. If being denied the promised game-playing time and forced to watch others enjoy the game makes the "watcher" boys frustrated and angry, the results of the study are probably telling us that there's no difference between players of violent games and "annoyed / frustrated people" – they can't really tell us anything about whether violent video games actually increase aggression compared to an average person who didn't play a violent game. This, again, could lead researchers to mistakenly underestimate the size of violent media effects due to a bad study design decision. Again, such studies exist.

Let's try one more example, just to drive the point home. Imagine that we ran a study of grade 6 children. We decide to measure violent media consumption by asking them how many hours of violent television they watch per week. We then decide to measure aggression by asking these grade 6 children how many times they had been arrested for assault with a deadly weapon. Further imagine that our study finds that *none* of the kids had been arrested. Because of this, the kids who watched a *lot* of violent television would look exactly the same as the kids who watched *no* violent television, on this extreme measure of aggression.

Does this mean that watching violent television had no effect on the kids' aggression? Probably not. After all, the reason there was no difference between the "high violent media" and "low violent media" children is because we used an aggression measure that was too extreme to be useful for this sample. As an analogy, imagine trying to compare which of two marbles is heavier by weighing them on a scale meant for dump trucks. Chances are, the scale wouldn't be sensitive enough to detect the differences between the two marbles – this doesn't mean that the marbles are therefore equal in mass. This is why scientists have to be careful when choosing their measures: Using a measure that's insensitive can lead to underestimating the size of violent media effects.

Up to now, we've discussed only the ways that studies tend to *underestimate* effect sizes. It should be pointed out that researchers can also *overestimate* the effect size of media violence. For instance: Imagine a study where participants in one condition play a violent video game that is frustrating. In the other condition, participants play a nonviolent video game that is satisfying. At the end of the study, the researchers find that participants in the violent game condition are more aggressive than participants in the satisfying game condition. One interpretation is that violent games *increased* participants' aggression. But isn't it also possible that the effect might also be due to the fact that playing a satisfying game lowers aggression and frustration increases it? This would mean that the difference between the two conditions is actually due to two different effects at the same time. If we ignore this fact, and treat the estimate as *only* an estimate of media violence effects, it would cause us to overestimate the effect.

This is an example of how a poorly-designed manipulation can lead to overestimation of media violence effects.

Another factor that can inflate estimates of effect size has to do with researchers "cherry-picking" their results. To see what this looks like, let's imagine running a media violence study and measuring aggression in three different ways. When we analyze the data, we discover that the violent game and non-violent game conditions were different on only one of the three aggression measures. We decide to "simplify" our story, by only publishing the results of the one scale where we found a difference. By throwing away data that would *lower* our estimate of the effect size, we are actually inflating, or *over*-estimating the true effect size. Of course, the opposite could also happen. That is, a few researchers really want to find no effects of media violence. Thus, they could "cherry-pick" their results by reporting only the measure that failed to show a difference.

In a similar manner, we might run a media violence study and find no evidence of a difference between our "violent media" and "non-violent media" conditions. Rather than publish the study, we might say "well, clearly we made some mistakes in designing that study" and choose not to bother publishing the study. This problem, called the file-drawer problem, means that scientific journals and other outlets are more likely to contain studies that show the existence of an effect and are less likely to contain studies that show no effect, or which go against a researcher's original hypothesis. Both of these problems have the unfortunate effect of leading to an overestimation of the size of media violence effects in the literature.

To be fair, all of these examples involve flawed studies or biased practices. We're not suggesting that anyone in this field intentionally designs such poor studies – they're being exaggerated here to help us make our point. But these same flaws – in much subtler forms – can be found in some of the studies which claim that the effect of violent media on aggression is virtually zero, or in some of the studies with very high estimates of effect sizes. Media violence researchers are usually quite aware of these limitations and frequently point them out when reviewing studies. Laypersons, however, are not taught to look for these sorts of design flaws, especially when such details are left out of media stories with headlines like "Study proves that violent games don't cause violence." Researchers bear at least some of the blame for this as well, often unable or unwilling to pressure media outlets to correct erroneous or overly simplistic conclusions about their studies.

One of the strongest concerns critics of media violence research have is that of publication bias – the fact that papers which find an effect significantly different from zero are more likely to be published than studies which find an effect that's near zero. These concerns are not limited to media violence research, but are in fact a problem across all fields of science and medicine. Researchers have been aware of these problems for quite some time, but the issue has recently been generating a *lot* of attention. Although researchers bear some share of the

142

blame, many have pointed a finger at scientific journals, which often avoid publishing studies that find near-zero effects. Since many researchers need publications to get promoted, this creates pressure for researchers to send out only research that's likely to get published, worsening the file-drawer problem.

As with any criticism, it's important to maintain a sense of perspective. To be sure, concerns about publication bias are a problem that needs to be addressed. But rather than declaring that an entire field is flawed or that there's nothing we can learn from the studies which have been done, it's preferable to acknowledge these biases and work to overcome them. One of the best ways to do this is to make sure that, when reviewing a body of research, we include unpublished datasets and articles published in less prestigious journals. In fact, many of the meta-analyses discussed in Question #11 do exactly that and include many unpublished studies in their analyses. Furthermore, there are statistical procedures that can tell us whether or to what extent a set of studies is likely to have suffered from publication biases. When properly applied to the media violence domain, it is clear that publication bias has not been a major problem.[6, 9]

At this point, we'd like to finish with one last point about critics of media violence effects: A criticism of the critics, you might say. It's often the case that critics will conduct a study which estimates media violence effects to be about zero. From this, they conclude that there is no effect of media violence. Although the data from such a study may well justify this conclusion, it's important to note that such findings themselves fly in the face of a great deal of past research and theory. Theories like the General Aggression Model and Social Learning Theory (Question #12) are based on decades of accumulated research and state that violent media *should* increase a person's risk of aggression. These theories and the decades of supporting research also show why media violence effects are not very large. The conclusion that violent media *are* a risk factor for aggression does not come out of a vacuum, but rather builds upon the work of psychologists in cognitive psychology, personality psychology, social psychology, developmental psychology, and biopsychology. So when critics say that there is no evidence of media violence effects because their particular study failed to find evidence for it, they often fail to provide a valid theoretical explanation for *why* there may be no effect when there *ought* to be one. In many cases, there are obvious methodological flaws in the studies. It makes no sense to claim that people can't learn aggression from video games, for example, when they can learn reading, problem solving, navigation skills, and hand-eye coordination from them. In the same way that critics have helped the field of media violence research improve by highlighting some weaknesses, this is one area where the critics, themselves, could stand to improve their research practices.

In summary: there are some studies which estimate the effect size of media violence on aggression to be close enough to zero to treat it as non-existent. In the context of media violence literature as a whole, however, a few such studies are expected purely by chance. These studies are overshadowed by the bulk of the research, which finds that media violence is a small, but significant causal risk factor for aggression. No study is without its limitations, however, and some studies will over-estimate or under-estimate the true effect size of media violence due to random chance factors, flaws in study design, or flaws in the publication process. Critics of media violence have done the field a service by starting discussions about these topics, which helps to keep science as objective and impartial as possible. Their skepticism has encouraged researchers to rule out alternative explanations and, ultimately, do better science. Where they do a disservice, however, is when they overstate their skepticism to the point of denying what the research literature as whole clearly shows. When they do this, they harm not only the scientific field, but the many consumers of violent media, just as tobacco industry scientists harmed generations of smokers and their families.

References
1. Ferguson, C. J. (2015). Do angry birds make for angry children? A meta-analysis of video game influences on children's and adolescents' aggression, mental health, prosocial behavior, and academic performance. *Perspectives on Psychological Science, 10*(5), 646-666.
2. Wood, W., Wong, F., & Cachere, J. (1991). Effects of media violence on viewers' aggression in unconstrained social interaction. *Psychological Bulletin, 109*(3), 371-383.
3. Sherry, J. (2001). The effects of violent video games on aggression: A meta-analysis. *Human Communication Research, 27,* 409-431.
4. Ferguson, C. J. (2007). Evidence for publication bias in video game violence effects literature: A meta-analytic review. *Aggression and Violent Behavior, 12,* 470-482.
5. Greitemeyer, T., & Mügge, D. O. (2014). Video games do affect social outcomes: A meta-analytic review of the effects of violent and prosocial video game play. *Personality and Social Psychology Bulletin, 40*(5), 578-589.
6. Anderson, C. A., Shibuya, A., Ihori, N., Swing, E. L., Bushman, B. J., Sakamoto, A., Rothstein, H. R., & Saleem, M. (2010). Violent video game effects on aggression, empathy, and prosocial behavior in Eastern and Western countries. *Psychological Bulletin, 136,* 151-173.
7. Paik, H., & Comstock, G. (1994). The effects of television violence on antisocial behavior: A meta-analysis. *Communication Research, 21*(4), 516-546.
8. Hearold, S. (1986). A synthesis of 1043 effects of television on social behavior. In G. Comstock (Ed.), *Public Communication and Behavior, 1,* 65-133. New York: Academic Press.
9. Greitemeyer, T., & Mügge, D. O. (2014). Video games do affect social outcomes: A meta-analytic review of the effects of violent and prosocial video game play. *Personality and Social Psychology Bulletin, 40,* 578 –589.

Chapter 2

The "Who," "When," and "What"

of Media Violence Effects

18 - Does it matter how realistic or fantasy-themed media violence is?

The Short Answer:

Research suggests that violent media increase a person's risk for aggression *regardless* of whether it's realistic or fantasy-themed. There are theoretical reasons to believe that fantasy violence (e.g., cartoons, violence against aliens, violence with unrealistic consequences) may actually be *worse* than realistic violence (e.g., violence against humans, violent sports, violence with realistic consequences). However, there are also theoretical reasons to believe that the *opposite* is also true. If the question is "do fantasy or realistic media lead to learning aggressive scripts," the answer is "both do." But if the question is "which is more likely to lead to the learning of aggressive scripts that can increase aggression in day-to-day life," it seems like realistic media violence *should* be a bigger risk factor. As of now, there's just not enough evidence one way or another to argue that one is, in general, more harmful than the other.

The Long Answer:

Common sense seems to suggest that the more realistic the violence in a film or video game is, the more it should be a risk factor for aggression. Parents, for example, are probably more concerned about their child playing a game in which they shoot an enemy with a realistic gun – causing realistic blood and gore to spray everywhere – than they are to let their child play a game where a cartoony Italian plumber jumps on a turtle, causing him to comically pop out of his shell. Film, TV, and video game ratings boards would certainly seem to agree: Any media featuring realistic guns and gore will almost *certainly* be rated inappropriate for young children, unlike the aforementioned turtle-jumping plumber (for more on content rating systems, see Question #48.) But is "realistic" violence *actually* more of a causal risk than fantasy-themed, cartoony violence when it comes to the viewer's risk for aggression?

Let's start by taking a quick look at what the General Aggression Model (GAM) – a theory about the risk factors for aggression – has to say (see Question #12 for more on the GAM). According to the GAM, there is no "one" cause of aggression, but instead dozens of risk and protective factors that alter a person's risk of behaving aggressively in a given situation[1]. Guided by the GAM, we can ask whether fantasy-themed versus realistic-themed violence involve different risk factors for aggression.

One of the ways violent media increases our risk of aggression is by teaching the consumer aggressive scripts[2] (for more on scripts, see Question #12.) Scripts involve well-rehearsed behavioral responses that are fairly routine or even automatic. We use these scripts to make sense of the situations we find ourselves in and to select appropriate behaviors. Since scripts are used to respond to, and make sense of, real-world situations, it makes sense that realistic portrayals of violence should lead viewers to create scripts that they can use in day-to-day life. For example, if you watch a lot of movies featuring fistfights, you may develop a script that says "when someone's coming toward you, get ready to throw down and hit them first!" It's easy to imagine situations where this script would be activated: at a bar, walking down the street, or being approached by a stranger at work.

Now imagine the scripts a person forms when watching movies about elven wizards shooting magic fireballs at attacking dragons. These scripts, while aggressive, seem far less likely to be activated in day-to-day life.[a] So, if the question is "do fantasy or realistic media lead to learning aggressive scripts?," the answer is "both do". But if the question is "which is more likely to lead to the learning of aggressive scripts that can increase aggression in day-to-day life?," it seems like realistic media violence should be a bigger risk factor. After all, the greater visual similarity of realistic media violence to real people and places means that some specific aspects of the learned script will be more similar to what one sees in the real world.

There's another reason why realistic media violence may be a bigger risk factor: desensitization effects. Generally speaking, people find the consequences of violence somewhat repulsive: We recoil at the sight of blood or gore and find it unpleasant to view videos that feature gratuitous violence.[3] According to the GAM, disliking the outcomes of violence or of even imagining violence reduces the desirability of aggression: We tend to avoid actions that lead to undesirable outcomes or that make us feel bad. In other words, being sensitive to outcomes of violence is a protective factor against our risk for violence – something that makes us think twice before throwing a punch.

But what does this mean for a person who's become *desensitized* to violence – that is, they're no longer bothered by sights or sounds of violence? Well, it makes them *more* likely to engage in aggression[4] (for more on this, see Question #32). People can become desensitized to pretty much anything by being repeatedly exposed to it.[b] Desensitization to blood and gore happens when people

---

[a] Unless, of course, your village is frequently attacked by dragons, in which case you've got a far bigger problem than the aggressive scripts you're learning from violent media!

[b] One of the authors recalls living near an airport and gradually becoming desensitized to the sound of planes flying overhead, to the point where he no longer notices it anymore!

are repeatedly exposed to violent scenes and images, in much the same way that medical students become desensitized to the sights, sounds, and smells of surgery[5].

So how might realistic and fantasy-themed violence differ in the amount of desensitization they lead to? Well, in a realistic portrayal of a gunshot wound, the victim's head might explode into bloody chunks of skull and brain – a thoroughly unpleasant scene. Now what happens if you shoot an alien with your disintegration ray? Perhaps they disappear altogether. Or they turn into a pile of ash with a comical "poof" sound effect. Although both scenes involve the murder of another person with a weapon, the "alien" nature of the fantasy setting may make it less emotionally influential on us, likely because it's far less recognizable than anything we could plausibly experience. If we're repeatedly exposed to this fantasy-themed violence, our emotional response to real images of blood and gore is unlikely to change much – we'll always be emotionally responsive to it. But what happens if we're repeatedly exposed to *realistic* violent media? Over time, our emotional response is likely to change, going from strong disgust and discomfort to a numb acceptance. And, given that we're far more likely to encounter scenes of real-world blood and gore than to encounter fantasy-like alien rays and disintegration, it would seem that realistic media once again has greater potential to influence our real-world aggression than fantasy-themed media. And, there is some research (but not all) that supports this realism/fantasy distinction.

But there *are* theoretical reasons to predict that fantasy-themed violent media could be the bigger risk. One reason involves the lessons people learn about aggression when watching violent media: Is violence something desirable or undesirable? Some realistic portrayals of war, such as the film *Saving Private Ryan*, frame violence as horrific and undesirable: During the famous storming of the Normandy beachhead scene, the film captures the tragedy and horror of the violence. Many viewers come away with the lesson that war is awful.

In contrast, think about less-realistic portrayals of aggression, which rarely show realistic consequences of violent behavior. Old TV westerns, for example, never showed blood when people were shot and rarely showed the negative consequences of someone being shot (e.g., either the viewer's own sense of guilt or the emotional trauma of the victim's family and friends). Violent cartoons and video games are often worse: Characters often hit, shoot, or blow one another up, only to reappear moments later, seemingly no worse for wear. In these contexts, violence is framed as heroic, funny, and having relatively few drawbacks. Because of this, one might expect fantasy-themed violence to lead to negative lessons about violence in a way that more realistic portrayals do not – making fantasy-themed violence a bigger risk factor.[c]

---

[c] Unfortunately, there are far too many real-world examples of this with regard to children and televised wrestling. Countless children are injured every year after

148

But there's another reason why fantasy-themed media may be a bigger risk factor than realistic media: Fantasy-themed media often "fly under the radar," so to speak. When people consume fictional media, they tend to not think critically about it, letting the things which happen in the story have a pass because it's not real. It means that they're unlikely to challenge what they're seeing. Because of this, peoples' beliefs and attitudes about violence can be swayed by fantasy content, and perhaps even more than by realistic content.[6] And if that fantasy-themed content shows that aggression is appropriate or that all strangers are inherently violent, viewers may pick up these beliefs or feelings without question and without conscious awareness.

Not only are consumers more likely to let their guard down, but so are parents. A parent may appropriately deny their child access to violent video games with blood and gore, but assume that a video game with cartoon characters in it is completely innocent. This is despite the fact that both games may feature characters hitting, shooting, and blowing one another up. As a result, children are likely exposed to far more violence than parents are aware of simply because the violence is fantasy-themed in nature. This ability to "fly under the radar" may well make fantasy-themed violence a greater risk factor – because it's a risk factor we don't even think to defend ourselves against.

To this point, we've suggested why realistic portrayals of violence may be a bigger risk factor for aggression than fantasy-themed violence, as well as the reverse. But there are theoretical reasons to believe that violent media should increase a person's risk of aggression *regardless* of how realistic or fantasy-themed it is. For example, according to the GAM, violent media activate aggressive thoughts in peoples' minds, making aggression much more likely to occur. Studies have shown, for example, that seeing a gun (or even just a *picture* of a gun) in the room can increase a person's aggressive behavior[7,8] by activating concepts of aggression in their mind. It shouldn't matter whether the gun is realistic-looking or cartoony – so long as you recognize it as a gun, the concept of "gun" and gun-related words like "weapon" and "aggression" will become activated, along with related scripts and behavioral intentions.

In a similar vein, playing a violent video game that rewards players for violent behavior should cause the player to associate "violence" with "reward". Learning theories suggest that any time a behavior is rewarded, that behavior will become more likely to occur in the future. As such, if violent behavior is what's being rewarded, whether the violence involves attacking another human or attacking an alien / animal / zombie, aggressive action is being rewarded, and the player's brain is absorbing that lesson each and every time it happens.

---

watching their favorite wrestling superstars hit and throw one another around with seemingly no ill effects. It makes you wonder whether we'd see the same thing happening if the consequences of these attacks were more realistically portrayed (e.g., blood, broken bones, pain and suffering).

So, where does that leave us? Should fantasy-themed violence be considered a bigger concern than more realistic violent media? The answer, unfortunately, is that at this point in time, there aren't any clear answers. We *can* confidently say that repeated exposure to realistic images of blood and gore will have a greater desensitizing effect than lack of such exposure, but desensitization to violent images is only one pathway that leads from media violence to aggression. Furthermore, the situation is even more complicated: Whether fantasy-themed violence or realistic violence is a bigger risk factor on later aggression may depend on how old the consumer is, or how much violence they have been exposed to in the past, or whether we're looking at short-term or long-term effects.[9]

In the end, realistic and fantasy-themed violence may end up having roughly the same sized effects on aggressive behavior, but for different reasons. Some studies show an increase in aggressive thoughts, feelings, and behavior after exposure to *realistic* media violence (e.g., violence against humans[10], violence in sports[11], violent television shows intended to be realistic[12], games that show blood and gore[13]). Other studies show similar findings using *fantasy-themed* media violence (e.g., violence against demons[14], violence against aliens[15], children's cartoons that feature violence[16]). But there have been very few studies directly comparing realistic and fantasy portrayals of violence, and no one that we know of has tried to review the literature on media violence to see whether fantasy-themed and realistic violent media differ in their effects on consumers.

To summarize: We can't confidently say whether fantasy-themed or realistic violence poses a greater risk for later aggressive behavior. Although there *are* theoretical reasons to predict that they may differ, theory and evidence *both* suggest that, at very least, both are risk factors for aggression, and that even fantasy violence increases aggression in adults who clearly know the difference between fantasy and reality. This is an important point to remember, especially since many parents mistakenly believe that realistic violence is the only violence that can affect their children, based on the false assumption that cartoon violence is harmless. In doing so, parents overlook the fact that it's *the presence of violence* in the media, and not necessarily *the realism of the violence*, that makes it a risk factor. Another way to think of it is like this: Imagine a parent refusing to give their child soda because they know that soda is high in sugar content. Instead, they choose to give their child apple juice, because they're told that juice is healthy. Despite their good intentions, unbeknownst to them, the juice itself contains *just as much sugar* as the soda just refused.[17] Without realizing it, the parent is still contributing to the sugar in their child's diet, but is now doing so *blind* to the fact that they're doing it – a chilling thought to anyone who's a proponent of consumers being as informed as possible so they can make decisions in their best interest.

References

1. Anderson, C. A. & Bushman, B. J. (2002). Human Aggression. *Annual Review of Psychology, 53,* 27-51.
2. Huesmann, L. R. (1998). The role of social information processing and cognitive schema in the acquisition and maintenance of habitual aggressive behavior. In R. G. Geen & E. Donnerstein (Eds.) *Human Aggression: Theories, Research and Implications for Policy*, pp. 73-109. New York: Academic.
3. Lang, P. J., Bradley, M. M., & Cuthbert, B. N. (2008). *International affective picture system (IAPS): Affective ratings of pictures and instruction manual.* Technical Report A-8. Gainesville, FL: University of Florida.
4. Engelhardt, C. R., Bartholow, B. D., Kerr, G. T., & Bushman, B. J. (2011). This is your brain on violent video games: Neural desensitization to violence predicts increased aggression following violent video game exposure. *Journal of Experimental Social Psychology, 47*(5), 1033-1036.
5. Fanti, K. A., Vanman, E., Henrich, C. C., & Avraamides, M. N. (2009). Desensitization to media violence over a short period of time. *Aggressive Behavior, 35,* 179-187.
6. Green, M. C., & Brock, T. C. (2000). The role of transportation in the persuasiveness of public narratives. *Journal of Personality and Social Psychology, 79*(5), 701-721.
7. Berkowitz, L., & Lepage, A. (1967). Weapons as aggression-eliciting stimuli. *Journal of Personality and Social Psychology, 7*(2), 202-207.
8. Leyens, J.-P. & Parke, R. D. (1976). Aggressive slides can induce a weapons effect. *European Journal of Social Psychology, 5*(2), 229-236.
9. Bushman, B. J., & Huesmann, L. R. (2006). Short-term and long-term effects of violent media on aggression in children and adults. *Archives of Pediatric and Adolescent Medicine, 160,* 348-352.
10. Gabbiadini, A., Riva, P., Andrighetto, L., Volpato, C., & Bushman, B. J. (2014). Interactive effect of moral disengagement and violent video games on self-control, cheating, and aggression. *Social Psychological and Personality Science, 5*(4), 451-458.
11. Geen, R., & Berkowitz, L. (1966). Name-mediated cue properties. *Journal of Personality, 34*(3), 457-465.
12. Josephson, W. L. (1987). Television violence and children's aggression: Testing the priming, social script, and disinhibition predictions. *Journal of Personality and Social Psychology, 53*(5), 882-890.
13. Barlett, C., Branch, O., Rodeheffer, C., & Harris, R. (2009). How long do the short-term violent video game effects last? *Aggressive Behavior, 35,* 225-236.
14. Uhlmann, E., & Swanson, J. (2004). Exposure to violent video games increases automatic aggressiveness. *Journal of Adolescence, 27,* 41-52.

151

15. Sestir, M. A., & Bartholow, B. D. (2010). Violent and nonviolent video games produce opposing effects on aggressive and prosocial outcomes. *Journal of Experimental Social Psychology, 46,* 934-942.
16. Liss, M. B., Reinhardt, L. C., & Fredriksen, S. (1983). TV heroes: The impact of rhetoric and deeds. *Journal of Applied Developmental Psychology, 4,* 175-187.
17. Walker, R. W., Dumke, K. A., & Goran, M. I. (2014). Fructose content in popular beverages made with and without high-fructose corn syrup. *Nutrition, 30*(7-8), 928-935.

19 - Are most people immune to the effects of media violence?

The Short Answer:

No. People often assume that that they're immune to media violence effects because they themselves have never engaged in extremely violent behavior. This line of reasoning is faulty, however, because it assumes that violent media *only* affects extreme aggression. In actuality, violent media effects are *far* more likely to be observed in everyday forms of aggression as well as in thought and feeling patterns. The effects of media violence have been found in practically every demographic that's been studied, which suggests that the effect is universal. For this reason, it's unlikely that anyone is "immune" to the effects of media violence, a conclusion that's consistent with what researchers know about other psychological processes (e.g., learning). In many ways, this is similar to the fact that no one is wholly immune to the effects of advertising.

The Long Answer:

Before we answer this question, let's take a moment to understand *why* it comes up so often, especially when we talk to regular users of violent media. It makes sense that heavy consumers of violent media would be motivated to protect their hobby or favorite forms of entertainment. After all, if a person spends hours playing violent video games or watching violent television, being told that these media are having a harmful effect on them means acknowledging some uncomfortable truths:

1. Chances are, they've already been affected by the media they've consumed

2. These effects likely happened without them even being aware of it

3. If they want to continue pursuing this hobby, they have to acknowledge a degree of risk

None of these is a particularly pleasant thought to have about one of your favorite pastimes.[a] To get rid of this unpleasantness, consumers have several options available to them:

1. Reduce the amount of violent media they consume, or stop consuming it altogether.

2. Acknowledge that violent media carries with it a risk that they're willing to accept and consider taking steps to reduce those risks.

3. Deny that violent media has any effect on them and continue consuming violent media as they currently do.

For some of us, Option #1 isn't really an option at all. If you're used to playing hours of first-person shooter video games a day, or used to binge-watching your favorite violent television show, after work each day Option #1 may seem daunting. Research on addiction shows that giving up or even cutting back on media use when it plays such a pervasive role in your life is incredibly difficult (see Questions #42, #43, and #44 for more on this).

Option #2 is a bit less dramatic, and involves fewer behavioral changes. It's not exactly ideal either: Although it doesn't force the consumer to do away with their hobby, it *does* force them to acknowledge that they're willingly doing something that's harmful for them and to society in general. If you want to know what this is like, try asking a smoker if they know that it's bad for them and, if so, why they're still doing it. If nothing else, the awareness that one's interests are having a detrimental effect on them is enough to take away *some* of their enjoyment of it.

Now look at Option #3: What a perfect solution! It requires no change in your behavior *and* it gets rid of those pesky unpleasant thoughts. The only requirement is to push back against the research on media violence effects. The obvious way to do this is to attack the quality of all media violence research and deny that the effects exist altogether.[b] But denying an *entire* body of research is pretty tough, especially if researchers can show you decades' worth of evidence. But there's an easier version of this tactic available, one that doesn't force you to deny the

---

[a] The discomfort created when multiple contradictory thoughts are simultaneously on your mind like this is called *cognitive dissonance*. One of the authors recalls being similarly disturbed the first time he learned *just* how unhealthy soda, one of his favorite snacks, was for him.

[b] Smokers in the '60s and '70s used to do this, joking about cigarette-smoking rats getting cancer as a way to dismiss the research.

research: Just claim that you're a special case, *immune* to media violence effects.[c] We'll address some of these specific claims more directly in Questions #29 and #33. For now, however, let's ask how people might come to believe that they are immune to media violence effects.

In answering this question, let's recall what scientists mean when they talk about media violence effects: What does it mean to say that violent media increases a person's risk for aggression? In Question #14, we introduced the idea that a person's "level of aggression" is like a glass of water: The higher the water gets, the more likely it is that a person will engage in increasingly extreme levels of aggression. Media violence, as a risk factor, is like adding a thimble of water to that glass. In most cases, it doesn't cause the glass to overflow, but it *does* increase the *chances* of a spillover for everyone when it gets jostled – no matter how full or empty their glass is. Even more importantly, even if the thimble of water doesn't cause the water to spill over ("extreme aggression"), that person *still* has more water in their glass, which makes more mundane, day-to-day forms of aggression (e.g., insulting someone, damaging relationships) more likely to occur.

You'd be hard-pressed to find a researcher who actually believes that media violence causes extreme violent behavior in a direct, 1-to-1 fashion. This would be a gross oversimplification of how psychologists think about aggression, which, like other forms of human behavior, is complex and determined by numerous factors.[1,2,3] Instead, researchers think about media violence as one of many causal risk factors for aggression. It's important to know this because *not* understanding this is why people assume that they're immune to violent media effects.

If you think that violent media are supposed to cause gamers to become violent, but you haven't engaged in violent behavior yourself, you're going to assume that you're an exception to the rule. After all, how can you be affected by violent media if you're not behaving violently yourself? But you shouldn't be so confident: Remember that violent behavior is different from aggressive behavior – Violence is an extreme and rare behavior[1], meaning it requires a *lot* of risk factors being present to cause it. For this reason, you *could* correctly say that most people who consume lots of violent media don't engage in violent behavior, but only because for most people, the small increase in risk provided by violent media isn't enough to cause their glass to "spill over".

But as we discussed in Question #7, not all aggression is violent. Most of us, while not violent, often *do* engage in mundane forms of aggression like insulting another person, shoving them, saying hostile things toward them, bullying them, spreading rumors about them, or undermining their goals or their relationships in one way or another. Of course, these aren't what most people

---

[c] Researchers call this the *third-person effect*, when people believe that others, but not themselves, are affected by media.

think of when they hear "aggressive behavior," but they *are* far more common and require *far* fewer risk factors to activate.

If you ignore this day-to-day aggression, it's easy to overlook the fact that violent media may well be affecting you. To see what we mean, imagine if someone defined "health" as "not having a heart attack." By that definition, most people could claim that none of the junk food they've eaten has had an effect on them because they haven't had a heart attack yet. And they would be correct! But if you had a subtler, more nuanced definition of health that included physical fitness, mobility, weight, flexibility, blood sugar levels, and liver functioning, it would suddenly become clear that a diet of junk food *does* have a number of subtle long-term effects on your health. And after your fatal heart attack, you no longer need to worry about the psychological tension created by having the conflicting cognitions that junk food is a casual risk factor for heart attacks and you eat a lot of junk food.

Considering this more subtle, nuanced definition of "aggression" is what so many consumers of violent media fail to do, which is what the violent media industries and their defenders rely on; it's why many people erroneously conclude that, because they haven't shot or stabbed somebody, they must be immune to media violence effects!

Okay, so we know *why* people are motivated to believe they are immune to media violence effects, and we have a fair idea as to how they're able to convince themselves of this. But what do the studies themselves suggest? Are certain populations or groups *unaffected* by violent media? It might be possible, after all, that some people really *are* immune to violent media effects.

When we look at psychological studies, it turns out that a majority of them use undergraduate psychology students as participants. This is partly a matter of convenience: Undergrads are a readily-available, inexpensive, and willing sample pool, especially since most introductory psychology courses give out bonus marks or credits to students who participate in research. These studies fairly consistently find that violent media are a risk factor for aggressive thoughts[4], feelings[5], and behavior[6] in undergrads. These effects aren't limited to any one study methodology either: They've been found in cross-sectional surveys[7] and experiments[8], and have been found using a variety of laboratory measures of aggression (e.g., giving shocks to another person[9], blasting another person with noise[10], making someone eat hot sauce[11,12], sabotaging a researcher's career prospects[13]) and real-world measures of aggression (e.g., getting into fights[14], violent delinquency[15]).

Okay, but that's just undergraduate students. Most people *aren't* undergraduate students. Just because there's evidence of media violence effects in undergrads doesn't mean it says much about the average violent media consumer. What's needed are samples of non-university student adults, or samples of children, because it's possible that some of these groups *don't* experience the same media violence effects.

As it turns out, there *have* been studies on these other samples! And the results look pretty much the same, no matter how you slice it. Media violence exposure is a risk factor for aggression in *both* male and female samples[16, 17, 18] (a topic we'll return to in Question #21), so it doesn't seem like being male or female makes you immune. Nor does it seem to help if you're over a certain age: Media violence effects have been found in studies of preschool children[18], children in elementary school[19], teenagers in high school[20], and adults[21] (we cover the topic of age more fully in Question #22.) And, lest you think the problem is solely an "American" one, there's little reason to believe that other cultures are immune: Media violence effects have been found in studies conducted in the United States[22], Canada[21], Belgium[2], China[23], Japan[24], Israel[25], Singapore[26,] Germany[17], and Australia[27, 28](among many others).

Researchers have also found that people do not "become" immune to violent media over time either. Exposure to violent media increases a person's risk for aggression in samples of people with very little violent media exposure and in samples of people who regularly consume violent media. With age, we gain many more resources for how to deal with difficult emotions, which is why people on average become less aggressive as they age. This can somewhat artificially make it look like media violence has no effect on adults. In short, in addition to there being no evidence that a certain demographic group is immune to the effects of media violence, there also doesn't seem to be any evidence that experience with media somehow makes you immune to the effects.

Not only is there no evidence to suggest that any particular group is immune to media violence effects, but the theories upon which media violence research is built also suggest that we shouldn't *expect* anyone to be immune. To see why, we turn to the General Aggression Model, a model we introduced in Question #12. The GAM lays out the numerous psychological processes that drive aggression[1]. Many of these processes are basic, fundamental properties of our minds – the building blocks of how we learn, think and function. For example, people learn by associating concepts with one another. If a specific behavior is repeatedly paired with a reward, we're more likely to do that behavior in the future ourselves. This is deeply-ingrained and universal: People of *all* ages and from *all* cultures learn this way. And, this form of learning is just one of many similarly universal processes that drive media violence effects.[29,30] Psychological theory not only predicts that media violence effects *should* exist, but that they should be found *universally*. Decades of data would seem to agree.

To summarize: There is no scientifically-grounded reason to believe that you or anyone is wholly immune to media violence effects. The belief is enticing because it helps many of us to continue pursuing an activity we like without having to confront its downsides. It also seems common sense, in part because it's based on the overly simplistic idea that if a person does not display violent behavior, it's impossible for them to have been affected by violent media. In the end, it doesn't really matter how strongly someone believes they're immune: The evidence just isn't on their side.

References

1. Anderson, C. A. & Bushman, B. J. (2002). Human Aggression. *Annual Review of Psychology, 53,* 27-51.
2. Exelmans, L., Custers, K., & Van den Bulck, J. (2015). Violent video games and delinquent behavior in adolescents: A risk factor perspective. *Aggressive Behavior, 41,* 267-279.
3. Gentile, D., A. & Bushman, B. J. (2012). Reassessing media violence effects using a risk and resilience approach to understanding aggression. *Psychology of Popular Media Culture, 1*(3), 138-151.
4. Sestir, M. A., & Bartholow, B. D. (2010). Violent and nonviolent games produce opposing effects on aggressive and prosocial outcomes. *Journal of Experimental Social Psychology, 46,* 934-942.
5. Barlett, C. P., Rodeheffer, C., Baldassaro, R., Hinkin, M., & Harris, R. J. (2008). The effect of advances in video game technology and content on aggressive cognitions, hostility, and heart rate. *Media Psychology, 11,* 540-565.
6. Haridakis, P. M. & Rubin, A. M. (2003). Motivation for watching television violence and viewer aggression. *Mass Communication & Society, 1*(6), 29-56.
7. Anderson, C. A. & Dill, K. E. (2000). Video games and aggressive thoughts, feelings, and behavior in the laboratory and in life. *Journal of Personality and Social Psychology, 78*(4), 772-790.
8. Bushman, B. J. (1995). Moderating role of trait aggressiveness in the effects of violent media on aggression. *Journal of Personality and Social Psychology, 69*(5), 950-960.
9. Meyer, T. P. (1972). The effects of sexually arousing and violent films on aggressive behavior. *The Journal of Sex Research, 8*(4), 324-331.
10. Anderson, C. A. & Carnagey, N. L. (2009). Causal effects of violent sports video games on aggression: Is it competitiveness or violent content. *Journal of Experimental Social Psychology, 45,* 731-739.
11. Barlett, C., Branch, O., Rodeheffer, C., & Harris, R. (2009). How long do short-term violent video game effects last? *Aggressive Behavior, 35,* 225-236.
12. Brummert-Lennings, H. I., & Warburton, W. A. (2011). The effect of auditory versus visual violent media exposure on aggressive behaviour: The role of song lyrics, video clips and musical tone. *Journal of Experimental Social Psychology. 47,* 794-799.
13. Cicchirillo, V., & Chory-Assad, R. M. (2005). Effects of affective orientation and video game play on aggressive thoughts and behaviors. *Journal of Broadcasting & Electronic Media, 49*(4), 435-449.

14. Prokarym, M. (2012). *The effect of video games on aggressive behavior in undergraduate students.* Unpublished doctoral dissertation, University of Texas at Arlington.
15. Swing, E. L. (2013). *Plugged in: The effects of electronic media use on attention problems, cognitive control, visual attention, and aggression.* Unpublished doctoral dissertation, Iowa State University.
16. Krahé, B., Möller, I., Huesmann, L. R., Kirwil, L., Felber, J., & Berger, A. (2011). Desensitization to media violence: Links with habitual media violence exposure, aggressive cognitions, and aggressive behavior. *Journal of Personality and Social Psychology, 100*(4), 630-646.
17. Möller, I., Krahé, B., Busching, R., & Krause, C. (2012). Efficacy of an intervention to reduce the use of media violence and aggression: An experimental evaluation with adolescents in Germany. *Journal of Youth Adolescence, 41,* 105-120.
18. Krahé, B. & Möller, I. (2011). Links between self-reported media violence exposure and teacher ratings of aggression and prosocial behavior among German adolescents. *Journal of Adolescence, 34,* 279-287.
19. Singer, D. G. & Singer, J. L. (1980). Television viewing and aggressive behavior in preschool children: A field study. *Annals of the New York Academy of Sciences.*
20. Busching, R., Gentile, D. A., Krahé, B. & Möller, I., Khoo, A., Walsh, D. A., & Anderson, C. A. (2015). Testing the reliability of different measures of violent video game use in the United States, Singapore, and Germany. *Psychology of Popular Media Culture, 4*(2), 97-111.
21. Leith, L. M. (1982). An experimental analysis of the effect of vicarious participation in physical activity on subject aggressiveness. *International Journal of Sport Psychology, 13*(4), 234-241.
22. Anderson, C. A., Carnagey, N. L., Flanagan, M., Benjamin, A. J. Jr., Eubanks, J., & Valentine, J. C. (2004). Violent Video Games: Specific Effects of Violent Content on Aggressive Thoughts and Behavior. *Advances in Experimental Social Psychology, 36,* 199-249.
23. Wei, R. (2007). Effects of playing violent videogames on Chinese adolescents' pro-violence attitudes, attitudes toward others, and aggressive behavior. *Cyberpsychology & Behavior, 10*(3), 371-380.
24. Anderson, C. A., Sakamoto, A., Gentile, D. A., Ihori, N., Shibuya, A., Yukawa, S., Naito, M., & Kobayashi, K. (2008). Longitudinal effects of violent games on aggression in Japan and the United States. *Pediatrics, 122*(5), e1067.
25. Bachrach, R. S. (1986). The differential effect of observation of violence on Kibbutz and city children in Israel. In L. R. Huesmann & L. D. Eron (Eds.), *Television and the Aggressive Child: A cross-national comparison.* Hillsdale, NJ: Lawrence Erlbaum.

26. Gentile, D. G., Li, D., Khoo, A., Prot, S., & Anderson, C. A. (2014). Mediators and moderators of long-term violent video game effects on aggressive behavior: Practice, thinking, and action. *JAMA Pediatrics, 168,* 450-457. *doi:10.1001/jamapediatrics.2014.63*

27. Anderson, C. A., Suzuki, K., Swing, E., Groves, C., Gentile, D. A., Prot, S., Chun, P. L., Sakamoto, A., Horiuchi, Y., Krahé, B., Jelic, M., Liuqing, W., Toma, R., Warburton, W. A., Zhang, X., Tajima, S., Qing, F & Petrescu, P. (2017). Media violence and other aggression risk factors in seven nations. *Personality and Social Psychology Bulletin, 43,* 986-998.

28. Brummert-Lennings, H. I., & Warburton, W. A. (2011). The effect of auditory versus visual violent media exposure on aggressive behaviour: The role of song lyrics, video clips and musical tone. *Journal of Experimental Social Psychology. 47,* 794-799.

29. Warburton, W. A. (2012). Growing up fast and furious in a media saturated world. In W. A. Warburton & D. Braunstein [Eds.], *Growing up fast and furious: Reviewing the impacts of violent and sexualised media on children* (pp. 1-33). Sydney: The Federation Press.

30. Warburton, W. A. (2014). Apples, oranges and the burden of proof: Putting media violence findings in context. *European Psychologist, 19,* 60-67.

20 - Are media violence effects only a problem for aggressive people?

The Short Answer:

Not really. A person's risk for aggression increases as they're exposed to more and more violent media, and as they accumulate other violence risk factors. This is the case *regardless* of whether or not they're aggressive people. This conclusion is supported by both psychological theory and existing research. However, there *are* theoretical reasons to be extra concerned about those who already have a high number of risk factors for aggression. Although current evidence for this prediction is somewhat mixed, it does suggest that media violence effects on more extreme forms of aggression may be *stronger* for those who are already at risk for violent behavior.

The Long Answer:

In Question #19 we addressed the misconception among many violent media consumers that they, in particular, are immune to violent media effects. In this answer, we'll address a related claim, which looks something like this:

"Violent media are only a problem when they're in the hands of violent people. It's the violent people who run out and hurt others because of something they saw in a movie or video game. Because I'm not a violent person by nature (whatever that means), violent media don't affect me."

The flaws in this argument are very similar to those we addressed in Question #19. For example, if the only outcome we consider is *extreme* aggression – violence – then the argument seems to have some merit. After all, most people don't have sufficiently many risk factors to make their "glass of aggression" more likely to "spill over" into violence. Because of this, most people are unlikely to be pushed into violence by the small, added risk of violent media. But by focusing *only* on violence as an outcome, we overlook the less extreme, day-to-day forms of aggression that we're more likely to actually encounter and engage in. And, as we reviewed in Question #19, studies *do* show that violent media increase your risk of engaging in this sort of aggression, regardless of who you are.

We could probably just end our response here by repeating the fact that the effects of media violence on the risk of aggressive thoughts, beliefs, feelings, and behavior are essentially universal. But we think it's informative to elaborate on this point a bit more and show exactly *how* researchers are able to use studies to rule out the possibility that violent media effects are limited only to a small number of highly-aggressive people.

To start, let's look at an example of an experimental study. In this experiment, college students were randomly assigned to one of two conditions, both of which involved playing a car-racing game. In the "violent" condition, players were not only *able* to hit other cars and run over pedestrians, but they were *rewarded* for doing so. In the "non-violent" condition, players played the exact same game with *one* modification: In this version of the game it was impossible for players to hit other cars or pedestrians[1].

The elegance of this study was that the two conditions were identical in almost every way except for the violent content: The graphics were the same, they used the same game physics and controls, and the game's speed and level's design were constant across the two conditions. Because players were *randomly* assigned to one condition or the other at the start of the study we can, statistically speaking, assume that the two groups were comparable with regard to gender, experience, age, history with video games, and aggressive personality. Finally, after playing the game, participants completed a competitive reaction time task where they were given the chance to blast their opponent with unpleasant noise – the study's measure of aggressive behavior.

The researchers found that those who played the violent version of the game gave longer and more intense blasts of painful noise than those who played the non-violent version of the game. The researchers chalked up these differences in aggressive behavior to the differences in violent content between the two games because random assignment made it unlikely that one group was simply more aggressive than the other beforehand. Violent content effects therefore seem to be the most reasonable explanation for the study's results.

At this point in the story, it's still possible to argue that the difference between the two groups *only* happened for participants who were *high* in aggression in both groups. In other words, a critic could argue that for people who were not particularly aggressive at the start of the study, the game they played might have had no effect on their aggression: They might simply have been low in aggression at the end of the study regardless. This would mean that the difference found between the two groups was *actually* caused by a few highly-aggressive participants becoming *particularly* affected by the violent game. By looking just at the average scores of the two conditions, there's no way to rule out this possibility.

However, *not* reported in the brief published version of the study is the fact that aggressive personality at the start of the study *was* measured, allowing the researchers to test this possibility.[a] As it turns out, the violent game had the same

---

[a] You might reasonably be asking *why* such details were not included in the published report. When a paper is submitted for publication, the journal editor and two or more anonymous reviewers first read the original paper. If they believe that the paper is good enough to publish, they either accept the paper as-is (which almost never happens) or suggest changes that, in their view, help the paper meet

aggression-increasing effect on people who were high or low on aggressive personality at the start of the study. True, those who scored higher on aggressive personality also behaved the most aggressively *regardless* of which game they played. But even so, the violent game *still* increased their aggressive behavior!

This experiment and others like it often show that media violence effects are *not* limited only to highly aggressive people. Longitudinal studies often reach similar conclusions. For example, in a longitudinal study of German students, participants told researchers how often they played different violent video games and completed a self-report measure of how physically aggressive they were (e.g., "I get into fights a little more than the average person"). Two and a half years later, the same students completed the exact same measures again[2].

After analyzing the data, the researchers found that, even after statistically controlling for how aggressive participants were at the start of the study, participants who played more violent games at the start of the study were more aggressive at the end of the study. The ability to statistically control for participants' level of aggression at the start of the study gives researchers another way to directly test whether media violence effects occur regardless of how aggressive a person is. Like the experimental study above, it's *far* more likely that these effects are caused by a modest media violence effect that's present in most participants rather than a very strong effect that's present only in a few highly-aggressive participants.

To this point, we've made the argument that media violence probably increases *everyone's* risk for aggression, not just a handful of particularly violent people. But this doesn't *fully* address the spirit of the original question, does it? Even *if* media violence effects occur for everyone, are they *stronger* for more aggressive people? This is a far subtler question, and it's one that's a fair bit trickier to directly test.

The "driving over pedestrians" experiment is an example of a study that *can* test this subtler question. It did find that the effect of playing a violent game was about the same for participants high and low in aggressive personality. But what about other studies in the field – do they come to this same conclusion?

As it turns out, it's a bit mixed. Some studies agree that there is little evidence to argue that media violence effects are different for people high and low in aggressive personality[3,4,5,6]. In these studies, differences in between high- and low- aggression participants may show up only on some measures of aggression, but not others. Sometimes differences between the groups do not show up at all.

---

the standards of the journal. This can mean changing the analysis, cutting the length, clarifying things, or dropping parts of the study that they deem unimportant to the study's main point or to the readers of the journal. The authors have the choice, of course, to refuse to make these changes, which usually means withdrawing the paper and trying to publish it in another (usually lower-status) journal.

On the other hand, other studies *have* found evidence that high-aggression participants experience stronger media violence effects[7,8,9,10].

To further complicate things, some studies suggest that the differences in media violence effects between highly-aggressive and less-aggressive people may come down to how aggression is measured (e.g., whether the researchers measured "mild" aggression or "violence") and even the age of the sample. In one of the first video game violence studies of its kind, researchers found that high exposure to violent video games in college students was associated with higher frequency of *violent* behavior among participants, but *only* if they *also* reported high levels of trait aggressiveness.[11] But a *very* similar study of high school students—shown in Figure 20.1— found that the effect of video game violence on violent behavior was essentially the same *regardless* of whether the students were high, average, or low on aggressive personality.[12]

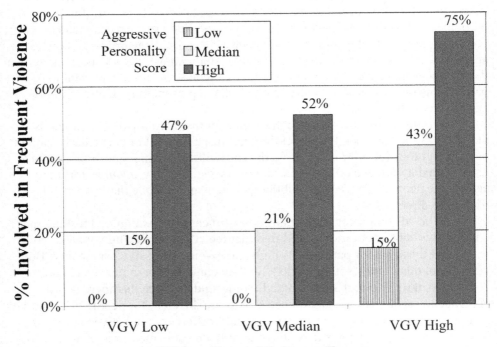

Video Game Violence Exposure

Figure 20.1. Effects of video game exposure on high school students' violent behavior as a function of aggressive personality.

As we've done with the research on media violence effects more broadly (see Question #11), we should look beyond the results of any one study to consider what these studies, taken together, tell us about aggressive personality and media violence effects. And, given that there is a considerable inconsistency in these "susceptibility" results, we can conclude that, at best, there is only weak evidence that media violence effects might be stronger in more aggressive people.

Beyond the data itself, let's also consider whether it makes *theoretical* sense to predict that media violence effects are stronger for highly-aggressive people. The General Aggression Model (introduced in Question #12) argues that one of the ways violent media increase the risk of aggression is by activating aggression-related thoughts and scripts in the user's mind[13]. In Question #13 we also introduced the idea that the link between media violence and aggression is likely bi-directional, meaning that aggressive people may *also* be more likely to prefer violent media[14,15].

What does this mean? Well, if aggressive people are consuming more violent content, and if exposure to violent content reinforces aggressive thoughts and scripts over time[16], then it makes sense that aggressive people may have better-developed aggression-related thoughts and scripts. If this is true, it would mean that a piece of violent media can elicit more aggressive thoughts, feelings, and behaviors (and stronger ones) in high-aggression people. So, at least in theory, there's at least *one* theoretical reason to believe that media violence effects, while universal, may be even stronger for those who are highly aggressive.

But this certainly isn't the *only* theoretical reason to believe that this is the case. Aggression researchers think about media violence as one risk factor among many that contributes to aggression (Question #14)[17]. With this in mind, highly aggressive people can be thought of as people with a number of these risk factors. And there *have* been studies looking at how having risk factors for aggression may influence additional risk factors. For example, in one longitudinal study researchers looked at a combination of different risk factors for aggression: media violence, being the victim of aggression, participant sex, past aggressive behavior, and having an aggressive view of the world[18]. They found that the effects of any single risk factor was *amplified* if the participant had other risk factors as well. Or, to put another way, media violence may be a larger risk factor for people who've already got a number of other risk factors. Far from being definitive proof, the study *does* illustrate another reason why finding stronger media violence effects for highly aggressive people is consistent with existing theories about aggression.

So, how do we wrap this up? Well, first we can conclude that media violence effects are not *limited* to highly-aggressive people. Media violence is *still* a risk factor for people who are low in aggression – even if it's unlikely to push them over the brink into criminal-level violence. Second, more research is needed before we can confidently say that the effect of media violence is (or is not) greater for highly-aggressive people, since the studies which *have* tested this hypothesis are somewhat mixed in their findings. Third, despite the fact that empirical evidence is weak, psychological theory *is* consistent with the idea that highly aggressive people *should* be more influenced by violent media, particularly when the measure of aggression is fairly extreme.

References

1. Carnagey, N. L. & Anderson, C. A. (2005). The effects of reward and punishment in violent video games on aggressive affect, cognition, and behavior. *Psychological Science, 16*(11), 882-889.
2. Möller, I., & Krahé, B. (2009). Exposure to violent video games and aggression in German adolescents: A longitudinal analysis. *Aggressive Behavior, 35*(1), 75-89.
3. Anderson, C. A., & Carnagey, N. L. (2009). Causal effects of violent sports video games on aggression: Is it competitiveness or violent content? *Journal of Experimental Social Psychology, 45,* 731-739.
4. Paradise, A. (2007). *Trait aggression and style of video game play: The effects of violent video game play on aggressive thoughts.* Unpublished doctoral dissertation, University of Massachusetts Amherst.
5. Bolton, A. G. (2009). *Individual differences in the effects of playing violent video games: Specific play rehearsals and changes in aggression.* Unpublished doctoral dissertation, University of Calgary.
6. Bushman, B. J. (1995). Moderating role of trait aggressiveness in the effects of violent media on aggression. *Journal of Personality and Social Psychology, 69*(5), 950-960.
7. Zillmann, D., & Weater, J. B. (2007). Aggressive personality traits in the effects of violent imagery on unprovoked impulsive aggression. *Journal of Research in Personality, 41,* 753-771.
8. Friedrich, L. K., & Huston, S. A. (1973). Aggressive and prosocial television programs and the natural behavior of preschool children. *Monographs of the Society for Research in Child Development, 38*(4).
9. Qian, Z. & Zhang, D. (2014). The effects of viewing violent movie via computer on aggressiveness among college students. *Computers in Human Behavior, 35,* 320-325.
10. Qian, Z., Zhang, D., & Wang, L. (2013). Is aggressive trait responsible for violence? Priming effects of aggressive words and violent movies. *Psychology, 4*(2), 96-100.
11. Anderson, C.A., & Dill, K.E. (2000). Video games and aggressive thoughts, feelings, and behavior in the laboratory and in life. *Journal of Personality and Social Psychology, 78,* 772-790.
12. Anderson, C.A., Gentile, D.A., & Buckley, K.E. (2007). *Violent Video Game Effects on Children and Adolescents: Theory, Research, and Public Policy.* New York: Oxford University Press.
13. Anderson, C. A. & Bushman, B. J. (2002). Human Aggression. *Annual Review of Psychology, 53,* 27-51.
14. Greitemeyer, T. (2015). Everyday sadism predicts violent video game preferences. *Personality and Individual Differences, 75,* 19-23.

15. Breuer, J., Vogelgesang, J., Quandt, T., & Festl, R. (2015). Violent video games and physical aggression: Evidence for a selection effect among adolescents. *Psychology of Popular Media Culture, 4*(4), 305-328.
16. Hopf, W. H., Huber, G. L., & Weiß, R. H. (2008). Media violence and youth violence: A 2-year longitudinal study. *Journal of Media Psychology, 20*(3), 79-96.
17. Exelmans, L., Custers, K., & Van den Bulck, J. (2015). Violent video games and delinquent behavior in adolescents: A risk factor perspective. *Aggressive Behavior, 41,* 267-279.
18. Gentile, D., A. & Bushman, B. J. (2012). Reassessing media violence effects using a risk and resilience approach to understanding aggression. *Psychology of Popular Media Culture, 1*(3), 138-151.

21 - Are violent media effects stronger for boys than girls?

The Short Answer:

Surprisingly, no. It's true that boys are, on average, more *physically* aggressive than girls. Boys also tend to consume more violent media than girls. But when you compare the size of violent media effects for boys and girls, they don't seem to differ – both are affected in about the same way, and to the same extent, by violent media. Or, to put it another way, 20 hours of violent media increases aggressiveness about the same amount for girls and boys. When you look at psychological theories of aggression, there isn't much reason to *expect* sex differences in how much media violence increases aggressive behavior, because boys and girls learn the same way and the psychological mechanisms underlying violent media effects are the same for boys and girls. The vast majority of studies support this conclusion, in that there is little evidence for sex differences in the media violence effect, and when differences do occur, they tend to be fairly inconsistent.

The Long Answer:

At first glance, the answer to this question might seem obvious: *Of course* boys should be more affected by violent media! Anyone who's spent time with children can attest to the fact that boys are more physically aggressive than girls: They roughhouse with one another and seem hell-bent on destroying anything they can get their hands on. And when you look at the screen media targeted toward young boys (e.g., *World Wrestling Entertainment*), it's *clearly* more violent than shows targeted toward young girls (e.g., *My Little Pony: Friendship is Magic*).[a] Based on these two facts alone, it's tempting to conclude that boys consume more violent media, and therefore it has a bigger effect on them. If this line of reasoning were true, it might even suggest that boys are the ones we should be focused on when it comes to media violence effects!

---

[a] Of course, we don't *endorse* these stereotypes or think that this is the way it *should* be. We recognize that plenty of boys watch shows that are "intended for girls," and plenty of girls watch shows that are "intended for boys". Moreover, it's true that *all* children would likely benefit from watching more shows with prosocial messages, and fewer shows that involved characters beating one another to a pulp (or, even better, spending less time watching screen media altogether!)

Before we jump to any conclusions, let's start by looking into some of the assumptions we're making about boys and girls and their use of violent media. Is it true that boys consume more violent media than girls? Well, actually, yes. Although boys and girls are *almost equally* likely to play video games[1], boys are *far* more likely to prefer games featuring violent content[2]. This difference isn't limited to video games either: Boys also tend to watch more violent television shows and more violent films than girls do[3].

Okay – so far it seems like our intuitions about boys and girls are correct. So is it true that boys are the more aggressive sex, as common sense tells us? This seems to be the case, at least at first. Boys are certainly more *physically* aggressive than girls – they're more likely to roughhouse, hit, threaten, and fight with one another[4,5]. So yes, if we're only counting *physical* aggression, we'd be right to say that boys are the more aggressive sex.

Doesn't it seem like there's a "but" coming up?

But in Question #7 we explain that "aggression" is a *broad* category of human behavior. Aggression is about far more than how much people hit each another. It includes things we often overlook, like verbal aggression (e.g., teasing, insulting) and relational aggression (e.g., spreading rumors, sabotaging relationships). If boys really *are* more aggressive than girls, we'd expect boys to score higher than girls on *these* types of aggression too.

Studies show otherwise. Some even suggest that girls engage in *more* non-physical aggression than boys[6,7], while others find no differences at all[4,8]. A meta-analysis of over 100 studies found that, when provoked, males and females aggress at about the same level.[9] Taken together, this evidence should make us reconsider our assumption that boys are *always* more aggressive than girls. As it turns out, the answers to these questions are not always as intuitive as they might seem!

So, according to research, boys consume more violent media than girls, and they're more *physically* aggressive than girls, but not necessarily more aggressive than girls in every way. Is this enough for us to conclude that violent media effects are larger for boys?

No, for a couple of reasons. First, in Questions #19 and #20 we point out that people often mistakenly look for media violence effects on measures of extreme aggression. If we're interested in the effects of media violence on *aggression* (not just violence), then we need to consider the *full range* of aggressive behavior. If we don't consider how media violence might affect other forms of aggression – including verbal and relational types of aggression, we're getting only part of the story – including many of the effects that violent media may be having on girls and women.

But there's a second, subtler problem with drawing conclusions about sex differences in violent media effects from the information we've reviewed in this question so far: We're accidentally answering the *wrong* question, "Are violent media more likely to push boys or girls into a more extreme and visible aggressive

169

behavior?" Because boys, on average, are more physically aggressive than girls, they can be thought of as having a fuller "glass" of aggression than girls (see Question #14 for the "glass" analogy). A small addition to boys' glass is thus more likely to cause an "overflow" than it is for girls. It's intuitive and simple, but ultimately an answer to the wrong question.

Remember, the original question is "Are violent media effects stronger for boys than girls?" Although the question *seems* simple, it's actually a fairly sophisticated question about whether the size of the effect of media violence on aggression is larger for boys than it is for girls (see Question #17 for an explanation of effect sizes). Another way to think about it is this: If you were to show a group of boys and a group of girls an hour of violent media (TV, films, or video games), would they *differ* in how much their aggression increased compared to a group of boys and a group of girls who were shown the same amount of *non-violent* media? As it turns out, it doesn't matter whether boys or girls consume *more* violent media, nor does it matter whether boys or girls behave more aggressively. What we're *really* interested in is whether X amount of violent content leads to the same amount of *increase* in aggression for boys and girls. You can see what this might look like in Figure 21.1, which shows data from a hypothetical media violence study. Comparison A looks at whether boys and girls differ in how aggressive they are without exposure to violent media – this is not what we're looking for. Comparison B is looking at whether violent media increases aggression in boys, and Comparison C is looking at the same effect in girls. Neither of these is what we're looking for either. Instead, we're looking at whether B and C are the same size.[b]

---

[b] This is, of course, an oversimplification of what is actually involved when comparing the relative size of two different effects, but we'll use whatever gets the point across short of turning this book into a stats textbook!

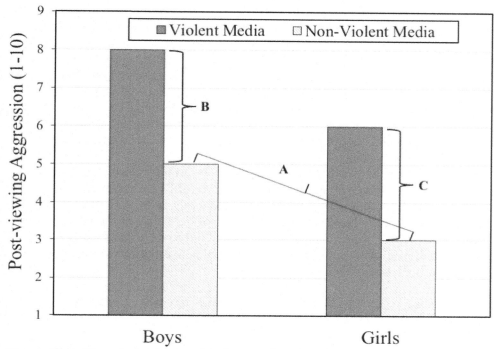

Figure 21.1. Hypothetical example of sex and violent media content on aggression.

One more way to think about it is to imagine that violent media are adding a thimble of water to both boys' and girls' aggression glasses – but is it adding the same *size* thimble each? If viewing an hour of violent media causes the water in girls' glasses to go from "10% full" to "20% full," and causes the level in boys' glasses to go from "30% full" to "40% full," then we can say the effect was the same: The glasses became fuller by the same amount. In this case, it doesn't matter whether the boys are more likely to strike someone physically while the girls are more likely to spread a rumor – all that matters is that violent media has increased the risk for aggressive behavior by the same amount for both.

Thinking about the original question this way makes it clear just how nuanced the issue is. It also nicely illustrates *exactly* why reputable scientists are so precise in choosing their words when describing media violence effects. For example, if our goal was to reduce the number of cases of extreme physical aggression that occur, a scientist would be correct to say that the biggest concern of media violence are its effects on boys. However correct that may be, though, it wouldn't be an appropriate response to the question of whether we should be concerned about the effect of violent media on girls. We should be, and are.

Although the data don't seem to show much in the way of evidence for sex differences in media violence effects, it also helps to look at whether there are *theoretical* reasons to expect differences. And, as it turns out, psychological theories of aggression also suggest that there ought to be no sex differences in media violence effect sizes. According to the General Aggression Model (discussed in Question #12), violent media increases the risk of aggression for numerous reasons: it reinforces the link between aggression and reward, it activates aggressive thoughts in our mind, it changes our beliefs about the appropriateness of aggression, it changes the way we interpret ambiguous situations, it desensitizes our responses to violent content, and it helps us develop scripts for aggressive behavior[10].

These mechanisms are fundamental aspects of how our minds work. As such, they're also universal. For example: If we reward a particular piece of behavior, people are more likely to do that behavior again in the future. This is basic learning, and it's how humans learn much of our behavior – not just aggression. Because it's so deeply-ingrained and universal, there's really no reason to believe that learning should be different across the sexes. Regardless of whether you're a boy or a girl:

1. Rewarding behavior will make you more likely to engage in that same behavior in the future.

2. Your past experience will influence what you believe about, and how you interpret, future situations.

3. Activating one idea in your mind will also activate related ideas.

4. Repeatedly being exposed to an image will, over time, cause it to have less of an emotional impact on you.

Because most of the mechanisms underlying media violence effects are present for boys *and* girls we can predict that, at very least, both boys and girls are susceptible to media violence as a risk factor for aggression. And because there's no reason to believe that these mechanisms differ significantly between boys and girls (e.g., they don't "learn" differently), there should also be little difference in the size of media violence effects between the sexes, other than a difference because boys tend to consume much more.

A dive into the studies on media violence effects seems to support what the theory suggests. For example, in the largest meta-analysis of video game violence effects to date, there was little to no evidence that video game violence effects were stronger for boys than girls.[11] Individual studies, each using different measures of aggression or different manipulations of violent media, occasionally find small, but inconsistent sex differences. Early studies, for example, didn't even bother to include female participants, since researchers were primarily studying physical aggression and assumed that girls would show little physical aggression regardless of media exposure[12]. Some studies find that violent media increases the risk for aggression only in boys[13], while others show just the opposite, that violent media increases the risk for aggression only in girls.[14] And many others find that the effect size is practically the same for boys and girls.[15,16] Taken together, there is no compelling evidence to suggest that there are large, consistent sex differences in media violence effects.

But in case we haven't complicated this question enough, there is one more important consideration to keep in mind. Our aggression water-glass metaphor suggests that, under some circumstances, some types of studies should show bigger effects of media violence (or any other causal risk factor for aggression) on males than on females. Being male means starting out with a glass that already has more water in it. This means that it will take fewer additional risk factors (thimbles of water) for boys to reach the level necessary to enable extreme acts of physical aggression. This means that studies that only measure extreme acts of physical aggression may show an effect of media violence for boys, but not for girls, even though everyone, boys and girls, have had their "aggression glass" raised by the same amount. It's an important demonstration of how a layperson, failing to take into account how aggression is being measured (see Question #8), can be led astray when interpreting the results of a study.

There are several key ideas to remember from this section. One can certainly argue that because boys consume more violent media than girls and are more likely to engage in physical aggression, there is greater reason to be concerned about boys' violent media use. If your goal is *specifically* to cut back on the amount of hitting and physical fighting that happens, it makes sense to focus your effort on boys' violent media consumption specifically.

If, on the other hand, you're concerned with reducing aggression of all types, there's no reason focus on just one sex, because boys and girls exposed to the same amount of violent media generally display similar increases in their risk of aggressive behaviors. How this aggression manifests may differ (on average) for boys and girls (more physical aggression in boys, more relational aggression in girls), but in the end, media violence adds a thimble of water to everyone's glass, just as psychological theory predicts.

References

1. Duggan, M. (2015). *Gaming and Gamers*. Retrieved from http://www.pewinternet.org/2015/12/15/gaming-and-gamers/
2. Buchman, D. D. & Funk, J. B. (1996). Video and computer games in the '90s: children's time commitment and game preference. *Children Today, 24*, 12-16.
3. Aluja-Fabregat, A. & Torrubia-Beltri, R. (1998). Viewing of mass media violence, perception of violence, personality and academic achievement. *Personality and Individual Differences, 25*, 973-989.

4. Lansford, J. E., Skinner, A. T., Sobring, E., Di Giunta, L., Deater-Deckard, K., Dodge, K. A., Malone, P. S., Oburu, P., Pastorelli, C., Tapanya, S., Tirado, L. M. U., Zelli, A., Al-Hassan, S. M., Alampay, L. P., Bacchini, D., Bombi, A. S., Bornstein, M. H., & Chang, L. (2012). Boys' and girls' relational and physical aggression in nine countries. *Aggressive Behavior, 38*(4), 298-308.
5. Eagly, A. H., & Steffen, V. J. (1986). Gender and aggressive behavior: A meta-analytic review of the social psychological literature. *Psychological Bulletin, 100,* 303-330.
6. Crick, N. R. & Grotpeter, J. K. (1995). Relational aggression, gender, and social-psychological adjustment. *Child Development, 66*(3), 710-722.
7. Bettencourt, B. A. & Miller, N. (1996). Gender differences in aggression as a function of provocation: A meta-analysis. *Psychological Bulletin, 119,* 422-447.
8. Straus, M. A. & Sweet, S. (1992). Verbal / symbolic aggression in couples: Incidence rates and relationship to personal characteristics. *Journal of Marriage and the Family, 54,* 346-357.
9. Anderson, C. A. & Bushman, B. J. (2002). Human Aggression. *Annual Review of Psychology, 53,* 27-51.
10. Anderson, C. A., Shibuya, A., Ihori, N., Swing, E. L., Bushman, B. J., Sakamoto, A., Rothstein, H. R., & Saleem, M. (2010). Violent video game effects on aggression, empathy, and prosocial behavior in eastern and western countries: a meta-analytic review. *Psychological Bulletin, 136*(2), 151-173.
11. Drabman, R. S. & Thomas, M. H. (1977). Children's imitation of aggressive and prosocial behavior when viewing alone and in pairs. *Journal of Communication, 27*(3), 199-205.
12. Eron, L. D., Huesmann, L. R., Lefkowitz, M. M., & Walder, L. O. (1972). Does television violence cause aggression? *American Psychologist, 27*(4), 253-263.
13. Olson, C. K., Kutner, L. A., Baer, L., Beresin, E. V., Warner, D. E., & Nicholi, A. M. (2009). M-rated video games and aggressive or problem behavior among young adolescents. *Applied Developmental Science, 13*(4), 188-198.
14. Feshbach, S. & Tangney, J. (2008). Television viewing and aggression: Some alternative perspectives. *Perspectives on Psychological Science, 3*(5), 387-389.
15. Fraczek, A. (1986). Socio-cultural environment, television viewing, and the development of aggression among children in Poland. In L. R. Huesmann & L. D. Eron (Eds.), *Television and the aggressive child: A cross-national comparison* (pp. 119-159). Hillsdale, NJ: Erlbaum.

22 - Are violent media effects stronger for children than for adults?

The Short Answer:

Possibly, although the evidence for this is weak. In *theory*, it makes sense that children should be more susceptible to media violence effects than adults, but few studies actually find strong, conclusive evidence to support this hypothesis. This is partly due to the difficulty of designing and running a study that accurately tests this specific hypothesis. We *can*, if nothing else, conclude that long-term violent media effects do occur in children and adolescents, and that such effects persist into adulthood. Given that the effects are partly a dose-response effect (that is, the more media violence one consumes, the more likely the effects are to accrue), starting earlier in childhood might increase the overall effects.

The Long Answer:

Parents have a deeply-ingrained, instinctual need to protect their children from harm.[a] We can see this for ourselves through the actions of parents who lift cars or bravely sacrifice themselves to save their children or harass their child's softball coach. But we can also see this protective instinct at a societal level. For example, many countries spend considerable time and energy trying to protect children from harm: such as safety standards for playground equipment, special speed limits in school zones, laws prohibiting the sale of alcohol, tobacco, and weapons to children, and countless government programs to ensure that children are raised in environments without undue harm or risk. In fact, the very existence of media content-rating systems for television, movies, video games, and music all reflect our collective desire to protect children from harm (although the utility of such systems is disputable, as we discuss in Question #48). It should come as no surprise, then, that most modern industrialized countries also use the law to protect their children from media violence.[b]

---

[a] We don't use the word "instinctual" lightly here. Our hard-wired need to protect our children is a behavioral quirk that improves our species' odds of survival. If we didn't have this instinct, children – who are quite fragile compared to youth of other species – likely wouldn't make it to adulthood, effectively ending of our species!

[b] The U.S. stands as the primary exception to this rule, providing no legal restrictions on exposing children to even the most extreme forms of entertainment-based media violence.

Because of all the effort put into protecting children from violent media, it's worth asking whether violent media are *actually* more harmful to children than to adolescents or adults. Are children more vulnerable to these risks, and do the risks have the potential to do more harm to children than to adults? Or is it the case that the risks are the *same* for children and adults, but we only feel the need to protect *children* from risks that we let adults to take? These questions are important – whether we're talking about exposure to alcohol, risky physical activities, or violent media – because they have important implications for the types of programs and policies we put in place to protect children.

Let's begin by looking at what psychological theories say about media violence and children. From a theoretical standpoint, there *are* reasons to believe that violent media may have a stronger effect on children's aggression than on adults. We can see why this is the case by looking once more at the General Aggression Model (introduced in Question #12). According to the model, someone's likelihood of aggression is determined by a combination of risk factors and protective factors[1]. Throughout much of this book, and indeed, in much of the psychological research, we tend to focus on risk factors: things like poverty, violent media exposure, and being the victim of violence, things that increase one's likelihood of inappropriate aggression.

Protective factors, on the other hand, things that reduce a person's likelihood of aggression, tend to get less attention from researchers. These include critical thinking skills, impulse control, and learning the norms of society. In theory, if a person lacked such protective factors, they might be particularly vulnerable to media violence effects. And it should come as no surprise to anyone that, unlike adults, children *lack* many of these protective factors (e.g., poor impulse control, poor critical thinking skills, lack of understanding social norms).

If you've ever taken care of a toddler, you know first-hand that we aren't born with the ability to control our impulses or to think critically about the world around us. We start as creatures of impulse, doing as we please until, with time, we learn to resist some of our desires (e.g., "What's that? Let's put it in my mouth!") and think through our actions (e.g., "If I eat all these cookies, I'll feel sick!"). We hone these abilities through our adolescent years[2], though our most sophisticated critical thinking skills don't finish developing until well into our 20s[3].

So if it's true that children and teenagers have weaker impulse control and less-fully developed critical thinking skills, how does this affect their aggression? Well, people who lack impulse control are more likely to act on aggressive impulses without stopping to second-guess their actions or the consequences they may have. In fact, we can see evidence for this by looking at the ages of people who commit aggressive criminal acts, which tend to peak in adolescence and early adulthood and then diminish with age (see Figure 22.1).[c] Similarly, if one simply counts the number of aggressive behaviors that a person commits per hour, we find that aggression is most frequent in early childhood years. However, this, in and of itself, is not enough to argue that children are therefore more *susceptible* to the effects of violent media than anyone else – simply that they lack some of the protective factors which override or counteract the risk factor of violent media.

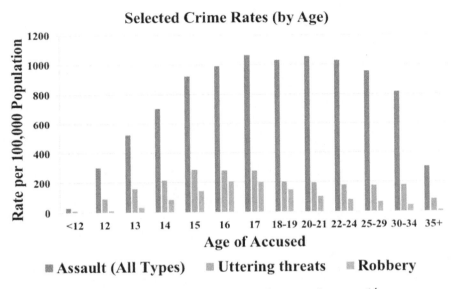

Figure 22.1. Prevalence of selected crimes by age of accused.[4]

For now, let's put impulse control and critical thinking on the back-burner and consider another theoretical reason why children may be more vulnerable to media violence effects. One possibility is their lack of experience learning society's norms for what's acceptable when it comes to aggression. It's well-accepted in psychology that people learn the norms of their society by watching others around them[5]. A lifetime of observation has taught us, for example, not to walk across the road at a red light, not to play with our food at the dinner table, to share with people who are less fortunate than us, and to not do things to others (e.g., hitting them) that we wouldn't want done to us. Some of these things we've learned by being explicitly told, while others were learned by watching people get

---

[c] Of, course, young children don't have the physical skills or knowledge necessary to carry out extreme acts of violence, which is why the frequency of *violent* acts (e.g., assault, murder) *increases* from childhood into adolescence and early adulthood before then declining.

rewarded or punished for *their* actions. We learn from both the people we admire *and* those we deplore.

All of this accumulated experience leads us to internalize the norms of society – that is, to incorporate them into our own beliefs about what is normal and acceptable. These internalized norms sometimes are thought to play a role in overriding our aggressive impulses. If someone makes us angry, for example, we may *want* to hit them. But knowing that our society frowns upon and punishes those who behave aggressively, we're more likely to resist these urges[3]. What if a child lacking experience with the real world hasn't yet internalized these norms? It's one less barrier between their aggressive impulses and the aggressive behavior.

Pulling it all together, it seems that children and adolescents are less likely to actively challenge or question what they experience and less likely to be aware of social norms about aggression. How might this affect the way they consume violent media and the lessons they learn from it? Well, a critical-thinking adult may watch a show about a violent person and actively challenge what they're seeing on the screen (e.g., thinking, "That's so unrealistic! If you hit someone like that in real life, they'd put you in jail!").[d] But a child? They're much more likely to passively accept what they're seeing and use it to inform their understanding of social norms (e.g., "So when two people disagree, they're *supposed* to hit each other"). By not questioning what they're seeing on the screen, children are more likely to form inaccurate beliefs about violence[6,7]. This, in turn, means that when a young person has an aggressive impulse and only a fraction of a second to decide whether to override it, they're less likely to do so.

It would seem that both intuition and theory point to the idea that younger people are not only more aggressive than older people, but they should also be particularly vulnerable to violent media effects. Despite this, however, there is surprisingly *little* data directly testing this hypothesis. A few studies *have* found evidence suggesting that younger children are more susceptible to media violence effects than older children[8,9,10]. The evidence is fairly weak in many of these studies, however, and the effect often depends on measuring aggression in a specific way or on looking only at short-term or only at long-term effects but not both types. Some studies fail to find age differences altogether[11], and meta-analyses generally fail to find evidence that studies with younger participants differ in their effect size from studies that use older participants (see Question #17 for more information about effect sizes)[12]. The best existing meta-analysis on this topic suggests that children show more harm from violent media than adults, but that's only in studies that look at long term effects (cross-sectional and

---

[d] One of the authors recently caught themselves having this *exact* thought while watching the classic Adam Sandler comedy *Happy Gilmore*. In the film, the main character routinely takes out his frustrations by punching nearby people and is never arrested or charged with assault.

longitudinal studies, see Question #9).[13] In short, the existing data don't find strong evidence of the age differences we would expect to find.

One possibility for this lack of strong evidence for age differences might be that there simply *aren't* any age differences in media violence effects. It might well be true that the effect of violent media is the same regardless of a person's age. But there's another possibility: It may simply be too difficult to conduct a study that *directly* tests whether there are consistent age differences in media violence effects.

To illustrate this difficulty, let's start by imagining how we would conduct a different, but comparable test of media violence effects –whether boys and girls differed. This would be a fairly straightforward test: Expose boys and girls to violent or non-violent media and then measure the differences between the four groups in their aggression after viewing. By comparing the differences between the violent and non-violent conditions for boys and girls separately, you can see whether the effects are bigger for boys than girls, or vice-versa.[e]

Now, how would we run the same study if, instead of comparing boys and girls, we wanted to compare Grade 1 students to Grade 12 students? The first problem becomes apparent when you try to decide what kind of violent media to expose them to. If you choose violent media that high school students might consume (e.g., slasher films, graphic first-person shooter games), chances are pretty good these will be too intense or upsetting to the Grade 1 children. You might therefore decide to go the opposite route, and have both groups watch the sort of violent media appropriate for children (e.g., a cartoon cat and mouse fighting). Although this might be exciting for Grade 1 students, it might put high school students to sleep. This makes it tough to know how to interpret our results. If Grade 1 students respond with more aggression to the violent cartoon than the high school students, is it because the Grade 1 students are more vulnerable to the effects, or is it because the Grade 12 students were bored and falling asleep during the cartoon?

A similar problem arises when it comes to *measuring* aggression. Can we find a measure of aggression that's comparable (and likely to be sensitive) for both Grade 1 and Grade 12 students? In Grade 12 students, maybe we want to measure aggression using noise blasts during a reaction time game (see Question #8 for more on this measure). Although an ethics committee might think that it's acceptable to blast Grade 12 students with loud, unpleasant noise, they would probably have reservations about doing the same thing to a Grade 1 student. And even if ethics approved it, it's unlikely the Grade 1 students would fully understand how the task itself works (e.g., how to set the levels of noise intensity and duration). Going the opposite direction presents other problems: Questions about aggression that are relevant for Grade 1 students (e.g., "how often do you

---

[e] Of course, even the gender question is much more complicated than the previous sentences imply, as shown in Question #21.

stick out your tongue at other students," "how often do you call someone a 'doo-doo head?'") are probably irrelevant to Grade 12 students.

It should be clear by now how tough it is for researchers to come up with studies that can directly test media effects on aggression in very young children, adolescents, and adults in the same way. One way to overcome these problems is to run studies where the age differences are much smaller: Instead of comparing Grade 1 students to Grade 12 students, why not compare Grade 1 students to Grade 3 students? This is, in fact, what many researchers do to get around these problems in their own studies.

The solution isn't without drawbacks, however. By reducing the age range of the groups being studied, the differences between the groups becomes smaller and any differences between them become harder to detect. Let's illustrate what we mean with an extreme example. Let's imagine we're trying to find differences between children who are exactly 5 years old and children who are exactly 5 years and one month old. How much of a difference would you *really* expect to find between these groups? Will one month of time difference between them *really* amount to any difference in media violence effects, especially since any two 5 year olds will differ a lot in their maturity? Studies looking for differences between 5 and 7 year olds or 10 and 12 year olds may similarly find it hard to detect differences in media violence effects between the two age groups, not because such differences don't exist, but possibly because the differences are just too small to be detectable by current state-of-the-art research methods.

Despite all of the problems that come with looking at age differences in violent media effects, there has been at least one experimental study comparing the short-term effects of playing a violent or nonviolent video game on aggressive behavior in children and college students.[6] Importantly, in most conditions of the study all participants played the same violent or nonviolent games; for ethical reasons, all of these games were considered child-appropriate. Also, the measure of aggressive behavior was the same for children and adults (giving people blasts of unwanted noise.) The results can be seen in Figure 22.2.

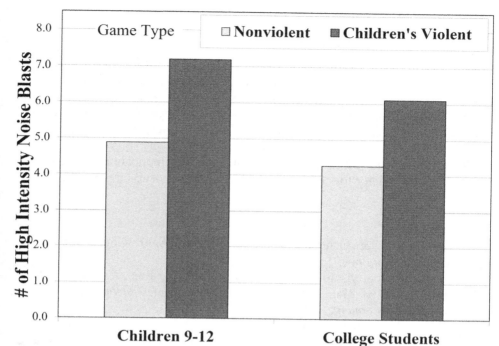

Figure 22.2. Effects of child-appropriate violent and nonviolent games on aggressive behavior by children (age 9-12) and college students.

As the figure shows, playing a violent video game increased aggression in *both* children and adults. Furthermore, the effect was almost as big for the adults (43% increase) as for the children (47% increase). Not shown in this figure is an additional interesting point; the effects were also essentially the same for girls and boys in the study. Thus, a study like this goes against *several* common claims about video game effects: First, they affect normal people, not just highly aggressive people. Second, they affect boys and girls to the same extent. Third, they affect adults about as much as children, at least in the short term.

So, what conclusions can we draw about this topic? It *does* make intuitive sense that children, who are vulnerable to many things because they are still developing physically and psychologically, should also be more vulnerable to media violence effects. This intuition seems to be supported by theory, which similarly states that children lack many of the protective factors that would otherwise counteract some of the risks associated with media violence exposure. Despite this, however, there's only weak evidence to support the hypothesis, though this lack of evidence *may* be the result of how difficult it is to conduct studies *directly* testing for age differences. At the very least, as we point out in Question #19, we *can* say that children are at *least as* susceptible to media violence effects as adults because media violence effects have been found in studies of preschool children[14], elementary school children[15], adolescents[16], and adults[17].

Since we can conclude from the evidence that the risk posed by media violence is present for children, it's worth asking whether we ought to *protect* children from these risks. After all, we as a society have decided that alcohol, tobacco, and other harmful substances are acceptable for adults, but not for younger people, despite the fact that they're harmful for both. When it comes to media violence we have put *some* special measures in place to protect children – we discuss one such measure, content rating systems, in Question #48. Throughout Chapter 5 we delve more into the practical implications of media violence as a risk factor for children and discuss what concerned parents can do to reduce this risk.

References
1. Anderson, C. A. & Bushman, B. J. (2002). Human Aggression. *Annual Review of Psychology, 53,* 27-51.
2. Arain, M., Haque, M., Johal, L., Mathur, P., Nel, W., Rais, A., Sandhu, R., & Sharma, S. (2013). Maturation of the adolescent brain. *Neuropsychiatric Disease and Treatment, 9,* 449-461.
3. Tanner, J. L. & Arnett, J. J. (2009). The emergence of 'emerging adulthood': The new life stage between adolescence and young adulthood. In A. Furlong (Ed.), *Handbook of Youth and Young Adulthood: New perspectives and agendas* (pp. 39-45). London and New York: Routledge.
4. Statistics Canada (2016). *Canadian Center for Justice Statistics, Incident-based Crime Reporting Survey. Table 2: Persons accused of crime for selected offences, by detailed age group of accused, Canada, 2014.* Retrieved September 1, 2018 from: https://www150.statcan.gc.ca/n1/pub/85-002-x/2016001/article/14309/tbl/tbl02-eng.htm
5. Bandura, A. (1971). *Social Learning Theory.* New York: General Learning Press.
6. Anderson, C. A., Gentile, D. A., & Buckley, K. E. (2007). *Violent Video Game Effects on Children and Adolescents: Theory, Research, and Public Policy.* New York, NY: Oxford University Press.
7. Li, D., Khoo, A., Choo, H., & Liau, A. K. (2012). Effects of digital game play among young Singaporean gamers: A two-wave longitudinal study. *Journal of Virtual Worlds Research, 5*(2), 1-14.
8. Liebert, R. M. & Baron, R. A. (1972). Some immediate effects of televised violence on children's behavior. *Developmental Psychology, 6*(3), 469-475.
9. Liss, M. B., Reinhardt, L. C., & Fredriksen, S. (1983). TV heroes: The impact of rhetoric and deeds. *Journal of Applied Developmental Psychology, 20,* 43-53.

10. Zhen, S., Xie, H., Zhang, W., Wang, S., & Li, D. (2011). Exposure to violent computer games and Chinese adolescents' physical aggression: The role of beliefs about aggression, hostile expectations, and empathy. *Computers in Human Behavior, 5*(27), 1675-1687.
11. Wallenius, M., & Punamäki, R-. L. (2008). Digital game violence and direct aggression in adolescence: A longitudinal study of the roles of sex, age, and parent-child communication. *Journal of Applied Developmental Psychology, 29*, 286-294.
12. Anderson, C. A., Shibuya, A., Ihori, N., Swing, E. L., Bushman, B. J., Sakamoto, A., Rothstein, H. R., & Saleem, M. (2010). Violent video game effects on aggression, empathy, and prosocial behavior in eastern and western countries: a meta-analytic review. *Psychological Bulletin, 136*(2), 151-173.
13. Bushman, B. J., & Huesmann, L. R. (2006). Short-term and long-term effects of violent media on aggression in children and adults. *Archives of Pediatric and Adolescent Medicine, 160*, 348-352.
14. Singer, D. G. & Singer, J. L. (1980). Television viewing and aggressive behavior in preschool children: A field study. *Annals of the New York Academy of Sciences.*
15. Busching, R., Gentile, D. A., Krahé, B. & Möller, I., Khoo, A., Walsh, D. A., & Anderson, C. A. (2015). Testing the reliability of different measures of violent video game use in the United States, Singapore, and Germany. *Psychology of Popular Media Culture, 4*(2), 97-111.
16. Leith, L. M. (1982). An experimental analysis of the effect of vicarious participation in physical activity on subject aggressiveness. *International Journal of Sport Psychology, 13*(4), 234-241.
17. Black, S. L., & Bevan, S. (1992). At the movies with Buss and Durkee: A natural experiment on film violence. *Aggressive Behavior, 18,* 37-45.

23 - I'm an adult – can violent media *really* affect me?

The Short Answer:

Absolutely. Rating boards overseen by the ESRB (for video games) and MPAA (for films) may determine that a piece of media is considered to be too violent for children under a certain age, but this does *not* mean that anyone above that age is unaffected by any screen media. Thinking otherwise would be like saying that drinking and smoking should have no effect on your liver or lungs if you're legally old enough to purchase it. Although most adults have more protective factors for aggression than children do, studies nevertheless find that violent media do increase the risk of aggression in adults. Being an adult shouldn't be taken to mean that you're immune to the risks of media violence exposure. Instead, it means you're old enough to be able to weigh the risks and make an informed decision for yourself.

The Long Answer:

In Question #22 we examined how media violence effects may be larger in children than they are in teenagers or adults. We explained why this makes intuitive sense and why parents, who are naturally protective of children, are often worried about exposing their children to these risks. Such concern (and more directly, threats by Congress) led to the creation of organizations such as the Motion Picture Association of America (MPAA) and the Entertainment Software Ratings Board (ESRB) and to the development of existing rating systems intended to help parents make informed decisions about their children's media use. Parents, in turn, can use these systems to prevent their children from being exposed to unnecessary risks from particularly extreme media content (see Question #48 for a critical discussion about the effectiveness of these rating systems).

Although these rating systems may have been founded with good intentions, they may be having an unintended effect: Causing adults to underestimate their *own* vulnerability to undesirable media effects. To illustrate, imagine you're an adult walking through a video game store.[a] Out of the corner of your eye, a game catches your attention. You pick up the box and turn it over, reading over the game's description. It sounds violent, action-filled, and fun! You see, on the corner of the box, that the game is age-restricted (e.g., "Restricted to players age 17 and up").

---

[a] For many of our readers, this will not be very hard to imagine!

Like many people, you probably never thought very much about where these ratings come from or what they imply. If pressed, you'd probably guess that a room full of child development experts got together, watched some gameplay, and gave the rating based on all sorts of research showing that kids can be harmed by this sort of content (you would be wrong). You also know that you're no longer a kid, and well over the restricted age. You take this to mean that you've outgrown whatever harmful effects this game might have (after all, you can tell the difference between fantasy and reality, and you're not a violent person!) For now, we'll overlook the latter two misconceptions, which we dispel elsewhere in this book (Questions #18, #19, #20, and #33). Instead, as we'll discuss in greater detail in Question #48, it turns out that these ratings are grounded in almost no psychological or developmental research at all. You may not be as safe from the harmful effects of that game as you think!

As we point out in Question #22, age plays, at most, a minor role in whether someone is affected by media violence. This is because many of the psychological mechanisms driving media violence effects (outlined in Question #12) are very basic and how our brains work (e.g., how we store and represent information, how we learn and form associations, and how our body reacts to the sight of blood and gore)[1]. These processes come online very early in life and operate in similar ways throughout our lives. Illustrating this point, studies find that viewing violent media increases the likelihood that people will interpret others' neutral behavior as provoking or aggressive in both 10-year old children[2] and in college undergraduates[3]. Similarly, being exposed to violent media is associated with believing that aggression is normal and acceptable, both in samples of teenagers[4] and in samples of adults[5]. As a final example, when adolescents[6] and adults[7] are exposed to violent media, both end up feeling less empathy for the victims of violence.

For these reasons, it should come as no surprise that the effects of media violence have been found in all age groups that have been tested (see Question #22). To be sure, there may be protective factors in place that lower the risk for aggression: Adults tend to have better critical thinking skills and are better able to control impulsive behavior. But the presence of these protective factors doesn't change the fact that violent media are still a risk factor, just as exercising every day doesn't make junk food any less unhealthy for you.

Ultimately, many adults erroneously believe that they are immune to media violence effects. Unfortunately, the data do not support this conclusion. As every disappointed 18-year old discovers on their birthday, nothing magical happens on your 18th lap around the sun. Your lungs don't suddenly become protected against the risks of smoking, or your liver against the damage done by alcohol. Age restrictions on these products aren't put in place because they become less harmful for you after the age of 18. Instead, restrictions reflect our culture's belief that people over a certain age have the right to choose for themselves which risks they're willing to expose themselves to. Age restrictions on media content are no different. This is why, as with products like tobacco and alcohol, it's important to know the risks associated with media violence if you're going to make an informed decision about its use – a point we discuss in greater detail in Question #56.

References

1. Anderson, C. A. & Bushman, B. J. (2002). Human Aggression. *Annual Review of Psychology, 53,* 27-51.
2. Martins, N. (2013). Televised relational and physical aggression in children's hostile intent attributions. *Journal of Experimental Child Psychology, 31*(10), 2047-2071.
3. Hasan, Y., Bègue, L., & Bushman, B. J. (2012). Viewing the world through "blood-red tinted glasses": The hostile expectation bias mediates the link between violent video game exposure and aggression. *Journal of Experimental Social Psychology, 4*(48), 953-956.
4. Möller, I., & Krahé, B. (2009). Exposure to violent video games and aggression in German adolescents: A longitudinal analysis. *Aggressive Behavior, 35*(1), 75-89.
5. Krahé, B., Möller, I., Huesmann, L. R., Kirwil, L., Felber, J., & Berger, A. (2011). Desensitization to media violence: Links with habitual media violence exposure, aggressive cognitions, and aggressive behavior. *Journal of Personality and Social Psychology, 100*(4), 630-646.
6. Padilla-Walker, L. M., Coyne, S. M., Collier, K. M., & Nielson, M. G. (2015). Longitudinal relations between prosocial television content and adolescents' prosocial and aggressive behavior: The mediating role of empathic concern and self-regulation. *Developmental Psychology, 51*(9), 1317-1328.
7. Wei, R. (2007). Effects of playing violent videogames on Chinese adolescents' pro-violence attitudes, attitudes toward others, and aggressive behavior. *Cyberpsychology & Behavior, 10*(3), 371-380.

24 - Do social factors like income or education change the effects of media violence?

The Short Answer:

Maybe, but probably in an indirect way. There's little reason to believe that having a lower income or being less educated directly increases how much media violence will affect your brain. However, having a low income and poor education is associated with greater likelihood of living in a violent neighborhood, viewing more violent media, and reduced parental involvement. All of *these* factors *can* increase both a person's exposure to other risk factors for aggression and also remove some of the protective factors that would otherwise reduce a person's likelihood of engaging in aggressive behavior.

The Long Answer:

In Question #12 we introduced the General Aggression Model (GAM), which outlines the various factors that interact to influence a person's likelihood of behaving aggressively in a given situation[1]. These mechanisms include factors like believing that aggression is useful, interpreting the world around us as violent, and forming aggressive scripts. Although the GAM discusses other such mechanisms, it appears, at first glance, to overlook two potentially important risk factors: education and income. Anyone with an understanding of demographic research should *expect* both of these factors to play a role in aggressive behavior. And yet, at first glance, it would seem like media violence researchers spend relatively little time discussing these variables and their relationship to media violence.

Let's first acknowledge that just because these measures of socioeconomic status (SES) are not specifically detailed in the model doesn't mean that SES factors don't play a role in media violence effects. After all, although the GAM focuses on the mechanisms driving aggressive behavior – it also acknowledges that these mechanisms are only one piece of the aggression puzzle. The GAM states that a person's risk is a combination of who they are and the situations they find themselves in. Both of these factors are influenced by a person's environment, which can protect a person from, or amplify, their risk of aggression[2,3,4].

Understanding how environmental factors contribute to a person's risk of aggression can be thought of in much the same way that biologists think about a person's risk of getting cancer. One way to study the risk of cancer is to look at the biological mechanisms that cause individual cells to mutate and become cancerous. Just as important, however, researchers must test whether being exposed to certain substances (e.g., carcinogens) or environments (e.g., radioactive) increase the risk of these biological processes happening. Both approaches have the same goal of better understanding where cancer comes from, but they ask distinctly different questions and rely on different types of data: One looks at cellular activity while the other looks at factors in the organism's environment.

In the same way, researchers study aggression and media violence effects both by asking questions about what's going on in the mind in the moments leading up to aggression *and* by studying what's happening in the person's environment that may affect these mental processes.

So what *do* researchers know about the relationship between SES, violent media, and aggression? The answer is "surprisingly little." There have been few studies directly testing whether SES plays a role in the size of media violence effects (e.g., whether media violence effects are larger in people with low SES versus those with high SES, or vice-versa). The few studies which *have* tried to directly assess this relationship have typically found little evidence *directly* linking SES to stronger media violence effects[5]. So, strictly speaking, there is little evidence that making more money or being better educated will change how much each additional hour of violent media will increase your risk for aggression.

But this doesn't mean we should abandon looking at the role of SES entirely. After all, researchers who study SES (e.g., sociologists) *know* that a person's SES can tell you a *lot* about *other* aspects of their environment, many of which *are* risk factors for aggression. For example, there is a well-known association between low SES and exposure to real-world violence[6]. People who are low in SES are more likely to live in rougher neighborhoods where they're more likely to both see and be the victims of violent crime. Aggression researchers know that exposure to real-world violence is one of the bigger risk factors for aggressive behavior[7]. Low SES might also make *other* risk factors for aggression, like violent media exposure, have a bigger impact[3,8] – sort of like how a tired or stressed person is more prone to becoming ill. This is why being poor or lacking education might still matter when it comes to understanding media violence effects, even if they don't directly contribute to a person's risk of aggression.

But there's another reason why SES may be related to a person's risk of aggression: Although it may or may not make a person more vulnerable to violent media effects, it does seem to increase the *amount* of violent media they consume. Studies show, for example, that lower-income people view more television[13] and play more video games[14] than higher-income people. This makes sense, when you consider that money is often a barrier for recreational activities like sports or hobbies. In contrast, once you have a television or a gaming console, you can get hundreds, even thousands of hours of entertainment out of it. And, for obvious reasons, people who consume more media are more likely to also consume more *violent* media[15], increasing their exposure to this particular risk factor for aggression[2,3].

Let's consider a final reason why SES might be related to a person's risk of aggression. SES tends to be associated with how much parental supervision children receive[9]. It's not hard to see why: Imagine a family where both parents have to work to make ends meet, or a single-parent household where the parent has to work multiple jobs just to keep the family afloat. In these situations, parents are often too busy to pay attention to their children's media-viewing habits or to sit down with children while they're consuming media – and who can blame them? If a parent is physically out of the house working or is at home but exhausted from working, can they really be expected to notice everything their children are watching or playing?

Now compare this to a household that can afford daycare, a caretaker, or the luxury of having a parent who stays home to raise the children. In these situations, someone is always around to monitor what the children are watching or playing and can make sure the children are taught to question what they're watching or to encourage them to do something besides stare at a screen all day. Active parental mediation in activities such as these can make a *huge* difference in how children interpret and are affected by media violence, reducing or possibly eliminating the relation altogether (for more on this, see Chapter 5)[10,11,12]. In short, lower SES not only increases a person's likelihood of being exposed to multiple risk factors for aggression, but it can even remove protective factors as well.

In sum, research suggests that SES factors like income and education may not *directly* increase one's risk of aggression, but they can have a number of undesirable indirect effects. Since SES predicts greater exposure to other risk factors – including media violence – and reduces the likelihood of having protective factors, it is clear why some researchers are particularly concerned about the effects of media violence for those from lower socioeconomic levels.

References

1. Anderson, C. A. & Bushman, B. J. (2002). Human Aggression. *Annual Review of Psychology, 53,* 27-51.
2. Exelmans, L., Custers, K., & Van den Bulck, J. (2015). Violent video games and delinquent behavior in adolescents: A risk factor perspective. *Aggressive Behavior, 41,* 267-279.
3. Gentile, D., A. & Bushman, B. J. (2012). Reassessing media violence effects using a risk and resilience approach to understanding aggression. *Psychology of Popular Media Culture, 1*(3), 138-151.
4. Anderson, C. A., Gentile, D. A., & Buckley, K. E. (2007). *Violent Video Game Effects on Children and Adolescents: Theory, Research, and Public Policy.* New York, NY: Oxford University Press.

5. Simonson, H. M. (1972). *The relationship of television program content and socioeconomic status to aggressive behavior.* Unpublished doctoral dissertation, Columbia University.

6. Eron, L. D., Guerra, N., & Huesmann, L. R. (1997). Poverty and violence. In S. Feshbach, J. Zagrodzka, (Eds.), *Aggression: Biological, developmental, and social perspectives* (pp. 139-154.). New York: Plenum.

7. Resnick, M. D., Ireland, M., & Borowsky, I. (2004). Youth violence perpetration: What protects? What predicts? Findings from the national longitudinal study of adolescent health. *Journal of Adolescent Health, 35*(5), 424 (e1-10).

8. Fikkers, K. M., Piotrowski, J. T., Weeda, W. D., Vossen, H. G. M., & Valkenburg, P. M. (2013). Double dose: High family conflict enhances the effect of media violence exposure on adolescents' aggression. *Societies, 3,* 280-292.

9. Harris, K. M. & Marmer, J. K. (1996). Poverty, parental involvement, and adolescent well-being. *Journal of Family Issues, 17*(5), 614-640.

10. Coyne, S. M., Padilla-Walker, L. M., Stockdale, L., & Day, R. D. (2011). Game on... girls: Associations between co-playing video games and adolescent behavioral and family outcomes. *Journal of Adolescent Health, 49,* 160-165.

11. Linder, J. R., & Werner, N. E. (2012). Relationally aggressive media exposure and children's normative beliefs: Does parental mediation matter? *Family Relations, 61,* 488-500.

12. Atkin, C. K., & Greenberg, B. S. (1977). *Parental mediation of children's social behavior learning from television.* Paper presented at the 60th Annual Meeting of the Association for Education in Journalism (Madison, Wisconsin, August, 1977).

13. Morgenstern, M., Sargent, J. D., & Hanewinkel, R. (2009). Relation between socioeconomic status and body mass index: Evidence of an indirect path via television use. *Archives of Pediatrics and Adolescent Medicine, 163*(8), 731-738.

14. McMurray, R. G., Harrell, J. S., Deng, S., Bradley, C. B., Cox, L. M., & Bangdiwala, S. I. (2000). The influence of physical activity, socioeconomic status, and ethnicity on the weight status of adolescents. *Obesity Research, 8*(2), 130-139.

15. Gentile, D. A., Lynch, P. J., Linder, J. R., & Walsh, D. A. (2004). The effects of violent video game habits on adolescent hostility, aggressive behaviors, and school performance. *Journal of Adolescence, 27,* 5-22.

25 - Are violent media a risk only for people exposed to a lot of it?

The Short Answer:

No – exposure to violent media technically increases your risk for aggression regardless of whether it's your first time being exposed to it or your five thousandth time. Like with any risk factor (e.g., smoking), regular exposure to violent media increases your overall risk of aggression more than being exposed a single time. There is no evidence showing that violent media exposure has *no* effect if you keep it under a certain level. This should not surprise you. If you watch a violent film or play a violent game and it truly has no effect on you, you call it "boring." We want to be influenced by the media, and any one show can make us laugh, cry, be excited, or scared. That's part of the effect, and in all honesty, we want to be affected by the media.

The Long Answer:

Throughout this chapter, we've debunked several popular misconceptions about whether certain people are immune to the effects of violent media. Time and time again, the data show that people of all ages, ethnicities, and backgrounds are susceptible to the effects of violent media (see Question #19). The mechanisms driving these effects are deeply-ingrained parts of how our minds work, and are involved in other facets of our lives (e.g., learning, prosocial behavior). Given how fundamental these processes are to how the human mind functions, it makes sense that everyone should be affected by seeing violence, regardless of whether it is in-person or through the media.

Even so, it's hard to shake the belief that some people should be more affected by media violence than others. In this question, we're introducing the idea of "dose": If a person consumes very little violent media – that is, they have a very small "dose" of it, might it have *no* effect on them? Or, another way to ask the question: "Is there an amount of violent media that someone can consume *without* experiencing an increase in their risk of aggression?"

On its surface, this idea seems to hold water. After all, *plenty* of things operate on such "threshold" models. We're told, for example, that meat has a minimum temperature to which it should be cooked to kill certain harmful micro-organisms. Above this threshold your meat is considered safe to eat; below this threshold you run the risk of getting food poisoning.[a] In a similar vein, pharmacists prescribe specific dosages for medications. Consume fewer than X tablets a day and you'll be fine; exceed this threshold and you risk an overdose.

Threshold models can also be found in our legal system. A person who drives with a blood alcohol content over a certain threshold can be found guilty of impaired driving, whereas a person driving below that threshold is not considered to be driving while impaired (unless, of course, they're driving recklessly – but that's an entirely different issue). Food manufacturing companies follow similar rules, being allowed to have a certain amount of a chemical, additive, or contaminant up to a threshold: Any more than this and they can be fined or shut down.[b]

Thresholds like these are appealing because they make risks easy for us to understand. Risks are, by definition, a matter of probability. Unfortunately, people aren't natural statisticians.[c] It's difficult for the average person to understand precisely what a 10% increased risk means or whether they should be worried about a procedure with a 2% lethality rate. However, the complex and nuanced subject of risk probability can be reduced to a set of easy-to-follow rules with thresholds: Stay under or over a certain value, and you'll be fine!

But reality is rarely so simple and seldom adheres to clear, simple thresholds. For example, if a city keeps lead levels in its drinking water below a certain legally acceptable threshold, this does not mean that whatever trace amounts of lead are in the water will have *no* harmful effects. Lead accumulates in the body, eventually leading to harmful effects. The "safe level" of lead in drinking water is a compromise between the estimated amount of harm done by the lead weighed against the increasing cost of reducing the amount of lead further. We've come to accept a certain level of risk when it comes to toxins in our drinking water. Similarly, "safe" radiation levels do not magically mean that any radiation exposure below that level has no effect whatsoever on the body's cells. Modern science suggests that radiation never stops being harmful for our bodies. The threshold simply represents a determination made by policymakers representing what is deemed to be "acceptable" levels of risk, relative to cost of further reductions.

---

[a] One of the authors is *especially* familiar with this particular threshold model, having gotten a very nasty case of salmonella from eating undercooked chicken a few years ago. Let this be a lesson to the reader: Properly handle and cook your meat!

[b] At the risk of ruining the reader's appetite for a good while: Believe it or not, the Food and Drug Administration *does* have guidelines for the acceptable levels of rat feces a company can allow in their product. Good luck getting *that* thought out of your head!

[c] If we were, stats classes would be a *lot* more popular at universities!

Legal policymakers make similar decisions about where to put the threshold for impaired driving: They may decide on a blood-alcohol level of 0.08 for their definition of impaired, but this doesn't mean that a person at 0.07 is not impaired at all. Any level above 0 increases a person's degree of impairment. How impaired a person will be at 0.08 will vary from person to person, with some not showing obvious signs of being impaired until well after 0.08 and others showing it clearly as low as 0.04. The 0.08 threshold is simply a judgment call about what policymakers have decided is an acceptable level of intoxication to risk letting people drive at.

At the risk of belaboring the point, let's look at one more example, one that we draw upon quite a bit in this book: cigarette smoking. Imagine that you've been given the job of setting a threshold for the number of cigarettes a person can safely consume before they experience negative health effects. You know from research that smoking increases a person's risk of getting lung cancer, heart disease, and host of other problems. But you also know that it's not *guaranteed* that smoking cigarettes *will* cause a person to experience these problems. You know, as a general rule, that more smoking equals more risk, but there's no clear-cut natural threshold. What do you do?

Well, it makes perfect sense to say that a person who smokes 3 packs of cigarettes a day is definitely at greater risk than a person who smokes only one cigarette a day. But what about when the differences become smaller? 10 cigarettes a day versus 1? 2 cigarettes a day versus 1? Using the exact same logic, you need to conclude that *every* additional cigarette carries with it a *very small* increase in the person's risk.

So how do we translate this into one of those thresholds that normal people so desperately want? The risk, however small, is *always* present with each additional cigarette. Technically speaking, only zero cigarettes will *totally* eliminate the risk. Any number you set for a threshold will simply be an arbitrary judgment about what you think is an acceptable amount of risk for health problems. You might decide that a 1% increase in the risk for cancer is a good place to put that threshold. Lung cancer researchers probably could come up with a reasonable estimate of how many cigarettes per day for 40 years would result in only a 1% increase of contracting lung cancer. For someone else, that preferred number might be a 5% increased risk. Either way, at that point the threshold has less to do with actual risk and more to do with your opinion. You might decide that 1 cigarette per month represents the threshold for this very small risk. But this would *not* mean that anyone who keeps their smoking to 1 cigarette per month would have no chance of ill effects.

Let's apply this same logic to the question of media violence, and whether there is such a thing as a no-risk amount of exposure. As we've discussed in other questions, violent media consumption is a small, but significant risk factor for aggression – it's certainly not the biggest risk factor, but also not negligible (Questions #11, #14). It seems sensible that 8 hours of violent media per day is a bigger risk for aggression than 8 hours per month. And the research would be on your side: People who watch a *lot* of violent television[1] and who play a *lot* of violent video games[2] are at a greater risk for aggression than people who consume far less.

But what about smaller amounts of exposure – can we find a "minimum amount," below which there are no measurable effects? Well, one study found that *three days* of intermittent exposure to violent media increased peoples' risk of aggression compared to people who watched the same amount of non-violent media[3]. And in laboratory studies, 45 minutes of violent video games increased aggression in the minutes following gameplay[4]. In fact, 45 minutes is *way* more exposure than most lab studies need to find effects! Some studies have found that as little as five *minutes* of violent cartoons can cause measurable short-term increases in aggression[5]. Remember from Question #12: One of the mechanisms underlying violent media effects involves activating aggressive thoughts in the mind. It only takes a few hundredths of a second to activate a thought in a person's mind. Even briefly being shown a *picture* of a weapon can increase a person's risk for aggression for a short period of time[6]!

But let's be real: Being exposed to a split-second of violent media carries with it less risk for aggression than months or years of regular exposure to hours of violent media.[d] In theory, more mechanisms are likely to be involved with regular viewing of violent media (e.g., changing norms and beliefs, learning scripts, desensitization) than in viewing a single picture of a weapon (increased activation of aggression-related thoughts for a few minutes). But, like with smoking, "less risk" is not the same thing as "no risk." There is no amount of exposure to violent media that doesn't carry with it at least *some* increased risk for aggression, either in the minutes immediately following exposure or, like a drop of water in an ocean, as a cumulative effect over time.

This isn't a terribly satisfying or practical answer. Sure, all violent media may carry with them an increased risk of aggression. But what people *really* want to know is how much will media cause dangerous real-world behavior? Well, to be fair, violent media *by itself* won't drive a normal person to extreme violence (see Questions #29, #35). For most people in most of life's situations and most normal levels of media violence exposure, the increase in risk can be measured as an increase in online arguments, road-rage behaviors, passive-aggressive relationship behavior, or very mild forms of physical aggression (e.g., a slap).[e] But for people already high in aggression or in highly provoking situations, this increased risk may be the factor that pushes them over the edge. We, as

---

[d] For one thing, brief exposures are typically studied with respect to *short-term* effects. Few (no one?) would argue that 5-minutes of violent video games will dramatically change your lifelong risk of aggression.

[e] Keep in mind that even these mild forms of aggression can lead to retaliatory behavior, which can escalate in a dangerous cycle.

researchers, can't come up with a hard-and-fast rule that will perfectly explain where this threshold is for every person in every situation. Instead, we can only say that, as a general rule, every piece of violent media carries with it a small increase in the consumer's risk of aggression. Whether that risk is worth taking, and who should be allowed to be exposed to that risk, is a matter of opinion left to others to decide (e.g., parents, politicians, see Question #56).

To sum it all up: Any exposure to violent media carries with it an increase in the consumer's risk of aggressive behavior. This does *not* mean that all violent media turns people violent. Instead, we simply recognize that there is no amount of exposure that *doesn't* have some small effect on your risk of aggression, at least in the minutes immediately after exposure. People can set up rules or thresholds for what they consider to be an acceptable level of risk, in the same way that we, as a society, have come up with reasonable levels of risk somewhere between "raw, uncooked chicken patties" and "incinerated briquette," or between "stone sober driver" and "completely sloshed menace." Although we, as researchers, don't believe it's our place to tell others what levels of risk ought to be acceptable, we can, at very least, help inform parents and policy makers so they can avoid making uninformed decisions.

References

1. McIntyre, J. J., Teevan, J. J. Jr., & Hartnagel, T. (1972). Television Violence and Deviant Behavior. In G. A. Comstock & E. A. Rubinstein (Eds.), *Television and Social Behavior Volume 3: TV and Adolescent Aggressiveness* (pp. 383-435). Washington, D. C.: National Institute of Mental Health.
2. Leiner, M., Peinado, J., Villanos, M. T., Alvarado, L. A., Singh, N., & Dwivedi, A. (2014). Psychosocial profile of Mexican American youths who play aggressive video games. *Hispanic Journal of Behavioral Science, 36*(3), 301-315.
3. Hasan, Y., Bègue, L., Scharkow, M., & Bushman, B. J. (2013). The more you play, the more aggressive you become: A long-term experimental study of cumulative video game effects on hostile expectations and aggressive behavior. *Journal of Experimental Social Psychology, 49*, 224-227.
4. Barlett, C. P. & Rodeheffer, C. (2009). Effects of realism on extended violent and nonviolent video game play on aggressive thoughts, feelings, and physiological arousal. *Aggressive Behavior, 35*, 213-224.
5. Ellis, G. T., & Sekyra, F. III. (1972). The effect of aggressive cartoons on the behavior of first grade children. *The Journal of Psychology, 81*, 37-43.
6. Anderson, C. A., Benjamin, A. J., & Bartholow, B. D. (1998). Does the gun pull the trigger? Automatic priming effects of weapon pictures and weapon names. *Psychological Science, 9*, 308-314.

26 - Are violent video games the only violent media we should care about?

The Short Answer:

No; the violent media effects are not limited to violent video games. Violent television, movies, books, and even music lyrics have all been found to increase one's risk of aggression. There *are* theoretical reasons to believe that the effect of violent video games may be *stronger* than other violent media effects, but more research is needed to test whether this is actually the case. Nevertheless, many of the psychological mechanisms responsible for media violence effects are the same *regardless* of what type of violent media is being consumed.

The Long Answer:

It's easy to forget (or, if you're younger than 40, to even be aware in the first place) that the question of media violence effects is *not* a new one. When people today talk about media violence effects, they're typically talking about video games: Concerned parents and organizations worrying about the effects of violent video games on today's youth. And it's easy to treat this topic as new for researchers, given that video games are still a relatively newer and evolving form of entertainment media.

If you take a broader look at the research on media violence, however, it becomes apparent that researchers have actually had a pretty good understanding of media violence effects for decades – well before the first violent video game studies were ever conducted. Video game violence research and other media violence research have a lot more similarities than they do differences. The evidence for media violence effects is fairly consistent across six decades, leading many researchers to the conclusion that the form that violent media takes isn't nearly as important as the violent content itself.[a]

If you know your history, it becomes clear that modern concerns about the effects of violent video games are simply the newest flavor of millennia-spanning public concern about violent or controversial media content that has included, at

---

[a] In fact, one of us had difficulty getting major journals to publish his early studies of video game violence because the editors and reviewers said that such studies were in theory no different from the hundreds of studies done previously on the effects of TV and film violence. Similarly, grant agencies were reluctant to fund video game studies because "we already know all about media violence effects."

various times, concerns about plays, books, radio, film, comic books, television, and video games.[1] Reflecting this concern, researchers since at least the 1950s have been tasked with applying psychological science to the question of whether television or radio violence was negatively affecting children's thoughts, feelings, and behavior[2,3]. The conclusion reached by most researchers today is the same as the conclusion reached by researchers decades ago: Violent media exposure increases the consumer's risk of engaging in aggression, whether we're talking about violent television and film[4], violent radio[2], violent comic books[5,6], violent music[7-12], or violent video games.[13,14]

When you consider the mechanisms that underlie media violence effects, it makes sense *why* violent TV, music, and video games would all increase the consumer's risk of aggression. As we discussed in Question #12, violent media increases one's risk of aggression for a variety of reasons: desensitizing, changing attitudes and beliefs about the appropriateness of aggression, reinforcing aggressive behavior, teaching new ways to behave aggressively, activating aggressive thoughts, and leading us to perceive the world around us as hostile[15]. But none of these mechanisms is unique to only one type of media. For example: Most violent video games teach players to associate aggressive behavior with reward by rewarding the player with points or story progression when they behave aggressively in the game.[b] But when you think about it, violent television, comic books, and music teach similar associations: Heroes in TV or film are rewarded for using violence, and popular musicians earn fame and wealth by bragging and glamorizing their own violent behavior.

Likewise, violent media of all sorts activate aggressive thoughts in our mind, making aggressive behavior more likely[15]. After all, if aggressive thoughts can be activated just by showing a person a *picture* of a gun[16], is it really a stretch to say that lyrics, stories, videos, or games that *prominently* feature violent images will similarly activate aggressive thoughts?[6,7,17-20]

In short, it makes sense, from a theoretical perspective, that video games are just like any other form of violent media that increases the consumer's risk of aggression. Although research shows that this is the case, it's hard to shake the feeling that video games are in a different category from other media. It *feels* like violent video games should have bigger effects than other violent media. We can see this belief reflected in public concern.

---

[b] Interestingly, one clever set of experiments reprogrammed a popular violent racing game where players were rewarded for running over pedestrians. In some conditions, the game was programmed so that players were punished (lost points) for hitting pedestrians, while in other conditions there were no pedestrians to hit. Participants who were randomly assigned to play the punish-for-hitting-pedestrians version or the no-pedestrians version were significantly *less* aggressive later on than players who had played the original reward-for-hitting-pedestrians version.[23]

197

Starting in the 1990s, there were growing concerns about the effects of violent video games. Many of these concerns stemmed from a combination of peoples' fascination with advancing video game technology and several high-profile mass shooting events (e.g., Columbine.)[21] People were left searching for an explanation in the wake of these tragedies, and many pointed their fingers at violent video games as a prominent cause. Specific genres of video games came under fire, including first-person shooters, which some claimed were little more than "murder simulators"[22]. Of course, other violent media existed at the time, including many violent films, television shows, and songs. But something about violent video games made them seem wholly different to the public - the one form of media we ought to be concerned about.

So what is it about video games that make people particularly concerned about them? One possibility is their interactive nature. Unlike books, songs, radio, film, or television, video games allow consumers to actively contribute to the carnage on screen. For comparison, imagine that you're a parent deciding whether to let your child watch the World War II film *Saving Private Ryan*, where soldiers violently fight with enemy combatants. You might be worried that your child will be frightened by the graphic scenes or desensitized by all of the blood on-screen.

Now, imagine walking into the room and seeing your child mowing down soldiers in a World War II themed video game. Something about the video game *feels* more concerning for many. Instead of other people – trained soldiers – being the ones committing the violence, it's now your sweet, innocent 8-year old child doing the killing! Instead of being an innocent, passive observer of someone else's violence, *they* are the aggressor, the one pulling the trigger. It seems like this increased immersion into the medium *should* make violent video games more harmful than other forms of violent media.

Preliminary research suggests that there might be some truth to this idea. For instance, the interactive nature of video games allows players to "get into the head" of the main character in a way they simply can't in a film. Players identify more with a character they can control than they do with an actor on a screen. This may cause players to internalize some of the character's attitudes or beliefs as their own. After all, if walking a mile in another person's shoes is supposed to help you see things the way they do, why shouldn't we expect the same from spending some time in their head, controlling their every action? And why stop there? Identifying with a video game character may also make the rewards for violence feel more personally relevant. If *you're* the one calling the shots, then *you're* the one being rewarded for their aggression, not some other character on a screen!

It's not so farfetched to believe that game players identify with their in-game characters. Studies have suggested that this occurs, especially when players are given the chance to customize the character themselves.[c] This identification, in turn, can amplify the effects of media violence on players.[24, 25] Even more concerning: When players identify with aggressive characters, they often associate *themselves* with aggression as well –not just by saying so, but in the way their minds connect the concept of "me" and "aggression" on mental tests.[26]

Another potentially unique mechanism for video games is the ability they give players to simulate violent acts themselves. Unlike watching an actor in a show do something violent (learning by watching another person), doing it first-hand makes the action much more vivid, which may speed along the formation of aggressive scripts. Studies have provided preliminary evidence for this possibility as well: Players who used a gun-shaped controller have more aggressive thoughts after playing the game than players who use regular controllers[27], suggesting there may be merit to the idea that the immersion and hands-on experience of a video game may amplify media violence effects.

Having said all of this, we hasten to add that there is limited research directly testing whether violent video game effects differ from other violent media effects. Few studies have directly pitted violent video games against other violent media to see which effects are larger, and those which have are often limited in their ability to draw any definite conclusions. Researchers studying violent video games usually focus their efforts on testing specific mechanisms underlying the effects. The results from these studies are far from clear about whether any of these mechanisms make video games a bigger risk factor than other violent media.

One of the reasons it's so difficult to compare violent games and violent television is the difficulty of appropriately matching video games and TV. In one study, for example, participants either watched a wrestling program or played a wrestling video game, after which researchers measured their aggressive thoughts and behaviors[28]. On the one hand, the study seems like an ideal test, since both conditions involved violent content that was comparable in nature and severity. But there are numerous *other* possible differences between the two conditions that make it difficult to meaningfully compare the conditions.[d] For example, the video game and the TV program may have differed in their perspective (e.g., where the camera is, whether it cuts between the wrestlers and the audience). It's also possible for players to "lose" in their game, something that can create frustration (a risk factor for aggression). In contrast, a viewer cannot personally "lose" while

---

[c] Many other gamers will likely recognize this experience: One of the authors, Courtney, frequently spends considerable time customizing the appearance of his character in any roleplaying video game that gives him the chance to do so. In *Fallout 4*, in particular, he often spends over an hour perfecting every detail of his character's face – only to immediately cover it up under a helmet!

[d] We call these unintended differences between conditions "confounding variables". We discuss them more in greater detail in Question #15.

watching a wrestling match on TV. In short, any difference between the conditions with respect to the consumer's aggression may be due to some other factor besides the fact that one involved a video game and the other a TV show.

Other experiments try to address these concerns by making the images that players and non-players see *identical*. In some studies, for examples, some participants are randomly assigned to play a violent video game while others are assigned to *watch* people play the video game[29,30]. To be fair, this is a pretty clever way to get around the problem of the two people seeing different content. For every play session, we can compare the person who played the game to the person who watched the exact same content as if it was a TV show.

But this type of study has a whole new set of problems. For example, imagine being one of those participants who was forced to watch someone else play a video game. Do you think that might make you feel just a bit annoyed or frustrated? Video games are designed, first and foremost, to be played – not to be watched. This means that the player is engaging in the media in the way it was intended, while the observer is doing so in an entirely different way. For this reason, it's hard to know how to interpret differences between the conditions (or lack thereof). Are we testing genuine differences between video games and other types of media, or simply testing whether watching a video game being played is more frustrating than getting to play it yourself?

Still other studies have tried to test differences between violent game effects and violent television effects by looking at measures *outside* the laboratory in cross-sectional or longitudinal studies (see Question #9 for more on these types of studies). In one study, researchers looked at violent video game and violent television use in those who had been diagnosed with aggressive behavioral disorders, comparing them to a non-clinical sample of adolescents[31]. Such studies might make it possible to see which variable – TV violence or video game violence – is a better predictor of who's in the "aggressive" group. But they introduce yet another problem: As it turns out, people who watch a lot of violent TV *also* happen to play a lot of violent video games. Because of this, it's incredibly difficult for researchers to statistically distinguish the effect of violent video games from the effect of violent TV. This is why, in studies that measure both violent TV and violent video game use, researchers tend to just combine them into a single measure of "violent media exposure"[32,33]. Because of this, little evidence exists directly testing whether violent video game exposure is *actually* more strongly associated with aggression than other forms of media violence.

In sum, we can confidently say that decades of research supports the idea that media violence of all types increases a person's risk for aggression. The effects have been observed across virtually every type of media studied. This means that, at the very least, we can say that the effects of violent media aren't *limited* to violent video games. But there are reasons to hypothesize that violent video games *should* be a bigger risk factor for aggression, and there is some early evidence suggesting that this may be the case, since violent video games may involve unique mechanisms (e.g., interactivity) that other forms of media do not. That said, little research has directly tested whether violent video games are a bigger risk factor for aggression than other violent media, mainly because of the difficulty inherent in designing such studies. Meta-analyses that compare media tend to show that the effect sizes are within the margin of error of each other, so it is unclear if any media have larger effects. The issue continues to be actively researched among media violence researchers today, with more studies needed before we'll have a definitive answer one way or another.

References

1. Kirsh, S. J. (2006). *Children, Adolescents, and Media Violence: A Critical Look at the Research* (pp. 4-8). Thousand Oaks, California: Sage Publications.
2. Albert, R. S. (1957). The role of mass media and the effect of aggressive film content upon children's aggressive responses and identification choices. *Genetic Psychology Monographs, 55,* 221-285.
3. Siegel, A. E. (1958). The influence of violence in the mass media upon children's role expectations. *Child Development, 29*(1), 35-56.
4. Andison, F. S. (1977). TV violence and viewer aggression: A cumulation of study results 1956-1976. *The Public Opinion Quarterly, 41*(3), 314-331.
5. Lovibond, S. H. (1967). The effect of media stressing crime and violence upon children's attitudes. *Social Problems, 15*(1), 91-100.
6. Berkowitz, L. (1970). The contagion of violence: An S-R mediational analysis of some effects of observed aggression. *Nebraska Symposium on Motivation, 18,* 95-135.
7. Johnson, J. D., Jackson, L. A., & Gatto, L. (1995). Violent attitudes and deferred academic aspirations: Deleterious effects of exposure to rap music. *Basic and Applied Social Psychology, 16*(1-2), 27-41.
8. Smith, B. S. (1995). *The effects of exposure to violent lyric music and consumption of alcohol on aggressiveness.* Unpublished doctoral dissertation, University of Mississippi.
9. Litman, C. S. (1996). *Effects of rap music on verbal and nonverbal aggressive and disruptive behavior in boy's social interactions.* Unpublished doctoral dissertation, Hofstra University.
10. Brummert-Lennings, H. I., & Warburton, W. A. (2011). The effect of auditory versus visual violent media exposure on aggressive behaviour: The role of song lyrics, video clips and musical tone. *Journal of Experimental Social Psychology. 47,* 794-799.
11. Warburton, W. A. (2012). How does listening to Eminem do me any harm? What the research says about music and anti-social behaviour. In W. A. Warburton & D. Braunstein [Eds.], *Growing up fast and furious: Reviewing the impacts of violent and sexualised media on children* (pp. 85-115). Sydney: The Federation Press.

12. Warburton, W. A., Roberts, D. F., & Christensen, P. G. (2014). The effects of violent and antisocial music on children and adolescents. In D. Gentile [Ed.], *Media violence and children* (2nd Edition)(pp. 301-328). Westport CT: Praeger.
13. Greitemeyer, T., & Mügge, D. O. (2014). Video games do affect social outcomes: A meta-analytic review of the effects of violent and prosocial video game play. *Personality and Social Psychology Bulletin, 40*(5), 578-589.
14. Anderson, C. A., Shibuya, A., Ihori, N., Swing, E. L., Bushman, B. J., Sakamoto, A., Rothstein, H. R., & Saleem, M. (2010). Violent video game effects on aggression, empathy, and prosocial behavior in eastern and western countries: a meta-analytic review. *Psychological Bulletin, 136*(2), 151-173.
15. Anderson, C. A. & Bushman, B. J. (2002). Human Aggression. *Annual Review of Psychology, 53*, 27-51.
16. Anderson, C. A., Benjamin, A. J., & Bartholow, B. D. (1998). Does the gun pull the trigger? Automatic priming effects of weapon pictures and weapon names. *Psychological Science, 9*, 308-314.
17. Stephens, R., & Allsop, C. (2012). Effect of manipulated state aggression on pain tolerance. *Psychological Reports: Disability & Trauma, 111*(1), 311-321.
18. Bösche, W. (2012). Application of the signal detection theory to the cognitive processing of aggressive stimuli after playing a violent video game: Response bias or enhanced sensitivity? *Advances in Psychology Research, 91*, 135-142.
19. Qian, Z. & Zhang, D. (2014). The effects of viewing violent movie via computer on aggressiveness among college students. *Computers in Human Behavior, 35*, 320-325.
20. Bushman, B. J. (1998). Priming effects of media violence on the accessibility of aggressive constructs in memory. *Personality and Social Psychology Bulletin, 24*(5), 537-545.
21. Cullen, D. (2009). *Columbine*. New York, NY: Twelve.
22. Grossman, D., & DeGaetano, G. (1999). *Stop Teaching our Kids to Kill: A Call to Action Against TV, Movie & Video Game Violence*. New York, NY: Crown Publishers.
23. Carnagey, N. L., & Anderson, C.A. (2005). The effects of reward and punishment in violent video games on aggressive affect, cognition, and behavior. *Psychological Science, 16*, 882-889.
24. Konijn, E. A., Bijvank, M. N., & Bushman, B. J. (2007). I wish I were a warrior: the role of wishful identification in the effects of violent video games on aggression in adolescent boys. *Developmental Psychology, 43*(4), 1038-1044.
25. Fischer, P., Kastenmüller, K., & Greitemeyer, T. (2009). Media violence and the self: The impact of personalized gaming characters in aggressive video games on aggressive behavior. *Journal of Experimental Social Psychology, 46*(1), 192-195.

26. Uhlmann, E. & Swanson, J. (2004). Exposure to violent video games increases automatic aggressiveness. *Journal of Adolescence, 27,* 41-52.
27. McGloin, R., Farrar, K. M., & Fishlock, J. (2015). Triple whammy! Violent games and violent controllers: Investigating the use of realistic gun controllers on perceptions of realism, immersion, and outcome aggression. *Journal of Communication, 65,* 280-299.
28. Meyers, K. S. (2003). *Television and Video Game Violence: Age Differences and the Combined Effects of Passive and Interactive Violent Media.* Unpublished doctoral dissertation, Louisiana State University.
29. Brooks, M. C. (1999). *Press Start: Exploring the Effects of Violent Video Games on Boys.* Unpublished doctoral dissertation, University of Texas at Austin.
30. Cooper, J., & Mackie, D. (1986). Video games and aggression in children. *Journal of Applied Social Psychology, 16*(8), 726-744.
31. Kronenberger, W. G., Mathews, V. P., Dunn, D. W., Wang, Y., Wood, E. A., Larsen, J. J., Rembusch, M. E., Lowe, M. J., Giauque, A. L., & Lurito, J. T. (2005). Media violence exposure in aggressive and control adolescents: Differences in self- and parent-reported exposure to violence on television and in video games. *Aggressive Behavior, 31,* 201-216.
32. Hopf, W. H., Huber, G. L., & Weiß, R. H. (2008). Media violence and youth violence: A 2-year longitudinal study. *Journal of Media Psychology, 20*(3), 79-96.
33. Krahé, B., & Möller, I. (2010). Longitudinal effects of media violence on aggression and empathy among German adolescents. *Journal of Applied Developmental Psychology, 31,* 401-409.

Chapter 3

Misconceptions about Media Violence Research

27 - Isn't violence more likely to be caused by something like abuse than to be caused by media?

The Short Answer:

Yes and no. Media violence is just one of the *many* factors that increases a person's risk of aggressive and violent behavior. And, to be sure, it's not the largest risk factor – it's almost certainly overshadowed by factors like severe provocation or joining a violent gang. But just because other, major risk factors exist doesn't mean that media violence *doesn't* affect aggression, nor does it mean that media violence effects should be ignored. Some studies also suggest that media violence isn't the smallest known risk factor and, in some studies, it's been found to be at least as big a risk factor as childhood abuse.

The Long Answer:

Let's imagine that one of the authors, Courtney, walked into the laboratory just in time to see his co-author, Chris, losing his temper and insulting one of the other co-authors, Johnie.[a] In that moment, Courtney is witnessing an act of verbally aggressive behavior. And, like any reasonable person, his first thought will likely be "What the heck is going on?" He, like aggression researchers for decades, is trying to understand aggression by learning its cause.

With this in mind, let's ask ourselves what *could* have caused Chris to yell insults at Johnie? Even without knowing a thing about Chris or Johnie, you might be able to come up with some believable-sounding causes. Some of them may explain what caused Chris to be aggressive to Johnie in this particular situation, while others may explain why this was a long time coming between these two, or why Chris is more likely to be aggressive toward Johnie in any situation.

---

[a] Readers will note that Craig, the senior author of this book, conveniently finds himself absent as either the perpetrator or victim of aggression in the laboratory. One of the perks of being the old-guy expert on aggression research is that no one dares to give you any guff! That said, Craig will be the first to point out that his students delight in those rare occasions when they do get to prove him wrong!

Let's consider some possible causes below:

1. Chris's computer died this morning.

2. Johnie insulted Chris just before Courtney walked in the door.

3. The lab room thermostat is broken, making it uncomfortably hot.

4. Chris did not have his regular cup of coffee this morning and is grumpy.

5. Johnie has been getting on Chris's nerves for months.

6. Chris is the type of person who loses his temper easily.

7. Death metal music from the lab next door is blaring loudly.

Let's assume that *all* of these statements are true. So, which one could be said to be *the* cause of Chris's aggression toward Johnie?

We could point to the event that happened just before Chris lost his temper: Johnie's insult. But would that be the full story? What if people insult Chris all the time without him reacting this way – could we still consider the insult to be *the* cause of Chris's aggression? What about the hot room and the death metal music – surely they're making both Chris and Johnie somewhat irritable, enough so that Johnie's minor insult caused Chris to snap. Then again, Chris didn't lose his temper until after Johnie's insult – so it's clear that, at very least, the music and the heat weren't enough by themselves to cause the aggression. Of course, Chris's mood wasn't the greatest when he came into work – his broken computer and lack of coffee might've been what pushed him to the edge. On any other day, Chris might've kept his cool and not responded to Johnie's insult. Then again, we're told that Chris is the sort of person who loses his temper easily: Maybe someone less temperamental might have remained calm despite all of this happening to them. And, let's not forget, Johnie's been driving Chris nuts for months: Chris would probably not have pushed back if it had been anyone but Johnie insulting him.

So, let's ask ourselves again: What exactly caused Chris' aggression?

This entirely fictitious example illustrates just how complex it can be when researchers try to sort out the causes of behavior – especially a particular incident. It's hard to point to any one factor in the story that's both *necessary* and *sufficient* to explain Chris's aggression. Chris's temper might not have flared up if some of these variables were absent (e.g., lack of coffee), meaning that no one variable in this list was *necessary* to cause Chris to get angry. Likewise, no one variable is enough by itself to explain Chris's outburst: He probably wouldn't have shouted if he had *only* broken his computer or *only* have been insulted by Johnie.

This same principle extends to pretty much all of human behavior. Very rarely can we point to any one single necessary and sufficient cause for behavior. For this reason, researchers rarely discuss behavior as the result of a single, "ultimate" cause. If we only point to the most recent factor (e.g.,. the insult), we're overlooking the importance of historical and situational context. And, on the flip-side of things, if we focus only on distant, long-term factors, we're ignoring the question of "why here, why now?"

Instead of focusing on single answers to explain complex behaviors, researchers adopt probability-based models: What factors make something *more* or *less* likely to occur, and how do these factors combine and interact with one another?[b] Aggression researchers use this probability-based model to understand risk factors for aggression[1,2]. Each risk factor adds to a person's likelihood of aggressing, like drops of water in a glass. As the glass gets increasingly full, the likelihood of aggression grows. Minor forms of aggression – like small insults or starting a rumor about someone – may occur even when the glass is only partially full. Extreme forms of aggression, on the other hand – hitting or attacking someone with a weapon – are very rare, and tend to happen only when the glass is full or overflowing.

We can answer the present question in terms of this probability-based model. The question asks whether other factors besides violent media cause aggression. Another way of putting it, while sticking to our glass analogy, is whether risk factors like gang membership or witnessing lots of real-world violence raise the water level in a person's glass *more* than media violence exposure does.

The simple answer to this question is, probably, yes. In Question #24 we discussed research showing that poverty and prior exposure to violence are, indeed, among some of the strongest risk factors for aggression. A person with a history of violence or who lives in poverty may walk around the world with a glass that's always mostly-full because of these risk factors. By comparison, media violence may be a relatively small risk factor –but it's still big enough to be detectable in most studies[3,4]. Exposure to violent media is more like adding a thimble full of water to the glass: If you're paying close attention, or know how to look for it, you'll notice that the water level has risen, and that people who walk around with this risk factor tend to walk around with slightly fuller glasses than people who don't. Media violence researchers don't claim that violent media are the *only* factor adding water to the glass – only that it's *a* factor.

---

[b] We've discussed these issues in depth in other questions (e.g., Question #14, #24).

This leads us to an important implication of the original question: If media violence is *not* the only risk factor for aggression, or even one of the largest risk factors, why should anyone care about it?

To be sure, there *are* practical reasons why we might absolutely agree with this sentiment. If your ultimate goal is to reduce aggression, it seems to make sense to start by tackling the *biggest* risk factors first. Analogously, if I were trying to make my car go faster, I would probably start by putting a more powerful engine in the car – I wouldn't focus on the aerodynamics of my car's side mirrors. Both of these factors will undoubtedly affect the top speed of my car, but *clearly* changing the engine is going to have a bigger effect. Is there *ever* a reason to focus on the mirrors?

Absolutely! Let's say I have a budget of $200 to fix my car. Or, let's say I know how to change my car's mirrors, but I don't know the first thing about building or installing an engine. In both of these cases, it makes more sense to focus on the car's mirrors. In the first case, I lack the resources needed to change the engine, but I *do* have the resources to change the mirror. In the second case, I don't have the *ability* to change the engine, but it's within my ability to change the mirrors.

This same line of reasoning can be applied to aggression research. Consider some of those big risk factors for violent behavior: becoming a gang member, growing up in poverty, being of an age where the risk of violence is high, and being male. Right off the bat, the last two risk factors – age and sex – are two things we can't change: We can't prevent people from being male, nor can we just lock up everyone between the ages of 15 and 25. But what about those other two risk factors: gang membership and poverty? How do you even *begin* to tackle those problems? There are government agencies and million-dollar programs aimed at trying to do just that, and even these are only partially successful at best. Ultimately, these major risk factors are impractical to tackle for a handful of researchers or a concerned parent.[c]

Okay, so it's a bit pie-in-the-sky for parents to try to put a stop to violence by going after some of its biggest sources. But instead of throwing up our hands in defeat, what if we focused on the risk factors that are both possible to address and within our ability to address? People's media consumption habits fall into this category. Although it's not easy to overhaul people's media-viewing habits, it *is* possible to devise small ways to incentivize non-violent media or to encourage people to spend less time in front of media.[d] At very least, we can try to make people aware of the fact that violent media are a risk factor for aggression so that

---

[c] Just ask the people who live in violent, gang-filled neighborhoods! They don't live there because they *want* to live in poverty or live with the threat of gang violence. They live there because they have little choice in the matter and little ability to change the situation!

[d] It's certainly easier than trying to change their age or stop poverty!

they can take steps to curb their own and their children's consumption. Even if this would only have the effect of lowering the average water level in peoples' aggression-glasses by a few drops across the country, it's a humble, practical step in the right direction!

We should also keep in mind that we shouldn't always treat media violence effects as trivially small. In fact, in a study discussed in Question #14, a recent study of youth and adolescents in six very different countries found that the media violence was the 2nd largest risk factor for excessive aggression, and was a larger risk factor than sex, abusive parenting, peer victimization (bullying), and neighborhood crime.[5] Only peer delinquency had a larger effect. To be sure, other studies using different measures and methods will rank the relative risk of media violence differently. But, as a general rule, peer violence (e.g., gang membership) is usually one of the largest, while media violence is usually somewhere in the middle of known risk factors. It's neither the biggest nor the smallest of risk factors.

Ultimately, if we want to understand and address the issue of aggression, we have to appreciate that it's complex and probabilistic. No one thing caused Chris to snap at Johnie (in our fictitious example), but a whole host of risk factors, both short- and long-term, led to it happening. And if our goal is to reduce the likelihood of aggression like this happening, we need to move past the idea that the only risk factors worth addressing are the biggest ones. Sometimes, we have only the resources or the know-how to change the mirrors on our car. We might not be able to change who Chris is or the fact that he and Johnie have a rough history together, but we *can* turn down the heat, keep the two of them apart, put a coffee maker in the laboratory, and add some soundproofing to keep out the death metal music from the lab next door!

References

1. Exelmans, L., Custers, K., & Van den Bulck, J. (2015). Violent video games and delinquent behavior in adolescents: A risk factor perspective. *Aggressive Behavior, 41,* 267-279.

2. Gentile, D., A. & Bushman, B. J. (2012). Reassessing media violence effects using a risk and resilience approach to understanding aggression. *Psychology of Popular Media Culture, 1*(3), 138-151.

3. Greitemeyer, T., & Mügge, D. O. (2014). Video games do affect social outcomes: A meta-analytic review of the effects of violent and prosocial video game play. *Personality and Social Psychology Bulletin, 40*(5), 578-589.

4. Anderson, C. A., Shibuya, A., Ihori, N., Swing, E. L., Bushman, B. J., Sakamoto, A., Rothstein, H. R., & Saleem, M. (2010). Violent video game effects on aggression, empathy, and prosocial behavior in eastern and western countries: a meta-analytic review. *Psychological Bulletin, 136*(2), 151-173.

5. Anderson, C. A., Suzuki, K., Swing, E. L., Groves, C. L., Gentile, D. A., Prot, S., Lam, C. P., Sakamoto, A., Horiuchi, Y., Krahé, B., Jelic, M., Liuqing, W.,

Toma, R., Warburton, W. A., Zhang, X., Tajima, S., Qing, F., & Petrescu, P. (2017). Media violence and other aggression risk factors in seven nations. *Personality and Social Psychology Bulletin, 43,* 986-998.

28 - Millions of people view violent media – why aren't there millions of murders each year?

The Short Answer:

Recall the distinction between *violent* (extreme, potentially lethal) behavior and *aggressive* (intended to harm) behavior. Violent behavior is very rare compared to verbal, relational, and other milder forms of aggression. Because of this, any increases in the rate of aggression caused *specifically* by violent media would be *far* more noticeable in day-to-day forms of aggression than in extreme forms of violence. This is true for *any* risk factor for aggression. Violent media exposure is a fairly modest risk factor, meaning that, for most people and in most situations, it will simply increase the frequency with which they engage in mild forms of aggression. Since so few people are on the cusp of violent behavior in the first place, almost no one would be expected to be pushed to violence by violent media alone.

The Long Answer:

Skeptics often raise this question as a way to make the claims of violent media researchers look absurd. It goes something like this:

1. Millions of people worldwide collectively spend billions of hours consuming violent media.

2. If violent media *were* linked with real-world aggression, there would have to be an epidemic of rioting in the streets, constant fights, and soaring murder rates.

3. Since we *don't* see this level of violence in our society (thankfully), there clearly cannot be a relationship between violent media and aggression.

Unfortunately for those who use this argument (and for those who are fooled by it), it's faulty for several reasons. For starters, it mixes up the terms "violence" and "aggression" – treating them like they mean the same thing. As we've discussed in Question #7, these terms mean *very* different things to aggression researchers. To put it simply, violence refers specifically to *extreme* aggression (e.g., assault, stabbing, shooting). By definition, anything that's *extreme* is rare – otherwise we would call it *average*. Most aggressive behavior is not extreme or violent: Insults, sabotaging relationships or reputations, rude gestures, shoving and slapping – these are all *far* more common than shootings and stabbings. But when you treat "aggression" and "violence" as exactly the same thing, you conveniently ignore this fact, making the modest claims of media violence researchers (e.g., violent media are a risk factor for aggression) sound ridiculous (e.g., violent media cause school shootings). This tactic is called creating a straw-man: Misrepresenting the position of media violence researchers as one that's extreme and easily debunked so that they can be trivialized without actually having to challenge their true position, research methods, or decades of data.

Since violence is a type of aggression, one *could* argue that media violence researchers *technically* agree that violent media should increase the risk of *all* forms of aggression – including extreme aggression. This is true. But violence itself is rare. For example, people who are bullied are *far* more likely to be called names, teased, or have rumors spread about them than they are to be physically beaten up[1].[a] Indeed, extreme violence tends to occur only when *many* risk factors are present in the same person at the same time in the absence of protective factors. Since violence occurs so rarely, even a modest increase in the risk of violence will seem to have almost no effect on the number of violent incidents we observe.

We can see that this is the case with a bit of math. For simplicity's sake, we'll use some simple numbers in a fake city called *Unpleasantville*, a city with a population of one million people. In a city this large, there are occasional murders. Last year, Unpleasantville saw 50 people murdered (each one a case of rare and extreme aggression). In addition, the city of Unpleasantville is home to 100,000 incidents of non-criminal aggression every year (e.g., shouting, insults, mild threats, teasing).

Now let's assume, for simplicity's sake, that violent media increases the frequency of *all* aggressive behavior by flat rate of 5%. So what does this 5% increase in aggression mean for the citizens of Unpleasantville? Well, when it comes to murder, 5% more is the difference between 50 murders per year and 52-53 murders per year. When you put it this way, the difference sounds somewhat trivial. Murder is pretty serious, but only 2 or 3 more? We could *easily* chalk that up to coincidence or random chance.

But what about common, day-to-day forms of aggression? An increase of 5% for something which happens 100,000 times per year in Unpleasantville means there will be 5,000 more incidents: That's 5,000 more bullied kids or 5,000 more people hurling hurtful words at their spouse or 5,000 more bigoted slurs shouted at

---

[a] To be clear, we're *not* saying that these non-physical forms of bullying are okay or that they're somehow less horrible than violent bullying! We're simply saying that, while awful, they are not as extreme as the sorts of bullying that causes grievous bodily harm.

minority groups. Suddenly, the effects seem a *lot* more widespread, and a lot more likely to affect us personally!

This example illustrates why the impact of media violence can't be based *solely* on its effects on *violence* (or other extreme aggression). Unfortunately, this is a subtle point that often gets lost amid shouting and fear-mongering by those who deny media violence effects, giving them the wiggle room they need to discredit media violence effects by focusing everyone's attention on the place where the effects are the *least* likely to be seen.

Let's try thinking about it another way. In other questions, we've talked about aggression being like a glass of water (e.g., Question #14, #27). As the water level in this aggression glass fills, people are at greater risk for increasingly aggressive behavior. Many risk factors contribute to how full this glass is, with violent media exposure being only one such factor. For most people, their glass will never become full. They go through life with relatively empty glasses, meaning it's fairly unlikely that they will find themselves in a situation that drives them to engage in extreme violence. But remember, mild aggression doesn't *require* a full glass. A person may engage in fairly mild aggression with only half a glass,[b] or even a quarter of a glass. Unlike violent behavior, it's *much* more likely that most of us will hit *this* level of water at some point in our lives.

Let's imagine that violent media are adding a thimble full of water to everyone's glass – a fair assumption since media violence effects are thought to be largely universal (see Question #19). Technically, everyone's glass is now more likely to overflow, but this doesn't mean that everyone's glass *will* overflow: We're only going to see overflowing in the few people with a lot of other risk factors whose glasses are already mostly full or who receive some extreme provocation, which is like shaking the glass. But this small increase in water level *will* push many people over the "half-full" or "quarter-full" threshold, dramatically increasing the number of cases of mild aggression.

This analogy illustrates why violent media alone don't cause huge changes in nation-wide violence, but they *can* lead to significant increases in people losing their temper, feeling angry or hostile, and insulting others. Most of us shouldn't fear becoming the victims of extreme violence, but we probably *are* concerned about being on the receiving end of someone's temper, bad mood, or being insulted or mocked by people around us. Unfortunately, it's easy to overlook the threats staring us in the face since they're rarely considered in the media or in national statistics, which focus primarily on the most extreme forms of violence.[c]

---

[b] This is one case where seeing the glass as half-full can actually be a *bad* thing!

[c] We shouldn't underplay the damage caused by these "mundane" forms of aggression either. Increases in aggressive attitudes and beliefs towards outgroups

Let's return to the original question and consider one additional reason why it's faulty. The question makes the unspoken assertion that media violence effects, if they exist, operate by basic mimicry or the inability to distinguish fantasy from reality. In other words, it sets up media researchers as claiming that viewers see violence on the screen and then mindlessly repeat that violence in the real world. Since this clearly isn't what happens (i.e., millions of viewers do not go out and mindlessly mimic the violence they see on their screens in the real world), critics conclude that media researchers are wrong. We address this misconception more thoroughly in Question #12 and #33, but for now we'll simply say that the actual mechanisms underlying violent media effects are *far* more complex than this. Finding a small or non-significant relationship between violent media and murder in real life isn't enough to prove that violent media are not a risk factor for aggression. Instead, the only thing this "disproves" is the straw-man model that violent media works because people mimic anything and everything they see on their screen. Media researchers tend to see viewers as being a bit more complicated than that.

References

1. Bradshaw, C. P., Sawyer, A. L., & O'Brennan, L. M. (2007). Bullying and peer victimization at school: Perceptual differences between students and school staff. *School Psychology Review, 36*(3), 361-382.
2. Saleem, M., & Anderson, C. A. (2013). Arabs as terrorists: Effects of stereotypes within violent contexts on attitudes, perceptions and affect. *Psychology of Violence, 3,* 84-99.
3. Saleem, M., Prot, S., Anderson, C. A., & Lemieux, A. F. (2017). Exposure to Muslims in media and support for public policies harming Muslims. *Communication Research, 44,* 841-869.

(minorities, refugees, immigrants) can drive voting behavior, policies, and decisions about national crises and war. For example, recent studies show that certain types of video games and news sources increase bias against American Muslims and lead to support for use of violence against Muslim nations.[2,3]

29 - I've used violent media for years and I'm not violent. Doesn't this disprove media violence effects?

The Short Answer:

No, for four reasons. First, even if it were true that someone was unaffected by media violence, it wouldn't change the fact that most people *are* affected by it. Second, researchers propose that media violence increases a person's *risk of aggression*, not that violent media causes all users to become violent (especially since most people are fairly low in aggressive tendencies to begin with). Third, it's a bad idea to rely on people to accurately gauge how a lifetime of something has influenced something as complex and slow-changing as their personality: It would be like eating junk food and waiting to see whether you could "feel" the increase in your risk for heart disease. Finally, this question confuses violence and aggression. Aggression is any behavior, physical, relational, or verbal, that is intended to cause harm (and the intended victim would want to avoid such harm). Violence is only physical, and is extreme, such that if successful it would cause severe bodily harm or death. Consuming violent entertainment is more likely to increase mild forms of aggression (e.g., make you more willing to say something rude when provoked) than it is to make you try to kill someone.

The Long Answer:

Critics and laypersons alike frequently ask this question as a "gotcha" to media researchers. It takes many different forms, but they often look something like this:

"If violent media makes the people who consume it violent, then I, as a regular consumer of violent media, should be violent. But I haven't killed anyone in real life, so I'm not violent. Therefore, you're wrong that violent media causes everyone to become violent!"

Because we, as media researchers, so frequently encounter this argument, we've become pretty good at dismantling its logic. It's actually not all that hard to do so: The argument falls apart for at *least* four different reasons.

To illustrate the first reason, let's assume for a moment that our skeptic is 100% correct: For whatever reason the skeptic is, as they claim, completely immune to media violence. Years of violent video games haven't done a thing to the skeptic – they are a rare exception to all of the research suggesting that there's no reason to believe that anyone should be immune to media violence effects (see Question #19).

What, exactly, does the existence of our immune skeptic prove?

Well, the skeptic's immunity *does* disprove the claim that "Violent media increases the risk of aggression for *every single person who consumes it without exception.*" But what if media researchers argue "Okay, so violent media increases the risk of aggression for *most people*" or "Violent media increases the risk of aggression for *the average person*"? The existence of a single immune person, or even *dozens* of immune people, doesn't change the fact that these other statements are *still true.* For instance: If media violence increased the risk of aggression for 99% of the population, the 1% of unaffected people would not change the fact that *most* people are still affected by violent media. If one were to accept the skeptic's line of reasoning, they should also should believe that smoking cigarettes isn't a risk for lung cancer because *two-thirds of* smokers don't die of lung cancer.

This is all assuming that our skeptic is *correct* when they claim to be immune to media violence effects. By delving into this assumption we'll see the second reason why the skeptic's argument fails.

Research introduced in earlier questions (e.g., Question #19) makes it clear that our skeptic's assumed immunity is unlikely true. After all, there's little evidence suggesting that any particular type of person is immune to media violence effects. To be fair, our skeptic is probably correct when they say that they're not a violent person. After all, violence is pretty rare and extreme, and most people would probably know if they've done something violent (e.g., had a serious fight, tried to maim or kill someone). (This is, of course, another serious problem with this argument – it treats violence as equivalent to all other forms of aggression.)

But not being violent doesn't mean that your *risk of aggression* hasn't been increased by years of media violence (see Questions #28 and #35 for more on this). It's entirely possible that violent media consumption has raised our skeptic's overall risk of aggression (e.g., from "not at all" to "mildly hostile") *without* making them violent. As an analogy, imagine if a person claimed "I've eaten junk food my whole life and I haven't once had a heart attack! That means junk food has had *no effect* whatsoever on my health!" This claim is pretty ridiculous because we *know* that there are other ways to measure a person's health than whether or not they've had a heart attack. By only looking at the most extreme outcome (violence, heart attack), it's easy to overlook all of the subtler results of one's actions (e.g., verbal aggression, high blood pressure).

But there's a third reason why our skeptic's claims that they're unaffected by violent media are faulty. To illustrate this fault, let's start by being generous and assuming that our skeptic *is* making the more subtle, nuanced argument: Their overall level of aggression has stayed constant across their entire life and, because of this, it's impossible that they've been affected by violent media.

217

This assumption relies on the skeptic to measure their own aggression. This is a problem because our personalities change extremely slowly and gradually over time[1,2], making it unlikely that our skeptic would notice the change themselves. Think about it for yourself: Would you say that you've become *more* outgoing, *less* outgoing, or are just as outgoing as you were when you were a teenager? As it turns out, research shows that most people become more outgoing throughout adolescence and into their 20s[3]. Was this your experience? Do you *remember* this change first-hand, and can you pinpoint the moment when you *became* more outgoing? Do you remember what, exactly, *caused* the change to happen? Or, more likely, do you feel like you're the same sort of person you've always been? Chances are pretty good that, despite our skeptic believing their aggression hadn't changed, they wouldn't have noticed it even if it had.[a]

And this isn't the *only* reason we should be dubious about our skeptic's claim that their aggression hasn't changed. In Question #12 we discussed several of the mechanisms behind media violence effects, one of which is desensitization to violence[4]. In a nutshell, becoming desensitized means having a weaker and weaker reaction to violence[5], seeing an action as less violent[6], and believing an act of violence is more appropriate or normal[7] each time you're exposed to it. If being exposed to violent media *does* desensitize people to violence, how could our skeptic recognize whether their own aggression was increasing? If their aggression gradually escalated from minor acts in the past (e.g., insults, shouting) to more intense forms of aggression today (e.g., threats, shoving), they might not notice the increase, since they might not consider threats or shoving to be aggression at all. In this case, we can't trust the measurement tool we're using because the way we use the tool itself is changing over time.

But there's one more reason to doubt the skeptic's claim that their aggression hasn't changed over time: What's their point of reference? What are they comparing their aggression to? To see why this lack of an objective reference point is important, let's once again assume that it's *completely* true that the skeptic's aggression has not changed despite consuming thousands of hours of violent media. How can we know that violent media hasn't affected them *without* knowing how aggressive they *would* have been if they hadn't seen all that violent media? For example, studies show that people tend to become *less* aggressive as they get older[8]. This means that, if anything, we should expect our skeptic's level of aggression to *drop* over time. If it "only" stayed the same, that could *actually* be evidence that violent media *has* increased their aggression compared to what it

---

[a] This isn't to say that our skeptic couldn't detect large, dramatic changes in their personality over time (e.g., going from a very timid person to a violent bully). But when it comes to personality, huge changes like these are the exception rather than the rule. Slow, gradual shifts in tendencies over years tend to be the norm.

would otherwise have been (see Figure 29.1). And even if their aggression *has* declined over time, there's still no way to know that it wouldn't have declined *more* if they weren't exposed to violent media. In short, it's impossible for our skeptic to provide the evidence needed to prove the claim they're making about whether violent media has affected them.

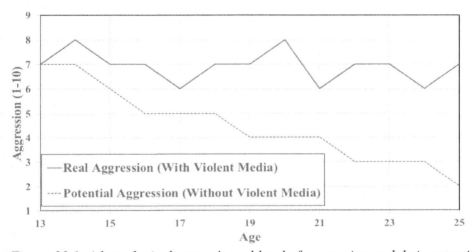

Figure 29.1. A hypothetical person's real level of aggression and their potential level of aggression if they hadn't been exposed to violent media.

In sum: It's tempting to test the hypothesis that violent media affects our risk of aggression using our own experience. Unfortunately, anecdote and introspection are not accurate ways to objectively and systematically collect data to test hypotheses. This is precisely why good social scientists rely on carefully-constructed studies, rather than merely asking people whether they *think* they've been affected by violent media. These studies aren't as intuitive as our own experience is, but they *are* specifically designed to tell us what your own intuitions simply can't.

References
1. Costa, P. T. Jr., Herbst, J. H., McCrae, R. R., & Siegler, I. C. (2000). Personality at midlife: Stability, intrinsic maturation, and response to life events. *Assessment, 7*(4), 365-378.
2. Roberts, B. W., & DelVecchio, W. F. (2000). The rank-order consistency of personality traits from childhood to old age: A quantitative review of longitudinal studies. *Psychological Bulletin, 126*(1), 3-25.

3. Roberts, B. W., Walton, K. E., & Viechtbauer, W. (2006). Patterns of mean-level change in personality traits across the life course: A meta-analysis of longitudinal studies. *Psychological Bulletin, 132*(1), 1-25.
4. Anderson, C. A. & Bushman, B. J. (2002). Human Aggression. *Annual Review of Psychology, 53,* 27-51.
5. Cline, V. B., Croft, R. G., & Courrier, S. (1973). Desensitization of children to television violence. *Journal of Personality and Social Psychology, 27*(3), 360-365.
6. Romer, D., Jamieson, P. E., Bushman, B. J., Bleakley, A., Wang, A., Langleben, D., & Jamieson, K. H. (2014). Parental desensitization to violence and sex in movies. *Pediatrics, 134,* 877-884.
7. Gentile, D. A., Anderson, C. A., Yukawa, S., Ihori, N., Saleem, M., Ming, L. K., Shibuya, A., Liau, A. K., Khoo, A., Bushman, B. J., Huesmann, L. R., & Sakamoto, A. (2009). The effects of prosocial video games on prosocial behaviors: International evidence from correlational, longitudinal, and experimental studies. *Personality and Social Psychology Bulletin, 35,* 752-763.
8. Harris, M. B. (1996). Aggressive experiences and aggressiveness: Relationship to ethnicity, gender, and age. *Journal of Applied Social Psychology, 26*(10), 843-870.

30 - Haven't violent crime rates fallen during the same period that violent media grew in popularity?

The Short Answer:

Yes, rates of some types of violent crime *have* declined in the United States since the early 1970s, although mass shootings[a] have increased dramatically. During this same period of time there was considerable growth in the prevalence of violent media (e.g., shooter-type video games). These two statistics do not, however, provide a valid test of whether media violence effects occur. As media researchers have pointed out for over a decade, this line of reasoning makes sense only if you assume that media violence is the *only* factor that contributes to societal violence.[1] In reality, crime rates are affected by numerous economic, social, and political factors, meaning that they're not particularly responsive to the effects of any one risk factor. What's more, measures of violent crime only consider the most *extreme* forms of aggression, while media violence effects are most easily observed in day-to-day forms of aggression. As a final point, group-level data (e.g., population statistics) can't effectively tell scientists about changes that are happening within individual people. For all of these reasons, changes in violent crime rates cannot answer the question of whether media violence effects exist.

The Long Answer:

The word "mass" in "mass media" hints at just how large-scale the implications of violent media consumption can be: Millions of people consuming billions of hours of content every year. Because of this massive scale, it makes sense that one would want to use data on an equally large scale to test for the effects of violent media. After all, if violent media really *does* increase aggressive behavior for everyone in society who consumes it, shouldn't we be able to detect these effects in statistics about our society's level of violence? By this same logic, if societal violence doesn't increase but, in fact, *decreases* as our society's level of violent media use increases, isn't that evidence that violent media *can't* be a risk factor for aggression?

Like many skeptical arguments described in this chapter, this argument makes intuitive sense because it has several kernels of truth buried within it. For example, trends in crime statistics are undisputable: Official agencies *clearly* show

---

[a] What the FBI calls "active shooting incidents."

that, whether we're looking at the past 40 years[2], the past 20 years[3], or even just the past few years[4], average violent crime rates (averaged across different types of crimes) are declining in the U.S. What's more, this decline has been happening at a time when both video game and television use is on the rise. But even though these statistics paint an accurate picture of societal trends, they actually tell us very little about the effects that violent media have on individual people.

To understand why this is the case, let's first remember that aggression, like all human behavior, has multiple causes (see Questions #14 and #24). Media violence is just one risk factor among many[5,6] other large risk factors for aggression (e.g., poverty, history of experienced violence). Keeping this in mind, what exactly *do* changes in violent crime rates tell us about media violence *specifically*?

The original question suggests that falling crime rates tell us that violent media can't be a risk factor because, if it were, violent crime rates would be increasing. This makes a pretty big assumption, however: For this to be true, it would mean that violent media exposure is either the *only* risk factor for violent crime, or that it is such a large risk factor that it overwhelms all of the other risk factors. But we just agreed that a lot of factors affect violent crime: the increasing average age of the population, increasing standard of living, reduced alcohol use, the decline in drug wars, and changes in police practices, "three strikes and you're out" laws, to name just a few.[7] Many of these factors decrease the rate of violent crime. So if you say that violent media should be increasing crime rates despite all of these other factors that are reducing crime rates, you're claiming that violent media plays a larger role than all of these societal factors combined. That is an absurd position that no media violence researcher we know of holds. And yet, this is precisely the straw-man position that's being propped up when critics argue that media violence effects can't be real if the nation's crime rates are going down.

The position *also* overlooks the fact that it's possible for violent media to have a small, incremental effect on violent crime rates even as violent crime rates are otherwise falling (we introduce this idea, at the level of individuals, in Question #29, Figure 29.1). To illustrate what we mean, let's imagine that because of changes in all other risk and protective factors the rate of violent crime would be going down by 10% each year in a world without violent media. But, with the addition of violent media, the drop in violent crime each year shrinks from 10% to 7.5% per year. In this case, violent crime rates are *still* decreasing overall, but violent media are *still* having a harmful effect, because they're *reducing* the rate in which violent crime is declining.[b] Unless we can compare current violent crime

---

[b] As an analogy: Imagine you're in a car and you're hitting the gas, speeding up to 60 mph. At the same time, you've accidentally left the car's emergency brake on. In all likelihood, the car would continue to accelerate and eventually reach 60

rates to the rates of violent crime in an alternate universe *without* violent media, rates of violent crime by themselves can tell us very little about media violence effects.

But even if we *could* use statistical techniques to figure out what violent crime rates would be like with and without violent media, the original argument is *still* flawed for another reason: It's based on a measure of criminal-level violence, not aggression. As we've discussed elsewhere (Questions #7, #29, #35), violence is only a tiny fraction of aggressive behavior – only the rare, most extreme physically aggressive behavior. Trying to measure media violence effects on extreme violent behavior would be like trying to measure the weight of a feather using a scale built for trucks: The measurement device just isn't sensitive enough, since numerous risk factors are needed to create violent behavior and media violence is only one such risk factor – and a modest one at that. To have a better chance of detecting media violence effects it would be better to use measures of normal, day-to-day aggression like insulting, shouting, or relational sabotage – things that aren't measured in violent crime statistics. As we mention in Question #29, a person who eats junk food and does not have a heart attack cannot claim that junk food has had *no* effect on their health, only that it hasn't caused them to experience one particularly extreme health outcome.

But even if we ignore these other issues, there's still a third problem with using violent crime data in this way: It's a measure of a *group* outcome, not an *individual* outcome.

Measures of group behavior are best used to understand group-level phenomena (e.g., using the country's GDP to understand the impact of certain economic policies). It's a bad idea to use group-level data to try to understand the behavior of individuals because things that happen at the level of groups don't easily translate into things that happen at the level of individuals. In fact, the problem of using societal level data (such as crime rates) to draw inferences about individual level effects (media violence) is so well-understood among scientists that it has its own name: the *ecological fallacy*.

To illustrate the ecological fallacy, let's consider how group-level data can be misapplied to individuals. If the USA decides to go to war with Canada,[c] it would be silly to say that "the average American is at war with the average

---

mph. It would be silly to argue that the emergency brake had *no* effect on the car just because the car accelerated. The car was accelerating *despite* the emergency brake, not *because* the emergency brake had no effect. Ultimately, the engine has a bigger effect on the car's speed than the emergency brake did, and the car would have accelerated *faster* if the effect of the emergency brake weren't working against it.

[c] The sole Canadian author, Courtney, is understandably not a fan of this example!

Canadian." After all, America would still be at war with Canada even if 80% of Americans were *opposed* to the war! It just doesn't make sense to draw conclusions about the thoughts, feelings, and behaviors of individual people from information about the group. Media researchers avoid this problem by studying media violence effects at the level of individuals: By studying how violent media affect the way individual people think and feel, how people learn aggressive scripts, and how people become desensitized to violence[8] (see Question #12). It just doesn't make sense to say that media violence has desensitized a *country*, caused a *country* to have aggressive thoughts, or caused a country to have a higher crime rate.[d]

As a final note, it's actually not that hard to flip this flawed style of reasoning on its head and similarly find violent crime data that "prove" that violent video games increase violent crime at a societal level. First, ask yourself what type of violence is most frequently modeled in violent video games: A character shooting and killing lots of enemies. Theory and research tell us that violent media effects accumulate over time. That is, it can take years for violent media to change a child's personality enough to be noticeable. So if mass-shooter type video games started becoming popular in the 1990s, and we assume that it takes 10 or more years of such games to begin influencing real-world mass shootings, we can ask whether mass shootings have increased, declined, or stayed about the same since about 2000. The FBI have such data, as shown in Figure 30.1. Clearly mass shootings (active shooting incidents) have increased since 2000. We can thus "prove" that violent video games cause increases in mass shootings, right?[e] Wrong!

---

[d] If you're still struggling to understand why the ecological fallacy is a problem, let's try one more example. Imagine that you discovered that a *group* of people had an average "aggressive thought" score of 5 out of 10. What does this number *actually* tell us about the individuals in that group? Does half of the group score "10" and half of the group score "0"? Does everyone score "5"? These critical details are *completely* lost when you look at population-level statistics.

[e] To be crystal-clear, we're using this example only to show you how flawed this line of reasoning is. It would be silly to blame mass shootings solely on violent video games, just as it would be silly to say that a decline in violence rates tells us something about media violence effects (or, as some critics want to argue, show that violent media *reduces* violent crime rates!).

224

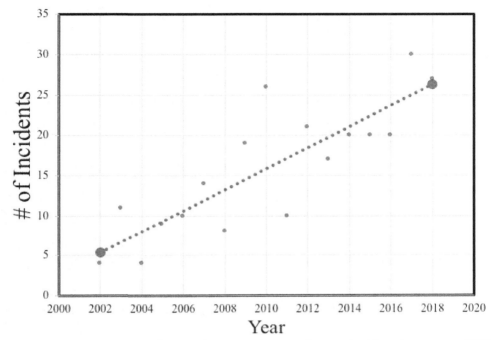

Figure 30.1. Frequency of mass shootings (active shooter incidents) per year, FBI data.

To summarize: It's intuitive to assume that media violence effects can't be real if violent crime has dropped while violent media use is up. This conclusion is based on several misrepresentations and misunderstandings about what, if anything, a nation's crime statistics can tell us about the effects of violent media on individual people. Although crime data are important for numerous reasons (e.g., establishing law enforcement policies), they are largely irrelevant to the question of media violence effects on *individual* people.[f]

References

1. Anderson, C.A., & Bushman, B.J. (2002). Media violence and the American public revisited. *American Psychologist, 57,* 448-450.

---

[f] Note that one *can* sometimes glean something of value from such multi-level analyses, but only if other key risk factors are measured and statistically controlled, so that all major plausible alternative explanations can be ruled out. Suffice it to say, high-quality multi-level analyses using large datasets and solid measures of media violence and aggression are few and far-between, especially when it comes to society-level data.

2. Federal Bureau of Investigation (2014). *United States Population and Rate of Crime per 100,000 People 1960-2014.* Compiled by, and retrieved from, http://www.disastercenter.com/crime/uscrime.htm
3. Federal Bureau of Investigation (2012). *Crime in the United States by Volume and Rate per 100,000 Inhabitants, 1993-2012.* Retrieved from http://ucr.fbi.gov/crime-in-the-u.s/2012/crime-in-the-u.s.-2012/tables/1tabledatacoverviewpdf/table_1_crime_in_the_united-states_by_volume_and_rate_per_100000_inhabitants_1993-2012.xls
4. Federal Bureau of Investigation (2013). *Violent Crime Offense Figure: Five-Year Trend, 2009-2013.* Retrieved from http://ucr.fbi.gov/crime-in-the-u.s/2013/crime-in-the-u.s.-2013/violent-crime/violent-crime-topic-page/violentcrimemain_final
5. Exelmans, L., Custers, K., & Van den Bulck, J. (2015). Violent video games and delinquent behavior in adolescents: A risk factor perspective. *Aggressive Behavior, 41,* 267-279.
6. Gentile, D., A. & Bushman, B. J. (2012). Reassessing media violence effects using a risk and resilience approach to understanding aggression. *Psychology of Popular Media Culture, 1*(3), 138-151.
7. Roeder, O., Eisen, L. B., & Bowling, J. (2015). *What Caused the Crime Decline?* New York University: Brennan Center for Justice.
8. Anderson, C. A. & Bushman, B. J. (2002). Human Aggression. *Annual Review of Psychology, 53,* 27-51.

31 - Don't violent media reduce aggression by getting it out of your system?

The Short Answer:

No. This belief is called *catharsis of aggression*, and it's based on a psychological concept that's been outdated for decades. It's true that someone may feel better after playing a violent video game or watching a violent film, especially if it distracts them from other worries or stresses. But this doesn't mean that the violent media has "vented" the aggression out of them or made them any less likely to be aggressive. This is because violent media *increases* your body's arousal (e.g., heart rate), activates aggressive thoughts in your mind, both of which make aggression *more* likely to happen in the minutes following exposure. Even worse, with repeated exposure, the odds of responding aggressively when provoked increase over time. Repetition increases learning, it doesn't reduce it.

The Long Answer:

Regular consumers of violent media will often insist that they play violent games, listen to violent music, or watch violent movies because it helps them vent the anger and frustration that they've been building up all day, making them less likely to be aggressive. As an example of what this might look like, let's imagine that Annie had a *really* bad day. It started with Annie getting stuck in a traffic jam and being late for work, which caused her to get yelled at by her boss. To top it all off, when Annie gets home, her neighbors are once again ignoring her past complaints and blaring their loud, annoying music. Annie decides to unwind from her crappy day by playing a violent video game. In the game she acts on the frustration she's been feeling all day. Instead of attacking the other drivers, her boss, or her neighbors, Annie instead punches, shoots, and blows up digital characters. After a couple hours of playing, Annie's mood is much better. Annie believes it's because the violent game helped her work the frustration and anger out of her system. She felt like she had to attack something, so it's better, she argues, that she attacks a video game character instead of a real person. For this reason, she believes that violent games *reduce* her aggression by giving her a "pressure release valve" for her aggressive desires.

If you're a regular player of violent video games, Annie's story may resonate with you. We *all* get frustrated from time to time. In those moments it often feels like the only thing that can make us feel better is to hit something.[a] This is why, on its face, Annie's claim seems to hold water. After all, if hitting something is the only way to make a frustrated person feel better, isn't it better that they hit something digital, rather than a piece of property, an animal, or a person? Of course! But *ideally* it would be better to reduce that person's frustration in the first place, or at the very least eliminate their *need* to hit something (digital or otherwise) to calm down. Given that aggression researchers have this goal in mind, the cracks in Annie's argument begin to show themselves. It only gets worse for the argument when you look at what decades of psychological research on frustration and aggression have to say on the subject.

The problems with Annie's argument begin with her assumption that a frustrated person has to lash out at something to get rid of the frustration. To be sure, when you feel that white-hot flash of rage, it can often *seem* like the only thing that'll satisfy your anger is to hit something to vent that anger. For a long time psychologists and psychotherapists generally agreed with this idea: Freud[2] believed that powerful emotions like anger built up over time like steam pressure in a boiler. As that pressure builds, he argued, it needs to go *somewhere*, otherwise it eventually leads to an outburst. He believed that you could release this pressure in a safe way, before it built to a dangerous level, through a purging process called *catharsis*. In catharsis, you release some of your emotional pressure by either engaging in acceptable versions of the desired behavior (e.g., punching a pillow) or by witnessing aggression in others (e.g., watching television violence). For Aristotle, this included watching plays that featured acts of violence, while Freud preferred having patients express their anger in therapy sessions. This hydraulic model of anger and frustration with a catharsis pressure release valve persisted well into 1970s psychology. And among laypersons, the idea remains popular to this day.

Although the concept of catharsis is both popular and intuitive, more than fifty years of psychological research have found almost no evidence to support it,[3,4,5] and a great deal of evidence against it. As an illustration of this, let's look at what a test of catharsis theory involves. In one study, college students were first asked to write an essay about their opinion on abortion[5]. When they were done, they were told that another person had critiqued their essay. Unfortunately for the participant, the reader (who was not an actual participant) described their essay as one of the worst pieces of writing they had ever seen. This feedback was designed to anger the participants. Participants were then divided into one of three conditions. In one condition, the participants were shown a picture of their critic, and were asked to keep the picture in mind while they hit a punching bag. This was the catharsis condition, since participants were encouraged to channel their anger into hitting the punching bag instead of the critic (while thinking of the

---

[a] As a testament to this fact, one of the authors will admit to having broken several of his fingers after punching a wall in frustration.

critic themselves). Participants hit a punching bag in another condition, but instead of thinking about their critic, they were asked to think about fitness and physical health. This was a distraction condition, designed to test the effects of taking your mind off of whatever was making you angry. In the third condition, participants were asked to sit in a room quietly for 2 minutes and just do nothing. This condition was a "do nothing" control condition against which to compare the other conditions.

After doing their requested activities, all of the participants completed a measure which asked them how hostile they felt at that moment. They were then given a chance to blast their critic with painfully loud noise as a measure of aggressive behavior (see Question #8 for more on this task). Since the researchers had set the experiment up so that *everyone* was mad at the critic at the start of the study, the different groups' scores on these measures would let the researchers test which group felt the most hostile and behaved the most aggressively after a cathartic activity, a distracting activity, or simply doing nothing. If catharsis really *does* reduce aggression, those who punched the punching bag while thinking about the critic should have "vented" their anger and felt the least angry and behaved the least aggressive at the end of the study, while those who just sat around or were distracted wouldn't have had a chance to "vent" this anger, and should be the *most* aggressive.

So what did the researchers find? The exact *opposite* of what catharsis theory would predict: Participants in the "catharsis" condition were actually the *angriest* and gave the most aggressive blasts of noise to the critic. In contrast, participants who just sat there doing nothing for two minutes seemed the most calmed down and showed the least aggressive behavior. The study found no evidence that "venting" your anger gets it out of your system, and instead suggests that venting might actually make things worse![b]

How can we explain the results of this study, which seem to fly in the face of catharsis? As it turns out, theories like the General Aggression Model (GAM), which we introduced in Question #12 offer us a plausible explanation[6]. According to the GAM, aggressive behavior becomes more likely to occur when a person has more risk factors. Some of these risk factors include having aggressive thoughts on your mind, being physiologically aroused (e.g., an elevated heart rate), or feeling angry.

Knowing this, let's compare the participants in the catharsis condition and the do nothing condition. In the catharsis condition, participants keep their aggressive thoughts activated by continuously dwelling on the critic, which also likely keeps them in an angry mood. And by hitting the punching bag, the participants are rehearsing aggressive responding and are keeping their heart rate

---

[b] This study reminds us of a quote which is often erroneously attributed to the Buddha, which reads: "Holding on to anger is like grasping a hot coal with the intent of throwing it at someone else; you are the one who gets burned."

229

elevated with the exercise. All three of these risk factors increase the participant's likelihood of aggression. In contrast, participants in the "do nothing" condition were, if anything, probably a bit bored. When people are bored, their minds wander, which means participants' thoughts were probably meandering away from the critic and onto something else entirely, causing them to feel less angry. And, since their bodies were doing nothing as they just sat there, their heart rate was probably levelling off. As such, the participants in this condition were lacking *three* of the risk factors that participants in the catharsis condition had, making them less likely to actually be aggressive. Although it might have *felt* good for people in the catharsis condition to imagine they were punching their critics, doing so did nothing to actually reduce their aggression.

It would seem that cathartic acts are an ineffective way to reduce aggressive feelings in the minutes following a provocation. And if that's all catharsis was, aggression researchers probably wouldn't make such a big deal about it. But catharsis can actually lead to *more* aggression in the long run, making it a much more serious problem. To see why, let's return to the GAM, which states that one of the risk factors for being more aggressive across a multitude of situations is having readily-available, well-learned aggressive scripts. People who have practiced aggressive behavior repeatedly start to develop automatic aggressive responses. These automatic aggressive responses rear their ugly head when someone has to make a split-second decision or a decision under pressure.

Now imagine a person who punches a pillow, throws a controller, or seeks out digital violence every time they're angry. Each time they do this, they're reinforcing a specific aggressive script: "When you're angry, hit or break something." Each time they engage in this script they're rewarded: An angry person who attacks someone in a video game and feels better for it and will come to associate this aggression with pleasure. To be fair, this isn't a problem if the *only* things you ever hit, insulted, or destroyed were digital. Unfortunately, when someone gets angry and *doesn't* have their video game console on-hand (e.g., at work, on the drive home from work, or dealing with an argument with their neighbors), these same behavioral scripts will drive real-world behavior. The fact is, many situations require a split-second decision about whether to be aggressive or not and don't give players the chance to retreat to their video game console. This is how real aggression results from supposedly-cathartic media violence.

Let's return once more to Annie's original argument and ask ourselves a final question about catharsis: Even if it isn't an effective way to reduce aggression, why does using violent media for catharsis *feel* good? Studies show that playing violent video games increases player anger[7], arousal[8], aggressive thoughts[9], and aggressive behavior[10], sure. But players also report feeling *great* after playing a violent game. Are they just lying to protect their hobby?

Probably not. Chances are good that players are being honest when they report feeling better after playing a violent video game. What may be happening, however, is that players are mixing up exactly *what* they're feeling. When players are saying "I'm becoming relaxed" or "my angry mood is improving," what they may *actually* be experiencing is the satisfaction that comes from accomplishing a goal. Accomplishing goals feels good, while failing to accomplish a goal is frustrating. When we fail to satisfy a goal, we often switch between goals to allow us to feel the satisfaction of accomplishing a different goal[11,12]. So if Annie spent all day being frustrated at work (e.g., being forced to do something she'd rather not do), being frustrated on the drive home (e.g., being prevented from getting home in a timely manner), and being frustrated by her neighbors (e.g., her goal of having a relaxing evening), she may feel good playing a game that lets her accomplish a goal. The positivity she's feeling probably has nothing to do with her being less angry or aggressive toward her boss or her neighbors, but instead has to do with her feeling better about accomplishing a goal that just happens to involve aggression (e.g., killing enemy soldiers). What's more, by playing the game, Annie was probably distracted from thinking about her rotten day, which might improve her mood without having anything to do with in-game aggression itself.

The take-away message is this: Although violent media may certainly *feel* good as a recreational activity, a distraction, and a way to satisfying our need to accomplish goals, this isn't evidence that violent media reduce aggression through catharsis. Numerous studies show that catharsis simply doesn't reduce aggression and may, if anything, increase a person's likelihood of aggressing, both in the short run and in the long run.

So what *can* people do to reduce their aggression? Research suggests that the best strategies involve reducing physiological arousal, getting away from the source of frustration, and distracting yourself from aggressive thoughts. Activities that are low in excitement such as walking, reading a book, or taking a relaxing bath can help to reduce your heart rate and make you less worked up, all while engaging you in a distracting, non-aggressive task. Similarly, building something or chatting with friends can help to distance you from the frustrating event and keep you from ruminating on it. You can even rely on games or media that *don't* include violence, like puzzle-solving games or comedy films. These media may reduce your physiological arousal while also providing the distraction needed to get your mind off of aggressive thoughts.

We'll finish this section with references to catharsis papers which nicely summarize the effects of catharsis for those who want even more details.[5,13] In one paper, the authors state that relying on catharsis to reduce aggression is "like using gasoline to put out a fire."[5]

References
1. Catharsis. (n.d.). In *Encyclopædia Britannica*. Retrieved from https://www.britannica.com/art/catharsis-criticism
2. Breuer, J., & Freud, S. (1893-1895). *Studies on Hysteria* (Standard ed., Vol. 2). London: Hogarth. (Original work published 1955).

3. Hornberger, R. H. (1959). The differential reduction of aggressive responses as a function of interpolated activities. *American Psychologist, 14,* 354.

4. Geen, R. G., & Quanty, M. B. (1977). The catharsis of aggression: An evaluation of a hypothesis. In L. Berkowitz (Ed.), *Advances in Experimental Social Psychology* (Vol. 10, pp. 1-37). New York: Academic Press.

5. Bushman, B. J. (2002). Does venting anger feed or extinguish the flame? Catharsis, rumination, distraction, anger, and aggressive responding. *Personality and Social Psychology Bulletin, 28*(6), 724-731.

6. Anderson, C. A. & Bushman, B. J. (2002). Human Aggression. *Annual Review of Psychology, 53,* 27-51.

7. Markey, P. M., & Scherer, K. (2009). An examination of psychoticism and motion capture controls as moderators of the effects of violent video games. *Computers in Human Behavior, 25,* 407-411.

8. Barlett, C., Branch, O., Rodeheffer, C., & Harris, R. (2009). How long to do the short-term violent video game effects last? *Aggressive Behavior, 35*(3), 225-236.

9. Kirsh, S. J., Olczak, P. V., & Mounts, J. R. W. (2005). Violent video games induce an affect processing bias. *Media Psychology, 7,* 239-250.

10. Schutte, N. S., Malouff, J. M., Post-Gorden, J. C., & Rodasta, A. L. (1988). Effects of playing videogames on children's aggressive and other behaviors. *Journal of Applied Social Psychology, 5*(18), 454-460.

11. Schmidt, A. M., & Dolis, C. M. (2009). Something's got to give: The effects of dual-goal difficulty, goal progress, and expectancies on resource allocation. *Journal of Applied Psychology, 94*(3), 678-691.

12. Louro, M. J., Pieters, R., & Zeelenberg, M. (2007). Dynamics of multiple-goal pursuit. *Journal of Personality and Social Psychology, 93*(2), 174-193.

13. Gentile, D. A. (2013). Catharsis and media violence: A conceptual analysis. *Societies, 3,* 491–510; doi:10.3390/soc3040491. Available at: https://www.mdpi.com/2075-4698/3/4/491/htm

32 - Why is becoming desensitized to violence a big deal?

The Short Answer:

Media violence reduces how much people respond physiologically (e.g., heart rate) and emotionally (e.g., fear, discomfort) to being exposed to scenes of blood, gore, and violence. By itself, this desensitization isn't a problem. In fact, for some jobs (e.g., doctors, soldiers) it's essential to be desensitized to blood, gore, and violence so that people can do their jobs effectively. But the revulsion that people normally feel toward violence and its consequences is a normal, built-in deterrent that makes people feel uncomfortable about even the thought of severely harming others. In essence, these automatic, negative emotional reactions to images of violence and sounds of distress reduce our likelihood of engaging in severe aggression against others. When someone becomes desensitized to violence, this "brake system" for violent behavior is removed. Desensitization can also make us feel less empathy toward the victims of violence, which may make us feel less motivated to help them.

The Long Answer:

Desensitization is based on a psychological principle known as habituation or extinction.[a] In essence, when a person is repeatedly exposed to something, their physical or emotional response to it becomes weaker. For example, one of the authors has an office where the pipes rattle loudly several times a day. The first time this happened, it scared the heck out of him. But each time after the first, he slowly, but surely, became less and less startled by the sound. Eventually, he stopped noticing it altogether: He habituated to the sound. This principle is well-known to psychologists, and has been used in the treatment of phobias[1] and other anxiety disorders[2].

But in the current context, we're not talking about desensitizing a person to an irrational fear of spiders, snakes, or airplanes. Instead, we're talking about

---

[a] The terms "habituation" and "extinction" actually have different meanings for psychologists. For the purposes of this book, we treat them as being synonymous. We're including this footnote to a) alert non-psychologist readers to the fact that they're not quite the same, and b) alert psychology experts that we know and understand the difference! So you don't need to send us emails wagging your fingers at us. Instead, encourage your colleagues to buy this book so you can all gather around and have a good laugh at our expense.

233

becoming desensitized to violence and its consequences (e.g., bruises, blood, gore, or other signs of injury, screaming, and other pain cues). What exactly does it mean to become desensitized to violence? Well, a normal response to being exposed to violent, bloody, or gory sights and sounds is an increase in physiological arousal (e.g., sweating, feeling startled, racing heart), to become anxious, and to feel generally uncomfortable[3]. A person who is desensitized by being repeatedly exposed to violent scenes, however, experiences far weaker reactions[4,5].

We can learn about media desensitization to violence from the experience of one of the book's authors. Courtney vividly recalls the first time he saw the gory horror film *Saw*. The film features graphic scenes of mutilation and torture, including a scene in which the main character uses the titular weapon to cut off his own foot in a prolonged scene. Needless to say, Courtney spent a fair chunk of the movie feeling nauseated, sweating, and generally being uncomfortable. Despite his better judgment, Courtney went on to watch the next six (yes, six!) films in the series, each of which contained just as many bloody and gruesome scenes.[b] And yet, by the third or fourth film, he had stopped being fazed by the on-screen violence. He no longer felt squeamish and felt none of the same anxiety. In fact, the violence had become almost boring to him by that point – it felt to him more like a distraction from the film's plot rather than the central feature of the film. This is a clear case of Courtney becoming desensitized to blood and gore due to his repeated exposure to the content of these films.

This kind of desensitization can occur even with brief exposures to violent media. In one experiment, college student participants played a randomly assigned violent or nonviolent game for 20 minutes.[4] Afterwards, they watched a 10-min video containing scenes of real violence while measures of physiological arousal were monitored. As shown in Figure 32.1, while watching real stabbings, shootings, and beatings, those who had just played a violent video game showed relatively smaller increases in heart rate and skin conductance (i.e., sweating) than those who had just played a violent game. In other words, they were less emotionally affected by the real violence.

---

[b] For those readers wondering why Courtney would subject himself to this, the answer is quite simple: He was dating someone who liked the films. Love makes people do strange things!

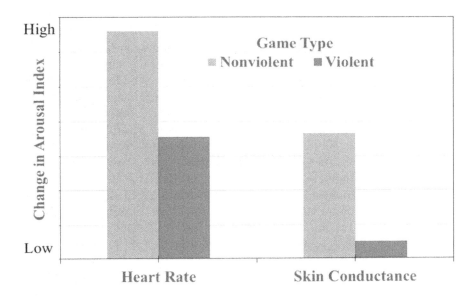

Figure 32.1. Increase in emotional arousal while watching real violence immediately after playing a violent or nonviolent video game. Playing a violent video game for 20 minutes decreases emotional reactions to real violence.

Funnily enough, consumers becoming desensitized to media violence is one of the *few* claims made by media violence researchers that consumers themselves frequently agree with. Instead of disputing whether people *actually* become desensitized to media violence, many consumers recognize that this is the case, and may even wear it as a badge of honor:

> *Everybody always complains so much on TV about video games "Desensitizing the youth of the world" blah, blah. Well, here's my question. Say I'm desensitized (which I think I am)... is it really so bad to be "desensitized"?*[6]

This quote comes from an online gaming forum. The poster's point illustrates how many critics don't dispute desensitization effects themselves, but instead asks whether it *matters* that they've become desensitized. As the forum discussion continues, participants go on to argue that they retain the ability to distinguish fantasy from reality, believing that this desensitization can't affect their real-world behavior (we address this claim in greater detail in Question #33). So it's worth addressing whether it *is* a big deal to become desensitized to violence. After all, it makes sense to be concerned about violent media increasing our aggressive thoughts, changing our beliefs about aggression, and teaching us aggressive scripts, since these are all risk factors for aggression.[7,8] But is desensitization to violence really a risk factor for aggression?

Before we begin, let's make it clear that desensitization to violence and its consequences is *necessary* for some occupations or situations. Personally, we prefer that our surgeon *not* vomit while performing open-heart surgery (into either our chest or the waste basket!). Similarly, one of the authors, Craig, served in the U.S. Army for several years, and recognizes the need for soldiers to be able to focus on fighting the enemy or stopping their buddy's bleeding wound in a foxhole *without* being paralyzed by fear or vomiting (or both).[c]

Those particular cases aside, let's talk about some of the effects that becoming desensitized to violence can have on a person. From a theoretical standpoint, desensitization to violence takes away a protective factor against aggression.[7] For example, if a person finds themselves in a situation where they have an aggressive impulse (e.g., desire to punch someone), they will normally hesitate to do so. Even if that person is not *consciously* thinking about the consequences of aggression, some part of them is likely repulsed by the thought of inflicting bruises, blood, or a broken bone on someone – or having that inflicted upon them. This revulsion is hard-wired into us, and likely has an evolutionary purpose[9]: People who are bothered by the sight of blood and injury probably avoided more unnecessary fights and reduced their likelihood of being killed, which improved their likelihood of surviving to reproduce. Lab studies find that people who *lack* this automatic repulsion due to desensitization by violent media are more likely to behave aggressively[10]. So, to answer the original question: It's bad to be desensitized to violence because it takes away one of the protective factors stopping us from engaging in unnecessary aggression.

But this isn't the *only* reason we should be concerned about desensitization. When we're not as bothered by or upset about the outcomes of violence, we also end up being less concerned about other people who are victims of violence. To illustrate this, participants in one study were randomly assigned to either view a violent slasher film every day for several days or they were assigned to not view any films at all[11]. At the end of the study, all participants were then asked to read and evaluate several cases of domestic abuse. Participants who watched the violent films showed less sympathy for the victims of domestic abuse and rated their injuries as less severe than participants who hadn't watched the violent films. And while these were only case studies, this insensitivity might similarly dampen our concern about someone we know who may be experiencing abuse and make us less likely to step in and help. What's a few bruises or cuts on a friend's arm to a person who's used to seeing blood and gore?

Other studies have indeed shown that people desensitized by media violence do become insensitive to, and refuse to intervene in, real-world violence. In one series of studies for example, children were randomly assigned to either view a violent movie or not[12,13]. Then, the children were given a simple job: Watch a live video feed of two young children playing in the next room (unknown

---

[c] Thankfully, despite serving in the Army, Craig was never in combat.

to the participants, it was a pre-recorded film and there were no children in the other room). Participants were asked to fetch the researcher if any problems arose with the children they were monitoring.

Shortly after the researcher left, the children on the monitor began to fight with one another, shouting at first, but eventually hitting one another. The researchers found that children who watched the violent film beforehand took longer to get help and were less likely to go get help at all compared to the children who did not watch the violent film. And if you're thinking that the researchers only found these effects because the participants were children, the same results were found in a similar study that used college student participants[14]. In this study, participants either played a violent or a non-violent video game. Later in the study, a fight was staged between two people outside the room, which included shouting, a chair being thrown against the laboratory door, and one of the actors crying out that they were hurt. Like the previous study, college students who had just played the violent game rated the victim's injuries as less severe, were less likely to help, took longer to help, and were less likely to even *notice* the fight. These results illustrate the chilling, real-world implications of becoming desensitized to violence: Not only are people more likely to become aggressive themselves, but they're less likely to offer assistance to a victim of violence.

To summarize: most people – researchers and laypersons alike – generally agree that violent media desensitize people to violence and its outcomes. This point isn't hotly contested; what *is* debated is whether we ought to care about this desensitization. Although it may not seem like a major problem, desensitization does makes people more likely to engage in aggression themselves. In fact, in some contexts, this is *precisely* the goal of violent media. The military, for example, uses violent video games to desensitize solders to ensure that they don't hesitate to shoot in a life-or-death situation[15]. But in addition to increasing the risk of aggression, desensitization also makes people less sympathetic to the victims of violence and less likely to intervene to stop violence from happening. In short, the effects of desensitization include a lot more than simply how much you squirm during a horror movie. Desensitization has significant implications for real-world violence and how we respond to it, which is why it's an issue that media violence researchers care greatly about.

References

1. Bandura, A., Reese, L., & Adams, N. E. (1982). Microanalysis of action and fear arousal as a function of differential levels of perceived self-efficacy. *Journal of Personality and Social Psychology, 43,* 5-21.
2. Pantalon, M. V., & Motta, R. W. (1998). Effectiveness of anxiety management training in the treatment of posttraumatic stress disorder: A preliminary report. *Journal of Behavior Therapy and Experimental Psychiatry, 29,* 21-29.

3. Bernat, E., Patrick, C. J., Benning, S. D., & Telelgen, A. (2006). Effects of picture content and intensity on affective physiological response.

4. Carnagey, N. L., Anderson, C. A., & Bushman, B. J. (2007). The effect of video game violence on physiological desensitization to real-life violence. *Journal of Experimental Social Psychology, 43,* 489-496.

5. Cline, V. B., Croft, R. G., & Courrier, S. (1973). Desensitization of children to television violence. *Journal of Personality and Social Psychology, 27*(3), 360-365.

6. blackngold29. (2008, January). Is being desensitized to violence a bad thing? (Read, don't jump to conclusions) [Msg 1]. Message posted to http://www.gamespot.com/forums/offtopic-discussion-314159273/is-being-desensitized-to-violence-a-bad-thing-read-26203648/

7. Anderson, C. A. & Bushman, B. J. (2002). Human Aggression. *Annual Review of Psychology, 53,* 27-51.

8. Anderson, C. A., Shibuya, A., Ihori, N., Swing, E. L., Bushman, B. J., Sakamoto, A., Rothstein, H. R., & Saleem, M. (2010). Violent video game effects on aggression, empathy, and prosocial behavior in eastern and western countries: a meta-analytic review. *Psychological Bulletin, 136*(2), 151-173.

9. Marks, I. (1988). Blood-injury phobia: A review. *The American Journal of Psychiatry, 145*(10), 1207-1213.

10. Engelhardt, C. R., Bartholow, B. D., Kerr, G. T., & Bushman, B. J. This is your brain on violent video games: Neural desensitization to violence predicts increased aggression following violent video game exposure. *Journal of Experimental Social Psychology, 47*(5), 1033-1036.

11. Mullin, C. R., & Linz, D. (1995). Desensitization and resensitization against women: Effects of exposure to sexually violent films on judgments of domestic violence victims. *Journal of Personality and Social Psychology, 69*(3), 449-459.

12. Drabman, R. S., & Thomas, M. H. (1974). Does media violence increase children's toleration of real-life aggression? *Developmental Psychology, 10*(3), 418-421.

13. Molitor, F. & Hirsch, K. W. (1994). Children's toleration of real-life aggression after exposure to media violence: A replication of the Drabman and Thomas studies. *Child Study Journal, 3*(24), 191-207.

14. Bushman, B. J., & Anderson, C. A. (2009). Comfortably numb: Desensitizing effects of violent media on helping others. *Psychological Science, 20*(3), 273-277.

15. Grossman, D., & DeGaetano, G. (1999). *Stop Teaching Our Kids to Kill: A call to action against TV, movie & video game violence.* New York, NY: Crown Publishers.

33 - Aren't you immune to media violence if you can tell the difference between fantasy and reality?

The Short Answer:

No, and it's really easy to see for yourself why this is the case! Chances are, you can recall a time when you've been affected by media despite knowing that its content isn't real (e.g., crying at a sad book, feeling fear during a scary movie, finding yourself compelled to buy a cool-looking product based on an amusing advertising campaign). To be sure, people who *can't* distinguish what's real from what's fake are probably *more* prone to media violence effects. But by age 7, most people *can* tell fantasy from reality, yet they're *still* affected by media violence. This is because media affects our feelings, thoughts, and behaviors in a variety of ways, almost none of which have to do with fooling us into believing that what we're seeing on-screen is real.

The Long Answer:

In Question #32 we looked at a quote from a video game forum which illustrated how the average person understands desensitization. When we revisit the same quote in its entirety, we see that the user has misconceptions about another media-related concept: users blurring the lines between fantasy and reality:

> Everybody always complains so much on TV about video games "desensitizing the youth of the world" blah, Blah. Well, here's my question. Say I'm desensitized (which I think I am): I still know what is right and wrong, and I will still help someone if they are in trouble, and I'm not going to hurt anyone else because I shot a grunt in Halo. So my question is as long as the lines between right and wrong, or media and the real world, aren't blurred, is it really so bad to be "desensitized"?[1]

The user acknowledges that violent media have probably had at least *some* effect on them, including making them less bothered by graphic displays of violence. But, they argue, this desensitization doesn't matter, since they can still tell the difference between the real world and the world of fantasy. The user recognizes that the actions carried out in violent media are *completely* inappropriate for them to do in real life. Because they have this knowledge, they argue, the media violence they're exposed to can't spill over into their real-world behavior.

Let's start unpacking the user's argument by first acknowledging one of the things that's likely *true* in their statement: Yes, a person who can't tell fantasy from reality is probably more likely to be influenced by media content. For evidence of this, we can look at research on a phenomenon called *fantasy proneness*.[2] Fantasy prone people, or "fantasizers," are people who become *extremely* involved in their fantasy worlds. They're not people who like fantasy a lot or who spend a lot of time daydreaming: They spend much of their time fantasizing and daydreaming *so* vividly that they have trouble telling what's fiction and what's reality.[3] As a result, fantasy prone people are more likely to have or believe in paranormal experiences (e.g., alien abductions, the ability to see the future).[3,4,5]

The highly-suggestable nature of fantasy-prone people[2] allows us to predict that they're more likely to act on what they see portrayed in the fantasy worlds of media. But we *also* know that fewer than 5% of people could be considered fantasy-prone.[3] The reality is that almost everyone, including very young children, know what's real and what's fantasy[6,7].[a] This means that the forum user is *correct* that they – and more than 95% of the human population – can tell fantasy from reality and know that what they're seeing on the screen is *not* reality.

However, even though most of us know that the screen is different from reality, this doesn't mean that our thoughts, feelings, and behaviors can't still be affected by media. In fact, it's not hard to find examples of average people being affected by the media in real-world ways. Shortly after the release of *The Fast and the Furious*, a film which prominently featured illegal street racing, police reported increases in the amount of stunt driving and street racing they had to deal with.[8,9] Even more disturbing, suicide rates have been known to increase in the days following the airing of popular TV shows where a character commits suicide.[10]

You could argue that these are fairly specific and extreme examples, and they are, but we'd wager that most readers can probably think of a time when they realized their own beliefs, feelings, and behavior were influenced by something they watched or played. In one study, one-third of the times when adults cried were in response to some form of media.[11] And anyone who ever found themselves looking under their bed or checking behind a shower curtain after watching a horror movie knows first-hand how you can experience real fear from

---

[a] And it's a good thing they can from an evolutionary perspective. We, as a species, probably wouldn't have lasted very long if it was extremely common for humans to blur the lines between fantasy and reality. Wishful thinking and daydreams can only get you so far when you've got to deal with very real issues like locating food and shelter or fending off predators!

something you *know* isn't real.[b] In one study, researchers found that reading a story about a violent psychiatric patient affected participants' beliefs about violent crime rates and how psychiatric patients should be dealt with.[12] Importantly, this effect occurred *regardless* of whether participants were told that the story was fictional or real[12]: As it turns out, it doesn't matter whether you believed the story was real or not – your beliefs were affected either way. Examples like these show us that media affects us *despite* our knowing that it's not reality.

But if we assume that people are affected by violent media, why aren't they doing the same violent acts they're seeing on the screen? Why does a violent video game make me insult and argue with strangers online, but not grab a gun and go on a shooting spree? As we discuss in Question #28, just because most people *aren't* homicidal doesn't mean that people aren't affected by violent media. Extreme aggression, like the kind we see in violent media, only occurs when a perfect storm of risk factors is present. Although violent media may *increase* a person's risk of aggression, there are plenty of barriers (e.g., the risk of prison) and other protective factors (e.g., learning prosocial messages in school) that prevent most of us from acting violently. Furthermore, after the age of 5, we usually don't simply *copy* what we see. Instead, we learn underlying themes and incorporate them into our attitudes and behaviors in a way that is particular to our own ways of thinking.

This means that the forum user is correct that they, and indeed most people, have never shot anyone *solely* because they played the first-person shooter game *Halo*. But this overlooks the fact that *Halo* players may engage in a considerable amount of less severe forms of aggression, like losing their temper, insulting others, or threatening people. Unfortunately, these exact behaviors are all-too-common problems in online video game play[13,14].[c]

One of the biggest flaws of the user's post is that it relies on a popular misconception based on how the average person *thinks* researchers believe violent media influences aggression. When laypersons hear researchers talk about someone being affected by violent media, they often assume that researchers are talking about behavioral mimicry: "I see it happening on the screen, and now I'm going to mindlessly mimic what I'm seeing in the real world." This, however, is a

---

[b] And if clowns in particular scare you, know that you're not alone: Many people attribute a lifelong fear of clowns to films such as *It*, *Poltergeist*, or *Killer Klowns from Outer Space*, which all feature horrific or homicidal clown characters.

[c] As a somewhat ironic example, one of the authors, Craig, has received threats from gamers who have sent him emails insisting that they've played violent games all their life and have never killed anyone... followed by threats in the same email to "kick his ass" if he kept publishing studies that tried to "take away their favorite games." We address this misunderstanding of media researchers' goals in Question #3.

gross oversimplification of how researchers think about the effects of violent media, which include a multitude of mechanisms which we discuss in Question #12[15]. So while most people don't mindlessly mimic what they see on the screen, they're still nevertheless affected by it.

But *how* can we be affected by media if we *know* that it's not real? To understand this, it helps to know a little bit about evolution, specifically the bit about evolution being a very slow process. The human brain evolved over many millennia, meaning that our modern brains are practically the same as those of our ancestors from tens of thousands of years ago – ancestors who didn't have screens, actors, and computer graphics. As a result, our mental machinery evolved to operate in a world without media: It didn't make sense to distinguish between whether something in front of you was fake or real because, up until very recently, we didn't have to make this distinction. If an angry-looking person appeared to be running toward us with a weapon in their hand, it's because an angry-looking person *was* running up to us with a weapon in their hand! There wasn't any need to distinguish "real angry people" from "fake angry people" because there wasn't a way to create convincing-looking fake, angry people. As a result, when we see or hear something, our minds tend to respond to and learn from it.

We can understand why our brains do this by understanding that we represent ideas in our brains as webs of interconnected neurons[16]. You have, for example, a group of neurons that activates whenever you're exposed to something related to the concept of "fight." These neurons might become activated when you see a picture of people fighting, observe a *real* fight between two people, hear the word "fight," or even have other thoughts that are somewhat related to fights (e.g., punch). The point is, these neurons will become activated by the concept of "fight" *regardless* of whether the source of the concept is a real fight or an on-screen fight. That's why this particular mechanism underlying media violence effects – the activation of aggressive thoughts – operates even though we can distinguish fantasy from reality.

In a similar fashion, another mechanism – learning to associate aggression with reward and other positive outcomes – operates outside of the fantasy/reality distinction. Our minds also evolved *this* ability to learn by observing associations in the world in a time before media existed. We evolved the ability to learn from having our own behavior rewarded or punished first-hand, but also by watching *other* people getting punished or rewarded[17] (including being rewarded in ways that *don't* involve getting something physical, such as getting approval from others[18]). This means that a person playing a violent video game can learn something by watching their character's violent behavior being rewarded: The players themselves do not have to receive a physical reward to make this connection. This type of learning happens whether we're actively aware of it[18] and regardless of whether we're watching real people[19] or fictional characters[20]. To our brains, seeing a digital character being rewarded is the same as seeing a *real* person getting rewarded. Thus, another mechanism of media violence effects –

learning positive associations with aggression – is unaffected by our knowing that the media aren't real.

And so, with all of this in mind, let's respond in full to the forum user's challenge. It's true that most players of violent video games don't blindly mimic the violence they see in media. People are generally very good at distinguishing the game world from the real world, and most have a well-developed sense of right and wrong and know about the consequences of violent behavior. Nevertheless, players' attitudes, beliefs, and behavior *are* influenced by the violent games they play outside of their awareness of such influence. For most players, violent games are not enough of a risk factor to drive them to the point of violence, but they *are* likely to see increases in day-to-day aggression, regardless of their ability to distinguish fantasy from reality. This is because media violence affects numerous mechanisms deep in their mind that evolved well before media existed.

References
1. blackngold29. (2008, January). Is being desensitized to violence a bad thing? (Read, don't jump to conclusions) [Msg 1]. Message posted to http://www.gamespot.com/forums/offtopic-discussion-314159273/is-being-desensitized-to-violence-a-bad-thing-read-26203648/
2. Lynn, S. J., & Rhue, J. W. (1988). Fantasy proneness: Hypothesis, developmental antecedents, and psychopathology. *American Psychologist, 43*(1), 35-44.
3. Wilson, S. C., & Barber, T. X. (1983). The fantasy-prone personality. Implications for understanding imagery, hypnosis, and parapsychological phenomena. *PSI Research, 1*(3), 94-116.
4. Irwin, H. J. (1990). Fantasy proneness and paranormal beliefs. *Psychological Reports, 66*(2), 655-658.
5. Bartholomew, R. E., Basterfield, K., & Howard, G. S. (1991). UFO abductees and contactees: Psychopathology or fantasy proneness? *Professional Psychology: Research and Practice, 22*(3), 215-222.
6. Woolley, J. D., & Wellman, H. M. (1990). Young children's understanding of realities, nonrealities, and appearance. *Child Development, 61*(4), 946-961.
7. Woolley, J. D. (1997). Thinking about fantasy: Are children fundamentally different thinkers and believers from adults? *Child Development, 68*(6), 991-1011.
8. Brown, K. (2013, May 25). Toronto police warn against stunt driving ahead of *Fast & Furious 6* release this weekend. *National Post*. Retrieved from http://news.nationalpost.com/2013/05/25/fast-furious-6-release-prompts-toronto-police-to-warn-against-stunt-driving/
9. The Guardian (June 26, 2001). Fast and furious fuels increase in street racing. *The Guardian*. Retrieved from http://www.theguardian.com/film/2001/jun/26/news

10. Gould, M., Jamieson, P., & Romer, D. (2003). Media contagion and suicide among the young. *American Behavioral Scientist, 46*(9), 1269-1284.
11. Frey, W. H., Hoffman-Ahern, C., Johnson, R. A., Lykken, D. T., & Tuason, V. B. (1983). Crying behavior in the human adult. *Integrative Psychiatry, 1,* 94-100.
12. Green, M. C., & Brock, T. C. (2000). The role of transportation in the persuasiveness of public narratives. *Journal of Personality and Social Psychology, 79*(5), 701-721.
13. GameFAQs forum. (2012). Call of Duty: Black Ops II: Worst Insult u heard on this game. Retrieved from http://www.gamefaqs.com/boards/669289-call-of-duty-black-ops-ii/65602800
14. Maher, B. (2016, March 30). Can a video game company tame toxic behavior? *Nature, 531*(7596). Retrieved online from http://www.nature.com/news/can-a-video-game-company-tame-toxic-behavior-1.19647
15. Anderson, C. A. & Bushman, B. J. (2002). Human Aggression. *Annual Review of Psychology, 53,* 27-51.
16. Pinker, S. (2002). *The Blank Slate* (pp. 78-79). Toronto, Ontario: Penguin Group (Canada).
17. Bandura, A. (1965). Vicarious processes: A case of no-trial learning. *Advances in Experimental Social Psychology, 2,* 1-55.
18. Bandura, A., & McDonald, F. J. (1963). Influence of social reinforcement and the behavior of models in shaping children's moral judgment. *The Journal of Abnormal and Social Psychology, 67*(3), 274-281.
19. Bandura, A. (1971). *Social Learning Theory.* New York: General Learning Press.
20. Bandura, A., Ross, D., & Ross, S. A. (1963). Vicarious reinforcement and imitative learning. *The Journal of Abnormal and Social Psychology, 67*(6), 601-607.
21. Coates, B., Pusser, H. E., & Goodman, I. (1976). The influence of "Sesame Street" and "Mister Rogers' Neighborhood" on children's social behavior in preschool. *Child Development, 47*(1), 138-144.

34 - Isn't media violence only a problem for those with mental illnesses?

The Short Answer:

No. Studies of violent media find that it increases people's risk for aggression regardless of whether the study used a clinical or non-clinical sample. There are *theoretical* reasons to be particularly concerned about violent media use in *certain* clinical populations – namely those who already have a high number of risk factors for aggression. Although some studies have attempted to compare media violence effects in clinical populations and non-clinical populations, there is not yet enough systematic research to reach a firm conclusion about whether some populations might be especially susceptible to violent media. Nonetheless, it is clear that even "normal" children, adolescents, and young adults are susceptible to the effects of media violence.

The Long Answer:

The train of thought driving this particular question usually goes something like this:

1. Violent behavior is extreme and unusual; it's not something most people do.

2. People who *do* engage in violent behavior are therefore abnormal.[a]

3. Researchers say that violent media causes violence, but most people who use violent media don't act violently.

4. Violent media therefore *only* affects unusual groups of people who are already prone to violence.

We dispel many of the misconceptions in this train of thought in detail in other parts of this book. For example, this argument assumes that researchers only

---

[a] To quickly dispel this particular misconception, most people who commit violent crimes do not have a diagnosable mental illness. This is true even for mass shooters. In fact, for most mental illnesses the violence rate is either lower than or equal to that of the general population. What violence perpetrators *do* have are lots of risk factors for aggression and violence. But risk factors themselves are not mental illness.

look for violent media effects in *violent* behavior, overlooking the fact that violent media effects are most easily observable in moderate, day-to-day forms of aggression (see Questions #7, #28). The argument also conveniently ignores the fact that most studies of violent media use *non-clinical* samples of schoolchildren[1,2,3] or college students[4,5,6]. If the effect really were only present in people struggling with mental illness, there shouldn't be evidence of media violence effects in these samples. In Question #19 we explain that, quite to the contrary, all of the available data suggests that there is little reason to believe that anyone is immune to the effects of violent media.

We could end our answer right here if we wanted! But if something's worth doing, it's worth doing right. In this spirit, we can look at the implications made by another version of the argument. Rather than asking, "Do violent media effects *only* occur for people with certain psychological conditions?", what if we instead asked, "Are people with certain psychological conditions *more* susceptible to violent media effects?" This question yields a much more interesting, subtle, and nuanced answer. And, as scientists, we're all about subtlety and nuance!

First, let's make it clear that there *are* studies looking at the effects of violent media in clinical or at-risk samples of participants. Such studies typically find the same effects that are been found in non-clinical samples, but do so in samples – primarily involving children – who have various emotional,[7] developmental,[8,9,10] or behavioral conditions.[11,12]

The number of such studies is relatively small, however. This is partly due to how difficult and expensive it can be to locate large samples of participants with a particular condition. As a hypothetical example, let's imagine we wanted to get a sample of 200 average college undergraduates. It's actually a pretty simple task! All we'd need to do is go to any of the hundreds of colleges in the United States and ask a professor there to wrangle up some volunteers from one of their classes.[b]

Now let's imagine that we wanted to get a *second* sample of 200 people, but this time we only want participants who have been diagnosed with schizophrenia. Suddenly, the task is *much* more difficult, time-consuming, and expensive. Why? Because only about 1% of adults in the United States have been diagnosed with schizophrenia[13]. This means that if we were asking people

---

[b] While it's certainly convenient to recruit participants for our studies this way, this method isn't without its downsides. A major critique of this method is that it raises questions about whether psychological research done *only* on undergraduates can tell us anything meaningful about non-undergraduate populations. There's also an ethical concern about coercion: Whether participants feel undue pressure to participate in studies for fear that choosing not to participate will impact their grade in the course. For these reasons and more, most psychological research is eventually conducted using other, less-convenient forms of sampling that aren't limited to undergraduate students!

completely at random, we would have to talk to 100 people before bumping into a single one who would meet the requirements for our study. To collect a sample of 200, that would mean talking to nearly 20,000 people, and this assumes that all 200 we meet would agree to be in the study.

Of course, researchers are more clever than that, and realize that there are more efficient ways to find people with schizophrenia. For example, we could focus our search by going straight to psychiatric hospitals where we're much more likely to find people who have been diagnosed with schizophrenia. But this would require getting special permission to access this population from the hospital – which may decide that they don't want researchers poking around their patients. Even if we *did* get permission from a particular psychiatric hospital to recruit participants with schizophrenia for our study, it's unlikely that a single location will have 200 patients with schizophrenia, meaning we'll have to go through the same process again at a number of different locations – possibly in other cities or states.

The difficulties don't stop there! In addition to getting permission from the facilities themselves, there are also several ethical considerations that any ethics board will have to consider before giving approval for such a study to be conducted. Ethics boards have a set of strict guidelines for deciding what's acceptable and unacceptable when it comes to conducting research with vulnerable samples, including juveniles, prisoners, parolees, children, or people with diagnosed mental illnesses.

For these reasons (and many more), it is far more difficult to run media violence studies on clinical populations. It was a bit easier to conduct media violence studies on clinical populations in the past, in part due to looser ethical guidelines at the time. As such, we could rely on earlier studies of media violence in clinical samples, many of which do tend to find effects like those observed in non-clinical settings. However, with the absence of modern, large-scale, systematic studies using clinical populations and modern techniques, there's no good way to meaningfully compare the size of media violence effects in clinical samples to effects in non-clinical samples.

But despite the lack of such studies, it *is* possible to draw upon existing theory and what little data exists to at least *hypothesize* that people with certain psychological conditions may be more susceptible to the effects of violent media. In earlier questions (e.g., Question #12) we introduced the General Aggression Model, which states that many different mechanisms determine a person's risk of aggression, including beliefs about aggression, aggressive thoughts, and hostile perceptions of the world[14]. Media violence is one such risk factor, one whose effects may be amplified by the existence of other risk factors[15,16] (see Question #20).

With this in mind, it makes sense why a person with a condition that makes them prone to aggression (i.e., they have many risk factors) would be *more* affected by the additional risk factor of media violence than a person who did not have such a condition. There are a number of conditions that fit the description of a condition that makes a person prone to aggression, including intermittent explosive disorder, antisocial personality disorder, borderline personality disorder, and conduct disorder.[17] As such, if future studies on media violence were to focus on these populations, we would hypothesize that the effects of violent media might be particularly pronounced in these groups. But, as noted earlier (Question #21), it's debatable whether people with these conditions are *actually* more affected by media violence effects, or whether it simply seems that way because they're already more easily-pushed into aggressive behavior.

In addition to clinical populations chosen because they are prone to aggression, researchers may also be interested in another group that may be susceptible to violent media effects. In Question #33 we introduced the idea of the fantasy-prone person, who struggles to distinguish fantasy from reality. Studies have shown that fantasy prone people are more susceptible to developing extreme or unusual beliefs based on the content of their fantasy activities,[18,19] which may lead them to develop pro-aggression beliefs if exposed to violent media. Although there have yet to be any studies directly testing whether fantasy prone people are more susceptible to violent media effects, there are studies showing that people who have frequent and violent fantasies are more prone to aggressive behavior.[20,21] At very least, this suggests that there are theoretical reasons to predict that fantasy prone people and those people suffering from delusions may be particularly vulnerable to media violence effects.

To summarize: A person doesn't need to be diagnosed with a mental illness to be affected by violent media. After all, most studies of media violence have found effects in non-clinical samples. Although there have been a few studies showing that violent media increase the risk for aggression in clinical samples, much of this research is dated and based on fairly small samples. Although greater study on the subject is needed, ethical and practical considerations make it difficult to conduct such studies. Nevertheless, there are, at the very least, theoretical reasons to believe that certain psychological conditions, while not *necessary* for media violence effects to occur, may amplify the effects of violent media.

References

1. Christakis, D. A., & Zimmerman, F. J. (2007). Violent television viewing during preschool is associated with antisocial behavior during school age. *Pediatrics, 120*(5), 993-999.
2. Sheehan, P. W. (2004). Age trends and the correlates of children's television viewing. (1983). *Australian Journal of Psychology, 35*(3), 417-431.
3. Hastings, E. c., Karas, T. L., Winsler, A., Way, E., Madigan, A., & Tyler, S. (2009). Young children's video/computer game use: Relations with school performance and behavior. *Issues in Mental Health Nursing, 25*(1), 45-53.

4. Giumetti, G. W. & Markey, P. M. (2007). Violent video games and anger as predictors of aggression. *Journal of Research in Personality, 41,* 1234-1243.

5. Turkat, I. D. (1977). Affinity for violent television and approval of violent behavior in relation to television exposure. *Aggressive Behavior, 2*(38), 141-149.

6. Krcmar, M., & Lachlan, K. (2009). Aggressive outcomes and videogame play: The role of length of play and the mechanisms at work. *Media Psychology, 12,* 249-267.

7. Gadow, K. D., & Sprafkin, J. (1987). Effects of viewing high versus low aggression cartoons on emotionally disturbed children. *Journal of Pediatric Psychology, 12*(3), 413-423.

8. Fechter, J. V. (1971). Modeling and environmental generalization by mentally retarded subjects of televised aggressive or friendly behavior. *American Journal of Mental Deficiency, 72*(2), 266-267.

9. Evans, C. (1973). *Effects of aggressive vs. nonaggressive films on the aggressive behavior of mentally retarded children.* (ERIC No. ED149511).

10. Talkington, L. W., & Altman, R. (1973). Effects of film-mediated aggressive and affectual models on behavior. *American Journal of Mental Deficiency, 77*(4), 420-425.

11. Baer, S., Saran, K., Green, D. A., & Hong, I. (2012). Electronic media use and addiction among youth in psychiatric clinic versus school populations. *The Canadian Journal of Psychiatry / La Revue Canadienne de Psychiatrie, 12*(57), 728-735.

12. Kronenberger, W. G., Mathews, V. P., Dunn, D. W., Wang, Y., Wood, E. A., Larsen, J. J., Rembusch, M. E., Lowe, M. J., Giauque, A. L., & Lurito, J. T. (2005). Media violence exposure in aggressive and control adolescence: Differences in self- and parent-reported exposure to violence on television and in video games. *Aggressive Behavior, 31,* 201-216.

13. Reiger, D. A., Narrow, W. E., Rae, D. S., Manderscheid, R. W., & Goodwin, F. K. (1993). The de facto mental and addictive disorders service system. Epidemiological Catchment Area prospective 1-year prevalence rates of disorders and services. *Archives of General Psychiatry, 50*(2), 85-94.

14. Anderson, C. A. & Bushman, B. J. (2002). Human Aggression. *Annual Review of Psychology, 53,* 27-51.

15. Exelmans, L., Custers, K., & Van den Bulck, J. (2015). Violent video games and delinquent behavior in adolescents: A risk factor perspective. *Aggressive Behavior, 41,* 267-279.

16. Gentile, D., A. & Bushman, B. J. (2012). Reassessing media violence effects using a risk and resilience approach to understanding aggression. *Psychology of Popular Media Culture, 1*(3), 138-151.

17. American Psychiatric Association. (2013). *Diagnostic and statistical manual of mental disorders* (5th ed.). Washington, DC: Author.

18. Wilson, S. C., & Barber, T. X. (1983). The fantasy-prone personality. Implications for understanding imagery, hypnosis, and parapsychological phenomena. *PSI Research, 1*(3), 94-116.
19. Irwin, H. J. (1990). Fantasy proneness and paranormal beliefs. *Psychological Reports, 66*(2), 655-658.
20. Smith, C. E., Fischer, K. W., & Watson, M. W. (2009). Toward a refined view of aggressive fantasy as a risk factor for aggression: Interaction effects involving cognitive and situational variables. *Aggressive Behavior, 35*(4), 313-323.
21. Kelty, S. F. (2010). You have to hit some people! Measurement and criminogenic nature of violent sentiments in Australia. *Psychiatry, Psychology and Law, 18*(1), 15-32.

35 - Do violent media turn people into mass shooters?

The Short Answer:

No – certainly not by themselves. Many risk factors must be present to make it even *remotely* likely that a person will engage in such an extreme act of violence. Although violent media may be one contributing risk factor, it's likely a relatively small factor compared some of the other contributing risk factors (e.g., access to rapid-fire guns, provocation, social exclusion). Blaming violent media as the *sole* cause for violence would be like blaming one specific fast food restaurant for someone's heart attack while ignoring all other dietary, genetic, and behavioral factors involved. The U.S. Federal Bureau of Investigation and the U.S. Secret Service have noted, however, that most mass shooters tended to have an obsession for violent media, and media violence research has found some significant associations with violent behavior.

The Long Answer:

On April 20th, 1999 the nation watched with stunned horror as two teenage boys rampaged through Columbine High School. The two young gunmen killed 12 fellow students and a teacher and injured a further 24 people before finally turning their guns on themselves. Sadly, this was certainly not the first school shooting to occur in the United States. In fact, less than a year earlier, a student at Thurston High School in Springfield, Oregon fatally shot 4 people and injured 23 more. Nor was Columbine the deadliest shooting to take place in an academic environment – a grim title held at the time by the University of Texas where, in 1966, a student killed 17 people and wounded 31 more.

Despite the existence of more deadly shootings both before and after, the Columbine shooting stands out in many of our memories today. This is due, in no small part, to the vicious debate which continued for years afterward. It was a debate fought between parents, teachers, the media, psychologists, and politicians, all of whom were trying to answer the same question: Why?[1] Why would two people choose to carry out such an extreme act of violence? Although it wasn't the first time people pointed the finger at violent media for an act of extreme violence, violent media definitely figured into this particular debate far more than it ever had before. As it came to the media's attention that the shooters were enthusiastic players of the popular first-person shooter game *Doom* (among others), speculation arose that the violent games themselves were the cause of the students' rampage.[1-3] In fact, the families of those killed at Columbine High School sued the creators of the game on these grounds.[4]

As the debate raged on, public opinion more or less settled into one of two general camps: those who believed violent media was the primary cause of the attack and those who denied that violent media played any role whatsoever. It's easy to understand wanting to place the blame solely on media violence. After such a horrific tragedy, it can be empowering to point to a single cause to rally against so that efforts can be channeled to prevent similar tragedies in the future. What's more, there's an intuitive simplicity to the idea that a person who repeatedly consumes media featuring graphic gun violence will eventually mimic that very same behavior. And, of course, it can't be denied that news media loves a controversy with clear "good" and "bad" sides because they generate outrage, attention, and, most importantly, revenue.

But in a similar vein, it's also easy to understand why people were so opposed to this explanation. Gamers, fans of violent television, and the creators and companies that produce violent media *all* had something to lose from violent media being blamed for the tragedy of Columbine: If the result was some type of restriction of their media, these groups would all suffer.[a] Just as importantly, these groups could rally around the seemingly common-sense argument that millions of people consumed violent media each day and did *not* engage in mass shootings.

In truth, both positions are fundamentally wrong. They're both guilty of oversimplifying the concept of causality. As we discussed in Question #15, media violence effects shouldn't be thought of in "all or nothing" terms (i.e., they either cause aggression or they don't.) In truth, evidence overwhelmingly suggests that media violence increases a person's *risk* for aggression,[5-10] a fact we cover extensively in Questions #12 and #14. But violent media are just one factor among *many* that contribute to the risk of aggression[11,12]. Depending on the group being studied or the magnitude of the aggression being looked at, violent media may be a fairly small, or even non-significant factor[13,14].

With all of this in mind, saying that violent media single-handedly cause mass shootings is overly simplistic to the point of being factually incorrect. As an analogy, it would be like blaming one brand of junk food or one particular fast food restaurant for a person's coronary heart disease while conveniently ignoring all of the other dietary, genetic, and behavior risk factors that played a role[15]. This doesn't mean that violent media get a pass and therefore play *no* role in violent behavior. Such an assumption ignores abundant evidence showing that violent media exposure *is* a significant risk factor (see Questions #29 and #30), and would

---

[a] In his younger years, one of the authors, Courtney, fell squarely into the "deny media violence effects" camp for this very reason. As an avid player of *Doom*, he recalls quite vividly how concerned he was that his parents would take away one of his favorite video games after watching news stories linking the game to the tragedy.

be like denying that eating a lot of one particular junk food probably played at least *some* role in a person's development of coronary heart disease[16].

Although it's important to recognize what scientists mean by "causality" and media violence as a "risk factor" for aggression, it's just as important to recognize the distinction researchers make between aggression and violence. In Question #7 we stated that aggression and violence were related, but distinct: Violence represents the extreme end of the aggression scale. Because violence is extreme and largely disapproved of by our society, violence is also (thankfully) relatively rare compared to day-to-day forms of aggression (e.g., insults, ignoring, hurtful gossiping, shoving, slapping). And, as we discussed in Question #14, it takes numerous risk factors (e.g., a "full glass of water") to make it even remotely likely that someone will engage in extreme violence. For this reason, it's very unlikely that media violence, let alone any other *single* risk factor could be reasonably called *the single* cause of the Columbine tragedy.

So the original question suffers from an overly-simplistic treatment of the issue. What does a more subtle, nuanced question look like? Well, we could rephrase it to something like "To what *extent* does media violence play a role in extreme acts of violence?" We can answer this by saying that it differs from case to case. It's certainly not hard to find *some* case studies in which media violence clearly played *some* role. For example, there are culprits who imitate a specific violent act seen in a violent film, such as several cases of people murdering their victims by pouring drain cleaner down their victims' throat as seen in the Dirty Harry movie *Magnum Force*.

There remains, of course, a reasonable question about whether the violent crime would have been committed if the perpetrators had *not* been heavy consumers of media violence: Would the perpetrators of the aforementioned drain cleaner killings have simply gone about them in a "less creative" way if they hadn't seen the Dirty Harry movies? The question is impossible to answer from a scientific standpoint as psychology is better-equipped to answer questions about average behavior and behavior that *actually* happened – not specific instances of behavior and hypothetical "what-if" scenarios. These latter question are often left to be decided by juries and judges.

When researchers talk about media violence effects, they're typically talking about the effects of media violence on the average person, with respect to increases in moderate, day-to-day forms aggression. But there *have* been studies showing that long-term violent media use can increase the risk of even violent behavior[17-19], prompting the FBI to issue a report on school shootings that listed heavy use of media violence as one of the risk factors.[b] But no researchers would

---

[b] Interestingly, Craig was present in a hearing in which the video game industry lawyer lied about that FBI report. She was caught in the lie by the opposing attorney. Craig witnessed that same lawyer giving the same lie at a media conference some months later.

claim that the media violence was the sole, or even one of the bigger causes of such violence: Clearly, if a person was willing to commit murder via drain cleaner, they've probably got several risk factors besides violent media use driving their behavior (e.g., why aren't they concerned about going to jail, why aren't they empathizing with their victim, why did they feel so much hostility toward another person?)

We can summarize this dark chapter by sympathizing with the fact that, in the wake of tragic mass shootings, it is understandable that people want to identify a single clear cause, such as violent media, as a target for their anger and desire to prevent similar tragedies in the future. Likewise, it makes sense why people would push back against this overly-simplistic explanation for violence, but there's a tendency for critics to push back too far and outright deny the role that media violence plays as a risk factor for aggression. Ultimately, the sort of extreme violence involved in these tragedies is very rare, and usually involves a "perfect storm" of multiple powerful risk factors (e.g., abuse, witnessed violence, ideological beliefs, psychological conditions, history of ostracism, and other situational factors). Violent media consumption is only one potential risk factor amongst this set. Playing violent video games or watching violent TV or films will not turn a normal, well-adjusted person into a mass shooter, but it can lead to a small increased risk of violence, especially if numerous other risk factors are present. Only by appreciating the nuance of this argument can we avoid rushing to the extremes of either banning violent media content outright or ignoring decades of well-established psychological research, neither of which is advisable nor likely to be effective in the long run.

References

1. Cullen, D. (2009). *Columbine*. New York, NY: Twelve.
2. Kushner, D. (2003). *Masters of Doom: How Two Guys Created an Empire and Transformed Pop Culture*. New York, NY: Random House, Inc.
3. Kushner, D. (2012). *Jacked: The Outlaw Story of Grand Theft Auto*. Hoboken, NJ: John Wiley & Sons, Inc.
4. Ward, M. (2001, May 1). Columbine families sue computer game makers. *BBC News*. Retrieved from http://news.bbc.co.uk/2/hi/science/nature/1295920.stm
5. Wood, W., Wong, F., & Cachere, J. (1991). Effects of media violence on viewers' aggression in unconstrained social interaction. *Psychological Bulletin, 109*(3), 371-383.
6. Sherry, J. (2001). The effects of violent video games on aggression: A meta-analysis. *Human Communication Research, 27,* 409-431.
7. Greitemeyer, T., & Mügge, D. O. (2014). Video games do affect social outcomes: A meta-analytic review of the effects of violent and prosocial video game play. *Personality and Social Psychology Bulletin, 40*(5), 578-589.

8. Anderson, C. A., Shibuya, A., Ihori, N., Swing, E. L., Bushman, B. J., Sakamoto, A., Rothstein, H. R., & Saleem, M. (2010). Violent video game effects on aggression, empathy, and prosocial behavior in Eastern and Western countries. *Psychological Bulletin, 136,* 151-173.
9. Paik, H., & Comstock, G. (1994). The effects of television violence on antisocial behavior: A meta-analysis. *Communication Research, 21*(4), 516-546.
10. Hearold, S. (1986). A synthesis of 1043 effects of television on social behavior. In G. Comstock (Ed.), *Public Communication and Behavior, 1,* 65-133. New York: Academic Press.
11. Exelmans, L., Custers, K., & Van den Bulck, J. (2015). Violent video games and delinquent behavior in adolescents: A risk factor perspective. *Aggressive Behavior, 41,* 267-279.
12. Gentile, D., A. & Bushman, B. J. (2012). Reassessing media violence effects using a risk and resilience approach to understanding aggression. *Psychology of Popular Media Culture, 1*(3), 138-151.
13. Ferguson, C. J., Rueda, S. M., Cruz, A. M., Ferguson, D. E., Fritz, S., & Smith, S. M. (2008). Violent video games and aggression: Causal relationship or byproduct of family violence and intrinsic violence motivation? *Criminal Justice and Behavior, 35*(3), 311-332.
14. Ferguson, C. J., Garza, A., Jerabeck, J., Ramos, R., & Mariza, G. (2013). Not worth the fuss after all? Cross-sectional and prospective data on violent video game influences on aggression, visuospatial cognition and mathematics ability in a sample of youth. *Journal of Youth and Adolescence, 42,* 109-122.
15. National Health Service (2014, August 26). *Causes of heart disease.* Retrieved from http://www.nhs.uk/Conditions/Coronary-heart-disease/Pages/Causes.aspx
16. Ascherio, A., Rimm, E. B., Giovannucci, E. L., Spiegelman, D., Stampfer, M., & Willett, W. C. (1996). Dietary fat and risk of coronary heart disease in men: Cohort follow up study in the United States. *BMJ, 313,* 84-90.
17. Gunter, W. D. & Daly, K. (2012). Causal or spurious: Using propensity score matching to disentangle the relationship between violent video games and violent behavior. *Computers in Human Behavior, 4*(28), 1348-1355.
18. Kruttschnitt, C., Heath, L., & Ward, D. (1986). Family violence, television viewing habits, and other adolescent experiences related to violent criminal behavior. *Criminology, 243,* 235-267.
19. Ybarra, M. L., Diener-West, M., Markow, D., Leaf, P. J., Hamburger, M., & Boxer, P. (2008). Linkages between internet and other media violence with seriously violent behavior by youth. *Pediatrics, 122*(5), 929-937.

Chapter 4

Is it all bad?

Other Effects of Media

36 - What kinds of effects do video games have on players?

The Short Answer:

There are no universal effects that *all* video games have on their players. The effects of a particular game will depend on what type of game it is, the game's content, and the amount of time players spend playing it. Like any other form of screen media, video games can have both positive and negative effects on users at the same time, and spending more time playing these games will increase the strength of these effects. Factors like the game's context, structure, and mechanics also play a role in how video games affect players, although more research is needed on these subjects to better understand their influence.

The Long Answer:

Asking "what kinds of effects do video games have on players?" is sort of like asking "what kinds of effects does food have on the body?" It very much comes down to *what* you're eating and *how much* of it you're eating. Fruits and vegetables typically have positive effects on your body while junk food typically has negative effects while also still providing energy. Eating *more* vegetables tends to yield *more* benefits, while eating *more* junk food tends to cause *more* negative effects. Nonetheless, it's also possible to overdo a good thing, both when it comes to food and when it comes to our gaming habits. For instance, while carrots are generally good for you, you would start to develop nutritional deficiencies if you lived on nothing *but* carrots. An ideal diet is a balanced one that contains a variety of healthy foods. Our media diet is no different and can be thought of in a similar fashion.

Like with foods, video games can have both positive and negative effects on players. The type of effect is often dependent on the game's content. For example, playing video games with violent content increases players' aggressive thoughts, feelings, and behavior (see Question #11)[1], something most of us would consider to be an unhealthy outcome. In contrast, playing nonviolent *prosocial* games (i.e., games where the player helps others in nonviolent ways) has the *opposite* effect, increasing prosocial thoughts, feelings, and behaviors[2] — outcomes most of us would consider to be healthy (for more on prosocial games, see Question #41). As a general rule, the effects of media content tend to increase as exposure increases.

The effects of video games, however, are not limited to "aggression" and "helping." Other types of game content tend to yield effects in line with the game's content. For example, players of video games that glorify risk-taking behavior are more likely to take risks in their everyday lives (see Question #38). In a similar vein, playing educational video games can improve students' academic performance (see Question #40). Though it might seem a bit obvious, studies do suggest that people are affected in fairly predictable ways by the content of their video games.

As it turns out, the parallels between food and media diets run even deeper. Consider ice cream, a favorite food of all of the authors.[a] From a food diet perspective, there are both positive and negative effects of eating ice cream. On the positive side, ice cream contains the important mineral calcium, as well as a moderate amount of protein. On the negative side, ice cream also contains excessive amounts of sugar. We would be lying if we said that ice cream was *entirely* bad for us or if we pretended that ice cream was only beneficial to us. As with many things in life, the truth is more complex and nuanced than simple black-and-white. The same can be said about the effects of video games, which can have *both* positive and negative effects on the player. A fast-paced shooting game may well improve the player's ability to extract movement information from a video screen (possibly useful for air-traffic controllers). This benefit does not, however, prevent the game from *also* increasing the player's likelihood of aggressive behavior outside of the game.

As another important comparison between one's food diet and their media diet, researchers must consider both *what* we consume and *how much* we consume. After all, even healthy foods can be harmful in large quantities: An apple a day may keep the doctor away, but 100 apples a day will probably leave you worse for wear.[b] In the same way, even relatively "healthy" media content can still have harmful effects if we regularly binge on it. When video games – even beneficial ones – take away from the time spent studying or doing homework, academic performance is likely to suffer (see Question #40). Likewise, time spent playing video games is time *not* spent exercising or engaging in other physical activities, which can contribute to health problems like obesity (see Question #39). In short, media use matters not *only* because content and messages affect consumers, but also because it can sap time away from other essential life activities.

Although media researchers tend to focus their efforts on understanding how content and frequency of use contribute to media effects, these aren't the *only*

---

[a] And, arguably, among most people who are fortunate enough to not be lactose-intolerant!

[b] In fact, the seeds of apples contain amygdalin, a compound which, when broken down by stomach acid, becomes hydrogen cyanide – a poisonous substance! Granted, a person would have to deliberately consume *hundreds* of apple seeds to receive a lethal dose, but the point still stands that a few hundred apples a day just might kill you if you aren't careful to avoid the seeds!

factors that need to be considered in our media diets. Some have suggested that design features of the games we play (above and beyond the games' content) play an important role in determining how they affect players[3]. One such factor is the game's context – that is, what the game tries to get the player to do and how it rewards or punishes them accordingly. For example, one violent game may *reward* players for killing opponents, while another may punish them for doing so (see Question #15, Figure 15.1, for example.) When aggression is paired with positivity, the effect will be to *increase* the players' risk for real-world aggressive behavior. In contrast, players *punished* for killing opponents are not as likely to experience the same increase in aggression, since aggression itself is not being paired with "positivity." In fact, if the punishments for aggression were severe enough, one might even expect a violent game could *reduce* the player's risk of aggression. Examples such as this illustrate how the exact same violent content can have dramatically different effects on players depending on the game's context. Unfortunately, there has been very little research looking directly at this topic. For any budding media scholars or students looking for future projects to pursue, this is a much-needed area of research for the field!

Another currently-understudied aspect of video games that may change the way they affect players has to do with the game's structure. Many video games, especially "action" games, present a wealth of visual information to players at an extremely fast pace. Anyone who's watched an action-filled game that they're unfamiliar with can attest to just how overwhelming it can feel to be bombarded with flashing lights, text, and sounds that all seem to be screaming for the player's attention. Players of such games learn to quickly take in, comprehend, consider, and apply this information if they want to succeed at the game. As an example, someone playing a multiplayer shooter game may turn the corner and see a character in front of them. In the blink of an eye, the player needs to consider dozens of important pieces of information:

- What is the person wearing, and are they on my team?
- Are there other players around?
- What kind of weapon am I carrying?
- Do I need to reload?
- How far away is the other player?
- What weapon are *they* carrying?
- Is there any cover nearby?
- How much time is left in the game?
- Am I currently being attacked from any other direction?
- Does my team need me elsewhere?

Players process *all* of these variables in a fraction of a second, and learn to do so automatically over time. Practicing this sort of quick decision-making may have some positive effects on players: Research shows that action games *can* increase players' visual-spatial skills (see Question #41 for more on this).

Other games require players to navigate through complex virtual environments, a skill that involves forming mental maps and rotating or updating them in response to changing events in the game world. These skills may well improve players' navigational ability in the real world, though, to date, several studies have failed to find such transfer for navigational skills to the real world.[c] More research is needed to determine whether – and when – structural elements such as these can cause games to have these sorts of desirable effects on players' skills which can be applied outside a gaming context.

A final aspect of video games worth considering involves the mechanics of the game. Put simply, this means considering the physical skills necessary for players to play the game. For example, many games require the use of two-handed controllers with more than a dozen different buttons and sticks that players manipulate to move their characters. The use of such input devices may improve motor skills and hand-eye coordination in players (see Chapter #41). And in recent years there have been a growing number of games that rely on a range of body movements to play the game. For example, when playing Wii Fit yoga, players must balance while holding yoga poses. Practicing these skills is likely to improve players' balance and physical dexterity over time. But like the design elements described above, more research is needed to test when and how different game mechanics alter the effects of media on players.

By now it should be clear that video games can have both what people might consider "good" and "bad" effects on players. Indeed, the same effect may be good for some users (e.g., desensitization to blood and gore is useful for surgeons and military combatants) and bad for others (desensitization to violence is likely bad for most 14-year-olds). Although a game may improve the visual processing skills of players, this doesn't mean the same game can't also have negative effects on the same players (e.g., increasing aggressive thoughts, feelings, and behavior.) Because of this, there's no valid reason for researchers or laypersons to make blanket statements about whether video games as a whole are entirely good or bad. As with food, it's important to remember that specific video games, like specific foods, can have a mix of positive and negative effects. Since most of the existing research has focused on testing whether media effects exist,[d]

---

[c] One of the authors happens to be a lifelong gamer *and* a very poor navigator (he is very thankful for GPS devices). Whether or not the disconnect between these two variables is the rule or the exception remains to be seen, however.

[d] In the face of seemingly endless criticism from a handful of critical researchers, gamers, pundits, and the media industry itself, researchers have to continually prove and re-prove the existence of media violence effects with studies. This is because any attempts to move beyond this question are met with

there has been comparatively little research looking at how design decisions in games and other screen media affect well-known media violence effects. We hope that future research will focus more on studies that test for these different nuanced and complex effects so that we can move beyond the continual treading and re-treading of old ground when it comes to media violence effects.

References

1. Anderson, C. A., Shibuya, A., Ihori, N., Swing, E. L., Bushman, B. J., Sakamoto, A., Rothstein, H. R., & Saleem, M. (2010). Violent video game effects on aggression, empathy, and prosocial behavior in eastern and western countries: a meta-analytic review. *Psychological Bulletin, 136*(2), 151-173.
2. Greitemeyer, T., & Mügge, D. O. (2014). Video games do affect social outcomes: A meta-analytic review of the effects of violent and prosocial video game play. *Personality and Social Psychology Bulletin, 40*(5), 578-589.
3. Gentile, D. A. (2011). The multiple dimensions of video game effects. *Child Development Perspectives, 5*(2), 75-81.
4. McGloin, R., Farrar, K. M., & Fishlock, J. (2015). Triple whammy! Violent games and violent controllers: Investigating the use of realistic gun controllers on perceptions of realism, immersion, and outcome aggression. *Journal of Communication, 65*, 280-299.

---

skepticism from critics who argue "But you're *assuming* that violent media increases aggression – where's your proof?" It's rather like asking a biologist to re-prove the existence of cells, asking chemists to re-prove atomic theory, or asking geologists and astronomers to re-prove that the Earth is not flat every time they want to publish a paper in their field. Depressingly, the existence of the Flat-Earth Society reveals that this problem is far from unique to media researchers.

37 - Can video games cause ADHD?

The Short Answer:

Yes and no – it's complicated. To date, studies have not conclusively shown that video games *cause* people to develop ADHD in the first place. However, studies *have* shown that there is a link between screen time (including video game play) and ADHD *symptoms*, including attention problems, impulsiveness, and a lack of self-control. In addition, there's evidence that video game play can worsen attention problems and impulsivity, and well as studies showing that this effect is not limited to video games (e.g., it happens with television, too). But evidence *also* shows that people with ADHD symptoms may prefer to consume video games because of their exciting nature, leading to a "which came first – the chicken or the egg" situation. More research specifically designed to disentangle the directionality of the effects (or whether both causal directions are present) is needed.

The Long Answer:

Attention deficit hyperactivity disorder (ADHD) has increased in the past two decades and is now at the point where nearly 1 in 10 children receive this diagnosis[1]. As it becomes increasingly prevalent, parents and researchers have become increasingly interested in the causes of this condition.[a]

ADHD is characterized by difficulties focusing and maintaining attention and by hyperactive and impulsive behavior. Given that many of these outcomes are believed to result from media exposure, researchers have conducted numerous studies testing whether this is the case. The results show that video game play and TV exposure are, indeed, linked to attention problems, impulsiveness, and self-control problems[2-8]. Unfortunately, however, much of this research is cross-sectional in nature. And, as we've discussed in other parts of this book (e.g., Question #9), cross-sectional studies can tell us whether two things are related, but they can't tell us about the causal direction. Researchers in this field have developed theories that account for the different possibilities underlying the link

---

[a] Ironically, many of the same critics who (incorrectly) claim that falling violent crime rates prove that video games don't increase aggression also (correctly) claim that rising ADHD rates do not prove that video games increase attention problems. See Question #30 for why these sorts of inferences from societal data are weak at best. If only they would apply the same logic consistently across *all* of their arguments!

between electronic screen time (e.g., video games, TV…) and ADHD. One theory, in particular, points to four possible explanations for the link[4]:

1. Excitement: Video games cause attention problems because they are so exciting. They grab our attention easily, which makes activities like reading and studying seem boring by comparison. Getting used to the excitement of video games makes it hard to focus on less-exciting activities.

2. Displacement: Video games take away time that we'd otherwise spend on other activities that would strengthen attention and self-control skills (e.g., reading). Since we don't really have to put in effort to pay attention to video games, we rarely get to exercise our "attention muscles," leaving them weak and insufficient when we need them for tasks that require attention and self-control.

3. Attraction: Because video games are quick-paced, they appeal to people who have ADHD symptoms. Because of this, people with ADHD symptoms are more likely to prefer video games over other activities (e.g., reading).

4. Third Variable: The link between video games and ADHD symptoms may be caused by their shared relationship to something else entirely. For example, boys are more likely to play video games *and* more likely to have attention problems. If this is the case, there may be no reason to believe that ADHD symptoms or video game play affect one another.

Importantly, with the exception of the fourth explanation, it's possible for more than one of these explanations to be true at the same time. For example, even if people with ADHD symptoms did prefer to play video games over other activities, it could *also* be true that playing video games takes away from time spent on other activities that improve attention skills. As we discussed in Question #13, effects can sometimes happen in *both* directions. This is called a bidirectional effect. In this case, the bidirectional effect might mean that ADHD symptoms lead to more video game play which, in turn, worsens ADHD symptoms.

So, we have four theoretically-driven explanations for the link between ADHD symptoms and video game play. Are there *any* data that can show us which of these explanations is most likely to be true? Well, we *can* say that there has been little evidence for the third variable hypothesis. Some studies *have* tested this possibility by measuring ADHD symptoms and video game use, along with several possible third variables (e.g., the participant's sex). In theory, if there is no longer a relationship between ADHD symptoms and video game use after controlling for participant sex, this would support the idea that the relationship is driven entirely by this third variable. One study *has* found support for this third variable hypothesis, but only by controlling for numerous different possible variables at the same time[9].[b] Other studies, however, find that the link between ADHD symptoms and video game use persists even *after* controlling for third variables[4,8]. At best, we can say that the evidence for this hypothesis is mixed.

Although there has been little research on the other three explanations, the evidence that *does* exist has been somewhat more consistent. For example, in a longitudinal study, researchers measured attention, impulsivity, and video game use in the same group of participants over two years to see how these three variables affected one another over time[4]. The study found support for both the attraction and displacement hypotheses. Specifically, participants with attention and impulsivity problems at the start of the study played more video games later in the study, supporting the attraction hypothesis. The researchers *also* found that participants who played more video games at the start of the study had *more* attention problems later in the study. This study[4], along with others[5], found some evidence to support the excitement hypothesis. Violent media exposure had reduced attention and increased impulsivity above and beyond other types of media use. Since violent media are often more fast-paced and exciting than other media, this suggests that the excitement factor of certain forms of media (e.g., video games) may contribute to the relationship between video games and ADHD symptoms.

It's worth noting that there *have* been several other studies beyond the ones described here that have tested whether there is a link between ADHD and video game use. Unfortunately, most of these studies were not designed in a way that allowed researchers test the different hypothesized causal directions or the reasons for the link[11-14]. There are also studies showing that the link between media use and attention problems isn't unique to video games. Numerous studies provide converging evidence that television use is also associated with ADHD symptoms[7,8,15]. As an example, one study looked at children's television use, video game use, and their attention problems over the course of 13 months[8]. As shown in Figure 37.1, the researchers found that video game and television (screen media) use at the start of the study (Time 1) predicted teacher-reported attention problems at the end of the study (Time 4), even after controlling for sex, grade in school, and for attention problem level at Time 1. Although not shown here, the study also found that the video game effect on later attention problems was greater than the TV effect.

---

[b] We'll spare you the boring statistical details here, but *most* statistical effects can be made to seem insignificant if you control for too many other variables at once. This isn't necessarily because these third variables validly explain the relationship, but may result from statistical quirks. Thus, to make an argument that a third variable can explain the relationship between two variables, it's good to have a strong theoretical reason to believe that this is the case and to use only an appropriate number of "third" variables given the size of the sample[10].

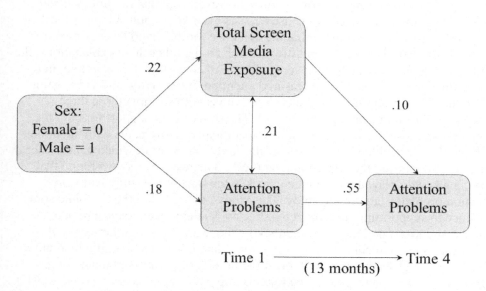

Figure 37.1. Long term effect of screen time (TV & video games) on real world attention problems in middle school students, controlling for earlier attention problems and sex. Numbers next to the arrows indicate the relative strength of the effect after controlling for all other variables. All effects in this figure are statistically significant. Children who spent more time with TV & video games have increased attention problems over time.

A cross-sectional study of over 400 college students also found unique effects of violent media on attention problems which, in turn, were associated with aggressive thoughts and feelings (see Figure 37.2.)[4]. Attention problems were strongly associated with impulsive aggressive behavior, in particular, and much less strongly associated with planful (premeditated) aggression. This is exactly the pattern predicted by the research team.

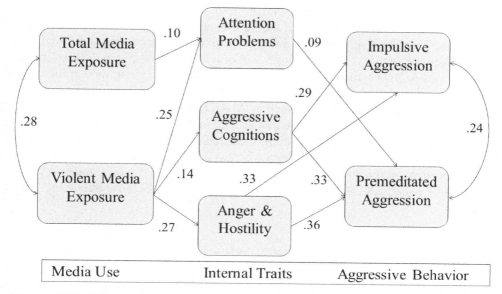

Figure 37.2. Effects of total media exposure (TV & video games) and violent media exposure on real world attention problems, aggression-related internal traits, and aggressive behavior. Numbers next to the arrows indicate the relative strength of the effect after controlling for all other variables. All effects in this figure are statistically significant.

Concerning TV effects on ADHD, a study found that for children under the age of three, every one-hour increase in average TV use roughly doubled the odds that they would have attention problems five years later[15]. That said, however, media use in the same children at the age of 4-5 was *not* associated with attention problems five years later. This suggests that the relation between media use and ADHD symptoms may matter the most for younger children. More research is needed, however, before we can confidently accept this conclusion.[c]

_____

[c] SCIENTIFIC MUMBO-JUMBO WARNING! The concept of "attention" is actually a *lot* more complex than we've laid out here! Psychologists recognize many different kinds of attention, including visual/spatial attention (making sense of complex visual scenes), executive control (suppressing impulses and quick decision-making), and real-world/school-room attention (paying attention to something without being distracted by the squirrel in the window – even if it is a *really* cute squirrel). People with ADHD have serious problems with this last type of attention, which has also tended to be the main type of attention focused on in media research. This doesn't mean, however, that media studies

To summarize: We know that ADHD symptoms and media use are associated with one another. People who are high in ADHD symptoms also tend to score higher than average in terms of media use, and vice-versa. The nature of this relationship is still actively debated among researchers and requires additional study. It's *possible* that the effect happens in only one direction (e.g., screen media use increases ADHD symptoms), but the best available data suggests that the effect is a bi-directional one, that is, high screen time (especially violent) increases later real world attention problems such as ADHD, *and* real-world attention problems increase later use of screen media. The result is a sort of downward spiral. And although additional research is needed to further test these hypotheses about screen use and attention problems, there is *also* a need for research looking at whether there are *positive* effects of some types of media use on impulsivity (e.g., slower-paced educational TV and video games may *decrease* attention problems[5]).

References

1. Akinbami, L. J., Liu, X., Pastor, P. N., & Rueben, C. A. (2011). Attention deficit hyperactivity disorder among children aged 5-17 years in the United States, 1998-2009. *National Center for Health Statistics Data Brief, 70*. Retrieved from http://www.cdc.gov/nchs/data/databriefs/db70.pdf
2. Bailey, K., West, R., & Anderson, C. A. (2010). A negative association between video game experience and proactive cognitive control. *Psychophysiology, 47*(1), 34–42.
3. Chan, P. A., & Rabinowitz, T. (2006). A cross-sectional analysis of video games and attention deficit hyperactivity disorder symptoms in adolescents. *Annals of General Psychiatry, 5*.
4. Gentile, D. A., Swing, E. L., Lim, C. G., & Khoo, A. (2012). Video game playing, attention problems, and impulsiveness: Evidence of bidirectional causality. *Psychology of Popular Media Culture, 1*(1), 62–70.
5. Hastings, E. C., Karas, T. L., Winsler, A., Way, E., Madigan, A., & Tyler, S. (2009). Young children's video/computer game use: Relations with school performance and behavior. *Issues in Mental Health Nursing, 30*(10), 638–649.
6. Hummer, T. A., Wang, Y., Kronenberger, W. G., Mosier, K. M., Kalnin, A. J., Dunn, D. W., & Mathews, V. P. (2010). Short-term violent video game play

---

haven't looked at other kinds of attention. Some studies suggest, for example, that hours of intensive training on a fast-paced violent video game can improve visual/spatial attention. It's worth noting, however, that *this* type of attention is *not* the same as the real world/school room type of attention that constitutes ADHD. So when laypersons (and a very few scholars) argue that "some studies show that video games *improve* attention!," you now know that this isn't the same type of attention that helps students do better in school!

by adolescents alters prefrontal activity during cognitive inhibition. *Media Psychology, 13*(2), 136–154.

7. Swing, E. L., & Anderson, C. A. (2014). The role of attention problems and impulsiveness in media violence effects on aggression. *Aggressive Behavior, 40*(3), 197–203.

8. Swing, E. L., Gentile, D. A., Anderson, C. A., & Walsh, D. A. (2010). Television and video game exposure and the development of attention problems. *Pediatrics, 126*(2), 214–221.

9. Ferguson, C. J. (2011). The influence of television and video game use on attention and school problems: A multivariate analysis with other risk factors controlled. *Journal of Psychiatric Research, 45*(6), 808–813.

10. Prot, S., & Anderson, C. A. (2013). Research methods, design, and statistics in media psychology. Chapter in K. Dill (Ed.) *The Oxford Handbook of Media Psychology* (109-136). New York: Oxford University Press.

11. Andreassen, C. S., Billieux, J., Griffiths, M. D., Kuss, D. J., Demetrovics, Z., Mazzoni, E., & Pallesen, S. (2016). The relationship between addictive use of social media and video games and symptoms of psychiatric disorders: A large-scale cross-sectional study. *Psychology of Addictive Behaviors, 30*(2), 252–262.

12. Bioulac, S., Arfi, L., & Bouvard, M. P. (2008). Attention deficit/hyperactivity disorder and video games: A comparative study of hyperactive and control children. *European Psychiatry, 23*(2), 134–141.

13. Mazurek, M. O., & Engelhardt, C. R. (2013). Video game use in boys with autism spectrum disorder, ADHD, or typical development. *Pediatrics, 132*(2), 260–266.

14. Tolchinsky, A., & Jefferson, S. D. (2011). Problematic video game play in a college sample and its relationship to time management skills and attention-deficit/hyperactivity disorder symptomology. *CyberPsychology, Behavior & Social Networking, 14*(9), 489–496.

15. Zimmerman, F. J., & Christakis, D. A. (2007). Associations between content types of early media exposure and subsequent attentional problems. *Pediatrics, 120*(5), 986–992.

38 - Can media use encourage risky behavior?

The Short Answer:

Many video games, TV shows, and films glorify risk-taking behavior. Research shows that consuming these media increases the consumer's risk-taking behavior, including increasing their risky driving, alcohol and cigarette use, and risky sexual behavior (e.g., unprotected sex). Studies not only show that a relation exists between risk-taking media and risk-taking behavior, but fairly consistently point to risk-taking media causing the increased risk-taking behavior. Similar effects have been found across different media (i.e., television, films, video games, and music).

The Long Answer:

A significant portion of this book has been devoted to the effects of violent media on aggression. But, as we point out in Question #36, media content is far too diverse to be shoehorned into just the categories of "violent" and "non-violent." In this section, we'll consider a different type of media content: media that glorifies risk-taking behavior. While it might not be the type of media content concerned parents think about first (sex and violence seem to come first, according to content rating systems; see Question #48), behavior that may potentially encourage dangerous and risky behavior probably ought to be on parents' radar.[1,2]

Let's briefly review some examples of the type of risk-taking behavior we see in video games. Car-racing games often take place in non-professional settings (e.g., speeding down the highway or through city streets), where the excitement comes from the thrill of beating your opponent and the possibility of being arrested or of crashing your car. In other games, characters fearlessly navigate dangerous scenarios including violent street fights, climbing tall and precarious ledges, and engaging in criminal behavior. In TV and films, characters use alcohol, tobacco, and other drugs, and often engage in unsafe sexual practices. In these situations, characters are rarely shown taking precautions to reduce their risks (e.g., wearing safety gear), sending a message that people who engage in these activities usually do so *without* such precautions[3].

And, of course, in many of these media products the characters are rewarded handsomely for their reckless behavior, earning money, fame, or power. It is rare to show the true consequences of these actions. In video games, even when players crash, fall, get shot, or are arrested, they're typically able to restart the level and try again with little consequence. In other words, there's no cost associated with taking risks in video games or other screen media. Unfortunately, in the real world, we don't have "extra lives" to spare.

Parents and content ratings systems aren't the only ones guilty of overlooking this concerning content. Research on the effects of risk-taking content in media is also relatively new. But the work that *has* been done tells a fairly clear story. Numerous survey studies show that risk-glorifying video games are associated with risky behavior and related outcomes. For example, one study of Belgian adolescents found that those who played racing games had more positive attitudes toward reckless driving and had greater intentions to drive recklessly themselves[4]. A similar study of Canadian car enthusiasts found that those who played more risk-glorifying games were more likely to have actually *engaged* in risky driving behavior[5]. Although you could argue that *any* racing game could lead to reckless driving, these same studies found that racing games that don't reward risky driving behavior don't have the same effects. This suggests that it's not the "racing" part of the game that's leading to risky driving, but specifically the "risk-taking" elements of the game content.

These effects are hardly limited to racing games and reckless driving. Video games have also been shown to be associated with reckless gambling behavior, especially for people who play first-person shooter games[6]. That said, not every study finds the link between video game playing and all risk-taking behavior. One study, for example, found that video game play may reduce certain risk-taking behaviors (e.g., binge-drinking, unprotected sex)[7]. In short, although studies find that risk-glorifying video games are associated with more risk-taking behavior in general, more research is needed to clarify which types of game content tend to cause particular risky behaviors and which players are the most likely to be affected by it.

As we've done in earlier questions, we'll be the first to point out that a correlation between two variables does not necessarily mean that one variable caused the other to happen (see Question #13). For this reason, researchers rely on laboratory experiments to test whether risky video games are, in fact, increasing risk-taking behavior, and not the other way around. As an example of such a study, German university students were randomly assigned to either play a risk-rewarding racing game or a racing game that did not reward risky behavior. When all participants were later tested in a driving simulator, those who played the risk-taking racing game were more likely than the other participants to take risks while driving and to consider themselves to be risk-taking drivers[8]. Risk-rewarding racing games have also been shown to increase risk-taking behavior, relative to playing fairly benign, neutral video games (e.g., Tetris) [9]. Risk-rewarding games have also been shown to affect risk-taking in domains outside the game's content, such as reducing the likelihood that participants would take a free test for a serious disease[10]. Experiments such as these show us that risk-glorifying games aren't just associated with risk-taking behavior: they *increase* it.

You could argue, however, that these laboratory studies only look at short-term effects in sterile laboratory settings that are nothing like the real world. This might mean that any increased risk-taking behavior would simply wear off a few minutes after playing, and this is an entirely valid possibility. Longitudinal studies have addressed this by looking at the long-term relations between video games and risk-taking behavior. In the Belgian driving study described above, for example, the authors looked at the same participants two years later and found that those playing risk-rewarding racing games at the start of the study were more likely to engage in risky driving behavior two years later[11], an effect that was also found in a sample of American teenagers.[12] In fact, the American researchers took their study one step further and found that risk-glorifying games *also* predicted increased alcohol use, cigarette use, delinquent behavior, and risky sexual behaviors almost four years later.[13]

Taken together, the limited number of cross-sectional, experimental, and longitudinal studies that exist all converge on the same conclusion: Media that glorify risk-taking behavior lead to increases in real-world risk-taking behavior. These effects aren't limited to video games: They've been found for television, movies, advertisements, and music[1,2,14]. The effects may be stronger for video games than for more passive media like film and television, and are especially likely to be strong when the risk-taking behavior in the media is similar to the real-world risky behavior (e.g., racing games and risky driving behavior). Further research will help us better understand which risks are the most likely to lead to specific risky behaviors (e.g., risky sexual behavior) and, perhaps even more importantly, may find types of media content that *reduce* risky behavior (e.g., prosocial games)[15].

References

1. Fischer, P., Greitemeyer, T., Kastenmüller, A., Vogrincic, C., & Sauer, A. (2011). The effects of risk-glorifying media exposure on risk-positive cognitions, emotions, and behaviors: A meta-analytic review. *Psychological Bulletin, 137*(3), 367–390.
2. Fischer, P., Vingilis, E., Greitemeyer, T., & Vogrincic, C. (2011). Risk-taking and the media. *Risk Analysis: An International Journal, 31*(5), 699–705.
3. Karazsia, B., & Muller, A. (2014). Depictions of injuries and safety gear usage in the world's most popular video games. *Journal of Media Psychology: Theories, Methods, and Applications, 26*(1), 4–9.
4. Beullens, K., Roe, K., & Van den Bulck, J. (2008). Video games and adolescents' intentions to take risks in traffic. *Journal of Adolescent Health, 43*(1), 87–90.
5. Vingilis, E., Seeley, J., Wiesenthal, D. L., Wickens, C. M., Fischer, P., & Mann, R. E. (2013). Street racing video games and risk-taking driving: An Internet survey of automobile enthusiasts. *Accident Analysis & Prevention, 50*, 1–7.
6. Bailey, K., West, R., & Kuffel, J. (2013). What would my avatar do? Gaming, pathology, and risky decision making. *Frontiers in Psychology, 4*.

7. Casiano, H., Kinley, D. J., Katz, L. Y., Chartier, M. J., & Sareen, J. (2012). Media use and health outcomes in adolescents: Findings form a nationally representative survey. *Journal of the Canadian Academy of Child and Adolescent Psychiatry, 21*(4), 296–301.

8. Fischer, P., Greitemeyer, T., Morton, T., Kastenmüller, A., Postmes, T., Frey, D., Kubitzki, J., & Odenwälder, J. (2009). The racing-game effect: Why do video racing games increase risk-taking inclinations? *Personality and Social Psychology Bulletin, 35*(10), 1395–1409.

9. Deng, M., Chan, A. H. S., Wu, F., & Wang, J. (2015). Effects of racing games on risky driving behavior, and the significance of personality and physiological data. *Injury Prevention, 21*(4), 238–244.

10. Kastenmüller, A., Fischer, P., & Fischer, J. (2014). Video racing games increase actual health-related risk-taking behavior. *Psychology of Popular Media Culture, 3*(4), 190–194.

11. Beullens, K., Roe, K., & Van den Bulck, J. (2011). Excellent gamer, excellent driver? The impact of adolescents' video game playing on driving behavior: A two-wave panel study. *Accident Analysis and Prevention, 43*(1), 58–65.

12. Hull, J. G., Draghici, A. M., & Sargent, J. D. (2012). A longitudinal study of risk-glorifying video games and reckless driving. *Psychology of Popular Media Culture, 1*(4), 244–253.

13. Hull, J. G., Brunelle, T. J., Prescott, A. T., & Sargent, J. D. (2014). A longitudinal study of risk-glorifying video games and behavioral deviance. *Journal of Personality and Social Psychology, 107*(2), 300–325.

14. Sargent, J.D., Wills, T.A, Stoolmiller, Gibson, M. & Gibbons, F.X. (2006). Alcohol use in motion pictures and its relation with early-onset teen drinking. *Journal of Studies on Alcohol, 67,* 617-637.

15. Greitemeyer, T. (2013). Exposure to media with prosocial content reduces the propensity for reckless and risky driving. *Journal of Risk Research, 16*(5), 583–594.

39 - Are screen media bad for your health?

The Short Answer:

Yes and no. Technically speaking, consumed in moderation, screen media (e.g., video games, television, computers…) aren't bad for your health *in and of themselves*. However, spending too much time sitting in front a screen can create the sort of inactive lifestyle that *is* associated with negative health outcomes. These outcomes include physical problems (e.g., obesity) as well as problems with your psychological and social quality of life. Furthermore, as noted in many sections of this book, the content of the media itself can have negative effects on consumers' mental and social health (e.g., violent content and aggression). Screen media can *also* be bad for your health by contributing to accidents such as texting while driving (or even while walking). That said, appropriate screen media in appropriate amounts can have positive health benefits as well. For example, recent research on a variety of modern video games holds some promise that games designed with specific health goals in mind may help consumers to achieve *specific* health goals.

The Long Answer:

Although it may not have seemed like it at the time, your parents were probably doing you a favor if they scolded you for being a couch potato. As it turns out, their intuition that it's bad for anyone to spend hours sprawled out on the couch is correct! Sedentary behavior – the technical term for being a couch potato – is a risk factor for all sorts of undesirable health outcomes including obesity, diabetes, and heart disease[1,2]. Doctors recommend that adults get at least 150 minutes of moderately intense physical activity each week, but many of us fall short of this guideline[a] – something we can see reflected in rising obesity rates.

Screen media (e.g., television, video games, computers) play an important role in many of our inactive lifestyles, in no small part because time spent consuming media usually is time *not* spent engaging in physical activity and often may include other harmful behaviors such as junk food consumption. Although this may seem like a conclusion so obvious that it doesn't even require a study to prove, as it turns out, research is surprisingly mixed on the relations between media use and health! Some studies find that a TV and video game console in the home is associated with more sedentary behavior, but others find that adding a

---

[a] Unfortunately, this statement also applies to more than one of the authors of this book!

274

TV-limiting device only *sometimes* reduces body mass index (BMI) scores[3]. Some reviews of the literature say there is a link between screen time and BMI rates[4], while others don't find a relation[5,6].

If it seems so intuitive that media use *should* be associated with physical health, why does the research seem so mixed? Part of the reason may have to do with the small size of the effect. As we discussed in Question #17, most studies try to estimate the size of an effect. If, in reality, an effect is fairly small, it can sometimes be hard to detect or to know how to interpret. Are they estimates of a *real*, but small effect, or is there no effect at all and we're trying to interpret noise in the data? The result is that some studies may find little-to-no evidence of the effect despite the fact that an effect is real – especially if the study's sample size is small or the measures being used are imprecise or too insensitive.

The solution is to follow the example of the media violence literature and look beyond the results of a single study. Instead, let's consider what *all* of the literature as a whole says on the subject (see Question #17 for more on this approach within the media violence literature). In one such analysis of the link between screen media and physical health, the authors found a small relation between television and video game use and body fatness[7]: Those who used more media were, on average, slightly fatter than those who didn't. The same analysis also found that those who use more media also tend to be less physically active. This provides at least *some* evidence that excessive media use can lead to negative health outcomes, in part because time spent using media is time *not* spent being physically active.

But there may be *other* reasons why media use is associated with poor health outcomes. One alternative is based on the idea that media use is associated with junk food consumption: People who play a lot of video games and watch a lot of television tend to eat while distracted (not paying attention to what – or how much – they're eating) and are exposed to more advertisements for junk food[8]. Studies suggest that there's truth in both of these hypotheses. In one study of American teenagers, for example, screen media use wasn't *directly* related to BMI scores, but people who paid more *attention* to TV tended to have higher BMIs[8]. This suggests that exposure to unhealthy food ads and distracted eating while watching TV may contribute to BMI scores, but also suggests that mindless eating may not be as prevalent an issue for video games or computer use. A Canadian study found evidence for this: Weekly TV use, but not video game or computer use, was associated with greater obesity[9].

To this point, we've been talking about media use and body mass scores. But it's important to note that weight is just one component of a person's overall health and well-being.[b] Other studies have taken a much broader approach to

---

[b] As an example, a person may have a fairly high BMI score but nevertheless keep physically fit lifting weights at the gym and running long-distance. In

studying well-being, looking not only at *physical* health, but *social* (e.g., relationship quality) and psychological (e.g., self-esteem, life satisfaction) health as well. In a study of Australian children, for example, researchers looked at media use and several different measures of quality of life across five years[10]. They found that children who used more media at the start of the study had poorer physical health-related quality of life by the end of the study. But they *also* showed poorer functioning socially, emotionally, and academically. In addition, participants who were the most physically active at the start of the study tended to report better physical and social functioning at the end of the study. By no means is this the last word on the link between media and well-being, and more research is clearly needed, but these studies provide a compelling case that the sedentary lifestyle associated with media use, at the very least, can't be said to be *helping* our physical and psychological well-being.

Although much of the research has focused on the *negative* effects of media use on health, there may be a silver lining to this cloud. In recent years, people have created video games specifically designed to promote physical and mental health in clinical settings. To point to just a few examples, video games haves have successfully been used to reduce nausea in children with cancer, manage anxiety, improve the effectiveness of physical therapy, alleviate burn pain, reduce bladder and bowel dysfunction, and manage diabetes and asthma symptoms[11]. With the development of consoles such as the Nintendo Wii there has been tremendous growth in the use of physical motion as an input in games designed with clinical applications[12]. A systematic review has found that such video games have improved the outcomes of:

- 69% of psychological therapy cases (e.g., reducing symptoms of post-traumatic stress disorder)
- 59% of physical therapy cases (e.g., physical rehabilitation after a stroke)
- 50% of physical activity cases
- 46% of clinician skill programs
- 42% of health education programs
- 42% of pain distraction cases
- 37% of disease self-management cases (e.g., dealing with asthma or diabetes)

These results suggest that video games – and their interactive nature – can be harnessed as a useful tool when they're specifically designed to address health-related outcomes.

We'll finish this discussion by mentioning a promising new genre of video games that aims to include physical activity as part of the game itself: exergames.

---

contrast, a person with a BMI score within the "healthy" range may spend all day sitting in a chair, smoke, and get almost no physical activity.

These games often involve the player physically moving around a room in front of a motion-capture device (e.g., posing, dancing, dodging), and have been found to increase heart rate, oxygen consumption, and energy use in a manner comparable to other light-to-moderate exercises such as brisk walking[1,2,14]. Although encouraging, and certainly better than being completely sedentary, experts caution that, in their current form, these exergames cannot fully replace traditional exercise[15] and do not, in and of themselves, lead to lasting changes in physical activity or obesity[16,17]. This is due, in part, to the fact that players often do not play such games for long enough or as intensely as is needed to see lasting changes[14,18]. Nevertheless, recent games have offered a promising new direction for video game technology, especially as interest grows for virtual reality and augmented reality games, which seem ideally suited for building games that get people to get up and walk around the world – digital or otherwise. As games like *Pokémon GO* have proven, it's possible to design games that can get millions of players out of their chairs and out into the world interacting with one another – even if it's just to chase down imaginary monsters.[c]

References
1. Peng, W., Lin, J.-H., & Crouse, J. (2011). Is playing exergames really exercising? A meta-analysis of energy expenditure in active video games. *Cyberpsychology, Behavior, and Social Networking, 14*(11), 681–688.
2. Swe en, J., Wallington, S. F., Sheppard, V., Taylor, T., Llanos, A. A., & Adams-Campbell, L. L. (2014). The role of exergaming in improving physical activity: A review. *Journal of Physical Activity and Health, 11*(4), 864–870.
3. Maitland, C., Stratton, G., Foster, S., Braham, R., & Rosenberg, M. (2013). A place for play? The influence of the home physical environment on children's physical activity and sedentary behavior. *The International Journal of Behavioral Nutrition and Physical Activity, 10*.
4. Duch, H., Fisher, E. M., Ensari, I., & Harrington, A. (2013). Screen time use in children under 3 years old: a systematic review of correlates. *International Journal of Behavioral Nutrition and Physical Activity, 10*, 102.
5. Jackson, L. A., von Eye, A., Fitzgerald, H. E., Witt, E. A., & Zhao, Y. (2011). Internet use, videogame playing and cell phone use as predictors of children's body mass index (BMI), body weight, academic performance, and social and overall self-esteem. *Computers in Human Behavior, 27*(1), 599–604.

---

[c] One of the authors has experienced the health benefits of *Pokémon GO* second-hand: Several of his friends play the game and have dragged him out of the house to accompany them on monster-hunting expeditions around the park near his house. Funnily enough, this was so they didn't feel silly walking around for miles pursuing imaginary monsters *by themselves*.

6. Wack, E., & Tantleff-Dunn, S. (2009). Relationships between electronic game play, obesity, and psychosocial functioning in young men. *CyberPsychology & Behavior, 12*(2), 241–244.

7. Marshall, S. J., Biddle, S. J. H., Gorely, T., Cameron, N., & Murdey, I. (2004). Relationships between media use, body fatness and physical activity in children and youth: A meta-analysis. *International Journal of Obesity, 28*(10), 1238–1246.

8. Bickham, D. S., Blood, E. A., Walls, C. E., Shrier, L. A., & Rich, M. (2013). Characteristics of screen media use associated with higher BMI in young adolescents. *Pediatrics, 131*(5), 935–941.

9. Casiano, H., Kinley, D. J., Katz, L. Y., Chartier, M. J., & Sareen, J. (2012). Media use and health outcomes in adolescents: Findings form a nationally representative survey. *Journal of the Canadian Academy of Child and Adolescent Psychiatry, 21*(4), 296–301.

10. Gopinath, B., Hardy, L. L., Baur, L. A., Burlutsky, G., & Mitchell, P. (2012). Physical activity and sedentary behaviors and health-related quality of life in adolescents. *Pediatrics, 130*(1), e167–e174.

11. Kato, P. M. (2010). Video games in health care: Closing the gap. *Review of General Psychology, 14*(2), 113–121.

12. Pessoa, T. M., Coutinho, D. S., Pereira, V. M., Ribeiro, N. P. de O., Nardi, A. E., & Silva, A. C. de O. e. (2014). The Nintendo Wii as a tool for neurocognitive rehabilitation, training and health promotion. *Computers in Human Behavior, 31*, 384–392.

13. Primack, B. A., Carroll, M. V., McNamara, M., Klem, M. L., King, B., Rich, M., ... Nayak, S. (2012). Role of video games in improving health-related outcomes: A systematic review. *American Journal of Preventive Medicine, 42*(6), 630–638.

14. Barnett, A., Cerin, E., & Baranowski, T. (2011). Active video games for youth: A systematic review. *Journal of Physical Activity & Health, 8*(5), 724–737.

15. Dutta, N., & Pereira, M. A. (2015). Effects of active video games on energy expenditure in adults: A systematic literature review. *Journal of Physical Activity and Health, 12*(6), 890–899.

16. Lu, A. S., Kharrazi, H., Gharghabi, F., & Thompson, D. (2013). A systematic review of health videogames on childhood obesity prevention and intervention. *Games for Health, 2*(3), 131–141.

17. Peng, W., Crouse, J. C., & Lin, J.-H. (2013). Using active video games for physical activity promotion: A systematic review of the current state of research. *Health Education & Behavior, 40*(2), 171–192.

18. Kari, T. (2014). Can exergaming promote physical fitness and physical activity? A systematic review of systematic reviews. *International Journal of Gaming and Computer-Mediated Simulations, 6*(4), 59–77.

40 - Do video games harm school performance?

The Short Answer:

They can: Numerous studies show that those who spend a lot of time playing video games tend to perform worse in grade school, middle school, high school, and college than those who play fewer video games. However, this relation seems to occur specifically when playing video games interferes with studying, doing homework, or sleep. Keeping play time to moderate levels should reduce this interference. Some studies also suggest that certain genres of game (e.g., educational games, strategy games) can actually *improve* school performance. In other words, it wouldn't be accurate to say that simply playing video games harms school performance: It matters how much one plays, whether playing takes away from sleep and studying time, and what types of games are being played.

The Long Answer:

One of the authors, Courtney, vividly remembers his first few weeks at college as a period of freedom unlike anything he had ever known before. He was free to do pretty much whatever he wanted. He could eat what he wanted[a] when he wanted. He could stay up until *he* decided it was time for bed. He could decide for himself when it was time to take out the trash. But, most relevant to the present chapter, Courtney also discovered that he could play video games as much as he wanted without anyone stopping him. He took full advantage of this last freedom in particular. He often found himself putting off studying so he could play a few more hours of *Civilization III*, *Starcraft*, and *Diablo II* – three of his favorite games at the time.

All of this came to a screeching halt when Courtney got his grades back for his first semester. To put it gently, they weren't exactly the grades he had been hoping for. Ultimately, he realized that computer games were eating up far too much of his time. The pull of one more level or one more online match was taking time away from studying and keeping him up so late that he was struggling to stay awake in classes. He knew he wanted to someday get into graduate school, which was highly competitive. He realized, much to his chagrin, that he would have to impose many of the same rules about media use that that his parents had imposed

---

[a] For the college student with discerning taste buds (and reckless disregard for their physical health), Courtney recommends putting soda in your cereal when you run out of milk.

on him when he was in high school. Thankfully, his grades picked up and he ended up getting into graduate school.

But was college-age Courtney right to blame his low grades on his gaming habits? We can answer this question by turning to what the research has to say about the subject. Put simply, the answer from media researchers is a pretty strong "yes." Numerous cross-sectional studies have shown that, whether you're looking at children, teenagers, or college students, the more time they spend playing video games, the poorer they tend to do in school on average[1-4]. Of course, as we discuss in Question #9, cross-sectional studies can't *prove* that one thing *causes* another thing to occur, so these studies, in and of themselves, are not enough to prove that that media use *causes* poor academic performance. But we can look at the results of other types of studies to see whether they lead to the same conclusion without this particular limitation.

When it comes to experimental studies about video game use and school performance, there are surprisingly few studies on the subject – in part because of the practical difficulties in conducting such studies.[b] But they do exist! In one clever study, young boys were randomly divided into one of two groups. The first group received a PlayStation 2 (PS2) game console and 3 games for it. The Control group would receive the same game console and games, but 4 months later[5]. After four months had passed, the researchers compared the two groups. As shown in Table 40.1, the boys who had immediately received the PS2 spent more time playing video games and less time on academic activities than the boys who had *not* yet received a PS2. They also had lower reading and writing scores and their teachers indicated that they were having more school problems (attention & learning) than the boys who had not yet received the PS2. The researchers concluded that the boys in the "immediate PS2" condition had, predictably, spent a lot of time playing their new video game console, which had the unfortunate effect of harming their school performance.

---

[b] There are at least two reasons why it's so difficult to conduct such studies. First, researchers must find a way to reliably manipulate how much media use participants engage in – which is easier said than done outside of the laboratory. Second, such studies typically have to take place over a longer period of time (i.e., longer than a day or two), in order to for noticeable changes in school performance to occur. This makes such studies both time- and resource-intensive.

Table 40.1. Effects of receiving a PlayStation 2 on school performance four months later, 6-9 year-old boys.

Outcome at 4 months	PS2	Control
Game play (minutes per day)	39	9
After school academics (minutes per day)	18	32
Reading score (adjusted for pre-test)	96	102
Writing score (adjusted for pre-test)	95	101
Teacher-rated attention & learning problems	52	47

Of course, not every experiment has led researchers to the same conclusion. In a study of college students, researchers found *no* changes in academic performance after some participants were assigned to play at least an hour of a video game each week for a month[6]. Of course, researchers need to think critically about the design of such studies to determine whether the studies were a fair test of the hypothesis. After all, it's possible that in this second study, college students may not have been playing video games as much as the children in the first study were (one hour a week is much less than the average). Alternatively, one month may not have been enough time for noticeable differences in academic performance to emerge between the groups. Yet another possibility is that students in the "control" condition actually were playing video games as much as those in the "at least 1 hour per week" condition – something researchers can have difficulty controlling. Or, as a final possibility, the college students may have been inflating their own academic performance, something which the children in the first study couldn't do, since their grades were provided to the researchers by their teachers. In short, this second study has several important limitations and seems to be the exception, rather than the rule, when it comes to the few experimental studies about video games and school performance.

Although there haven't been many experiments on media use and school performance, there have been a number of *longitudinal* studies looking at screen media effects on academic performance. In one particularly illustrative study of elementary school students, researchers found that more time spent on video games and television at the start of the study predicted lower grades five months later[7]. Another study of middle school children found similar results over two years and went one step further: Media exposure was *also* associated with more drug use and problem behavior at school, both of which, in turn, reduced academic performance[8]. In this study, however, it was video game *addiction* that led to the decline in performance, not the exact number of hours students spent playing per week (see Questions #42, #43, and #44 for more on video game addiction.). Similar results were found in an all-male sample of college students.[9]

Displacement of other activities is difficult to measure, because you're basically trying to measure something *not* happening. Nonetheless, a couple studies have successfully looked at how screen time may hinder school performance indirectly. In one, over 1,000 families were measured several times across 13 months, finding that screen time (including TV, video games, and online computer time) predicted less sleep, which in turn predicted more attention problems.[10] In another longitudinal set of studies with large samples and lags of up to two years, researchers found that screen time had an effect on later grades by reducing sleep and reducing reading for pleasure. That is, the more time children spent on electronic media, the less they read and slept, and these in turn predicted poorer later school performance.[11] This effect was even stronger if the children had screen media (TVs or video games) in their bedrooms.

Based on these studies and many others like them, we can confidently say that television use is associated with poor academic performance. When it comes to video games, the picture is a bit more nuanced: Video games *do* seem to be linked to poorer academic performance, but the effect may be driven more by students who play with excessive frequency.[12] When it comes to low or moderate levels of gameplay, there's unlikely to be much difference between people who play 2 hours of games per week and those who play 5 hours per week. (The average among youth gamers is about 13 hours a week.)

Since video games and other screen media do seem to be hurting academic performance, we can ask *why* this might be the case. What is it about video games and other screen media that's causing this harm? After all, it doesn't *seem* like sitting in front of a screen or controlling a character should have anything to do with how students do on an exam.

Researchers believe that the effects of media on academic performance are primarily due to something called *activity displacement*. In a nutshell, this means that time spent playing games or watching television is time *not* spent studying, reading, doing schoolwork, creating, exploring, or any number of other activities that might have more educational benefit. If this hypothesis is true, it might explain why video game addiction is more strongly associated with poor school performance than whether people play video games at all. As long as students have enough time to do their homework and study, video game playing is unlikely to interfere with homework or other academic activities, meaning the total amount of game playing they do (after completing their schoolwork) should do little to harm their school performance.[c]

Supporting this notion, some studies of children and adolescents find that video game addiction is a *better* predictor of negative academic outcomes than frequency of video game play is[9,12,13]. This makes a lot of sense when you consider that addictive gaming is, *by definition*, gaming that interferes with other important activities – meaning it's defined, in part, by the fact that it takes away from activities like studying. To use an example, let's imagine a person who plays video games for 20 hours a week. This person is a student, but they have no other job or responsibilities. They rush home after school and get all of their studying and schoolwork done first, leaving them with plenty of time to play games. Such a student is unlikely to be adversely affected by the game-playing. Now imagine a person who plays video games for 20 hours per week but also has football practice, a part-time job, and a partner in addition to school. This person will have to sacrifice *something* to find time to play for 20 hours a week. Schoolwork may well be one of these sacrifices.

This would also explain why some studies fail to find a relation between frequency of video game play and academic performance. If the participants are all finding ways to complete their schoolwork (i.e., they are not playing games to an extreme extent), it's less likely that the amount of gaming they're doing will be related to their academic performance. In other words, such studies may be using samples of students who were *not* displacing their academic activities with video game playing[14,15]. The research, taken together, suggests that when it comes to academic performance and video games, how you balance video game play and schoolwork is perhaps more important than how many hours you play.

It might also matter what *kinds* of video games you play. Some studies suggest that some games can *improve* learning and school performance. In a study of kindergarten students, for example, researchers found that those randomly assigned to play an hour per day of age-appropriate educational games for a semester improved their spelling and reading skills over children who did not play the educational games[16]. In another study, students who took a game-based online course had better grades at the end of the semester than students who took a traditional version of the same course, suggesting that elements of games can actually improve learning[17]. As a final example, a four-year study of Canadian high school students found that those who played more strategy-based video games became better problem-solvers over time which, in turn, led to better grades[18]. This effect was specific to strategy-based games, as students who played

---

[c] This doesn't mean, of course, that all those hours of video game use are having *no* effects on kids. As we point out in Questions #11, #37, #38, and #39, media use contributes to other negative outcomes, including aggression, risk-taking behavior, attention problems, and health issues.

fast-paced, non-strategy games did not experience the same increase in school performance.

Before you rush out to buy the newest educational games on the market, we'd like to finish this section with one of our favorite analogies: chocolate-covered broccoli. Sounds disgusting, doesn't it? The concept stems from the fact that all of us know that broccoli is good for us, but few children *love* broccoli. In contrast, many think chocolate is pretty wonderful, even if it lacks nutritional benefits. A highly-imaginative person may try to combine these two foods to create a perfect super-food with the desirability of chocolate and the nutrition of broccoli. You probably see the problem with this approach: Chocolate and broccoli work against one another, with chocolate undercutting the nutritional value of the broccoli and the broccoli undercutting the taste of the chocolate. The result is a product that does neither nutrition nor taste very well.

Now replace "chocolate" with "video games" and "broccoli" with "learning." It's appealing to make education fun by dressing up math or history lessons with flashing lights and wacky sound effects, but the result is, more often than not, something that's both a bad game and an inefficient teaching tool. For this reason, many educational games fail to create the sort of engaged learning that parents and teachers hope for. So what does a *good* educational game do? In a good educational game, the lessons are a natural extension of the problems encountered in the game itself (i.e., they don't *feel* like a learning experience). For an excellent real-world example, take the wildly-successful computer game *Kerbal Space Program*. The game teaches players astrophysics and rocket science, not by forcing them to complete dry physics problems with flashy lights, but by asking them to build their own rocket, make mistakes, see the disastrous consequences of those mistakes, and then improve their design based on the principles of rocket science. If a game can make something as complex as rocket science fun and make millions of people *want* to learn about it, it's doing something right.

Parents who are concerned about their child's academic performance and the effects of media on it should consider three things. First, look beyond how many hours they're spending playing or watching and in addition ask whether they're playing or watching at the *expense* of schoolwork, studying, other beneficial hobbies, or sleep. Second, they should consider what *types* of media their children are consuming and, whenever possible, find ways to encourage them to consume media that has benefits (e.g., strategic games, educational games). And third, they should be wary of media *claiming* to be educational without exploring it for themselves. It should take only a few minutes of trying it out to determine whether their child will like it, or whether you've got a piece of chocolate-covered broccoli in your hands.

References

1. Anderson, C. A., Carnagey, N. L., Flanagan, M., Benjamin, A. J., Eubanks, J., & Valentine, J. C. (2004). Violent video games: Specific effects of violent content on aggressive thoughts and behavior. *Advances in Experimental Social Psychology, 36,* 200–251.

2. Gentile, D. A., Lynch, P. J., Linder, J. R., & Walsh, D. A. (2004). The effects of violent video game habits on adolescent hostility, aggressive behaviors, and school performance. *Journal of Adolescence, 27*(1), 5–22.

3. Hastings, E. C., Karas, T. L., Winsler, A., Way, E., Madigan, A., & Tyler, S. (2009). Young children's video/computer game use: Relations with school performance and behavior. *Issues in Mental Health Nursing, 30*(10), 638–649.

4. Jackson, L. A., von Eye, A., Fitzgerald, H. E., Witt, E. A., & Zhao, Y. (2011). Internet use, videogame playing and cell phone use as predictors of children's body mass index (BMI), body weight, academic performance, and social and overall self-esteem. *Computers in Human Behavior, 27*(1), 599–604.

5. Weis, R., & Cerankosky, B. C. (2010). Effects of video-game ownership on young boys' academic and behavioral functioning a randomized, controlled study. *Psychological Science, 21*(4), 463–470.

6. Smyth, J. M. (2007). Beyond self-selection in video game play: an experimental examination of the consequences of massively multiplayer online role-playing game play. *CyberPsychology & Behavior, 10*(5), 717–721.

7. Anderson, C. A., Gentile, D. A., & Buckley, K. E. (2007). *Violent video game effects on children and adolescents: Theory, research, and public policy.* New York, NY: Oxford University Press, Inc.

8. Sharif, I., Wills, T. A., & Sargent, J. D. (2010). Effect of visual media use on school performance: A prospective study. *Journal of Adolescent Health, 46*(1), 52–61.

9. Brunborg, G. S., Mentzoni, R. A., & Frøyland, L. R. (2014). Is video gaming, or video game addiction, associated with depression, academic achievement, heavy episodic drinking, or conduct problems? *Journal of Behavioral Addictions, 3*(1), 27–32.

10. Barlett, N., Gentile, D. A., Barlett, C. P., Eisenmann, J. C., & Walsh, D. A. (2012). Sleep as a mediator of screen time effects on American children's health outcomes: A prospective study. *Journal of Children and Media, 6,* 37-50. DOI:10.1080/17482798.2011.633404.

11. Gentile, D. A., Berch, O. N., Choo, H., Khoo, A., Walsh, D. A. (2017). Bedroom media: One risk factor for development. *Developmental Psychology, 53,* 2340-2355. doi: 10.1037/dev0000399

12. Schmitt, Z. L., & Livingston, M. G. (2015). Video game addiction and college performance among males: Results from a 1 year longitudinal study. *Cyberpsychology, Behavior, and Social Networking, 18*(1), 25–29.

13. Skoric, M. M., Teo, L. L. C., & Neo, R. L. (2009). Children and video games: Addiction, engagement, and scholastic achievement. *CyberPsychology & Behavior, 12*(5), 567–572.

14. Ferguson, C. J. (2011). The influence of television and video game use on attention and school problems: A multivariate analysis with other risk factors controlled. *Journal of Psychiatric Research, 45*(6), 808–813.
15. Wack, E., & Tantleff-Dunn, S. (2009). Relationships between electronic game play, obesity, and psychosocial functioning in young men. *CyberPsychology & Behavior, 12*(2), 241–244.
16. Din, F. S., & Calao, J. (2001). The effects of playing educational video games on kindergarten achievement. *Child Study Journal, 31*(2), 95.
17. Hess, T., & Gunter, G. (2013). Serious game-based and nongame-based online courses: Learning experiences and outcomes. *British Journal of Educational Technology, 44*(3), 372–385.
18. Adachi, P., & Willoughby, T. (2013). More than just fun and games: The longitudinal relationships between strategic video games, self-reported problem solving skills, and academic grades. *Journal of Youth & Adolescence, 42*(7), 1041–1052.

41 - Aren't there also *good* effects of playing video games?

The Short Answer:

Yes, absolutely! Although this book has focused primarily on the negative effects of media because that's what most parents want to know about, there is a growing body of work showing that screen media can have several positive effects on users. These positive effects are most easily found in media that are specifically designed with these goals in mind (e.g., prosocial or educational media). That said, it's also possible to get several benefits from violent media, although these benefits come from the medium itself (e.g., learning to respond quickly to fast-paced events on the screen) rather than the violent content specifically.

The Long Answer:

In his youth, one of the authors, Courtney, recalls spending much of his free time playing video games, many of which contained more violence than they probably should have, in retrospect. When his parents would show concern about just how much time he spent playing games, he would proudly tell them "they're improving my hand-eye coordination!" Courtney had *no* idea what hand-eye coordination was, or why, exactly, it was something good. (Of course, throwing a ball would have improved it even more.) And, realistically speaking, no one was buying the argument that Courtney was playing his video games just to improve his hand-eye coordination. He was playing them for the same reason everyone else plays them: He thought they were fun. Still, in the lawyer-like mind of an eight-year old, Courtney had conveniently justified why he should be allowed to play his games without hassle.[a]

The present question is often asked by defenders of screen media in much the same way that Courtney's younger self appealed to hand-eye coordination. Sure, violent media probably have some unpleasant side effects, but they can't be *all* bad! Surely spending all that time perfecting your skills at an activity must have *some* benefits, right? And, to be sure, there *are* benefits, which we'll get to in just a moment. But throughout this discussion, let's keep a couple of things in mind. First: Just because media have *some* benefits doesn't mean that they can't still be harmful or a net negative. After all, sugar-filled food provides people with

[a] In case you are wondering, his parents didn't buy the excuse for a second. They, like Courtney, didn't know what the heck eye-hand coordination was or why it was important, so his argument usually proved less than persuasive!

287

a cheap and delicious source of energy, but this benefit doesn't change the fact that it *also* increases the eater's risk of heart disease[1]. In other words, violent media certainly aren't "all bad," but pointing out the benefit doesn't make the downsides any less real.

The second thing to keep in mind is that many of the benefits of violent media aren't *unique* to violent media. All of the benefits we'll be describing below could be obtained from non-violent media *without* the negative side effects of violent media. Returning to our junk food analogy, junk food provides people with energy, but so does fruit! And fruit does so with far fewer drawbacks for your health.

To be perfectly clear: We're not suggesting that people should restrict themselves to *only* non-violent media. As we discuss in Questions #56 and #57, we believe it's important that people make *informed* decisions about media use that include understanding both its benefits and the drawbacks of its use[2]. A person can absolutely consume violent media as part of a healthy regimen of media consumption, just as any healthy diet includes the occasional dessert or guilty pleasure snack. But it makes little sense to defend an "all junk food" diet as healthy, just as it makes little sense to argue that violent video games have only benefits and no downsides. Clear understanding and respect for the consequences – both good and bad – of the activities we partake in is important for making healthy decisions for ourselves and our children.[b]

With that out of the way, let's begin by talking about some of the benefits that come from prosocial media in particular – that is, media with strong messages of helping, sharing, or which otherwise model positive social behavior. Strangely enough, we can discuss prosocial media effects using the General Aggression Model that we introduced in Question #12. The GAM states that aggressive behavior is influenced by a multitude of factors including activated aggressive thoughts, learned aggressive scripts, aggressive attitudes and beliefs, and perceived hostility in the world around us[3].

But there's no reason to believe that these processes *only* apply to aggressive behavior. As it turns out, these exact same processes can be used to create all sorts of behavior, *including* prosocial behavior. For example, a picture of a gun activates the concept of "gun" and the related concept of "aggression" in a person's mind, making them more likely to see aggression in the world and to activate aggressive scripts. Using the exact same mental process, a picture of a gift may activate the concept of "giving" and the related concept of "sharing" in a person's mind, making them more likely to see kindness in others and to behave generously toward others! Or, looking at another mental process, imagine a viewer sees a film character get rewarded for their violent behavior. The result is the

---

[b] And we do strongly suggest that parents pay attention to the amount and type of violent content in their children and adolescents' media diet, just as parents would for their food diet.

288

viewer will associate aggression with positivity, making them more likely to behave aggressively in the future. In the same way, however, a viewer who sees a film character get rewarded for their generosity will be more likely to associate generosity with positivity, making them more likely to act generously toward others. In short, many of the psychological mechanisms that drive violent media effects are also known to drive the effects of prosocial media on prosocial behavior.[c]

Numerous studies have shown exactly what we've described here: Exposing people to prosocial media increases their prosocial thoughts, feelings, empathy for others, and helpful behavior in a manner analogous to that of violent media[4-8]. The first experimental study of this type compared the effects of playing either a prosocial game, a neutral game or a violent game for 20 minutes on a later task where participants could choose to help or to hurt another person's chances of winning a $10 gift card[4]. Specifically, participants were responsible for assigning puzzles for another person to complete. If the other person completed enough puzzles, that other person would win a gift card. The participant could choose to assign the other person easy puzzles or difficult puzzles. As can be seen in Figure 41.1, those who had just played a prosocial game chose more easy (helpful) and fewer difficult (hurtful) puzzles than participants who had just played a violent or a neutral game. Conversely, those who had just played a violent game chose more difficult and fewer easy puzzles than either of the two other game groups.

---

[c] Interestingly, the same research teams who pioneered work on the harmful effects of violent video games on aggression also pioneered studies on the *beneficial* effects of prosocial video games. These two teams both worked out of Iowa State University, headed up by two of this book's authors, Craig and Douglas. Funnily enough, neither researcher has *ever* gotten hate mail or been attacked on the internet for their work on the *benefits* of prosocial video games, despite constantly catching flack for their work on violent video games!

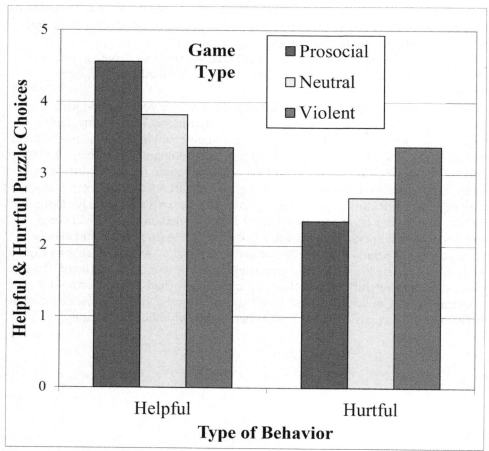

Figure 41.1. Effects of playing a prosocial, neutral, or violent video game on later helpful and hurtful puzzle choices.

In another of our favorite examples, undergraduate students were randomly assigned to play one of three different video games for 8 minutes[9]. One of the video games featured prosocial content: Players played the video game *Lemmings*, where the goal was to help digital critters avoid harm and get to the end of the level safely. Another game, *Lamers*, was a violent version of *Lemmings*: Players were instructed to kill all of the digital critters before any of them could reach the end of the map. The last game, *Tetris*, was devoid of any prosocial or violent content: Players simply stacked blocks in a moving puzzle.

Later in the study, after players had played one of these three games, the research assistant was trained to "accidentally" knock a cup full of pencils onto the ground. They were interested in measuring participants' willingness to help: Who would get down on their hands and knees and help the research assistant pick up the spilled pencils? As it turns out, participants who played the prosocial game were *twice* as likely to help as participants who played either the neutral or the violent game. In the same way that violent games increase a person's likelihood of engaging in aggressive behavior, these results suggest that a prosocial game can similarly increase a person's likelihood of engaging in prosocial behavior. Later studies found the same pattern of effects with other forms of prosocial behavior, including being more likely to volunteer your time and being more likely to step in and help a woman who was being harassed by her boyfriend[9].

The effects of prosocial media aren't limited to video games either. In one study, preschool children who were assigned to watch the prosocial television program *Mister Rogers' Neighborhood* for a week tended to interact more with other children during free-play and were more likely to share, hold hands, praise one another, and be generally positive[10]. A review of nearly three decades of research on the television show *Sesame Street* similarly concluded that the show increases cooperation, reduces aggression, and improves relationships between children of different racial groups[11]. These effects were universal, being observed in children across cultures. Clearly media with non-violent, prosocial messages can have beneficial effects on the user's prosocial behavior.

But we've only been looking at media designed to model and improve *prosocial behavior*; what about media designed to have *other* positive effects? It turns out media can be purpose-built to have all sorts of specific benefits to consumers! Certain well-designed educational video games can be an effective teaching tool[12] that hold the players' attention and responds to their needs. Games like these can improve school performance[13], job skills[14], and health-related knowledge[15]. As we discussed in Question #39, games can also designed with player mobility and physical activity in mind: Games such as *Dance Dance Revolution* (a rhythm-based game that requires players to dance in time with arrows on a screen) or *Wii Fit* are designed to motivate the player's physical activity[16,17], while games such as *Pokémon GO* have shown us that encouraging players to go out and explore the (digitally augmented) world around them is both popular[18] and effective at getting players off of the couch[19].

Up to this point, however, we've only been looking at media that were *specifically designed* to have positive outcomes for players. But remember that young Courtney, like many gamers, wanted to argue that his *violent* games, built primarily for player entertainment, not education, were beneficial. So what does the research show?

As it turns out, young Courtney was at least somewhat right. Studies *have* shown that video games, violent or otherwise, can improve a wide range of mental abilities. In one study gaming was found to improve the amount of attention players could devote to their entire visual field, meaning players became better at noticing and reacting to things at the edge of their field of vision[20] (see Question #37). In another study, players of action video games were faster at storing visual information in their short-term memory than non-players[21]. At least one study suggests players of shooter video games may also be better at filtering out irrelevant information from a visual scene[22]. And finally, most vindicating of all for young Courtney: Yes, video games do improve eye-hand coordination[23], and have been suggested as a possible way to improve speed and reduce errors in surgeons (although the correlational nature of this work makes causal inferences risky)[24]. Studies like these, in short, show us that video games, violent or otherwise, absolutely *can* have positive effects on the way our minds work.

But the benefits don't stop there! For example, while violent video games *do* increase players' likelihood of aggression, *team-based* violent games may also improve *cooperation* in some contexts. In one study, players were randomly assigned to play the popular violent shooter game *Halo II* either competitively (attacking other participants) or cooperatively (working together with other participants to attack computer players). Participants who played cooperatively during the game ended up behaving more cooperatively in a later, unrelated task in the study[25]. This same effect has been found by other researchers using other games[26].

Researchers studying massive multiplayer online games such as *EVE Online*[27] and *World of Warcraft*[28] have also found that players can practice and improve their leadership skills by coordinating the actions of large groups of other players called guilds. Some researchers have even suggested that playing video games can improve player well-being[29] by offering them a way to satisfy needs for growth, improvement, and feelings of control in their life (although Question #39 discusses how a sedentary lifestyle associated with video gaming can reduce player health and well-being.) Again, the correlational nature of most of these studies warrants caution in interpretation.

To summarize: Several lines of research show that people can, and do, benefit from screen media use. This is *especially* likely to be the case when the media themselves are designed to have benefits on users. These benefits don't undo or counteract other negative effects of media (e.g., violent media on aggression, excessive media use and health problems) but they do, at very least, offer a more complex view of screen media effects as not being entirely bad. In recent years, research on these benefits has been growing. Unfortunately, as the public continues to deny the existence of undesirable media effects, researchers find themselves forced to repeatedly conduct study after study re-proving that negative media violence effects exist, which leaves far less time and resources for studying the *benefits* of media use. Hopefully this will change in time, allowing researchers to better study and understand the all the upsides and downsides to media use. This will allow designers to use this research to craft media that maximize the benefits while minimizing the potential harms to the user. It will also allow consumers to make properly-informed decisions about their own media diet.

References

1. Ascherio, A., Rimm, E. B., Giovannucci, E. L., Spiegelman, D., Stampfer, M., & Willett, W. C. (1996). Dietary fat and risk of coronary heart disease in men: Cohort follow up study in the United States. *BMJ, 313,* 84-90.
2. Prot, S., McDonald, K. A., Anderson, C. A., & Gentile, D. A. (2012). Video games: Good, bad, or other? *Pediatric Clinics of North America, 59,* 647-658.
3. Anderson, C. A. & Bushman, B. J. (2002). Human Aggression. *Annual Review of Psychology, 53,* 27-51.
4. Gentile, D. A., Anderson, C. A., Yukawa, S., Ihori, N., Saleem, M., Ming, L. K., Shibuya, A., Liau, A., Khoo, A., Bushman, B. J., Huesmann, L. R., & Sakamoto, A. (2009). The effects of prosocial video games on prosocial behaviors: International evidence from correlational, longitudinal, and experimental studies. *Personality and Social Psychology Bulletin, 35*(6), 752-763.
5. Greitemeyer, T., & Mügge, D. O. (2014). Video games do affect social outcomes: A meta-analytic review of the effects of violent and prosocial video game play. *Personality and Social Psychology Bulletin, 40*(5), 578-589.
6. Greitemeyer, T. & Osswald, S. (2009). Playing prosocial video games reduce aggressive cognitions. *Journal of Experimental Social Psychology, 4,* 896-900.
7. Greitemeyer, T. & Osswald, S. (2011). Playing prosocial video games increases the accessibility of prosocial thoughts. *Journal of Social Psychology, 151*(2), 121-128.
8. Greitemeyer, T., Osswald, S., & Brauer, M. (2010). Playing prosocial video games increases empathy and decrease schadenfreude. *Emotion, 10*(6), 796-802.
9. Greitemeyer, T. & Osswald, S. (2010). Effects of prosocial video games on prosocial behavior. *Journal of Personality and Social Psychology, 98*(2), 211-221.
10. Coates, B., Pusser, H. E., & Goodman, I. (1976). The influence of "Sesame Street" and "Mister Rogers' Neighborhood" on children's social behavior in preschool. *Child Development, 47*(1), 138-144.
11. Fisch, S. M., Truglio, R. T., & Cole, C. F. (1999). The impact of Sesame Street on preschool children: A review and synthesis of 30 years' research. *Media Psychology, 1*(2), 165-190.
12. Gentile, D. A. & Gentile, J. R. (2008). Violent video games as exemplary teachers: A conceptual analysis. *Journal of Youth and Adolescence, 9,* 127-141.
13. Corbett, A. T., Koedinger, K. R., & Hadley, W. (2001). Cognitive tutors: From the research classroom to all classrooms. In P. S. Goodman (Ed.).

Technology enhanced learning (pp. 235-263). Mahwah (NJ): Lawrence Erlbaum.

14. Flood, S. (2006). All play and more work. In: *Computing*. Retrieved from http://www.computing.co.uk/computing/analysis/2152597/play-work
15. Brown, S. J., Lieberman, D. A., Germeny, B. A., Fan, Y. C., Wilson, D. M., & Pasta, D. J. (1997). Educational video game for juvenile diabetes: Results of a controlled trial. *Medical Informatics, 22*(1), 77-89.
16. Biddiss, E. & Irwin, J. (2010). Active video games to promote physical activity in children and youth. *Archives of Pediatric and Adolescent Medicine, 164*(7), 664-672.
17. Graf, D. L., Pratt, L. V., Hester, C. N., & Short, K. R. (2009). Playing active video games increases energy expenditure in children. *Pediatrics, 124*(2), 534-540.
18. Meyer, D. (2016, August 12). Pokémon Go creator is now the most popular game publisher in the world. *Fortune*. Retrieved from http://fortune.com/2016/08/12/niantic-pokemon-go-popularity/
19. Kim, L. (2016, July 20). Is Pokémon Go going to help people who seldom exercise to walk a lot more? *Medical Daily*. Retrieved from http://www.medicaldaily.com/pokemon-go-sedentary-lifestyle-get-fit-392304
20. Green, C. S., & Bavelier, D. (2006). Effect of action video games on the spatial distribution of visuospatial attention. *Journal of Experimental Psychology: Human Perception and Performance, 32*(6), 1465-1478.
21. Wilms, I. L., Petersen, A., & Vangkilde, S. (2013). Intensive video gaming improves encoding speed to visual short-term memory in young male adults. *Acta Psychologica, 142,* 108-118.
22. Bavelier, D., Achtman, R. L., Mani, M., & Föcker, J. (2012). Neural bases of selective attention in action video game players. *Vision Research, 61,* 132-143.
23. Griffith, J. L., Voloschin, P., Gibb, G. D., & Bailey, J. R. (1983). Differences in eye-hand motor coordination of video-game users and non-users. *Perceptual and Motor Skills, 57*(1), 155-158.
24. Rosser, J. C. Jr., Lynch, P. J., Cuddihy, L., Gentile, D. A., Klonsky, J., & Merrell, R. (2007). The impact of video games on training surgeons in the 21st century. *Archives of Survery, 142*(2), 181-186.
25. Ewoldsen, D. R., Eno, C. A., Okdie, B. M., Velez, J. A., Guadagno, R. E., & DeCoster, J. (2012). Effect of playing violent video games cooperatively or competitively on subsequent cooperative behavior. *Cyberpsychology, Behavior, and Social Networking, 15*(5), 277-280.
26. Greitemeyer, T., Traut-Mattausch, E., & Osswald, S. (2012). How to ameliorate negative effects of violent games on cooperation: Play it cooperatively in a team. *Computers in Human Behavior, 28*(4), 1465-1470.
27. Lisk, T. C., Kaplancali, U. T., & Riggio, R. E. (2012). Leadership in multiplayer online gaming environments. *Simulation Gaming, 43*(1), 133-149.

28. YeiBeech, J., & SeongHo, R. (2011). Exploring game experiences and game leadership in massively multiplayer online role-playing games. *British Journal of Educational Technology, 42*(4), 616-623.
29. Ryan, R. M., Rigby, C. S., & Przybylski, A. (2006). The motivational pull of video games: A self-determination theory approach. *Motivation and Emotion, 30*, 347-363.

42 - Is video game addiction a real thing?

The Short Answer:

Almost certainly, yes, although it's a fairly small percentage of gamers who would be diagnosed with the disorder. Video game addiction is officially referred to in the U.S. as Internet Gaming Disorder (IGD) and has been recognized by the American Psychiatric Association in the most recent edition of the Diagnostics and Statistical Manual of Mental Disorders (5th ed.; DSM-5)[1] – the reference manual that clinical psychologists use to diagnose and treat patients with mental illnesses. As of 2013, IGD was described as a condition requiring further study to better understand its causes, symptoms, treatment, and relationship with other conditions. In 2019, however, its conceptual counterpart, Gaming Disorder (GD), was officially recognized by the World Health Organization's International Classification of Diseases (11th Revision; ICD-11)[2].

The Long Answer:

When most of us think about "addictions," the first things to come to mind are biological addictions to drugs, such as nicotine, alcohol, cocaine, or heroin.[a] But what about addictions that *don't* involve consuming a particular substance? What if, instead, the addiction is to a particular behavior or activity – known as a *behavioral addiction*? Video game addiction is an example of one such *behavioral* addiction. Despite the fact that it doesn't match the image many of us conjure up of an addict craving their drug of choice, addiction to video games (or any pleasurable, rewarding behavior) is very much possible! In fact, in many ways it is very similar to *gambling addiction* or *gambling disorder*.

It might seem a bit silly, at first, to consider it a *bad* thing to want to spend all of one's time thinking about and playing a video game. After all, addictiveness is often a *selling point* for games: If a game makes you not want to put it down, many of us would simply call it a good game, not an addiction in the player! For this reason, it can often seem to laypersons that researchers are simply out to blame online games for being too fun, or blaming gamers themselves for having a hobby they're passionate about.

---

[a] Caffeine is arguably one of the most common, and socially acceptable, addictions that people have. Think for a moment about how common it is to see a cartoon character humorously musing about the fact that they can't function without a cup of coffee, and then realize how disturbing that would be if it were replaced with "heroin" or "cocaine"!

This belief is based on a fundamental misunderstanding about what, precisely, makes an addiction an addiction. The scientific definition of "addiction" differs greatly from the everyday use of the word "addiction." We discuss specific symptoms of video game addiction in greater detail in Question #43, but for now, it's enough to say that "addiction" is not the same thing as "liking something a lot". An addiction refers specifically to a situation where one's use of a substance or engagement in an activity is causing significant harm to other important aspects of their lives. This is the same for a drug addiction and gambling addiction as it is for a video game addiction: Liking the taste of alcohol or consuming it with some regularity isn't what defines a person as having an addiction to it. Alcohol use becomes an addiction when the person starts to show up to work drunk (or miss work altogether), when they start hurting their relationships with their friends and family because of alcohol, and when their physical health is harmed because of their alcohol use. In the same fashion, liking a video game is not enough to be considered an addiction, nor is spending a lot of time playing one's favorite video game. But if your video game playing is causing you to shirk your responsibilities as a student, parent, spouse, or employee, or if it's destroying your relationships with other people, then psychologists become concerned that the activity has become an addiction for that person.

If you still think it's weird to think about being addicted to a *behavior* rather than a drug, it's helpful to point out that video gaming isn't the *only* example of a behavioral addiction. In fact, the model for studying Internet Gaming Disorder (IGD), which video game addiction is officially recognized as by the American Psychiatric Association[1b] comes from an abundance of past research on gambling disorders. Like with gaming, people who go to casinos to gamble would argue that it would be silly to blame casinos for making their games too fun, and certainly no psychologist is against people having fun. But we, as a society, recognize that gambling has an incredibly powerful financial impact on people and their families. When a person knowingly loses their family's savings, steals from their friends and family, and loses almost everything they have just to be able to continue gambling, it's hard to deny that the person has moved from "entertainment" into "addiction."

For those of us who are not addicted, it's hard to imagine that a behavior, something we *choose* to do, can become addictive. After all, if gambling is causing problems, why don't these people just stop doing it? Unlike, say, a drug addiction, where one's body is craving the drug and is *dependent* on it to function without painful withdrawal symptoms, behavioral addictions don't have a biological basis, right?

As it turns out, that's not *entirely* true. There are remarkable similarities between behavioral addictions (e.g., video games, gambling), and addiction to

---

[b] The condition is recognized as Gaming Disorder (GD) by the World Health Organization in the International Classification of Diseases, 11th revision.[2]

substances. Addictions occur, in part, because a behavior or substance essentially "hijacks" the brain's natural, built-in reward system. Evolution has provided us with this area in our brain which responds to positive outcomes with a shot of chemicals that make us feel good. It's our brain's way of telling us "Hey, that thing you did – keep doing more of that!" It's an incredibly useful way to get people to do the things necessary to ensure the survival and propagation of our species (e.g., eating, being social with others, having sex and reproducing). Any behavior that activates this system is reinforced with a burst of pleasure.

Unfortunately, this system has a dark side. When we rely solely upon specific substances or specific behaviors as the main way to get the reward from this brain system, addiction starts to occur. As a result, you end up with a person who gets stuck in a sort of "behavioral loop" – they need to engage in the behavior in order to get that rush of pleasure, and, gradually, nothing else seems to give them that same feeling. Pretty soon, it's hard to feel "normal" without that substance or behavior in your life, and it becomes less about the pleasure associated with it and more about simply avoiding the pain of being deprived of the one thing that makes you feel good – or even *normal*. To people in these situations, it's easy to understand why "just stop doing it" isn't a plausible option.

The fact that video games can become addicting shouldn't be terribly surprising if you consider the fact that video games are designed by their creators to be as rewarding as possible for players. In other words, designers build games to specifically tap into the brain's reward system as much as possible, to keep the player coming back to the game and wanting more! We can see this approach to game design in popular game mechanics, especially in games that are among the most addictive.[3]

For example, massively multiplayer online games (MMORPGs) such as *World of Warcraft*, use "loot" systems that give players rewards at random points in time. Each time a player gets a desired weapon or piece of armor, their brain rewards them with a jolt of pleasure. Naturally, players seek to get as many of these rewarding experiences as possible. But the game is somewhat stingy in how it gives these rewards out. Designers know that they can't simply give players rewards every time they push a button – the player would quickly adjust to this and grow bored of it, much in the same way a person with a drug addiction requires more of their chosen drug to get the same "high".

So, what do developers do? They give out the rewards sporadically, at random and unpredictable intervals. Each time a player kills a monster they usually receive a small handful of coins or some poor-quality weapon or piece of armor they don't really want, but can sell for a trivial amount of money. Most players would quickly grow bored of this system, were it not for one key feature: Every so often, on a rare occasion, a monster will "drop" a highly-valued item like a chest full of coins or a new weapon that dramatically increases the player's power. The result? Players will kill monsters for hours, chasing that next "high," knowing that they can't quit now because the next big hit could come from the next monster they kill.

This system of randomly rewarding players has long been known to psychologists to be the most efficient way to guarantee that a behavior will be repeated.[4] In fact, if it sounds familiar, it's because the exact same system of rewards is used in slot machines. Slot machines are designed to not only hook players quickly with the promise of exciting, if randomly-occurring rewards, but the random nature of the reward means that players will continue to play even after "losing" repeatedly, knowing the next reward is just around the corner, making all of their effort worthwhile. Those who are addicted will play long after the game has stopped being about fun, playing until it's become a necessity.

Also like many disorders, interest in GD sparked from startling stories of extreme addiction. For example, in 2010, a 3 month old baby in South Korea died of malnutrition while the parents played marathon sessions of the game *Prius Online* in an Internet cafe.[5c] In 2007, a Chinese man died after a lengthy session of playing online games during a holiday break.[6] Of course, tragic events such as these are rare and quite extreme even among those who might be diagnosable with a gaming disorder. There are, however, many milder examples of people who show the same symptoms of addiction (e.g., marathon gaming sessions, ignoring important responsibilities in one's life to play a game) that have spurred interest in considering IGD as an officially diagnosable disorder in the DSM-5 and that led to the WHO classifying GD in the ICD-11.

At this point, readers who've read Question #9 will be correctly pointing out that anecdotes are not scientific, nor are they, in and of themselves, evidence for the existence of an effect. Thankfully, we don't have to rely on anecdotes for evidence of IGD.[7] For instance, research has shown that people who are being treated for IGD report feeling a loss of self-control (i.e., inability to stop playing despite wanting to do so) and frequent cravings to play – both symptoms commonly seen among those with substance addictions.[8] Likewise, people with IGD-like symptoms also tended to be more emotionally reactive (both positively and negatively) to playing games as compared to normal participants, suggesting just how much more involving these games are to people who may be addicted to them.[9] And in brain imaging studies, people with IGD and people with substance addictions have numerous similarities in the parts of their brain that became activated when exposed to symbols of the things they're addicted to (e.g., a game trailer)[10]. In other words, the brains of people with video game addiction look remarkably similar to the brains of people with substance addictions.

Studies such as these formed the basis for the decision by the American Psychiatric Association to include IGD in the DSM-5 appendices and the WHO to include gaming disorder in the ICD-11 (see Question #43 for the criteria for IGD).

---

[c] In a tragic bout of irony, the game involves raising a digital character and helping them to grow and develop.

Despite this foundational research and the importance of the topic, however, there remain several questions that have received limited attention[11]. First, little is known about the causes of IGD and what (if any) stages people might go through as the disorder develops. Second, the time course of the disorder is not well understood. Some studies find that IGD lasts for at least two years for most of those affected[12], but we simply don't know how long it takes for a full-fledged disorder to develop or how long it might last without treatment. Lastly, researchers need to know a lot more about the outcomes of IGD and any other problems that might accompany the disorder. We *do* know that those with IGD tend to report higher levels of depression and anxiety, but it's less clear whether these problems *cause* people to become addicted to video games, are the *consequences* of becoming addicted to video games, or both.

When we look at the full body of evidence on the subject of IGD, there appears to be fairly strong support for its existence. In fact, most of the debate about IGD and its inclusion in the DSM-5 and the ICD-11 has less to do with whether or not people can become addicted to video games and more to do with whether or not it should be categorized as something distinct from other behavioral addictions (e.g., gambling). Anecdotal evidence and studies alike seem to validate the idea that people can be addicted to playing video games – something which shouldn't surprise us when you consider that designers themselves aim to create games that people want to keep playing. All of this considered, however, there is still more research required to better understand gaming disorders. Such work will ideally establish the disorder's causes, time course, and will better establish how gaming disorders are related to other common disorders (e.g., depression).

References

1. American Psychiatric Association. (2013). *Diagnostic and statistical manual of mental disorders* (5th ed.). Washington, DC: Author.
2. World Health Organization. (2018). *International statistical classification of diseases and related health problems* (11th Revision). Retrieved from https://icd.who.int/browse11/l-m/en
3. Gentile, D. A., Groves C. L., Gentile, J. R. (2014). The General Learning Model: Unveiling the learning potential in video games. In F. Blumberg (Ed.), *Learning by Playing: Video Gaming in Education* (121-142). New York, NY: Oxford University Press.
4. Skinner, B. F. (1953). *Science and Human Behavior* (p. 293). New York: Macmillan.
5. CNN (2010). Jail for couple whose baby died while they raised an online child. *CNN*. Retrieved from http://edition.cnn.com/2010/WORLD/asiapcf/05/28/south.korea.virtual.baby/.

6. Reuters (2007). *Online addict dies after "marathon" session.* Retrieved from: http://www.reuters.com/article/2007/02/28/us-china-internet-addiction-idUSPEK26772020070228

7. Petry, N. M., Rehbein, F., Gentile, D. A., Lemmens, J. S., Rumpf, H. J., Mößle, T., ... & Auriacombe, M. (2014). An international consensus for assessing internet gaming disorder using the new DSM-5 approach. *Addiction, 109*(9), 1399-1406.

8. Beranuy, M., Carbonell, X., & Griffiths, M. D. (2013). A qualitative analysis of online gaming addicts in treatment. *International Journal of Mental Health and Addiction, 11*(2), 149-161.

9. Groves, C. L., Gentile, D., Tapscott, R. L., & Lynch, P. J. (2015). Testing the Predictive Validity and Construct of Pathological Video Game Use. *Behavioral Sciences, 5*(4), 602-625.

10. Zhang, Y., Ndasauka, Y., Hou, J., Chen, J., zhuang Yang, L., Wang, Y., ... & Zhang, X. (2016). Cue-induced Behavioral and Neural Changes among Excessive Internet Gamers and Possible Application of Cue Exposure Therapy to Internet Gaming Disorder. *Frontiers in psychology, 7,* 675.

11. Groves, C. L., Blanco-Herrera, J. A., Prot, S., Berch, O. N., Bowie, S., & Gentile, D. A. (2015). What is known about video game and internet addiction after DSM-5. In Rosen, L. D., Cheever, N. A., & Carrier, M. (Eds.), *The Wiley Handbook of Psychology, Technology, and Society.* Hoboken, NJ: John Wiley & Sons.

12. Gentile, D. A., Choo, H., Liau, A., Sim, T., Li, D., Fung, D., & Khoo, A. (2011). Pathological video game use among youths: a two-year longitudinal study. *Pediatrics,* peds-201

43 - What are the symptoms of video game addiction?

The Short Answer:

There are currently nine recognized symptoms of video game addiction (called Internet Gaming Disorder) in the U.S. They are similar to the symptoms one sees in people with other types of addictions (e.g., gambling addiction, alcohol addiction). These symptoms include a preoccupation with games, withdrawal symptoms when games are taken away or absent, increased need for more gaming, loss of interest in non-gaming activities, continuing to play despite it causing problems in your life, playing games as the main way you deal with problems, and games causing harm to your relationships, work, education, or career. Importantly, addiction involves having most of these symptoms, not just one or two of them. Likewise, simply enjoying games a lot or playing them a lot does not mean that a person is addicted to them. The term addiction (or disorder) is really only used when gaming is causing considerable dysfunction in a person's day-to-day life.

The Long Answer:

When gamers hear researchers talk about term like "video game addiction," "Gaming Disorder" (GD), and "Internet Gaming Disorder" (IGD), their response is often to become defensive and to deny that such a condition could possibility exist. The defensiveness from gamers tends to stem from a few different misconceptions about researchers and about addiction. The first misconception is that researchers hate video games and are trying to impose their opinions on others – that is, trying to demonize video games so that others don't "waste" their time on them. This misconception assumes that media researchers dislike video games or consider them a complete waste of time, a point we dispel in Question #3. But even if it were true that researchers had a grudge against video games, it's a pretty big stretch to assume that they would simply "invent" a condition just to stop people from doing an activity that they don't personally enjoy. To be fair, scientists *do* have a bit of a reputation for being downers that rain on peoples' parades.[a] But it's unlikely that the concerted push of dozens of psychologists to bring gaming addiction to the field's awareness is simply the result of cranky psychologists trying to run gamers' fun.

A second misconception is grounded in the mistaken belief among gamers that, if researchers had their way, every gamer would be diagnosed as having an

---

[a] Just ask smokers, junk food connoisseurs, or anyone who really wants to believe that human activities aren't damaging the environment.

addiction to video games. This misconception is largely grounded in simple ignorance about what addiction actually entails. Most laypersons assume that "addiction" is just another way of saying "someone who uses or does something a lot," as is evident by the number of self-described "chocoholics" or "shopaholics" in the world.[b] In, reality, as we outline below, addiction is less about the sheer amount of something someone consumes and more about the problems it causes in a person's functioning.

But first, an example: It would be silly to define an alcohol addiction solely based on how many drinks a person consumes. Chris and Courtney may both have consumed 10 alcoholic drinks last week, but there's a *big* difference between them if Chris consumed all 10 of his drinks at a single party (which he only does once a year), while Courtney consumed 1-2 drinks every day last week. Likewise, it matters that Chris consumed his 10 drinks over the course of a long evening in the company of friends at a party, while Courtney consumed his 1-2 drinks each night by himself because they were the only way he could put himself to sleep. Finally, Chris and Courtney's 10 drinks have very different implications if Chris was 300 lbs. and Courtney was 120 lbs. In short, when it comes to addiction, amount of consumption isn't as important as the regularity of consumption, context of consumption, the reasons for consumption, and life consequences of the consumption. This is true when we're talking about substance addiction, and it's especially true when we're talking about gaming addiction.[1]

What does this mean for the average gamer? Well, it means that most of them would *not* fall under the category of having a gaming addiction according to most criteria. Gamers may well spend several hours every day playing their favorite games and those games may well have some other detrimental effects on them (e.g., violent games serving as a risk factor for aggression in Question #11, excessive media use and health problems in Question #39.) But loving games a lot and spending a lot of time on this hobby isn't enough to earn them a diagnosis of addiction. It's only when game-playing itself starts causing significant dysfunctions in a person's life that a label of addiction may be warranted.

With this in mind, let's look at the criteria themselves which are grounded in research, both on addiction more broadly and on video game playing specifically. Early studies of IGD defined it like any other addiction[2], adapting criteria used to diagnose people with gambling addictions. The result of this work and work in the years following has been the inclusion of IGD in the appendices of the Diagnostic and Statistical Manual of Mental Disorders, 5th Edition[3], the reference manual that U.S. psychologists and psychiatrists use for the diagnosis and treatment of clients, and to likewise be included as a diagnosable condition (Gaming Disorder) in the World Health Organization's International Classification for Diseases (ICD-11)[4]. The American Psychiatric Association identifies nine symptoms that are indicative

---

[b] Words that, according to this author, seem to imply an addiction to "chocohol" and "shopohol," whatever *those* are!

of IGD, instructing clinicians to consider someone as meeting the criteria for IGD if five or more of these symptoms apply to them:

1. **Preoccupation with games**. This means that gaming is the dominant activity in the person's daily life. When they're not currently playing, their thoughts are frequently about previous gaming sessions or future gaming sessions. The person generally has difficulty focusing on anything that's *not* gaming.

2. **Withdrawal symptoms result when games are taken away**. This doesn't necessarily mean that the person is showing signs of physical withdrawal (e.g., sweating, shaking) like one would see in a drug addiction, but instead there are psychological symptoms of withdrawal, including irritability, anxiety, or depression. These symptoms go away when the person is allowed to game again.

3. **Tolerance builds over time**. In a nutshell, this means that people require increasingly large amounts of gaming in order to "scratch the itch" to so speak – to satisfy their need to game. This is very much like drug addiction, where users begin to build up a tolerance for their drug, getting used to it over time. As a result, more is needed to obtain the same "rush". It can also refer to a need for increased intensity of gaming sessions, although little research has been conducted regarding this specific issue.

4. **Unsuccessful attempts to cease or reduce the frequency of play**. One of the clearest indicators of gaming addiction is someone's inability to quit or even reduce the amount of playing they do when they *want* to. This "wanting" component is critical, because people who do not attempt to reduce or quit their playing cannot considered to be meeting this criterion (i.e., a person who can't reduce the amount they play because they don't *want* to isn't considered to be "unable" to do so).

5. **Loss of interest in other forms of entertainment or hobbies**. The person prefers gaming over almost all other activities. This is usually coupled with a *loss* of interest in activities or hobbies that they *used to* enjoy, suggesting that gaming is "taking over" more and more of their life.

6. **Excessive gaming despite problems**. This is often related to the symptom of being unable to quit or reduce playing. This item specifically refers to people continuing to play despite knowing that their playing is causing professional (e.g., missing work), social (e.g., ignoring friends), academic (e.g., failing classes) or psychological damage (e.g., feelings of worthlessness or depression).

7. **Deceives others about playing.** Like other addictions, family and friends often express concern about their loved one's addictive behavior. This symptom emphasizes the tendency for people with addictions to lie to their friends and families about how much they play, or the problems games are causing in order to hide it.

8. **Escapism or relief from negative moods.** Media use (generally speaking) is designed to help consumers escape the humdrum of everyday life. In other words, it's fairly normal to occasionally use media to improve a bad mood or cheer oneself up. People with a gaming addiction, however, tend to use video games to deal with the emotional fallout (e.g., guilt, anxiety) of life's problems, rather than dealing with the problems themselves. In other words, people addicted to games use games to try to hide from their problems indefinitely, instead of treating them as the temporary escape that they are.

9. **Lost or jeopardized a job, relationship, educational or career opportunity.** In addition to the above symptoms, an important symptom in addiction is whether gaming itself has *actually* caused harm in the person's life. This item is a necessary condition for symptom #6, since a person needs to first experience problems before they can be said to continue playing *despite* these problems.

Far from being arbitrary or baseless, researchers have focused considerable efforts on identifying these symptoms and providing empirical support for them. For instance, in a study using functional magnetic resonance imaging (fMRIs scan the brain for activity), the brains of patients with IGD were found to be comparable to those of substance abusers when both were experiencing cravings[5]. People with IGD also report feeling a loss of interest in previous hobbies due to their game playing[6], noting that life seemed "boring" and "dark" when they couldn't play[6]. Some evidence indicates that IGD individuals are more likely to play in order to avoid negative moods while "normal" individuals tend to play as a method of seeking fun and pleasure[7]. Other research has found that while game players tend to display poorer academic performance[8] and get poorer sleep[9], those who met the criteria for IGD reported even *worse* performance, even after authors statistically controlled for their frequency of playing.

In sum, gamers who are worried that media researchers are going to brand them as addicts simply because they enjoy playing video games need not worry. As it turns out, addiction has *less* to do with the amount of time people spend playing video games and *more* to do with how and why people play[1]. The list of symptoms for IGD are designed to reflect this fact.

References

1. Plante, C. N., Gentile, D. A., Groves, C. L., Modlin, A., & Blanco-Herrera, J. (2018). Video games as coping mechanisms in the etiology of video game addiction. *Psychology of Popular Media Culture, 8,* 385–394.
2. Brown, R. I. F. (1991). Gaming, gambling and other addictive play. In J. H. Kerr & M. J. Apter (Eds.), *Adult place: A reversal theory approach* (pp. 101–118). Amsterdam, the Netherlands: Swets & Zeitlinger.
3. American Psychiatric Association. (2013). Diagnostic and statistical manual of mental disorders (5th ed.). Washington, DC: Author.
4. World Health Organization. (2018). *International statistical classification of diseases and related health problems* (11th Revision). Retrieved from https://icd.who.int/browse11/l-m/en
5. Ko, C. H., Liu, G. C., Hsiao, S., Yen, J. Y., Yang, M. J., Lin, W. C., ... Chen, C. S. (2009). Brain activities associated with gaming urge of online gaming addiction. *Journal of Psychiatric Research, 43*(7), 739–747.
6. Hussain, Z., & Griffiths, M. D. (2008). Gender swapping and socializing in cyberspace: An exploratory study. *CyberPsychology and Behavior, 11*(1), 47–53.
7. Wan, C., & Chiou, W. (2006b). Psychological motives and online games addiction: A test of flow theory and humanistic needs theory for Taiwanese adolescents. *Cyberpsychology and Behavior, 9*(3), 317–324.
8. Anand, V. (2007). A study of time management: The correlation between video game usage and academic performance markers. *Cyberpsychology & Behavior, 10*(4), 552-559.
9. Choo, H., Gentile, D. A., Sim, T., Li, D. D., Khoo, A., & Liau, A. K. (2010). Pathological video-gaming among Singaporean youth. *Annals of the Academy of Medicine Singapore, 39*(11), 822–829.

44 - What are the causes and consequences of video game addiction?

The Short Answer:

Several theories exist that help researchers explain what may cause individuals to develop Internet Gaming Disorder (IGD). Some of these theories are based on the idea that some of the player's basic psychological needs are not being met in the "real world," forcing them to turn to digital worlds to scratch the itch. Other theories describe maladaptive patterns of thinking that may drive players to become addicted to games. Still other theories suggest that people who are depressed, anxious, have difficulty socializing, or earn poor grades are more likely to have IGD, although the direction of the relations between these factors and addiction is difficult to establish. Some research has found that having parents monitor and limit their children's media use may help prevent the development of IGD symptoms.

The Long Answer:

When trying to answer questions about what causes Internet Gaming Disorder (IGD) and its consequences, it's important to keep in mind the sorts of limitations researchers face. In Question #15 we introduced the experiment, a type of study that allows researchers to directly test causes and effects between variables. However, we also explained some of the drawbacks of experiments, including the fact that it's not always possible to randomly assign people to conditions. In the case of IGD, it is simply impossible for researchers to bring people into the laboratory and tell them "Okay, you're going to be in our 'addicted' condition" or "you're going to be in the 'non-addicted' condition". Unfortunately, people come to our studies already addicted or not, meaning it's not something within our power to manipulate in an experiment.[a] Nor would it be ethical to do so even if we *could*: No ethics board would allow researchers to conduct a study that ended with participants developing an addiction of any sort – for reasons we hope are obvious.

---

[a] This is due, in no small part, to the fact that addictions may take *years* to develop and are likely a reaction to other factors in a person's life (e.g., stresses). In other words, it is impossible for researchers to "create" a video game addiction in the laboratory.

Because of these restrictions, researchers studying the development of gaming addiction are limited to correlational and longitudinal study designs (i.e., cross-sectional, see Question #11, and longitudinal, see Question #13). In these studies, participants typically complete one or more surveys with questions measuring addiction-related symptoms (see Question #43) and measuring the presence of possible risk factors and consequences. This limitation can lead to the question of "Which came first – the chicken or the egg?" To see what we mean, imagine that a researcher found that participants with more IGD symptoms also scored higher on measures of depression and anxiety. One possible interpretation of these results is that IGD *caused* participants to experience more anxiety and depression. But it's just as plausible that people who are anxious and depressed may develop IGD as a way of coping. A third possibility is that some other, unmeasured variable, like having poor socializing skills, may have led to *both* IGD symptoms *and* anxiety/depression. Longitudinal studies can begin to help researchers tease apart possible causal directions.

Despite these limitations, researchers *have* come a long way in understanding the potential causes of video game addiction. This progress comes from a combination of numerous studies converging on the same conclusions *and* on existing theories that explain other types of addiction. For example, some theories suggest that IGD is like other addictions (e.g., drug abuse, gambling), caused by a basic deficiency called reward deficiency syndrome (RDS)[1]. People with RDS experience relatively little excitement or enjoyment from activities that would be pleasant for most other people. As a result, people with RDS become addicted to behaviors that give them a way to feel "alive," something most people have much less difficulty feeling. Researchers have found specific genes that affect the parts of the brain responsible for the experience of reward. As you might imagine, people with genes that lead to abnormal development of this part of the brain are therefore more likely to develop RDS and addictions, including possibly IGD. In other studies, researchers have likewise found that areas of the brain responsible for overriding and preventing undesirable responses are less active in those who say they play excessive amounts of games[2].

Other research has focused less on biological causes of IGD and focused instead on *cognitive* causes – problems with the ways people *think*. One such model, called the model of generalized problematic internet use, argues that there are two types of dysfunctional thought processes that may lead to IGD[3,4]:

1. Dysfunctional thoughts about the self. These include self-doubt and negative thoughts about the self. These types of thoughts cause people to seek out positive social interactions through online games. In other words, people with IGD tend to see themselves in a positive light only when they're playing online games, motivating them to play the games frequently.

2. Dysfunctional thoughts about the outside world. This includes a tendency to treat specific events as if they represent the entire outside world. This may cause people to treat the internet as the only safe place available to them or cause them to believe that they can be appreciated only by others online.

Researchers have also looked at the possibility that IGD is the result of people failing to meet basic psychological needs[5,6,7,8]. According to this theory, called self-determination theory, people are motivated by three basic needs. First, they need what's called autonomy: People need to feel in control of their actions and make decisions for themselves. Second, people need mastery (or competence), to be able to develop skills over time with practice and effort. Third, people need to relate to others, to feel a sense of connection with people around them. People may fulfill these needs through various activities in their life, such as work, which may give them a chance to feel in control, to develop skills, and to interact with others. But some people, the theory argues, may not be able to fulfill these needs in various parts of their life. For example, if your job forces you to follow someone else's orders doing simple, unskilled labor, all while working by yourself, you're likely not fulfilling any of these three needs. People whose needs are unmet will find activities that satisfy these needs particularly attractive. And, as it turns out, video games (especially online ones) satisfy all of these needs: They give players a chance to make decisions for themselves, to develop and improve new skills, and to interact with other people. This may explain why (and for whom) video games can be such a rewarding and difficult-to-quit activity. Indeed, recent research has found a strong link between need satisfaction, need frustration, and IGD[7]. As shown in Figure 44.1, gamers who scored low on need satisfaction in the real world but high on need satisfaction in the game world also tended to score high on IGD.

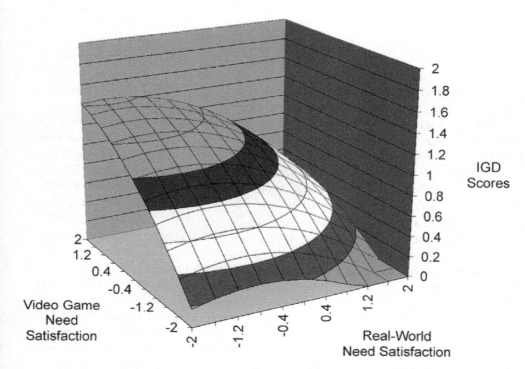

Figure 44.1. Internet gaming disorder scores are highest for gamers whose real-world need satisfaction is low and their video game need satisfaction is high.

Beyond biological, cognitive, or environmental causes for IGD, researchers have also begun looking at whether certain personality traits are associated with a person's likelihood of developing IGD. For example, one study found that people with IGD tended to score higher on measures of neuroticism (i.e., emotional instability) and lower on measures of conscientiousness (i.e., diligence, hard-working) and agreeableness (i.e., friendliness, warmth)[9]. Others have found that people with more impulsive personalities also report having more IGD-like symptoms[10,11].

Ultimately, people with IGD are more likely than those without IGD to experience depression and anxiety[12,13]. These factors can be understood as either *causes* or *consequences* of IGD (or both, creating what psychologists call a downward spiral model). The idea is that depressed or anxious people may be more likely to seek relief from these unpleasant feelings in games. Doing so excessively (see Question #43) may prevent players from dealing with the life problems causing the depression and anxiety in the first place, leading to negative consequences that only worsen the depression and anxiety.

In a study testing this possibility, researchers studied students at the start and end of a two-year time period[14]. The researchers measured students' IGD symptoms, as well as related problems such as academic achievement, anxiety, depression, and social phobia. Those who developed IGD over the course of the study also scored higher on depression, anxiety, social phobia, and earned worse grades in school compared to those who never developed IGD or those who started with IGD but no longer had it at the end of the study. Mirroring findings reported above, students with impulsivity problems were more likely to develop IGD and, once IGD had developed, were more likely to become even *more* impulsive. Ultimately, depression, anxiety, and poor grades were *outcomes* of IGD, rather than causes of it. Of course, more work is needed to more firmly establish this causal direction.

Parents and teachers are particularly concerned about the academic achievement of children who are at risk for IGD (see Question #40 for more on video game use and school performance). As mentioned in the study above, as well as in other studies, poor grades seem to be an *outcome* of IGD[14,15], rather than a cause of it. IGD may also influence other important aspects of academic life. In one notable longitudinal study, those who had IGD symptoms when they entered college were also less likely in their first year to engage in community service, develop close friendships, complete an internship, or show interest in studying abroad[16].

Up to this point, we've focused primarily on both the risk factors for IGD and its negative consequences. But it's also worth noting that, like with aggression, there are protective factors that can *reduce* a person's chance of developing IGD (see Question #14 for more on risk and protective factors for aggression). When it comes to factors around the home, researchers have several pieces of advice for parents. In one study, researchers found that parental supervision (e.g., knowing what your kids are doing during their free time) and parental devotion (e.g., creating an environment where your kids feel they can talk to you about anything) were associated with *lower* rates of IGD in children[17]. The same study also found that children who did not have a TV set or gaming console in their bedroom, as well as children who did not own a handheld gaming console, were all less likely to develop IGD[17]. Even better: These protective factors seemed to last for more than five years, illustrating how important these seemingly small changes in parenting styles can be on children's long-term well-being.

When you put all of this research together, it becomes clear that a number of factors are involved in the development of IGD. Likewise, the relationship between IGD and outcomes such as anxiety, depression, and academic performance is nuanced, but seems to suggest that IGD can have serious consequences for those experiencing it. As we point out in Question #43, however, IGD is about more than mere frequency of play. Although it's true that those with IGD do tend to play more games than those without IGD, it's entirely possible to play a lot of video games and still not qualify for a diagnosis of IGD[14].

In other words, for people concerned about whether they may have IGD or be experiencing some of the negative consequences of excessive game play, it's worth considering whether other risk factors (e.g., environmental, cognitive, or personality factors) are present and thinking critically about *how* and *why* they find themselves playing video games.

References
1. Blum, K., Chen, A. L., Chen, T. J., Braverman, E. R., Reinking, J., Blum, S. H., ... & Prihoda, T. J. (2008). Activation instead of blocking mesolimbic dopaminergic reward circuitry is a preferred modality in the long term treatment of reward deficiency syndrome (RDS): a commentary. *Theoretical Biology and Medical Modelling, 5*(1), 24.
2. Littel, M., Ivo, I. V. D. B., Luijten, M., Van Rooij, A. J., Keemink, L., Franken, I. H. A., ... & Tibboel, D. (2012). Error processing and response inhibition in excessive computer game players: An event-related potential study. *Addiction Biology, 17*(5), 934-947.
3. Davis, R. A. (2001). A cognitive-behavioral model of pathological Internet use. *Computers in human behavior, 17*(2), 187-195.
4. King, D. L., & Delfabbro, P. H. (2014). The cognitive psychology of Internet gaming disorder. *Clinical psychology review, 34*(4), 298-308.
5. Przybylski, A. K., Rigby, C. S., & Ryan, R. M. (2010). A motivational model of video game engagement. *Review of general psychology, 14*(2), 154.
6. Ryan, R. M., Rigby, C. S., & Przybylski, A. (2006). The motivational pull of video games: A self-determination theory approach. *Motivation and emotion, 30*(4), 344-360.
7. Allen, J. J., & Anderson, C. A. (2018). Satisfaction and frustration of basic psychological needs in the real world and in video games predict internet gaming disorder scores and well-being. *Computers in Human Behavior, 84,* 220-229.
8. Bender, P. K., & Gentile, D. A. (2019). Internet gaming disorder: Relations between needs satisfaction in-game and in life in general. *Psychology of Popular Media Culture,* doi: http://dx.doi.org.proxy.lib.iastate.edu/10.1037/ppm0000227
9. Andreassen, C. S., Griffiths, M. D., Gjertsen, S. R., Krossbakken, E., Kvam, S., & Pallesen, S. (2013). The relationships between behavioral addictions and the five-factor model of personality. *Journal of behavioral addictions, 2*(2), 90-99.
10. Billieux, J., Chanal, J., Khazaal, Y., Rochat, L., Gay, P., Zullino, D., & Van der Linden, M. (2011). Psychological predictors of problematic involvement in massively multiplayer online role-playing games: illustration in a sample of male cybercafé players. *Psychopathology, 44*(3), 165-171.
11. Robbins, T. W., & Clark, L. (2015). Behavioral addictions. *Current Opinion in Neurobiology, 30,* 66-72.

12. Yu, H., & Cho, J. (2016). Prevalence of internet gaming disorder among Korean adolescents and associations with non-psychotic psychological symptoms, and physical aggression. *American Journal of Health Behavior*, *40*(6), 705-716.
13. Plante, C. N., Gentile, D. A., Groves, C. L., Modlin, A., & Blanco-Herrera, J. (2018). Video games as coping mechanisms in the etiology of video game addiction. *Psychology of Popular Media Culture*. Advanced online copy.
14. Gentile, D. A., Choo, H., Liau, A., Sim, T., Li, D., Fung, D., & Khoo, A. (2011). Pathological video game use among youths: a two-year longitudinal study. *Pediatrics*, peds-2010.
15. Gentile, D. (2009). Pathological video-game use among youth ages 8 to 18: a national study. *Psychological science*, *20*(5), 594-602.
16. Schmitt, Z. L., & Livingston, M. G. (2015). Video game addiction and college performance among males: Results from a 1 year longitudinal study. *Cyberpsychology, Behavior, and Social Networking*, *18*(1), 25-29.
17. Rehbein, F., & Baier, D. (2013). Family-, media-, and school-related risk factors of video game addiction. *Journal of Media Psychology, 25*, 118-128.

45 - Can video game addiction be treated?

The Short Answer:

Yes. Like all addictions, treatment options are available for people with gaming addictions. The most common form of treatment is a therapeutic method called *cognitive behavioral therapy*, which focuses on teaching those with addictions to avoid the sorts of thoughts and behaviors that encourage excessive playing. Other work suggests that medications used for treating other addictions *can* be useful, but their degree of effectiveness is not yet fully understood. Research on this topic is still fairly new, and there is thus no "best-practice" approach agreed on by researchers yet. Future research will hopefully provide clinicians with tools and techniques to help clients suffering from gaming addiction.

The Long Answer:

Video game addiction, officially referred to in the U.S. as Internet Gaming Disorder (IGD)[1], is a relatively new condition compared to what people think of as "typical" addictions (e.g., substance use, gambling; see Questions #42 and #43 for more on this comparison). Because the condition is so new, mental health professionals are still learning how best to approach treatment, while research and development on treatment options is still in the early stages. That said, researchers are not starting from scratch: They've borrowed a considerable amount from existing knowledge about how to treat other addictions, using this work as a "starting point".

So, what do researchers and clinicians have to go on? Currently, the most effective treatment for addictions in general and IGD specifically as supported by scientific research is called *cognitive-behavioral therapy* (CBT). It's a remarkably practical, common sense approach to treatment that focuses on breaking down the sorts of thoughts and behavioral patterns that fuel addictions[2]. To illustrate how CBT might work, let's imagine you're a clinician working with a client who's been diagnosed with IGD. The client believes that they *need* their favorite games to make friends and that, if they weren't allowed to play their games anymore, they would be unable to make friends "in real life." You might identify this belief as being one of the main thoughts underpinning the addiction, since it's contributing to the client's lack of making real-world friends and, as a result, causing them to lack an offline social support network. This, in turn, may leave them feeling particularly vulnerable, which only reinforces their desire to play the game further. As part of CBT, you might ask the client to challenge this belief that they can't make friends in the real world and encourage them to try making

314

friends elsewhere. You may also help them practice social skills such as making small talk and approaching others politely to help them build their confidence. If all goes well, the client will make more attempts to form offline friendships, reducing their need to turn to games for social interaction and giving them an alternative form of recreation (i.e., hanging out with friends) that doesn't involve video games.

Researchers have noted that the use of CBT in treating IGD differs in important ways from the way it's used to treat of gambling disorder[3]. For example, treating gambling disorder often involves focusing on false beliefs about the likelihood of earning a big "payout" in the long-term. In a sense, the clinician is trying to teach their clients the basics of statistics and probability, that long-term gambling is far more likely to negatively affect their financial status rather than improve it.

Entirely different thoughts and beliefs have to be addressed in people with IGD[3]. For example, people with IGD tend to over-value the benefits of playing and think about playing excessively (see Question #43 for more on this). As a result, they're prone to believing that if they can just play one more game or complete one more task in the game, they'll be better able to concentrate – something that studies show is far from the truth (see Question #44 for more on the consequences of IGD). It's up to clinicians to help clients with these beliefs recognize that their assumptions are wrong and ultimately hurting them in the long run.

People with IGD may also develop rigid rules and routines that commit them to spending excessive amounts of time on their games. For example, a person may believe that if they don't practice for a certain amount of time every day, they'll become "rusty" and perform poorly at it in the future.[a] Other players may find themselves addicted to games that employ time-restricted reward systems (e.g., daily quests) that require them to complete a task within a particular amount of time or be denied a reward. Although there may be nothing wrong with wanting to practice to improve one's skill or finding some time to get a particular reward for playing a game on a certain day, players with IGD may play excessively precisely because of these mistaken beliefs and poor choices of priorities.

---

[a] Although this may be true to a small extent, it also overlooks much more important questions about perspective and priorities: What are the consequences, really, if you become worse at beating people at a particular game? One of the authors, Courtney, had this realization with respect to one of his favorite online games. When he found himself spending more and more time worrying about his competitive ranking in an online game, he realized that, in the grand scheme of things, no one – not his students, his friends, or his colleagues – cared whether he was in the top 20% of players or the top 50% of players!

People with gaming addictions may also have harmful beliefs about their sense of control and the world around them which ties them to the digital worlds they inhabit. In some clinical work, for example, researchers find that people who play excessively consider gameplay to be one of the few ways they can maintain a sense of predictability and control over their life, or see video games as a way to deal with their inability to handle uncertainty[4]. In particular, people who have trouble tolerating uncertainty in the world find it particularly appealing to obtain all of a game's "collectible items" or to unlock all of a game's secrets and achievements. Being able to claim that you've completely mastered and beaten every part of a game can provide a temporary sense of control and certainty in one's life, even if comes at a tremendous cost of time and effort, and even if it lasts only until the next game comes along.

Researchers have also found that people with IGD often tie their sense of social worth and self-esteem to the games they play. This is based on the well-established psychological principle that humans have an innate need to belong and feel like part of a social group[5,6]. Video games, especially massive multiplayer online video games like *World of Warcraft* or *Everquest*, give players a chance to satisfy this need by being part of a large group of like-minded players (e.g., guilds, clans). Unfortunately, these same groups can also cause players to feel obligated to play out of fear that they might be ostracized or that they might let members of their group down[7]. Players steeped in these online communities also tend to think more positively about other gamers than about non-gamers and to believe that others, including therapists who don't game, cannot truly understand their experience[3]. As you might imagine, this can create barriers to the therapeutic process.

In addition to addressing these specific thoughts and beliefs, therapists also try to help their clients identify and recognize the internal states and feelings associated with the urge to play. This might involve teaching the client to acknowledge urges when they arise rather than denying them or pretending that they don't exist. Likewise, they may help their clients find ways to make better decisions that help them reduce these feelings and urges without giving in to the desire to play, including techniques such as controlled, meditative breathing.

In short, therapists using CBT are attempting to dismantle the sorts of thoughts and behaviors that support their client's gaming addiction. Techniques include helping them recognize false beliefs, changing the way clients think, and practicing skills to encourage their client to seek out non-gaming activities. Therapists may also go one step further, suggesting ways to create barriers that make it harder for them to give in to the temptation to play (e.g., spending more time away from home; setting up scheduled playing times, and timing sessions so that they stop playing after a set amount of time). These last suggestions in particular (e.g., setting time limits) are often an initial goal of CBT therapies[8].

But are CBT-style therapies *actually* effective? Initial research is cautiously encouraging. One investigation found that CBT-style therapies produce significant reductions in internet use (including gaming) and found that 70% of clients were able to successfully manage their symptoms six months after treatment[8]. Another research team in China randomly assigned individuals with IGD-like symptoms to either receive CBT treatment or no treatment and found that those who received treatment had reduced symptoms both immediately after the program and at a six-month follow-up[9]. In short, there is growing evidence that CBT treatments seem to help most people with IGD and symptoms of gaming addiction to reduce and manage their gaming behavior.[b]

But CBT isn't the only treatment researchers have considered for people with IGD. For example, researchers have studied whether pharmaceutical interventions (e.g., drug treatments) may help clients with IGD. These studies typically use the same medications used in the treatment of other addictions (e.g., alcohol addiction). Some drug treatments focus on correcting deficiencies in the brain's ability to reward people for doing normal, day-to-day activities (e.g., doing well at school) for people with IGD. In another study, researchers presented people who have a gaming addiction with cues related to their addiction (e.g., a video game character)[10]. They also measured participants' brain activity during the cravings. Researchers then gave participants a drug called bupropion (often used to treat nicotine addiction) for six weeks. At the end of the study, the researchers found that the participants were more likely to report reductions in cravings, less time playing games, and reduced brain responsiveness to the addictive stimuli. Similar results have been obtained using another drug treatment, methylphenidate over an eight-week period.[11]

When reviewing the research literature on treating addictions, researchers make note of the treatment methods that seem promising, but they're also keenly aware of the limitations in the research. For example, due to the recency of IGD's inclusion into the Diagnostic and Statistical Manual of Mental Disorders, 5th edition[1], studies of IGD have not always been consistent in how they measure IGD. This can make it difficult to meaningfully compare the results of different IGD studies; in some ways, it's like comparing apples to oranges.[c] Another drawback of this research is that many of the studies do not measure how effective these treatments are in bringing patients below the threshold for a diagnosis of

---

[b] Many treatments aim to reduce excessive gameplay and help people manage their gameplay – not to prevent *all* gameplay. Clinicians and media researchers recognize that ours is a society where people are surrounded by mass media. It's unrealistic to expect anyone, let alone a person with an addiction, to *completely* cut off an entire type of media. Instead, like a dietician working with a patient, clinicians work to help their clients develop healthier media diets.

[c] Though it's perhaps more appropriate to say that it's like comparing one type of apple to another type of apple. After all, researchers may agree that they're studying IGD, but disagree on how precisely to measure it, leading to disagreements about how large improvements in IGD symptoms are.

IGD. Put another way, many of these studies show reductions in symptom severity or reductions in the number of problems in a participant's life, but they don't directly test whether the treatments specifically reduce participants' symptoms to the point that they're no longer considered to have an addiction. As a third (but certainly not last) limitation, more work is needed to test the long-term effectiveness of these treatments[12]. It's one thing to show that a treatment helps people over the course of six months or a year, but it's another matter entirely to show that improvements last for years and truly prevent patients from relapsing down the road.

To summarize: There are several methods that look promising for treating IGD. The most common method – and the one best-supported by research – is CBT, which focuses on reducing the patterns of thinking and behaving that drive addiction. Other methods, including drug treatments, similarly offer a glimmer of hope. Although research supports the effectiveness of these therapies, we're still in the early stages. It will likely be years – perhaps even decades – before researchers have determined a set of "best practices" for treatment[12]. Nevertheless, for those who live with IGD or symptoms of video game addiction, therapists and psychiatrists are unarguably the professionals best suited to help with treatment.

References

1. American Psychiatric Association. (2013). Diagnostic and statistical manual of mental disorders (5th ed.). Washington, DC: Author.
2. Butler, A. C., Chapman, J. E., Forman, E. M., & Beck, A. T. (2006). The empirical status of cognitive-behavioral therapy: a review of meta-analyses. *Clinical psychology review, 26*(1), 17-31.
3. Delfabbro, P., & King, D. (2015). On finding the C in CBT: The challenges of applying gambling-related cognitive approaches to video-gaming. *Journal of gambling studies, 31*(1), 315-329.
4. Floros, G., & Siomos, K. (2012). Patterns of choices on video game genres and Internet addiction. *Cyberpsychology, Behavior, and Social Networking, 15*(8), 417-424.
5. Baumeister, R. F., & Leary, M. R. (1995). The need to belong: Desire for interpersonal attachments as a fundamental human motivation. Psychological Bulletin, 117, 497–529.
6. Ryan, R. M., Rigby, C. S., & Przybylski, A. (2006). The motivational pull of video games: A self-determination theory approach. *Motivation and Emotion, 30*, 347-363.
7. King, D. L., Delfabbro, P. H., & Griffiths, M. D. (2009). The psychological study of video game players: Methodological challenges and practical advice. International Journal of Mental Health and Addiction, 7, 555–562.
8. Young, K. S. (2013). Treatment outcomes using CBT-IA with Internet-addicted patients. *Journal of behavioral addictions, 2*(4), 209-215.

9. Du, Y. S., Jiang, W., & Vance, A. (2010). Longer term effect of randomized, controlled group cognitive behavioral therapy for Internet addiction in adolescent students in Shanghai. *Australian and New Zealand Journal of Psychiatry, 44*(2), 129-134.

10. Han, D. H., Hwang, J. W., & Renshaw, P. F. (2010). Bupropion sustained release treatment decreases craving for video games and cue-induced brain activity in patients with Internet video game addiction. Experimental and clinical psychopharmacology, 18(4), 297.

11. Han, D. H., Lee, Y. S., Na, C., Ahn, J. Y., Chung, U. S., Daniels, M. A., ... & Renshaw, P. F. (2009). The effect of methylphenidate on Internet video game play in children with attention-deficit/hyperactivity disorder. *Comprehensive psychiatry, 50*(3), 251-256.

12. King, D. L., & Delfabbro, P. H. (2014). Internet gaming disorder treatment: a review of definitions of diagnosis and treatment outcome. *Journal of Clinical Psychology, 70*(10), 942-955.

Chapter 5

Parenting in the 21st Century

46 - Do parents and caregivers have any influence on the effects of violent media?

The Short Answer:

Yes. Children whose parents take an active role in discussing and critiquing violent media content with them appear to be less affected by violent media they consume. Similarly, children whose parents limit the *amount* and the *type* of media content their children consume are *also* less likely to be influenced by violent media. Setting limits appears to be a powerful protective factor for children's healthy development. That said, there *are* ways this strategy can backfire, such as turning violent media into "forbidden fruit." Other research shows that it's not enough to simply "be in the room" or consuming violent media *with* your children, as this may actually *increase* violent media effects. The best piece of advice we have at this time is to reasonably limit your child's exposure to violent media while discussing with them the reasons for these limits – in the same way you would explain to your child that eating candy for every meal would not be healthy for them. One of the best ways to reduce exposure to violent or other harmful types of media is to move screen media devices from private spaces (e.g., bedroom) into public spaces (e.g., living room, kitchen).

The Long Answer:

Throughout Chapter 1 we explained how media and public health researchers have reached the conclusion that violent media are a risk factor for aggression based on hundreds studies across decades of research (see Question #11). We imagine that many parents, upon reading this, responded with some concern, asking themselves if they *really* knew what was in the games their children were playing or second-guessing past decisions to let their kids to watch certain shows. Because of this, we suspect that at least some of our readers were tempted to do something drastic like take away their child's video game console or outright ban violent content from their homes. After all, it's entirely natural for parents to want to protect their kids from harm.

But before you run out and sell the game console or ban television from your home, it's worth asking whether these actions will *actually* help the situation? And are there less extreme, but still effective solutions? Can we avoid "throwing the baby out with the bathwater," so to speak?

Researchers have been searching for solutions to violent media effects for almost as long as they've been researching media violence itself. To date, however, no single, definitive answer has emerged, no "silver bullet" that confers immunity to media violence effects.

When it comes to strategies for reducing violent content effects, researchers recognize four types: *active mediation, restrictions on amount of viewing, restrictions on the content viewed*, and *co-viewing*. This first category, active mediation, is the hardest to do but seems to have the best results. It involves parents helping to guide critical reasoning about what is being seen on the screen. This includes questioning and discussing why things are shown the way they are, what points of view are represented and which are not being shown, whether things would work in the real world the way they are shown, what might be better (non-violent) responses to conflicts, etc. This is usually best done with questions, rather than statements. Ask your children whether they've seen things like that at school and how people really reacted, and why they think TV or video games showed it differently. The goal of active mediation strategies is to make children critical consumers of media – to make them stop and challenge what they're seeing on the screen, rather than passively accepting everything they see on the screen at face value. These strategies aim to stop beliefs about aggression being positive, normal, and acceptable from forming in the first place.[a] The research seems to show that when parents regularly discuss media content in this way it seems to mitigate most of the negative effects of media and also enhances the positive effects.

The second and third strategies are both types restrictive mediation, *limiting* the amount and type of media content children are allowed to consume. The most obvious of these strategies involves restricting violent content by forbidding children from playing "Mature"-rated games or watching R-rated films (for more on content rating systems, see Question #48). Parents may rely on content-filtering programs for television shows or websites to make these decisions for them or they can research a game, TV show, or film to determine for themselves whether it's appropriate for their child. Restrictions on amount tend to be unrelated to specific content – for example, limiting how much television or video game play their child is allowed each day or limiting media use to family rooms where it can be monitored. The ultimate goal of restrictive strategies is to reduce the risks of media exposure by reducing the amount of exposure in the first place.[b]

The fourth category of strategies is called co-viewing. It involves parents consuming media alongside their children. This involves watching television or playing video games with their children. At first glance, co-viewing may seem

---

[a] As an analogy for this type of strategy, imagine trying to improve your child's eating habits by teaching them to think about whether what they're eating is healthy or unhealthy.

[b] This type of strategy would be like trying to improve your child's eating habits by limiting or outright banning unhealthy food from being in your house.

similar to active mediation, since active mediation *can* involve co-viewing or co-playing. What differs between the two strategies is the role of the parent. In active mediation, the parent is a *critical voice*, encouraging their child to challenge what they're seeing and to think about non-violent alternatives. In contrast, co-viewing parents are simply consuming media with their children – they're not criticizing what's on screen, although they may selectively limit exposure (e.g., close your eyes for this part!)[c]

Take a moment to think about these different strategies for yourself: active mediation, restrictions on amount, restrictions on content, and co-viewing. Which strategies have *you* used (or would you *consider* using) with your own children? Which strategies did *your* parents use with you?

To be clear, all of these strategies involve more effort than simply letting your children watch or play whatever they want. But even so, some of these strategies require more effort than others. After all, active mediation involves discussing media content with your child, usually after you've reviewed the media yourself. This requires time, something that many parents find themselves in short supply of! It also is something most parents have not seen modeled unless they took a class on critical media theory. In contrast, it's pretty easy to just make a rule that your kids can't watch anything with a certain age-rating. Having said that, rules like these take some effort to enforce, and sometimes lead to complaints. Plus, it's not always easy to come up with an all-or-nothing rule about what media are appropriate, especially if you don't know details about the types of video games or TV shows your kids want to consume. The point is, any strategy will necessarily take some amount of time and effort to implement.

For now, let's put practical considerations like "having the time needed" aside. Instead of asking which strategy is the *easiest* or involves the *least* effort, let's instead ask which strategies, according to research, are the most *effective* at reducing the effects of media violence on aggression.

First up: active mediation strategies. Of all the strategies, active mediation is the one most consistently found to work, weakening the link between violent media exposure and aggressive behavior[1,2,3,4]. When parents reinforce the inappropriateness of violence in the real world and teach their children that society disapproves of violence it undermines one of the underlying mechanisms of aggression (i.e., beliefs that aggression is appropriate; see Question #12.)[5] With one fewer mechanism to support the link between media violence and aggression, media violence becomes a smaller risk factor for aggression.

So research seems to support the effectiveness of active mediation strategies. What about restrictive mediation strategies? On the one hand, it's hard to argue with the logic of these strategies: If media violence is a risk factor for

---

[c] In the context of improving your child's eating habits, this would be like trying to do so by sitting next to your child and eating what they're eating, while occasionally deciding for them what they can and cannot eat.

aggression, being exposed to less of it should reduce aggressive behavior, right? Evidence *does* support this position: Children of parents who restrict the amount or type of content they can view are less aggressive than children whose parents impose fewer or no restrictions[6,7,8].

But there can be drawbacks to restrictive mediation as well, especially when no explanation and discussion (i.e., active mediation) accompanies it. For example, restricting media use can cause children to develop negative opinions of their parents[9].[d] Although this is bad enough (no parents likes to be "the bad guy"), these strategies might not even have their intended effect, since kids can simply go to their *friends'* houses to watch violent TV or play violent games[9]. Even worse, banning violent content may actually make it *more* appealing to children, a phenomenon that psychologists colorfully refer to as "forbidden fruit" theory[10],[e] although there is little research indicating that this happens very often.

The best study we know on restrictive mediation was conducted with over 1300 families across a school year, with data gathered from 3rd-5th grade children, their parents, their teachers, and even school nurses. Three very interesting results emerged. First, parents and children do *not* agree on whether parents have rules about media use or whether parents discuss media content with them. In general, if 80% of parents say they have a rule, only about 40% of children agree.[11] So either parents are overly optimistic, or they are not clear enough with children about the rules.

The second interesting result is that setting limits on the amount and content of children's screen media at the beginning of the school year had powerful effects at the end of the school year.[12] Children whose parents set these limits were, at the end of the year, (1) getting more sleep, (2) which in turn led to lower weight gain and lower risk of obesity; they were (3) getting better grades, (4) were more prosocial in their behaviors at school (as rated by teachers), and (5) were less aggressive at school (again as rated by teachers). This is fascinating because these are not the same types of outcome variables. These include physical health, school performance, and social wellness. Those don't usually all co-occur together, but simply setting limits on amount and content of media influenced *all* of them positively!

---

[d] The only grandparent among the authors of the book (Craig) points out that the primary duty of a parent is to *parent*, not to be their child's or adolescent's best friend! Even so, it *is* possible and quite common to set clear rules and restrictions and still be loved and liked by one's children.

[e] This concept should be *very* familiar to anyone who remembers being a teenager and the appeal of doing something (e.g., listening to certain music, wearing certain clothes) precisely *because* you knew that someone else didn't want you to do it!

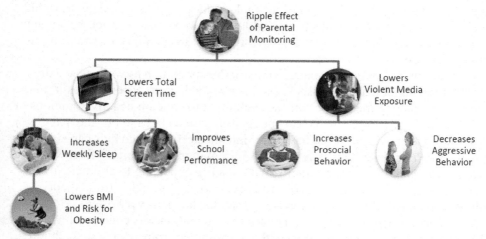

Figure 46.1. Ripple effects of parental monitoring.

The most interesting thing to realize from this study, however, is that no parents will ever know they are having this effect. You cannot know that your child gained less weight than he *would have*, or is less aggressive than she *would have been* if your rules had been different. You can only know what your child is. This is why parents often feel powerless – all they can see is the fight over the rules; they can't see the beneficial effects the rules are having. Nonetheless, this study demonstrates that parents are in a much more powerful position than they realize and that it's worth setting limits.

Though active mediation is "effective" and restricting media use is "effective, but with potential downsides," we must describe co-viewing as "ineffective at best, harmful at worst". To date there has been little research *directly* testing the effectiveness of co-viewing strategies, but the research which *has* been done isn't promising. Most studies of co-viewing show that it can actually *increase* the risk for aggression[9]. If this seems counter-intuitive, take a moment to think about what message a parent is sending their child by co-viewing violent media with them. In doing so, parents may be unintentionally telling their children "I approve of what you're seeing on the screen since I'm willing to watch and participate in it."

Although it may be hard to believe sometimes (especially in the case of teenagers), children *do* look to their parents as moral beacons, teachers of wrong and right. So if parents *don't* disapprove of the violence on the screen, it may be read as a signal that "I'm okay with this!" This tacit approval may well explain why co-viewing strategies can *increase* the child's risk of aggression – children are forming beliefs that aggression is acceptable, a risk factor for aggression (see Question #12).

At this point, a small set of studies is worth mentioning here. Up to now, we've focused on strategies that parents can implement to help reduce the effects of violent media on their children. But some researchers are thinking outside the home, to a place where children spend a considerable amount of their day: school. Some schools have introduced intervention programs designed to reduce exposure to violent media in children and thereby reduce the harmful effects of such media. Two such experimental interventions have been found to reduce students' real-world aggressive behavior.

One of these studies was conducted years ago, before video games existed.[13] In this study, seven to eight year old children were randomly assigned to a one of two conditions. In the "treatment" condition, the children were trained to recognize the lack of realism in TV violence and later made a video tape of themselves presenting essays explaining why it's bad to imitate TV violence (supposedly to show to other children who had been fooled or harmed by TV violence). The other condition was a control condition, where no intervention took place. Four months later, friends rated the children's aggressive behavior. Children in the treatment condition were found to be *less* aggressive than the children in the control condition.

More recently, a research team in Germany tested the effects of an intervention that consisted of 5 weekly 90-minute sessions with 7th and 8th grade students, as well as two evenings that involved parents.[14] Classes of students were again randomly assigned to the treatment (intervention) condition or to the control condition. The intervention itself had two goals: restricting consumption of violent media (TV, movies, electronic games), and thinking critically to create negative attitudes about violent media. The intervention took place through class discussion, small group tasks, demonstrations, and homework assignments. The effects of the treatment on aggressive behavior were tested 3 months, 18 months, and 30 months later. Like the first intervention, this one *also* reduced aggressive behavior over time.

Parents can learn from the success of these school-based interventions, since they both contain features that parents can provide in their own home. These include teaching children that media usually don't accurately portray violence the way it happens in the real world, teaching them that society opposes violence as a solution, getting them involved in thinking about how and why media violence is bad for them, getting them to reduce their own media violence consumption, and getting them to consider non-violent solutions to conflicts. All of these lessons can be taught by parents through the judicious use of active and restrictive mediation strategies.

We have alluded to the issue of screen media in children's bedrooms and the privatization of media in general as an additional risk factor for children. One recent study followed three groups of children across time. One group of over 400 3rd-5th graders was followed for six months, one group of over 1300 3rd-5th graders was followed for 13 months, and one group of over 3000 3rd-8th graders was followed for two years.[15] Across all three samples of children, the results were clear: Having a TV or video game system in the bedroom increased all of the negative effects. Bedroom media increased both the amount of screen media viewed and the amount of violent content consumed. These in turn predicted poorer sleep, less reading for pleasure, poorer school performance, higher risk of obesity, higher video game addiction symptoms, higher normative beliefs about aggression (thinking aggression is more acceptable), and more physically aggressive behavior. In short, having media in children's bedrooms acted like a turbocharger for multiple harmful media effects! Therefore, one of the most effective things parents can do is to not allow screen media in bedrooms.

We finish this section with a reminder that more research is needed before researchers know for sure what the "best" strategies for reducing media violence effects are. We suspect that there is not one overall best strategy, but the most effective strategies should involve parents, schools, and other groups that can influence the beliefs and values of children. Just because more research is needed doesn't mean that we don't have *some* idea about which strategies are likely more effective: Pairing active mediation with restrictive mediation seems to be quite effective, since active mediation strategies can decrease the negative aspects of restrictive mediation while restrictive mediation can reduce exposure to harmful media overall. Of course, future research needs to reconcile this with the fact that a couple of studies have found no effects of parental involvement at all[16]. Nonetheless, parents can still benefit from the information that's currently available to make informed decisions about their children's media diets – much in the same way parents make informed decisions about their children's food diets even as nutritionists continue to study the benefits and drawbacks of different foods.

References
1. Corder-Bolz, C. R. (1980). Mediation: The role of significant others. *Journal of Communication, 30*(3), 106-118.
2. Horton, R. W. & Santogrossi, D. A. (1978). The effect of adult commentary on reducing the influence of televised violence. *Personality and Social Psychology Bulletin, 4*(2), 337-340.
3. Nathanson, A. I. (1999). Identifying and explaining the relationship between parental mediation and children's aggression. *Communication Research, 26*(2), 124-143.
4. Linder, J.R., & Werner, N. E. (2012). Relationally aggressive media exposure and children's normative believes: Does parental mediation matter? *Family Relations, 61*(3), 488-500.
5. Anderson, C. A. & Bushman, B. J. (2002). Human Aggression. *Annual Review of Psychology, 53,* 27-51.

6. Gentile, D. A., Lynch, P. J., Ruh Linder, J., & Walsh, D. A. (2004). The effects of violent video game habits on adolescent hostility, aggressive behaviors, and school performance. *Journal of Adolescence, 27,* 5-22.
7. Singer, J. L., Singer, D. G., & Rapaczynski, W. S. (1984). Family patterns and television viewing as predictors of children's beliefs and aggression. *Journal of Communication, 34*(2), 73-89.
8. Rothschild, N., & Morgan, M. (1987). Cohesion and control: Adolescents' relationships with parents as mediators of television. *Journal of Early Adolescence, 7,* 299-314.
9. Nathanson, A. I. (2002). The unintended effects of parental mediation of television on adolescents. *Media Psychology, 4*(3), 207-230.
10. Bushman, B. J. & Stack, A. D. (1996). Forbidden fruit versus tainted fruit: Effects of warning labels on attraction to television violence. *Journal of Experimental Psychology: Applied, 2*(3), 207-226.
11. Gentile, D. A., Nathanson, A. I., Rasmussen, E. E., Reimer, R. A., & Walsh, D. A. (2012). Do you see what I see? Parent and child reports of parental monitoring. *Family Relations, 61,* 470-487.
12. Gentile, D. A., Reimer, R. A., Nathanson, A. I., Walsh, D. A., & Eisenmann, J. C. (2014). A prospective study of the protective effects of parental monitoring of children's media use. *JAMA-Pediatrics, 168,* 479-484. doi:10.1001/jamapediatrics.2014.146
13. Huesmann, L. R., Eron, L. D., Klein, R., Brice, P., & Fischer, P. (1983). Mitigating the imitation of aggressive behaviors by changing children's attitudes about media violence. *Journal of Personality and Social Psychology, 44,* 899-910.
14. Krahé, B., & Busching, R. (2015). Breaking the vicious cycle of media violence use and aggression: A test of intervention effects over 30 months. *Psychology of Violence, 5*(2), 217-226.
15. Gentile, D. A., Berch, O. N., Choo, H., Khoo, A., Walsh, D. A. (2017). Bedroom media: One risk factor for development. *Developmental Psychology, 53,* 2340-2355. doi: 10.1037/dev0000399
16. Hastings, E. C., Karas, T. L., Winsler, A., Way, E., Madigan, A., & Tyler, S. (2009). Young children's video/computer game use: Relations with school performance and behavior. *Issues in Mental Health Nursing, 30,* 638-649.

47 - Should I limit how much screen media my child is exposed to?

The Short Answer:

Yes. Children spend a *lot* of their free time in front of a screen. And although some TV shows, films, and electronic games *can* have benefits, these are largely accompanied by other harmful effects, especially when it comes to *excessive* screen media use. In addition to the risks posed by violent media, screen media usage in general is associated with health and well-being issues, attention problems, and school performance problems. However, outright prohibiting screen media use in children over the age of 3 is not only difficult, it also may be counterproductive. Aiming for a moderate amount of screen media use is a good idea. The American Academy of Pediatrics has previously suggested a maximum of 1 hour of total screen time per day for children through elementary school, and 2 hours for secondary school students. At the very least, it's worth being aware of just how much screen time your child is exposed to and avoiding creating situations where they are unsupervised and able to use screen media for excessive periods of time.

The Long Answer:

On a typical day, the average American child spends more than 7 hours in front of a screen, including watching television, playing video games, or browsing the internet[1]. To parents and researchers alike, this is a startlingly high number. Since screen media consume so much of a child's time, it's worth asking whether all of this media use is bad for them and, if so, what can a parent do to reduce it.

Let's start by talking about what all of this screen media is likely to do to kids. To be fair, we do know that it's not *all* bad. In Question #41 we discussed some of these benefits of media use, which include improved visual/spatial skills[2], hand-eye coordination[3], and – in the case of educational media specifically[4], improved school performance. We could even be generous and argue that modern media (e.g., online video games) are the "playground" of today's era[5], so to speak: Whereas children in the past would meet up after school to gossip, explore the nearby forest, or play sports, children today "meet" after school on social media to gossip, explore viral videos together, or play competitive video games. If we take this perspective, we *could* argue that children's recreational activities haven't changed in the past few decades, only the form in which it occurs. This perspective argues that media use seems fairly innocuous and may even be beneficial, giving kids a chance to socialize with one another. And from this perspective, media researchers might seem like backwards-looking Luddites who hate screen media and want to ruin everyone's fun by taking away some of the most addictive and engrossing technology known to humankind.[a]

As we've discussed throughout this book, there are *many* legitimate reasons to be concerned about media content and the sheer amount of it we consume. Perhaps the most obvious drawback is the effect of media content on our thoughts, feelings, and behavior, best exemplified by the vast body of research showing that violent media carries with it an increased risk of aggressive behavior[6] (see Question #11). But violent content isn't the only content worth being concerned about. Similar effects have been found between certain media content and early sexual behavior[7], body dissatisfaction[8], alcohol use[9], and impulsiveness[10], to name just a few (see Question #38). But even if we ignore the risks associated with specific content, spending hours each day staring at a screen has a host of undesirable side effects. As we've discussed elsewhere in this book, frequent media use is associated with attention problems[10] (Question #37), health and wellness concerns[11,12] (Question #39), poor academic performance[13] (Question #40), and may even lead to addiction[14] (Question #42). So it's not just a matter of *what* we're exposed to, it's *how much* of it we're exposed to as well. In addition, it's also a matter of what children *aren't* doing, such as reading, creating, exploring, doing homework, having hobbies, playing sports, etc. when they're spending time on screen media.

Which leads us back to our original question: If screen media has all of these undesirable effects, should parents set limits on how their children consume it? Well, if we want to reduce the risks associated with media use, having *some* restrictions is a good idea. Most parents would probably agree, for example, that their child *shouldn't* spend every waking moment watching TV and playing video games, especially if it gets to the point that it's hurting their performance in school, ability to make friends, or eventually get a job.

So we can agree that having *some* limits is a good idea. But most of us would *also* likely agree that it would be an overreaction to outright ban a child from viewing any and all screen media. Such a ban would not only be

---

[a] One common question we hear goes something like this, "Why is playing a violent video game worse than playing cops and robbers was in the old days?" One key difference involves learning about consequences. Beating the bad guy with a stick in a video game has no negative consequences for the character doing the beating. If your child *actually* hits another child while playing cops and robbers there are immediate consequences (the struck child cries, bleeds, hits back…) and long-term consequences (the parents punish the offending child in some way, and explain why it's bad to hurt others).

impractical,[b] but, as we discussed in Question #46, this could lead to blowback from children and increase the desirability of screen media.[15,16] Furthermore, an outright ban on screen media overlooks the fact that electronic media can have a lot of benefits, even some media created for entertainment purposes!

In other words, an ideal solution for managing your child's media use should fall somewhere between the two extremes; Allow *some* screen media use, but take measures to avoid excessive amount and worrisome content. In many ways, we already take this sort of approach to our children when it comes to their food diet. We recognize, for example, that no amount of junk food is "healthy" for them, but we also realize that it's *unreasonable* to expect them to *never* eat junk food.[c] Instead, we aim to minimize the risks associated with junk food by limiting its consumption (e.g., "not every meal can be sugary cereal") while encouraging reasonably healthy eating habits (e.g., "you can have your dessert if you eat your broccoli first!").

So just what *is* a reasonable level of media exposure, and how do we reduce a child's exposure to this level without outright banning or limiting media use? To answer the first question, the American Academy of Pediatrics recommends 1-2 hours of total screen media use per day (1 hour for children through elementary school, 2 for secondary school, and *no* screen media use for children under the age of two.)[17] If seeing how low that number is just made your stomach turn a bit (e.g., "oh my gosh, my child watches *way* more than that!), you're not alone! You'll notice that this recommended amount is *far* lower than the than 7 hours of media use the average child gets per day[1].[d] As it turns out, the vast majority kids are getting *way* more screen media than they probably ought to be getting.[e]

---

[b] Screen media are everywhere in our society, from our phones to our TV screens, computers to gaming consoles – it's impossible to get away from. Even if you banned it outright in your house, could you realistically keep your children from using a computer at school or at the library? From playing video games at a friend's house? From watching a movie at the theatre? Who has that kind of time?

[c] It's unreasonable because children lack the impulse control that adults have, because so much junk food advertising is geared toward making the products as appealing as possible to children, and because children will have access to junk food in situations beyond your control.

[d] Actually, the AAP recently backed away from their original recommendations in a misguided belief (in our view) that parents would be more likely to adhere to easier (less stringent) guidelines. In fact, recent longitudinal research of over 100,000 children shows that 2+ hours a day of screen media yields cognitive decrements, and that 7+ hours yields cortical thinning.[20]

[e] If you find yourself thinking "that's ridiculous, you can't say that *most* people have unhealthy media habits!," remember that, according to the World Health

Answering the second question is far more difficult. If kids are *this* overexposed to screen media, how can we possibly hope to reduce it to the recommended guidelines?

One approach is to make it *harder* for children to use screen media for hours on end while avoiding the need to explicitly limit media use. For example: The American Academy of Pediatrics recommends turning off screen media during shared family activities such as meal times[17]. They also recommend not allowing children to have a TV, video game console, or computer in their rooms[17] (we would add electronic tablets, cell phones, and any electronic entertainment devices to that list.) The rationale for this restriction is actually pretty simple: Having access to screen media in their own room (private space) makes it easy for children to use them without anyone noticing. If a child is forced to use the TV or computer or other electronic devices only in a public room (e.g., a family room), it's less convenient for them to consume media uninterrupted for hours (especially if they have to share with others). It also makes a child's media consumption habits far more obvious to parents, since it's harder to get away with watching TV at 3:00 am if they can do so only in the family room. Finally, it makes in less likely that the children will access extremely inappropriate content. Small changes such as these can reduce screen time *without* having to set explicit rules limiting screen time, and may also seem less draconian and arbitrary to a child than simply choosing a specific amount of screen time.

Another thing to keep in mind when trying to reduce children's screen media use is that children are bundles of energy that need to do *something*. If screen media currently makes up the majority of your child's recreational time, taking it away without any sort of replacement activity is bound to lead to boredom, unhappiness, and frustration. This is why you should reframe your goal from "limiting screen media time," to the goal of "replacing screen media time with other fun activities." If they're encouraged to take up a hobby or a sport, or to read books, or to interact with friends out in the real world, it's very likely they'll spend less time in front of a screen all on their own![f] All the better if you're able to get involved and help them take up these activities (e.g., arrange for them to have a ride to and from sports practice) or get involved yourself (e.g., share in your child's hobbies). These sorts of changes are more likely to make these alternative activities "stick" and lead to long-lasting declines in screen media use.

Organization, nearly three-quarters of American adults are also overweight, suggesting that most people also have unhealthy diet and exercise habits![18]

[f] For parents with young children, we strongly urge you to make reading to your child a part of their bedtime routine. As soon as they begin to talk, you can make reading a fun (but relatively calm) bedtime activity. Start by reading to them and, as they get older, you can take turns reading. We also recommend using real books, not an electronic screen, as the light emitted by screens can be disruptive to sleep.[12,19]

Remember, time spent on hobbies, hanging out with friends, creating something, or otherwise out in the real world is time *not* spent in front of a screen!

Another approach that some families have had success with is to give a screen-time "allowance," such as 14 hours a week or whatever you negotiate with your children. Consider a monetary allowance. We don't give an allowance to children because we think they need money. We give it to them so that over time they can learn to manage money responsibly. When a child first gets an allowance, they usually spend it all right away, often on candy. Later in the month they wish they still had some money. Over time they learn not to spend it all at once, and later they learn to save money. The point is that by the time they move out of your house, they have some sense about how to manage their money responsibly. The idea of a screen-time allowance is the same. You can print out coupons, make a log sheet, have tokens, or whatever might seem fun to your children. At the beginning of the week, they get their allowance. If they decide to spend it all on Saturday, then that's their choice and they'll be sad later in the week. After a while, they'll learn to be thoughtful about their screen time and not just turn on the TV to "see if something's on." By the time they move out of your house, they will have some sense about how to manage their entertainment time responsibly.

Above all else, it's important to have *realistic* goals when it comes to your child's media use. Children are growing up in an era with unprecedented access to media of all sorts, meaning that time in front of a screen will inevitably be a normal part of their day-to-day lives. Since this is the case, it's unlikely you'll be able to immediately cut their screen time from seven hours a day to two or fewer hours. If you try to do this all at once, it'll likely end with you throwing your hands up in exasperation and your child frustrated and upset. Remember that big changes in behavior don't happen overnight. Treat it as a long-term goal and aim toward small improvements. In the same way that no one goes from the couch to running a marathon, don't expect to go from seven hours of media use a day to two. Look for ways to reduce screen time by a half an hour at a time, adding to that once these changes become routine. Also keep in mind that the strategies we suggest here may not work for you: Not everyone has the time to be a little league coach or the money to send their children to an art class. As a parent, you should work to develop strategies that fit your family. Your solution may involve a half-hour walk with them each day, reading to them before bedtime, or just making it easier for them to spend time with their friends outside. Either way, it's a good place to start!

References

1. Rideout, V. J., Foehr, U. G. & Roberts, D. F. (2010). *Generation M2: Media in the lives of 8-18 year olds.* Merlo Park CA: Henry J Kaiser Foundation.

2. Green, C. S., & Bavelier, D. (2006). Effect of action video games on the spatial distribution of visuospatial attention. *Journal of Experimental Psychology: Human Perception and Performance, 32*(6), 1465-1478.

3. Griffith, J. L., Voloschin, P., Gibb, G. D., & Bailey, J. R. (1983). Differences in eye-hand motor coordination of video-game users and non-users. *Perceptual and Motor Skills, 57*(1), 155-158.

4. Corbett, A. T., Koedinger, K. R., & Hadley, W. (2001). Cognitive tutors: From the research classroom to all classrooms. IN P. S. Goodman (Ed.). *Technology enhanced learning* (pp. 235-263). Mahwah (NJ): Lawrence Erlbaum.

5. Tyler, T. R. (2002). Is the internet changing social life? It seems the more things change, the more they stay the same. *Journal of Social Issues, 58*(1), 195-205.

6. Anderson, C. A., Shibuya, A., Ihori, N., Swing, E. L., Bushman, B. J., Sakamoto, A., Rothstein, H. R., & Saleem, M. (2010). Violent video game effects on aggression, empathy, and prosocial behavior in eastern and western countries: a meta-analytic review. *Psychological Bulletin, 136*(2), 151-173.

7. Brown, J. D., L'Engle, K. L., Pardun, C. J., Guo, G., Kenneavy, K., & Jackson, C. (2006). Sexy media matter: Exposure to sexual content in music, movies, television, and magazines predicts black and white adolescents' sexual behavior. *Pediatrics, 117*(4), 1018-1027.

8. Groesz, L. M., Levine, M. P., & Murnen, S. K. The effect of experimental presentation of thin media images on body satisfaction: A meta-analytic review. *International Journal of Eating Disorders, 31*(1), 1-16.

9. Robinson, T. N., Chen, H. L., & Killen, J. D. (1998). Television and music video exposure and risk of adolescent alcohol use. *Pediatrics, 102*(5), e54.

10. Gentile, D. A., Swing, E. L., Lim, C. G., & Khoo, A. (2012). Video game playing, attention problems, and impulsiveness: Evidence of bidirectional causality. *Psychology of Popular Media Culture, 1*(1), 62-70.

11. Ianotti, R. J., Kogan, M. D., Janssen, I., & Boyce, W. F. (2009). Patterns of adolescent physical activity, screen-based media use and positive and negative health indicators in the U.S. and Canada. *Journal of Adolescent Health, 44*(5), 493-499.

12. Cain, N. & Gradisar, M. (2010). Electronic media use and sleep in school-aged children and adolescents: A review. *Sleep Medicine, 11,* 735-742.

13. Sharif, I., Wills, T. A., & Sargent, J. D. (2010). Effect of visual media use on school performance: A prospective study. *Journal of Adolescent Health, 46*(1), 52-61.

14. Gentile, D. (2009). Pathological video-game use among youth ages 8 to 18: A national study. *Psychological Science, 20*(5), 594-602.

15. Nathanson, A. I. (2002). The unintended effects of parental mediation of television on adolescents. *Media Psychology, 4*(3), 207-230.

16. Bushman, B. J. & Stack, A. D. (1996). Forbidden fruit versus tainted fruit: Effects of warning labels on attraction to television violence. *Journal of Experimental Psychology: Applied, 2*(3), 207-226.
17. American Academy of Pediatrics, Committee on Public Education (2001). Children, Adolescents, and television. *Pediatrics, 107,* 423-426.
18. United States Department of Health and Human Services, Center for Disease Control and Prevention, National Center for Health Statistics (2015). *Summary Health Statistics: National Health Interview Survey, 2015. Table A-15a: Age-adjusted percent distribution (with standard errors) of body mass index among adults aged 18 and over, by selected characteristics: United States, 2015.* Retrieved September 16, 2018 from: https://ftp.cdc.gov/pub/Health_Statistics/NCHS/NHIS/SHS/2015_SHS_Table_A-15.pdf
19. Higuchi, S., Motohashi, Y., Liu, Y., & Maeda, A. (2005). Effects of playing a computer game using a bright display on presleep physiological variables, sleep latency, slow wave sleep and REM sleep. *Journal of Sleep Research, 14,* 267-273.
20. Paulus, M. P., Squeglia, L. M., Bagot, K., Jacobus, J., Kuplicki, R., Breslin, F. J., . . . Tapert, S. F. (2019). Screen media activity and brain structure in youth: Evidence for diverse structural correlation networks from the ABCD study. *NeuroImage, 185,* 140-153.

48 - Should I use content rating systems to determine what kinds of media my children use?

The Short Answer:

Yes, but do so cautiously. Media rating systems in the U.S. are generally run and funded by media industries, not by researchers or independent organizations. As a result, age ratings are arbitrary, especially since the criteria for what makes something appropriate or inappropriate for children of a certain age are not clear. In general, age ratings work well as a lower limit guideline for appropriateness (e.g., a mature-rated game is *always* inappropriate for anyone under 17). But, many games and films rated as "appropriate" for teenagers and children are in fact *inappropriate* for them, mainly because of violent content. Wherever possible, parents should get as much information about a piece of media as they can (e.g., trailers, descriptions, youtube, reviews) and base their judgment about the appropriateness on that information, rather than relying solely on its rating. This is especially important not only because of harms that psychological science has found, but also because parents often disagree with ratings systems about whether content would be appropriate for *their* children. Independent web sites run by child advocate organizations can also provide additional information, reviews, and ratings without the influence or funding of the media industry.

The Long Answer:

It's tough being a parent: You want to raise a happy, healthy child in a world chock-full of risks. There are, of course, plenty of resources out there which promise to ease this burden. Overworked and concerned parents *are* grateful for guides, summaries, and suggestions that break down a complex subject and give them clear, simple answers to the questions they're faced with every day: Is this snack healthy for my child? Is this toy safe? Will this school give them a good education? How late should I let my child stay up?[a] Fully answering these questions could take hours of painstaking research, and might not end up giving parents the simple, straightforward answers they're looking for. For this reason, it's helpful to have reviews, rating systems, and expert recommendations to take some of this guesswork out of parenting.

It's not surprising, then, that many parents find content ratings systems such as the Classification and Ratings Administration (CARA) for movies (e.g.,

---

[a] In fact, we'd wager that many of you are reading this book right now for this exact reason!

"Rated R"), the Entertainment Software Ratings Board (ESRB) for video games (e.g., "Rated M"), and the TV Parental Guidelines Monitoring Board (e.g., "TV 14") so appealing. If your child wants to see a movie or buy a video game, it's hard to know whether the right answer is to say yes or no, even *if* you've had time to review the game's content for yourself. Is it *okay* for your 12-year old to watch a show where characters kill zombies? Can an 8-year old to watch cartoon characters chasing one another with weapons? Ratings systems give you a simple, black-and-white answer: If it's rated PG-13 and your child is 10, you should probably say "no."

These systems and their simple answers are appealing. However, if you delve into the inner workings of many of these systems, cracks and weaknesses begin to appear. Despite the fact that they seem very official, credible, and data-driven, these systems suffer from several significant flaws. We'll discuss some of these flaws, but first, it's helpful to know where these rating systems originate.

Although the numbers and letter-ratings may give these systems the appearance of being based on scientific data, most media rating systems are not based on science at all – that is, they have little to no grounding in media psychology research or developmental psychology principles[1]. All of the official media ratings systems in the U.S. were created by their respective media industries, usually as a response to political pressure (e.g., angry parent groups, politicians and lawyers going after specific companies, threats from Congress). When these ratings boards are created, it's almost always with little to no guidance or input from psychologists or media researchers. Instead, the systems are devised by the industry, funded by the industry, and run by industry-paid boards of raters, none of whom are, themselves, experts in developmental or media psychology. In the case of TV ratings, for example, it's the *producers* of the TV shows who decide on the rating of the show (if a rating is even to be provided), with studios and channels deciding for themselves whether to keep or change the rating later.

Usually, when a film, program, or video game is produced, companies submit the product (or, in the case of video games, sometimes just a *survey* about it) to a ratings board to be rated by a handful of non-expert raters[b] whose identity is usually kept confidential (though they're supposed to have no conflicts of interest.) After deliberating, the raters eventually assign a rating[2-5]. These ratings are then returned to the producers[5], sometimes with a list of suggested changes that, if implemented, will reduce the content age rating (e.g., from an "R" to "PG-13").[c] In the end, most games, films, and television programs receive an age rating

---

[b] In some cases, raters are required to either be parents themselves or to have had children in the past – though we would hardly say that being a parent qualifies someone to decide what's appropriate for *everyone's* children!

[c] To understand why these suggestions are given, it helps to know that, as a general rule, companies want their product to be sold to the widest market

without *any* input from a single media effects researcher, developmental psychologist, or expert in child development.

But it gets worse: How a particular piece of media winds up with the rating it does is often unclear, sometimes even to the reviewers and producers themselves. In many cases, there are no formal guidelines for what earns a piece of media a particular rating[6]. As a result, it's hard to know exactly how to interpret a particular rating: Is a film's "R" rating due to it having a *lot* of swearing, or due to a single, brief flash of nudity? Is it due to extreme and gratuitous violence or passing drug references? Are raters treating some of these problems as more important than others, and how does that show through if a piece of media simply gets a single-letter rating? We can see the confusion for ourselves by looking at some of the perplexing outcomes of this system. For example, the film *Billy Elliot*, an inspirational story about a boy becoming a ballet dancer, was given an "R" rating (restricted to anyone under the age of 17 without an accompanying adult). Why? Because the film included a lot of profanity – certainly not something you'd want a five-year old to listen to, but probably not anything a teenager hasn't heard before.

Now, compare the R rating of our swear-filled story about a ballet dancer to a film like *The Expendables 3*, which is about a mercenary group fighting against an illegal arms dealer. *The Expendables 3* received a rating of PG-13 (some material considered inappropriate for children under the age of 13), despite the fact that it showed more than 300 on-screen killings. If these ratings are taken at their face value, it suggests that hundreds of people being killed is somehow more appropriate for young audiences than a couple of bad words![d] Inconsistencies like these boggle the mind, but the frequency with which they occur is even more unsettling. For example, violent content is present in 64% of video games that are rated by the video game industry as appropriate for *all ages*[7], while TV ratings that claim to flag shows which contain violent content *fail* to catch between 75% and 81% of shows that contain violence[8]. Clearly, there's a need to develop better content-rating guidelines that yield ratings most people would agree with and which avoid contradictions like the ones pointed out above.

---

possible. For example, being told that your product can only be sold to adults completely cuts off the lucrative teenage market. For this reason, companies have a vested interest in trying to get their product the lowest age rating possible, which might include cutting parts of a scene or censoring a specific number of swear words – a small price to pay to broaden a product's potential market.

[d] Of course, you may think this is the case, but we'd argue that most of society disagrees with you. After all, the penalty for murder is a *lot* more severe than the penalty for profanity or disorderly conduct, suggesting that we, as a society, have decided which of these forms of behavior is more socially inappropriate.

This lack of clear, consistent guidelines also contributes to another, more subtle problem, called *ratings creep*. To put it simply, ratings creep means that, as time passes, the amount of "inappropriate" content that's allowed for a certain age rating increases[9,10]. This means that a game, television show, or film containing content that would have made it restricted to adults a decade ago is more likely to be rated appropriate for teenagers today. The problem is *most* pronounced at the boundaries between the more moderate ratings (e.g., "Teen" versus "Mature," or "PG" versus "PG-13"). This is because similar, somewhat fuzzy terms (e.g., graphic violence, strong violence, shocking violence[e]) are used to distinguish which content falls into which category, giving raters a lot of "wiggle room" for disagreement – which is precisely where ratings creep sneaks in[4]. Ratings systems do a fairly good job when it comes to shows or games that *clearly* are appropriate for very young children or that *clearly* are appropriate only for adults – precisely where parents need ratings systems the least. But when it comes to content that falls between these two extremes, where there's the most fuzziness and ambiguity for parents, ratings systems begin to struggle[7].

Another problem stems from the nature of the "yes or no" labeling system itself. By organizing the ratings system as a series of age thresholds, content is essentially divided into "appropriate" or "inappropriate." By doing this, content systems may be creating a "forbidden fruit" effect[11,12], a concept that was introduced in Question #46. We can see this demonstrated in a study of children who all saw an identical film clip. Some of the children were told that the film that the clip came from was rated "G," while others were told that the film was rated "PG-13" or even "R." The researchers then asked the children whether they were interested in seeing the whole film themselves. None of the boys wanted to see the film when it was rated "G." In contrast, about half of boys said they wanted to see the *exact same film* when they were told it had been given a rating of "PG-13" or "R." If you've ever gotten into an argument with a child who wanted to watch a show that they were too young for, you'll appreciate this problem with the age-rating system.[f]

---

[e] Feel free to let us know if you've figured out what the differences between the three are, especially when you consider that violence, by definition, is an act of extreme aggression (see Question #7).

[f] One of the authors, Courtney, distinctly remembers turning 18 and being *most* excited by the fact that it meant he could no longer be prevented from seeing R-rated movies at the theater or from buying R-rated video games at the store.

Perhaps the *biggest* drawback to age-based ratings systems, however, is the fact that, despite trying to make the job of picking appropriate content for their children easier, parents often find these systems confusing and they frequently disagree with the ratings themselves. Across the various media rating systems, content can be given any of dozens of possible labels: GA, PG, PG-13, R, NC-17, E, T, M, AO, Y, Y7, 14, MA, V, S, L (to name just some of the ratings categories). This alphabet soup of different ratings and criteria can make it tough for parents to know whether a piece of media is appropriate for their child, especially if they don't already know what the letters mean.[g]

Even if a parent is familiar with what all of these letters mean, it's worth asking *who* decided what was appropriate for their child in the first place, and whether parents themselves agree with the ratings. Studies have shown, for example, that when parents *themselves* are asked to rate shows, films, and games, there's considerable disagreement between what parents deemed appropriate for their children and what different ratings systems deemed appropriate[2]. Parents felt that almost half of the content rated appropriate for all ages contained content that they thought was not appropriate for some ages. Parents similarly disagreed with 13% to 37% of media rated appropriate for children ages 8 to 12 and 40% to 57% of media rated as appropriate for teenagers[13]. In other words, these systems that were designed to take the guesswork out of decision-making for parents aren't in line with parents' own judgments! That said, a national study of parents found that when asked at what age specific types of content are appropriate, parents basically *never* agree.[14] Some parents think kissing is ok for children under 6 and others not until 18. Some parents think graphic violence is ok for children under 6 and others think it's never appropriate. This means that no matter what age rating is placed on a media product, a majority of parents will think it's the wrong age!

So what should parents do – ignore ratings systems altogether? This would probably be an over-reaction. There's some value to be had in age-based ratings systems, as long as they're not treated as *ultimate truth*. After all, ratings systems do a fairly good job when it comes to labeling material that is *clearly* inappropriate for children.[h] And certainly, if a parent knows absolutely nothing about a piece of media, relying on an age-based rating system is better than *nothing*. But, ideally, if parents want to make informed decisions about media, they would do better with some sort of descriptive list of any potentially worrisome content, which would allow them to decide for themselves whether they want their own children to be exposed to it[14]. Rather than being told that a game is appropriate for "Teens," parents would prefer to know that a game

---

[g] The more conspiracy-minded might think that this confusing and misleading state of affairs is not entirely an accident!

[h] To the best of our knowledge, there has never been a case of a piece of media with frequent graphic murders or excessive sexual content being labeled "appropriate for all audiences"!

involves soldiers shooting other soldiers, maybe with some graphic (but not intensely gory) death sequences, and frequent profanity, so they can decide if they're comfortable with their child seeing this content.

And, to be fair, some ratings systems *have* started providing these sorts of descriptive lists in online information, though we would still argue that it's not enough detail to be useful. For example, terms like "fantasy violence" are still incredibly vague and say very little about what's *actually* happening on-screen.[i] Many people also think "fantasy violence" means it's ok for children, when the research shows that it can have most of the same negative effects that more realistic violence does (see Question #33). What's more, ratings – especially game ratings – are typically based on a sample of gameplay or simply a survey answered by the game producers, not on the whole game itself. As such, it's entirely possible for there to be content in a game that's never been seen by a rating board and which is not described clearly in the game's official rating. This famously happened with the video game *Grand Theft Auto: San Andreas*, in which players could, with only slight modification, access highly sexual content that was on the game's disc, but which was never seen by the game's ratings board[15]. In the ensuing outrage, the game was eventually recalled from store shelves to have its rating changed from "Mature" to "Adults Only". The company then modified the game to remove the offending content.[j]

For all of these reasons, content-based ratings should be seen as a good *start*, something to use in a pinch or when you have nothing else to go on. Our advice for parents, however, is to look online for themselves for examples of the media content. For films, television shows, and video games, it's worth watching a trailer or two online or to try to find a basic summary of the plot, which should provide information about the emphasis of the show and its style: Does it focus on realistic portrayals of violence and its consequences? Is sexual content present, and is it the film's main selling point? For video games, it may be possible to not only look at trailers for the game, but to see gameplay footage online. In recent years it's become popular for players to stream footage of their gameplay online, making it possible for parents to watch someone else play the game for a few minutes and see for themselves whether it's the sort of game that they're okay with their

---

[i] We're always amused to see movies rated PG-13 or R for "some language" which presumably refers to profanity but is vague enough to refer to *any* language (e.g., Spanish). Something tells us that movies don't have to be silent to be appropriate for children.

[j] Somewhat ironically, the *offending* content displayed consensual sexual intercourse between adults, including some female nudity. What was deemed *appropriate* content for the "Mature" rated version includes mass murder (including police officers) and having sex with a prostitute (without nudity) to regain health and then killing said prostitute in order to recover the money spent for her services.

children playing. And, of course, there are several parent groups and other child-first advocacy groups who independently assess and review media content to ensure that parents can make well-informed decisions about the media they let their children consume. These include, but are not limited to:

A. Australian Council on Children and the Media (https://childrenandmedia.org.au/)
B. Common Sense Media (https://www.commonsensemedia.org)
C. The Parents Television Council (http://w2.parentstv.org)
D. Screen It Movie Reviews for Parents (http://www.screenit.com/)
E. Kids in Mind (https://kids-in-mind.com/)
F. Movie Mom (https://moviemom.com/)
G. Plugged In https://www.pluggedin.com/
H. Dove https://dove.org/

Here are some sites with information on media, but that do not provide ratings or reviews:

A. Campaign for a commercial free childhood https://commercialfreechildhood.org/
B. Center on Media and Child Health https://cmch.tv/
C. Action Coalition for Media Education https://acmesmartmediaeducation.net/
D. Children's Screen Time Action Network www.screentimenetwork.org

In addition, there are a number of very useful sites with parenting information in general. Some of these are:
A. The Parent Coaching Institute https://www.thepci.org/
B. Growing Child https://growingchild.com/
C. Raising Children Network https://raisingchildren.net.au/guides/movie-reviews
D. Center for Innovative Public Health Research https://innovativepublichealth.org

In the end, decisions about what media children should be allowed to view really *should* come down to their informed parents. Ratings systems and content descriptions provide some information as general guidelines, but parents should never feel obligated to allow their children to play a game or watch a film that's been rated appropriate for their age if they disagree with the rating themselves. Nor should parents feel that they *have* to restrict their child's access to something that's been rated age-inappropriate if, after reviewing its content, they deem it appropriate. As long as you're mindful of the risks associated with the content (e.g., violent content effects), you, as your child's caregiver, have the final say in what counts as an acceptable risk, a topic we discuss in more detail in Question #49.

References

1. Gentile, D. A., Humphrey, J., & Walsh, D. A. (2005). Media ratings for movies, music, video games, and television: A review of the research and recommendations for improvements. *Adolescent Medicine, 16,* 427-446.
2. Funk, J. B., Flores, G., Buchman, D. D., & Germann, J. N. (1999). Rating electronic games: Violence is in the eye of the beholder. *Youth & Society, 30*(3), 283-312.
3. Cantor, J. (2003) Rating systems for media. In: D. H. Johnston (Ed.) *Encyclopedia of International Media and Communications,* pp. 47-57. San Diego, CA: Elsevier Science.
4. Federal Trade Commission (2000). *Marketing violent entertainment to children: A review of self-regulation and industry practices in the motion picture, music recording & electronic game industries.* Retrieved from https://www.ftc.gov/sites/default/files/documents/reports/marketing-violent-entertainment-children/vioreport_0.pdf
5. ESRB Ratings Process. Retrieved from http://www.esrb.org/ratings/ratings_process.aspx
6. Waxman, S. (2001, April 8). Rated S, for secret. *Washington Post,* G01.
7. Thompson, K. M. & Haninger, K. (2001). Violence in E-rated video games. *Journal of the American Medical Association, 286*(5), 591-598.
8. Kunkel, D. (2003). The road to the v-chip: Television violence and public policy. In: D. A. Gentile (Ed.) *Media Violence and Children,* pp. 227-246. Westport, CT: Praeger.
9. Yokota, F., & Thompson, K. M. (2000). Violence in G-rated animated films. *Journal of the American Medical Association, 283,* 2716-2720.
10. Thompson, K. M. & Tokota, F. Violence, sex and profanity in films: Correlation of movie ratings with content. *Medscape General Medicine, 6*(3).
11. Bushman, B. J., & Cantor, J. R. (2003). Media ratings for violence and sex: Implications for policymakers and parents. *American Psychologist, 58,* 130-141.
12. Bushman, B. J. & Stack, A. D. (1996). Forbidden fruit versus tainted fruit: Effects of warning labels on attraction to television violence. *Journal of Experimental Psychology: Applied, 2*(3), 207-226.
13. Walsh, D. A., & Gentile, D. A. (2001). A validity test of movie, television, and video-game ratings. *Pediatrics, 107,* 1302-1308.
14. Gentile, D. A., Maier, J. A., Hasson, M. R., & de Bonetti, B. L. (2011). Parents' evaluation of media ratings a decade after television ratings were introduced. *Pediatrics, 128,* 36-44.
15. Kushner, D. (2012). *Jacked: The Outlaw Story of Grand Theft Auto.* Hoboken, NJ: John Wiley & Sons, Inc.

49 - How should I choose what kinds of media my children consume?

The Short Answer:

When considering whether you or your children should be consuming a piece of media, you should consider not only its content (e.g., does it contain violent acts), but also its message (e.g., violence is heroic) and the context in which it will be seen (e.g., with others, alone.) Although it's certainly important to be aware of how much violent content is being consumed, some violent media are likely to be worse than others. Try to avoid media which focus primarily on violence, or that glamorize violence or treat it as something that's funny. Instead, try to choose alternatives that are non-violent, or that paint violence in a realistic but negative light, or that are not centered on the violence itself. It's also worth considering screen media with other redeeming traits, such as encouraging cooperation between players, requiring difficult moral choices, or engaging in creative problem solving. Though it may be unreasonable to *completely* avoid violent media for adolescents, it's at least possible to pick less-harmful violent media which may also have some benefits.

The Long Answer:

The message throughout much of this book is clear: Violent media consumption is a modest risk factor for aggression, in much the same way that we consider junk food to be a risk factor for poorer physical health (see Question #11 and #14 for more on this). If our goal is to protect ourselves and our children from harm, it may seem like we should outright avoid *all* violent media. This seems like a laudable but impossible goal. For young children (e.g., preschool) it is possible and desirable to avoid all violent media. For elementary school age children, it is possible to keep their media diet very healthy, at least at home.[a] For older children the task becomes more difficult, though it's still is possible to have a positive impact by setting appropriate rules and engaging in active mediation (Question #46). In fact, it is possible to use some violent media (e.g., viewing and discussing films with realistic portrayals of violence such as *Saving Private Ryan* or *Band of*

---

[a] One of the benefits of using active mediation regularly is that when you are in the habit of discussing media critically with your children, if they see something at someone else's house that you would not have probably allowed in yours, they will come home and tell you about it. You will then get the opportunity to discuss it with them in a way that is beneficial.

Brothers) as opportunities to teach your teens about your family's important values concerning life, death, war, and sacrifice.

Violent media are enticing by design – they're action-filled, attention-grabbing, and exciting. *Millions* of dollars are spent on advertising every year to make violent video games, films, and television shows enticing to potential audiences – including children. In fact, a US Federal Trade Commission report found that 70% of *adult*-rated games were being marketed to players under the age of 18.[1] Couple this with the fact that 1 in 3 stores routinely sell mature-rated content to children[2] and the fact that banning or prohibiting these games for children can make them *more* appealing[3], it can seem like preventing kids from consuming violent media is like trying to stop the tide from coming in.

As we describe in Question #46, prohibiting kids from viewing violent content is challenging[4], but at the same time, it would be better if we didn't entirely ignore a potential risk factor: Ideally, we'd like to *minimize* the risks of the violent media content our children are going to be exposed to. Is there an alternative for parents that lies somewhere between outright banning violent media versus letting them watch whatever they want?

We argue that there is, and we'll illustrate it with an anecdote from one of the authors, Courtney. In his youth, Courtney and his brother *loved* to watch wrestling. This isn't terribly unusual for kids, since nearly a quarter of *World Wrestling Entertainment's* (WWE) fan base is *under* the age of 18[5]. Courtney's father, on the other hand, disapproved of this: He was getting tired of the roughhousing that occurred after his sons watched wrestling, which usually ended when one of them got hurt.[b] It should be noted, by the way, that wrestling-inspired roughhousing like this wasn't unique to Courtney and his brother: Studies show that people who watch professional wrestling are more likely to engage in real-world aggression themselves[6,7].

Finally, when Courtney's father could take it no longer, he came up with a simple solution: He brought home a videotape featuring *real* martial arts bouts, which he showed to his sons. The difference between the two was staggering. In *WWE*, wrestlers attacked each other with chairs and weapons with virtually no consequence. When Bret Hart jumped off the top turnbuckle and landed on Steve Austin's head elbow-first in the 1996 Survivor Series, it did little more than stun his opponent for a few moments before he got back up and continued to fight for 15 more minutes. In contrast, seconds into the martial arts bouts, one fighter broke his hand. Minutes later, there were various bloody cuts, bruises, and swelling –

---

[b] Courtney distinctly remembers one of these roughhousing sessions ending with his brother shoving him *through* a wall – another factor that likely contributed to his father's ever-growing disdain for his sons watching wrestling!

real consequences of real aggression. Not long after, Courtney and his brother found themselves losing their stomach for roughhousing and playfighting.

The point of this anecdote *isn't* to suggest that parents should sit their children down in front of real violence. Nor are we trying to say that some kinds of violent media *decrease* aggression. Instead, we're trying to point out that it's too *simple* to just categorize media in terms of "violent" or "non-violent" and, by extension, "good" or "bad." Not all violent media are equal, and they shouldn't be expected to have the same effect on the viewer as such.

To see why, let's compare *WWE* wrestling and the martial arts bouts. On their surface, they probably seem pretty similar: They both involve professional athletes physically attacking one another in a combat-based competition. And, based on the General Aggression Model (GAM) introduced in Question #12, we should expect both films to increase the viewer's risk for aggression, since both films activate aggressive thoughts in the viewer's mind and increase the viewer's physiological heart rate. But what about *other* mechanisms, like the viewer's beliefs about the consequences of aggression?[8] In the case of *WWE* wrestling, viewers repeatedly see acts of aggression with few consequences: People who get hit stand back up, shake it off, and keep fighting. In addition, there are commentators saying things to make it seem more exciting and fun. This may cause viewer to learn, whether they realize it or not, that aggression's consequences aren't all that bad. The real martial arts fights, on the other hand, let viewers see the consequences of each strike, which injure both the attacker and the defender. They bleed real blood, break real bones, and they don't bounce back so quickly after a major blow to the head. Viewers of *these* fights quickly learn that aggression has dramatic consequences, which may cause them to think twice about starting a fight themselves.[c] So while, on the surface, these examples seem very similar in content (televised fighting), viewers may take dramatically different messages away from them.

These subtle content differences are one of the reasons why content-rating systems often lack the information needed to help parents make informed decisions about what their children are exposed to (see Question #48 for more about these systems). Knowing that a game contains "appropriate" amounts of violence for a teenager says very *little* about the nature of the in-game violence itself. An arcade-style fighting game such as *Street Fighter II* might be rated appropriate for teenagers because it doesn't show blood or gore, involve weapons, or use excessive profanity. But how is the violence in the game *framed*? If the player's *only* goal is to fight opponents, and the only way to win is to fight, and

---

[c] When he was young (but old enough to know better), Johnie and his high school friend decided to try fighting each other after thoroughly enjoying the movie *Fight Club*. Unsurprisingly, getting punched in the head was about as much fun as you'd expect, and both Johnie and his friend quickly decided that a fight club was a resoundingly stupid idea in practice.

the player is rewarded for winning by fighting, think about the associations the player is repeatedly making as they play (recall from Question #33 that people learn these associations even without actively *trying* to learn them).

We can compare *Street Fighter* to a game like *Fallout 4*, a game that's rated "Mature" by the ESRB because it contains, among other things, blood and gore and intense violence. In *Fallout 4*, players take on the role of a survivor in the wasteland of Boston, Massachusetts, more than two centuries after a nuclear war devastated the planet. Throughout the game, the player is tasked with finding their lost child and, ultimately, resolving numerous large-scale conflicts in the region. Importantly, the game is designed around player choice. Players are free to decide for themselves how they want to proceed at almost every point: They can choose to solve situations with violence, but they can also solve most situations with stealth, diplomacy, or avoidance altogether. In many instances, aggressive actions result in failed quests and can earn the player a negative reputation that precedes them and affects how other characters interact with them. Unlike *Street Fighter II*, the focus of *Fallout 4* is less about fighting and more about exploration, adventure, and role-playing. And while violence is certainly present in both games, in *Fallout 4* the player is often shown that violence isn't an ideal, or even satisfactory solution to problems that arise.

As a final comparison, let's compare *Fallout 4* to another computer game, *Hatred*. In *Hatred*, players control a sociopath who goes on a killing spree in New York City with the ultimate goal of killing as many people as possible. The character uses a variety of guns and explosives to butcher civilians, police officers, and soldiers alike. Violence is the *defining feature* of the game, playing prominently into advertisements for the game and into the game's mechanics themselves[9]. The violence in the game is glamorized and rewarded when the player receives health bonuses for up-close and personal executions of defenseless, injured victims. Unlike *Fallout 4*, where the goal of the game is first and foremost about exploration of a post-apocalyptic world, *Hatred* has next to no storyline or player decision-making: The only real option is to take part in the killing spree. Although both *Fallout 4* and *Hatred* involve weapons, explosives, and the ability to kill other characters in gory ways, players of *Hatred* are exposed to nothing *but* glamorized violence and are rewarded for it, whereas in *Fallout 4*, violence, while an important game mechanic, is often punished, unnecessary, or even detrimental to the player's goals.

These important differences in gameplay design and the context in which the violence is portrayed in these games is lost *entirely* if you were to read *only* the age-based content ratings or basic descriptions of the game's content. After all, both *Hatred* and *Fallout 4* contain "intense violence" and "blood and gore." This is why, as we discuss in Question #48, it's important for parents to become informed about what their children are watching and playing. Watching trailers and gameplay demonstrations online can help parents understand not only the surface features of the content (e.g., blood, level of violence), but also the context of the violence itself (e.g., is violence the focus, is it being glamorized). Violent content, however fake or realistic, does increase the player's risk of aggression (see Question #18), but we can at least choose violent media that work *against* some of the mechanisms driving violent media effects.

In a related vein, it's also possible for parents to choose media that, while containing violence, may also have *some* benefits. Examples of such games include *Minecraft* and *World of Warcraft*. In *Minecraft*, players start the game in an open world where they must harvest resources (e.g., wood, metals) and craft a shelter and tools to survive. The game itself *does* contain violent content, since players can choose to attack one another and must occasionally defend themselves from attacking monsters, both of which would be expected to increase players' risk for real-world aggression. That said, the game's primary focus is on problem-solving and creativity[10], encouraging players to find novel ways to solve problems and create and share elaborate creations with others in the *Minecraft* community. Similarly, the game *World of Warcraft*, while often focusing on combat with enemy players and monsters, is primarily driven by players' interactions with others in their guild. For example, there are numerous "raids" in the game, where players form large groups of up to 40 people to successfully defeat a dungeon. This requires an incredible amount of cooperation, teamwork, strategy, and leadership[11], with raids often seeming more like a chess match than a hack-and-slash game. These two games, and others like them, illustrate the fact that not all violent games are equal and that some may be preferable to others for having some potentially beneficial effects on players.[d]

Let's look at another illustrative example, one that doesn't involve video games, which shows how different people can experience the *same* piece of media in different ways. The opening of *Saving Private Ryan* is an incredibly gory, realistic (but fictionalized) scene of violence that took place during the storming of the Normandy beaches by U.S. troops on June 6, 1944.[e] The effects of this scene likely vary from person to person, depending on the thoughts and feelings they experienced while watching the scene and thinking about it later. Some people may have negative attitudes towards war while others have positive attitudes towards bravery and patriotism. Most will become slightly more desensitized to scenes of violence after watching the film. But almost no one comes away from such a film totally unchanged.

A positive feature of the film (from our perspective as media scholars and people who consider violence and war to be harmful), is that the film doesn't

---

[d] As an analogy, you might imagine that you've decided to splurge a bit and eat a snack. One possibility is to have some chocolate-dipped fruit. Another possibility is to eat a cup of sugar. While both of these desserts contain a lot of carbohydrates and would probably be considered less-than-ideal for you, the fruit *at least* contains vitamins and nutrients and is thus not *entirely* bad for you.

[e] The film also happens to be a favorite of Craig, one of the authors.

glorify and sanitize violence (two things that would likely *increase* the viewer's aggression). It's a complex film that allows, and even encourages, a lot of thinking and reflection which may, in turn, affect the viewer's future behavior. For example, if the viewer experiences a sense of horror at the carnage wrought by guns and bombs on the screen, they may choose to vote for a candidate who speaks out against war, or may refuse to own a gun based on their revulsion toward the gun violence shown in the film.

To summarize: it's unlikely, and probably not even recommended, for parents to completely prevent their older children from being exposed to *all* violent media content. Instead, when deciding whether to permit their child to be exposed to a particular piece of violent media, parents should think about the age of the child, the nature of the violence being portrayed and the associations being made. Media where violence is the primary focus, or which glamorize and reward violence, are not appropriate for children, and are likely to be among the *most* harmful forms of violent media. In contrast, media where violence is present but not the focus, or where violence is discouraged, are better candidates, both for children and for adults. This is why it's so important for parents and consumers in general to know about this sort of content information when making decisions about media use, rather than simply being told that others have deemed it "appropriate" for people of a certain age (see Question #48). And, as we'll discuss in Question #54, being choosy about which violent media we consume is a fairly reasonable middle-ground solution between the extremes of "absolutely no violent media" and "anything goes."

References

1. Federal Trade Commission. (2000). *Marketing violent entertainment to children: A review of self-regulation and industry practices in the motion picture, music recording and electronic game industries.* Report for the United States Federal Trade Commission. Washington DC: United States Federal Trade Commission.
2. Parents Television Council. (2008). *PTC Secret Shopper Campaign Reveals Children Still Able to Purchase M-Rated Video Games.* Retrieved from www.parentstv.org/PTC/publications/reports/secretshopper/main.asp
3. Bushman, B. J. & Stack, A. D. (1996). Forbidden fruit versus tainted fruit: Effects of warning labels on attraction to television violence. *Journal of Experimental Psychology: Applied, 2*(3), 207-226.
4. Nathanson, A. I. (2002). The unintended effects of parental mediation of television on adolescents. *Media Psychology, 4*(3), 207-230.
5. Lichter, N. (2013, January 11). A closer look at WWE's audience and why you can expect more of the same. *Cageside Seats: Fanpost.* Retrieved from http://www.cagesideseats.com/2013/1/11/3864386/a-closer-look-at-wwes-demographics-and-why-you-can-expect-more-of-the

6. DuRant, R. H., Champion, H., & Wolfson, M. (2006). The relationship between watching professional wrestling on television and engaging in date fighting among high school students. *Pediatrics, 118*(2), 265-272.
7. DuRant, R. H., Neiberg, R., Champion, H., Rhodes, S. D., & Wolfson, M. (2008). Viewing professional wrestling on television and engaging in violent and other health risk behaviors. *Southern Medical Journal, 101*(2), 129-137.
8. Anderson, C. A. & Bushman, B. J. (2002). Human Aggression. *Annual Review of Psychology, 53,* 27-51.
9. Haas, P. (2015). Hatred's developers wanted controversy and they succeeded. *Cinemablend.com: Games.* Retrieved from http://www.cinemablend.com/games/Hatred-Developers-Wanted-Controversy-They-Succeeded-67893.html
10. Risberg, C. (2015). More than just a video game: Tips for using Minecraft to personalize the curriculum and promote creativity, collaboration, and problem solving. *Illinois Association for Gifted Children, 2015,* 44-48. Retrieved from https://www.imsa.edu/sites/default/files/2015-iagc-journal_1.pdf#page=44
11. YeiBeech, J., & SeongHo, R. (2011). Exploring game experiences and game leadership in massively multiplayer online role-playing games. *British Journal of Educational Technology, 42*(4), 616-623.

50 - Should I be discussing media violence with my children?

The Short Answer:

Yes. Discussing violent media content with your children (once they are old enough to understand that hurting people is bad) can reduce the risks associated with violent media exposure. There are at least two different ways to go about this. The first involves expressing outright disapproval of the violence being portrayed on the screen. Although this has been shown to help somewhat, its effects are limited. A more effective way to have this discussion is to ask your child questions and encourage them to think critically about the content themselves. Try to work into the conversation the fact that aggression and violence are inappropriate and ineffective ways to deal with problems in the real world. This sort of discussion is likely to foster stronger, longer-lasting reductions in media violence effects and it helps to teach the child to take responsibility for what he or she watches, rather than just following orders.

The Long Answer:

In Question #46 we discussed several strategies that parents can use to reduce the effects of media violence on their children's risk of aggression. The strategy that is most consistently effective is active mediation[1,2,3,4]. Active mediation involves parents discussing violent media content with their children. This is best done with questions that encourage the child to challenge what they're seeing (e.g., "do you think you'd be arrested for that kind of behavior in real life?"), but it can also include expressing disapproval of violent actions being taken by a character (e.g., "oh, that's awful!"), drawing their child's attention to the negative consequences of the violent behavior (e.g., "that must have really hurt!"). Ultimately, active mediation aims to break the link between violent media and the risk of aggression by preventing harmful beliefs about aggression from forming (e.g., aggression is useful, aggression is a good way to solve problems, aggression is normal – everybody does it.)[4]

We could easily end the answer here: Yes, parents should discuss media violence with their children because doing so reduces the risks associated with violent media. But there is considerable nuance to be found in the original question. For example, we can tell parents that they *should* discuss media violence with their children, but *what* should they be discussing? *How* should they be bringing up these discussions? Is it enough for parents to watch TV with their kids and occasionally say "don't do that – it's bad," or is there more to it than that? Addressing these questions is our goal for the rest of this answer.

Let's start off with a bit of a surprise: When it comes to reducing media violence effects, it *can* be as simple as expressing disapproval of on-screen violence, at least for young children. As an example, children in one study watched an episode of *Batman* with their teacher. For about half of the children, the teacher made neutral comments about what was happening in the episode (e.g., looks like Batman and Robin got captured). For the other half of the students, the teacher made comments expressing disapproval (e.g., fighting is bad). Later in the study, the children who heard their teacher express disapproval toward violence were *less* likely than the other children to believe that hitting and stealing from one another was normal. They were also *more* likely to say that hitting and stealing from others was wrong[1]. In other studies, when an adult vocally disapproved of violent behavior in media, children were faster to try to stop two children from fighting[2].

Although these studies seem to suggest that expressing disapproval is enough to break the link between media violence and aggression, there *is* a catch. In these studies, children's beliefs about aggression were tested shortly after being exposed to the violent content and the adult's disapproval. Their attitudes and behavior were also measured by the *same* people who expressed the disapproval (e.g., their teacher.) This introduces two possibilities. One possibility is that children's beliefs about aggression are genuinely changing when they hear an adult disapprove of violence. The other possibility is that children's beliefs aren't actually changing – they're simply saying and doing what they *think* the adult wants them to do. At least one study suggests that this is the case: The drop in aggressive behavior *only* happened when the adult was around[6]. But as soon as the disapproving adult left the room, the children may go back to their aggressive beliefs and behaviors. So while it's *possible* that expressing disapproval can change children's beliefs about aggression, it's also possible that this only teaches kids to not be aggressive *when adults are looking*[5].

If we want to reduce the link between violent media and aggressive beliefs / behavior (instead of creating the façade of reducing it), we'll need to move beyond just teaching kids that their parents disapprove of violence. One approach involves trying to change the way children *think* about media violence. Instead of telling children that *we* disapprove of what's on the screen, we can teach them to instead *think* about what they're watching and to *question* how appropriate it is. In doing this, children learn to form negative beliefs about aggression on their own, without needing someone in the room to tell them to believe this or point it out to them.

Studies generally find that this idea works. When parents ask their children *questions* about the media they're watching, children get into the habit of challenging what they see on the screen[7]. These sorts of questions help children better understand the differences between what's on the TV screen and what's appropriate in the real world[8]. Parental questioning can also encourage children to take the perspective of others, including the victims of violence, creating empathy[9]. As a general rule, when people have empathy for the victims of violence, violent media are less of a risk factor for aggression[10]. For example, children in one study watched a *Woody Woodpecker* cartoon where Woody attacked and knocked out an innocent man who had disrupted Woody's nap. Some of the children in the study watched the cartoon normally, while others were asked to think about the feelings of the man who was being attacked. The children who had been encouraged to think about what they were watching disliked Woody more and saw his actions as meaner and less-justified than the children who passively watched the cartoon[5]. And while this study only looked at the short-term effects of these questions, other studies find similar results in the long-term: Children whose parents routinely encourage them to challenge the media they consume tend to be less aggressive[2].

One of the real benefits of active mediation is that it trains children to not only question what they see, but to generate their own values about what they want to view. One of the authors (Douglas) routinely asked his daughter Lauren questions about what they watched. When she was 10, he wanted to watch *Star Wars* with her. This had been an important film for him, one he loved and wanted to share with her once she was old enough. She refused to see it, because, as she said, "Why would I want to watch that? It's just people fighting all the time!" She had created her own internal values about what she liked seeing, and now policed herself.

In summary, we can say that discussing violent media content with your children *can* reduce the impact of violent media as a risk factor for aggression. The most effective strategy involves encouraging children to not be passive consumers of media, but rather to question the things they see on the screen. Get them to think about the consequences of on-screen violence when they see it and to consider the perspective of the victim! Because once this becomes a habit, children are likely to continue thinking critically about media whether or not their parents are around. This can prevent violent media from instilling beliefs that violence is normal and positive and, in the long run, can reduce the risk of aggressive behavior.

Of course, all of these benefits depend on a key assumption, that the adult in the room (parent, teacher, other caregiver) is speaking out against the violence. If, instead, the adult frames the violence as a positive thing, or indicates that aggressive and violent behavior is the best way to handle conflict, or simply shows that they don't have a problem with the violence on the screen, the presence of the adult can actually have the *opposite effect*, increasing the child's tendency to behave aggressively (see Question #46 for more on this).

References

1. Corder-Bolz, C. R. (1980). Mediation: The role of significant others. *Journal of Communication, 30*(3), 106-118.
2. Horton, R. W. & Santogrossi, D. A. (1978). The effect of adult commentary on reducing the influence of televised violence. *Personality and Social Psychology Bulletin, 4*(2), 337-340.
3. Nathanson, A. I. (1999). Identifying and explaining the relationship between parental mediation and children's aggression. *Communication Research, 26*(2), 124-143.
4. Ruh Linder, J., & Werner, N. E. (2012). Relationally aggressive media exposure and children's normative believes: Does parental mediation matter? *Family Relations, 61*(3), 488-500.
5. Nathanson, A. I. & Cantor, J. (2000). Reducing the aggression-promoting effect of violent cartoons by increasing children's fictional involvement with the victim: A study of active mediation. *Journal of Broadcasting & Electronic Media, 44*(1), 125-142.
6. Hicks, D. J. (1968). Effects of co-observer's sanctions and adult presence on imitative aggression. *Child Development, 39*(1), 303-309.
7. Hobbs, R., & Frost, R. (1997). *The impact of media literacy education on adolescents' media analysis and news comprehension skills.* Paper presented to the International Communication Association's annual convention, Montreal, Quebec, Canada.
8. Desmond, R. J., Singer, J. L., Singer, D. G., Calam, R., & Colimore, K. (1985). Family mediation patterns and television viewing: Young children's use and grasp of the medium. *Human Communication Research, 11,* 461-480.
9. Tamborini, R., Stiff, J., & Heidel, C. (1990). Reacting to graphic horror: A model of empathy and emotional behavior. *Communication Research, 17,* 616-740.
10. Schmutte, G. T., & Taylor, S. P. (1980). Physical aggression as a function of alcohol and pain feedback. *Journal of Social Psychology, 110,* 235-244.

51 - How can I maximize positive media effects while minimizing harm?

The Short Answer:

By fostering responsible media use habits. Whenever possible, seek out media with positive, pro-social messages or media that's been designed to have beneficial effects. If you *do* choose violent media, avoid media that glamorizes violence, or where violence is the focus of the piece. Try to avoid "passive" consumption: Question what you're seeing on the screen and consider choosing media that raises some of these questions itself. If possible, seek out media that involves integrating physical activity into the experience (e.g., augmented reality games such as *Pokémon Go*). And finally, set reasonable limitations on media use – even in the case of prosocial or beneficial games.

The Long Answer:

The simplest answer to this question is to use the advice given throughout this book to develop healthy media use habits. What do we mean by "healthy media use habits," and how do we form them? It helps to use the analogy of "eating habits." It makes no sense to talk about the "best diet" because, frankly, there's no one right answer. Needs will differ from person to person, as will social, genetic, and other environmental factors, which will make some diets better for some people and other diets better for other people. What's more, even *if* the dietician gave you a precise description of the "perfect diet," it would be unrealistic to expect you to follow it to the letter every day for the rest of your life.[a]

In other words, giving you a long list of "what to eat" is less useful than a list of general guidelines that you should follow when deciding on a given meal, especially if we make the guidelines relatively straightforward and easy-to-follow:

1. Seek out food loaded with good stuff (e.g., nutrients, vitamins)
2. Avoid food full of bad stuff (e.g., excessive sugar, fat)
3. Pay attention to what you're eating (e.g., snacking for hours while watching TV)
4. Eat reasonable portion sizes (e.g., food for sustenance, not competition)

---

[a] After all, we live in an age where deep-fried peanut butter and jam sandwiches and chocolate cheesecake exist – it's just not possible!

When it comes to media consumption, the exact same principles apply! It's not terribly useful for us to give you a list of "appropriate" and "inappropriate" content or to tell you what shows to watch or what games to play. Instead, based on the research we've discussed throughout this book, we can offer a similar set of guidelines for your media consumption habits:

1. Seek out media designed to elicit benefits (e.g., prosocial; Questions #40, #41)
2. Avoid media associated with risks (e.g., violent; Questions #11, #38)
3. Pay attention to and challenge what's being seen on-screen (Questions #46, #50)
4. Consume media in moderation (Questions #39, #40, #50)

Speaking to Guideline #1, examples abound of television shows, movies, and video games that are designed to be both interesting and beneficial to the consumer. Video games and television shows can educate users as they play or watch[1,2,3]. They don't have to be boring either! If done right, games and TV shows can be engaging and interesting while still being educational and having a positive message. For example, the computer game *Kerbal Space Program* teaches players astrophysics and rocket science[4] within the context of a comedy-themed spaceship-building game. The game's excellent and interesting design is reflected in the fact that it was, at one point, one of the most downloaded computer games[5]. Similarly, television shows like *Mythbusters* are popular with adult audiences, being both entertaining and exciting while also teaching viewers about the experimental method and physics.

Some media aren't designed to educate on academic topics, but rather to teach and elicit positive social behavior: television shows like *Sesame Street* and *Mister Rogers' Neighborhood* have been shown to increase prosocial behavior (e.g., sharing, compliments) in children[6], while video games like *Undertale* are designed to get players to question their own aggression and to encourage compassion, empathy, and pacifism.[b] Other games such as *Dance Dance Revolution* and Pokémon *GO* encourage physical activity in players by tracking their body movement and, in the case of *Wii Fit*, actively encourage players to pursue physical fitness[7,8]. So when it comes to choosing what to watch or play, there numerous options for people of all ages that are engaging while also having a number of positive effects.

Guideline #2 emphasizes avoiding media with harmful effects. Much of this book has emphasized violent content specifically, but this general principle includes media with racist[9], sexist[10], and generally antisocial messages[11]. Since negative media content generally contributes to your risk of undesirable behavior[12], exposing yourself to less of it should reduce the magnitude of the risk

---

[b] One of the authors, Courtney, will attest to the fact that he now considers himself to be a pacifist as a *direct* result of having played through *Undertale*.

it poses. Of course, it would be impractical to suggest that people avoid *all* violent media content, since most media content– even media targeted at children – contains *some* violence in one form or another. In the same way that it would be unreasonable to expect someone to *never* eat junk food, it would be unreasonable to expect people to *never* consume violent media. At the very least, we can make a conscious effort to be aware of the *amount* and *type* of violent media we're consuming and perhaps make a concerted effort to seek out media that, while violent, doesn't glamorize or focus exclusively on this violence.

To illustrate what we mean by this, compare the films *Kill Bill* and *Avatar*. The film *Kill Bill* tells the story of a woman exacting bloody revenge upon a group of assassins. The film is well-known for its gratuitous violence (e.g., decapitation, fountains of blood.) Throughout the film, the viewer sympathizes with the protagonist's quest and cheers her on in her quest for brutal vengeance – aggression *is* the goal. In contrast, the film *Avatar* is about humanity's exploitation of an alien planet and its impact on the species that live there. The film certainly contains violence (e.g., scenes of war), but the aggressors are portrayed in a negative light and the film's primary message is overwhelmingly anti-war. Violence is not the central focus of the film – it became famous for its visually stunning portrayal of the alien world Pandora and the sense of awe and discovery it instilled.

To be sure, it *is* likely that the violent content in both films increases viewers' aggressive behavior post-film, if only by activating aggressive thoughts in the viewers' minds. However, we might predict that viewing *Kill Bill* would be a *greater* risk factor for long term aggression than *Avatar*, because *Kill Bill* may *also* have increased its audience's beliefs about the usefulness, acceptability, and "coolness" of violence. In contrast, *Avatar* would be more likely to instill beliefs that violence is wasteful and tragic, something we would expect to *reduce* the risk of later aggression. Ultimately, we must recognize that not all violent media are created equal. As such, it's possible, even if we can't avoid violent media altogether, to at least be judicious about *which* violent media we're going to consume.

Guideline #3 emphasizes being a critical consumer of media. This means thinking about what's shown on-screen and regularly questioning or challenging it. As we discussed in Question #51, when people are encouraged to question the violence they see portrayed in media, they're less likely to be influenced by it[13,14]. Viewers, for example, can critique the content of a piece of media (e.g., "there's no way that person would be fine after getting hit like that.") But the media itself can *also* prompt viewers to challenge the violent content in the media itself. One notable example of this is the video game *Spec Ops: The Line*. Players in this game take on the role of American soldiers on a mission in Dubai, with the game beginning as a seemingly typical military-style shooter. As the game progresses, however, it occasionally breaks the player's immersion, calling into question their in-game actions. During loading screens, the game flashes messages like "Do you feel like a hero yet?" and "The US military does not condone the killing of unarmed combatants. But this isn't real, so why should you care?" Although players start the game believing that their characters are heroic, by the end of the game the immorality of their actions becomes apparent.[c]

In one particularly memorable scene from the game, players discover that they've accidentally killed dozens of innocent civilians with burning white phosphorous while thinking they were attacking a group of enemies. Players are then forced to walk down the blackened street, past the charred bodies of the civilians they killed, *literally* forcing players to walk slowly past the consequences of their violent actions. It's a particularly gruesome and chilling example, but games like *Spec Ops: The Line* and *Undertale*[d] mentioned earlier, illustrate that it's possible to not only challenge what we see on the screen, but to seek out media that encourage us to do exactly this.

Finally, Guideline #4 emphasizes consuming media in moderation. Although this point is again most obvious with respect to violent content effects, harmful effects of media are not limited to aggression. For example, screen time, whether spent in front of a television set or a computer, is associated with reduced physical health[15], as time spent in front of a screen is time not spent on physical activity. The solution is simple, at least in theory: Just cut back on media use and you'll cut back on your exposure to these risk factors. In practice, however, this can be tough, as trying to limit someone else's media use can lead to conflict.[16,17]

To ease the task of reducing screen time in your life, consider introducing reductions in your (or your children's) media use gradually, alongside increases in other activities. Something as simple as devoting an hour a day to go for a walk, take up a project, or hang out with friends is a good way to begin cutting back on media use. Augmented reality games such as *Pokémon Go* may make it possible to ease this transition, as they require players to go outside, walk around, and interact with others in order to get the most out of the game. The popularity of the game

---

[c] For any budding media scholars reading this book, this would make an *excellent* research topic: How can we predict which players are more likely to understand and internalize these sorts of subtle, anti-violence messages and which players will completely miss them?

[d] In the game *Undertale*, players take on the role of a young child in a cavern full of monsters. On its face, it looks like a traditional role-playing game, where players confront monsters, battle them, and defeat them for experience. As the game progresses, however, the player learns more about the monsters they're killing and discovers that they can not only avoid hurting the monsters, but that they can become *friends* with the monsters. Getting one of the story's best endings involves beating the game without killing a single monster and befriending the monsters in the cavern. Even more remarkable, the game itself "remembers" previous playthroughs of the game, confronting the player with their violent behavior in past runs through the game.

worldwide speaks wonders about the plausibility of this solution. If one wants to jump in a little more abruptly, however, consider variations of the allowance or token economy idea described in Question #47.

To summarize: The guidelines presented here should be seen as a starting point for developing healthy media consumption habits. Adults reading this book can adopt these guidelines for themselves and can begin teaching them to their children, both directly and by leading through example. The rules are simple enough to be easily remembered and flexible enough to accommodate differences in each person's unique set of circumstances. What's more, these guidelines are just that – guidelines. They're not laws or hard-and-fast rules – they allow for day-to-day life and the occasional treat, just as any diet should allow for the occasional piece of cheesecake. These guidelines are a good first step toward minimizing the risks associated with media use while maximizing its benefits, and should help you avoid falling into an "all-cheesecake" media diet.

References
1. Corbett, A. T., Koedinger, K. R., & Hadley, W. (2001). Cognitive tutors: From the research classroom to all classrooms. In P. S. Goodman (Ed.). *Technology enhanced learning* (pp. 235-263). Mahwah (NJ): Lawrence Erlbaum.
2. Short, D. (2012). Teaching scientific concepts using a virtual world – Minecraft. *Teaching Science, 58*(3), 55-58.
3. Fisch, S. M., Truglio, R. T., & Cole, C. F. (1999). The impact of Sesame Street on preschool children: A review and synthesis of 30 years' research. *Media Psychology, 1*(2), 165-190.
4. Ranalli, J. & Ritzko, J. (2013). *Assessing the impact of video game based design projects in a first year engineering design course.* Presented to the Institute of Electrical and Electronics Engineers Frontiers in Education Conference, Oklahoma City, OK.
5. Relaxnews. (2013, June 17). PC download charts: 'Kerbal Space Program'. *xinmsn Lifestyle: Tech.* Retrieved from https://web.archive.org/web/20131222085356/http://technology.xin.msn.com/gaming/pc-download-charts-kerbal-space-program-1
6. Coates, B., Pusser, H. E., & Goodman, I. (1976). The influence of "Sesame Street" and "Mister Rogers' Neighborhood" on children's social behavior in preschool. *Child Development, 47*(1), 138-144.
7. Biddiss, E. & Irwin, J. (2010). Active video games to promote physical activity in children and youth. *Archives of Pediatric and Adolescent Medicine, 164*(7), 664-672.
8. Graf, D. L., Pratt, L. V., Hester, C. N., & Short, K. R. (2009). Playing active video games increases energy expenditure in children. *Pediatrics, 124*(2), 534-540.

9. Weisbuch, M., Pauker, K., & Ambady, N. (2009). The subtle transmission of race bias via televised nonverbal behavior. *Science, 326*(5960), 1711-1714.
10. Hald, G. M., Malamuth, N. N., & Lange, T. (2013). Pornography and sexist attitudes among heterosexuals. *Journal of Communication, 63*, 638-660.
11. Hansen, C. H. & Hansen, R. D. (2010). Rock music videos and antisocial behavior. *Basic and Applied Social Psychology, 11*(4), 357-369.
12. Anderson, C. A., Shibuya, A., Ihori, N., Swing, E. L., Bushman, B. J., Sakamoto, A., Rothstein, H. R., & Saleem, M. (2010). Violent video game effects on aggression, empathy, and prosocial behavior in eastern and western countries: a meta-analytic review. *Psychological Bulletin, 136*(2), 151-173.
13. Horton, R. W. & Santogrossi, D. A. (1978). The effect of adult commentary on reducing the influence of televised violence. *Personality and Social Psychology Bulletin, 4*(2), 337-340.
14. Nathanson, A. I. & Cantor, J. (2000). Reducing the aggression-promoting effect of violent cartoons by increasing children's fictional involvement with the victim: A study of active mediation. *Journal of Broadcasting & Electronic Media, 44*(1), 125-142.
15. Russ, S. A., Larson, K., Franke, T. M., & Halfon, N. (2009). Associations between media use and health in US children. *Academic Pediatrics, 9*(5), 300-306.
16. Nathanson, A. I. (2002). The unintended effects of parental mediation of television on adolescents. *Media Psychology, 4*(3), 207-230.
17. Bushman, B. J. & Stack, A. D. (1996). Forbidden fruit versus tainted fruit: Effects of warning labels on attraction to television violence. *Journal of Experimental Psychology: Applied, 2*(3), 207-226.

52 - If my child has problems with aggressive behavior, should I take their violent games away?

The Short Answer:

Maybe. On the one hand, if your child is already prone to aggressive behavior, you probably don't want to expose them to yet *another* risk factor for aggression. On the other hand, completely taking away their violent games (especially without a provoking incident) will probably seem unfair to them and may foster resentment. One approach is to buy the games from them, and help them choose new games. This way you can shift the games they play without it being seen as a punishment, but may actually get them excited about getting new games. In the broader scheme of things, your goal should be to gradually replace their violent media with non-violent activities. You may want to begin by explaining to them the harmful effects that some games have on players. You can stop purchasing violent media for them in the future and encourage interests that they may have in other media (e.g., racing, crafting, exploration) or other non-media activities (e.g., sports, crafts). Becoming involved in these alternative activities may also increase their appeal and make it more likely that they'll catch on. If all goes well, growing interest in these other activities should lead to reduced interest in violent media on its own.

The Long Answer:

In Question #19 we discuss the fact that violent media are likely to increase everyone's risk for aggression, regardless of who they are. In Question #20 we elaborate on this point and explain that although everyone's risk for aggression increases due to violent media exposure (e.g. like a thimble of water added to a glass), the increase is a more serious problem for people who are already prone to aggression (e.g., people who go around with a moderately-full glass all the time). With this in mind, it's understandable that parents of children who are prone to aggression or are already having behavior problems may be particularly concerned about exposing their kids to any more violent media. Or, as the case may be, they may be trying to find a way to take away the violent media their children are *already* being exposed to. Unfortunately, the solution isn't quite as simple as "just take away their violent video games and television."

For starters, doing this is more difficult than you might expect. Of course, it's easy to take away their physical media: It's not hard to grab all of their game consoles, game discs, and DVDs and hide them. But what about downloadable games? Many game companies have done away entirely with discs and, instead, allow players to download games. If you're determined, you can uninstall these games from your kids' computers and force them to disable their accounts with these companies. Even so, it's *still* possible to access browser-based games online or on their phones. You *could* go one step further and install content-blocking software for both the internet and for TV sets in the house. You could, as we suggested in Question #47, remove electronic media from your child's room. With the computer and television in a public part of the house, it'd be easier to monitor your child's media use and ensure they're not watching or playing anything they shouldn't be. However, with many parents working jobs, it's virtually impossible to actively monitor your child's media use 24 hours a day. And if your children have friends who own violent video games, or a cell phone that can they can browse the internet on, any ban on violent content becomes that much harder to enforce.

To put it simply: If your children *really* want to see violent media, they're going to find a way to do so. Of course, the difficulty of the task isn't a valid reason in and of itself for not doing *something*. After all, just because the parents of your child's best friend lets them eat chips and drink soda for lunch doesn't mean you have to serve soda and chips at your house. But it also doesn't mean that you should ban your child from playing and lunching at their friend's house.

What's worse, actively trying to ban violent media, whether successful or not, may have the effect of making your children angry and resentful [1]. After all, most people don't like to be told they can't do something that they want to do! Of course, that's not the end of the world either. After all, you *are* supposed to be the parent. But, generally speaking, everyone's probably better off if we can minimize the number of resentment-inspiring incidents.

When you put all of this together, it becomes pretty clear that it's somewhat unrealistic to expect parents to completely take away their child's violent media, especially if it's already in the house, and especially not all at once. It might be tempting to do so, especially if your child is already prone to aggression, or if there is a significant incident (such as assaulting another student at school) that calls for major changes at home and school. But, generally speaking, making broad-sweeping changes to your family's media use policies out of the blue is likely to have a number of undesirable consequences unless it's seen as valuable in some way, such as by getting the child on a sports team he has wanted to join or by making a token economy that the child is interested in helping to design.

Instead, we propose a more moderate middle-ground: Aim to create alternative interests, or encourage the interests your child may already have. Instead of prohibiting violent media, try encouraging them to pursue other interests they might have. Incentivize these more desirable activities. This can be done both within the gaming context as well as outside of it. One key to making this work is to actively discuss with your child or adolescent (not just lecture about) the reasons for the changes, such as the harmful effects of media violence on them and your family's values concerning harming others. A second key is to give them some choices and get them actively involved in making the changes in their media diet and in alternative (non-media) activities.

Within the gaming context, explain why you and your child need to reduce violent content, and give them some nonviolent choices.[a] Explore a number of nonviolent gaming options, such as racing games, sports games, or building games. Let your child have some choice and control over the new games in exchange for giving up some of their violent ones. For instance, perhaps you discover that your child enjoys playing the team-based shooter computer game *Overwatch*, where they work with a team of other players to defeat an opposing team online. Ask yourself (and your child) what they like about the game. Is it *really* the fact that they're shooting and killing others? Or is it the fact that they get to compete as part of a team in a fast, highly-skilled setting?

If it's the fast-paced, highly-skilled setting they enjoy, other games may scratch that particular itch *without* being so violent. For example, the popular online game *Rocket League* allows players to join teams and compete in a digital game of soccer played with cars rather than human players. The game is highly competitive, requires significant skill to master, and heavily emphasizes team play – all without being violent. You could encourage your child to check out *Rocket League*, which they may find interesting enough to pursue – taking away from time spent playing *Overwatch*.

Or, if they're particularly drawn to the social aspects of the game *Overwatch*, and the fact that it gives them a chance to do something with their friends online, you may be able to encourage them to play games like *Minecraft* or *Empyrion*, where players work together toward a creative goal like building castles or spaceships or exploring a digital universe together. The point is, if you can encourage your child to find interests in related, but non-violent media, you can reduce the time they're spending on violent media without having to outright ban violent games and suffer the backlash that might otherwise ensue.

You can also encourage other interesting activities outside of a gaming or media-based context. Activities can range from building model planes or going out for a walk, to playing catch, shooting hoops, or playing board games. Although these activities might not seem quite as exciting as the digital worlds of screen media, you might be surprised how interested younger children become in doing these things if they get to do them with a parent, siblings, or other friends. Many families participate in a screen-free week, sometimes with their children's

---

[a] Of course, you don't have to throw a book like this one at them to convince them! Instead, it's helpful to use an analogy, like that of our food diet. In the same way that we have to have some restrictions on what we eat and how much of it we eat, we also need to pay attention to what we put into our minds, media-wise. An analogy like this can work wonders with helping people understand the rationale behind watching what we consume.

schools during the national screen-free week in May (see https://www.screenfree.org/ for more information). We have heard from several parents who participated that the children were unhappy for the first few days, but then found that they really enjoyed all of the things they got to do once they settled into it.

And, as we've suggested elsewhere (e.g., Question #46), getting involved in media activities with your children *can* include actively mediating in their violent media use – spending time playing video games or watching television with them while encouraging them to challenge what they're seeing and being critical about the content. Indeed, this strategy has been shown to be particularly effective in reducing the effects of violent media on children's risk for aggression[3,4] (see Questions #46 and #50 for more on this).

To summarize: If you suspect that your child may be particularly susceptible to aggression and wish to reduce their exposure to violent media as an additional risk factor, it's important to take a reasonable approach and have a realistic goal in mind. Throwing away their game consoles and banning violent media entirely isn't likely to be as effective as promoting alternative activities and engaging in both active and restrictive mediation. If these alternative activities involve other media, it can take a bit of work to become familiar with the available options, but the effort is likely to be worth it.

References

1. Nathanson, A. I. (2002). The unintended effects of parental mediation of television on adolescents. *Media Psychology, 4*(3), 207-230.
2. Bushman, B. J. & Stack, A. D. (1996). Forbidden fruit versus tainted fruit: Effects of warning labels on attraction to television violence. *Journal of Experimental Psychology: Applied, 2*(3), 207-226.
3. Horton, R. W. & Santogrossi, D. A. (1978). The effect of adult commentary on reducing the influence of televised violence. *Personality and Social Psychology Bulletin, 4*(2), 337-340.
4. Nathanson, A. I. & Cantor, J. (2000). Reducing the aggression-promoting effect of violent cartoons by increasing children's fictional involvement with the victim: A study of active mediation. *Journal of Broadcasting & Electronic Media, 44*(1), 125-142.

Chapter 6

Thinking about Media Violence in the "Big Picture"

53 - Is it fair to compare the media violence issue to the issue of cigarettes and lung cancer?

The Short Answer:

There are many parallels between the issue of cigarettes and lung cancer and the issue of violent media and aggression – although we'd like to make it crystal clear that the two issues are not *identical*. Media violence and smoking *are* similar in the fact that they both involve a large industry and consumer base who are strongly motivated to deny the harmful effects of a product. Moreover, the tactics used to challenge and undermine the scientific evidence are comparable in both cases: denying that a link exists at all or claiming that the issue is still hotly debated among scientists who can't reach a conclusion. That said, we're not arguing that the magnitude of the risks for smokers are the same as the risks for violent media: Smoking increases the risk of lung cancer and death, whereas media violence increases the risk of aggressive behavior. At this time, there are no comparably huge long-term studies of the effects of media violence on homicide or other causes of death, so that specific question remains an open one. But just because violent media may have less severe consequences on the consumer than smoking has, this does not mean that those harmful consequences should be ignored. Otherwise, by that logic, we would have to ignore the effects of child abuse and poor nutrition on aggression as well, simply because there are "bigger fish to fry."

The Long Answer:

If you ask a group of Americans whether they believe cigarettes are bad for you, the vast majority would say yes[1]. In fact, to most of us, the link between cigarettes and health (e.g., lung cancer) seems pretty obvious. But this wasn't always the case. Half a century ago, only about 60% of Americans believed there was *any* link at all between cigarette smoking and health problems, and fewer than half believed that cigarettes could affect something as severe as lung cancer or heart disease[1]. In fact, one of the authors, Craig, remembers when talk show hosts like Johnny Carson would joke about how many cigarettes a rat had to smoke before it would get cancer. By the 1990s, the link between cigarettes and cancer had caught up to comedy, with comedian Denis Leary quipping that he would continue to smoke cigarettes despite knowing the risk of cancer, including being willing to buy a brand of cigarettes called "Tumors" in a black-colored box with a skull-and-crossbones on it.[a]

So what changed? What caused people's opinions about cigarettes to shift so dramatically over 50 years? Did scientists first start finding evidence for the link between cigarettes and lung cancer in that time? Actually, no: Scientists began publishing research showing the link between smoking and lung cancer well before that, as early as 1950[2]. In fact, by the end of the 1950s, a study of more than 40,000 British doctors found that the link between cigarette smoking and lung cancer was almost certain[3]. And yet, despite the publication of these results, the public's belief about any link between cigarettes and lung cancer was virtually unaffected by the research for well over a decade[1]. Why?

In a word: advertising. On January 4, 1954, the American tobacco industry ran an advertisement in nearly five hundred newspapers across the country. The ad was titled *A Frank Statement to Cigarette Smokers*, and was the cigarette industry's response to growing evidence linking cigarettes to lung cancer. Among other things, the ad made four explicit claims about what "eminent doctors and research scientists" had concluded[4]:

1. That medical research of recent years indicates many possible causes of lung cancer.

2. That there is no agreement among the authorities regarding what the cause is.

3. That there is no proof that cigarette smoking is one of the causes.

4. That statistics purporting to link cigarette smoking with the disease could apply with equal force to any one of many other aspects of modern life. Indeed the validity of the statistics themselves is questioned by numerous scientists.

It would later be revealed that the tobacco industry placed this advertisement despite the fact that their own scientists acknowledged the harm cigarettes were causing[5]. In fact, the tobacco industry would continue to publicly deny the existence of a relationship between smoking and health problems until 1999[5]. Despite accumulating evidence saying otherwise, the tobacco industry was able to spend millions of dollars on advertising to misinform the public about what the research had actually found. Researchers, on the other hand, had the evidence on their side, but struggled to convince the public otherwise. People believed that the issue was still being debated among scientists and thought that there was no strong

---

[a] Perhaps not the safest hobby, but at least he's an informed consumer and acknowledges the risks associated with his actions!

evidence one way or another, despite the fact that researchers had a conclusive answer to the question by the end of the 1950s.

So what does any of this have to do with the issue of media violence? Can we compare the two issues? In general sense, yes: There are numerous parallels between the two issues and the way companies, consumers, and the public have responded to them.

To start, in both cases there is a powerful industry whose sales are threatened by the negative effects that its products might have on users. In the case of cigarettes, they were physically harming users. In the case of violent media, they're increasing users' risk of aggression and violence. Now, to be fair, cigarettes are a *much* deadlier risk to its users than violent media are. In no way do we mean to suggest that an increase in the risk of aggressive behavior is comparable to the painful and destructive diseases wrought by smoking. No media violence researcher believes that violent media effects are as serious as the thousands of deaths caused each year by cigarettes. Ultimately, the risks of violent media are far less lethal and much harder to visualize than the risks of smoking.[b]

That said, however, it doesn't make sense to say that an effect is unimportant just because there are *more* lethal effects to compare it to. If that were the case, we would have little reason to care about issues like drunk driving, since cigarettes are responsible for 50 times more deaths[6]. Although the effects of violent media are far less lethal than the effects of cigarettes, both involve undesirable side effects associated with the use of a product.

For this reason, both the cigarette industry and the digital games industry (and the TV and film industries) have a vested interest in keeping the public uninformed about the negative effects of their products, for fear that it could lead to a drop in the sales of their products. Companies do this in at least two ways: Advertising the heck out of their products and downplaying or denying any research that might suggest harmful effects.

When it comes to advertising, companies are especially eager to advertise to children, who, lacking critical thinking skills, are unlikely to consider a product's downsides or challenge what they see in an advertisement. Both cigarette companies and digital games companies have marketed themselves heavily to children. Cigarette companies created mascots like Joe Camel, deliberately designed to target children and teenagers and create the belief that smoking is cool[7]. Although the video game industry doesn't have a "Joe Camel" equivalent, they do relentlessly advertise violent, mature-rated games in places (e.g., magazines, websites, TV) where children and teenagers are likely to see them[8]. In their defense, the media violence industry *does* largely comply with standards aimed to reduce minors' exposure to ads for adult games[9]. Unfortunately, these standards come from the industry itself, and its rules are far

---

[b] Plus, there's no violent video game equivalent to showing a picture of a tar-blackened smoker's lung and letting the image speak for itself.

from ideal (e.g., don't advertise M-rated games on websites or in magazines with a readership of *more* than 45% minors, which is almost no websites or magazines because there are far more adults in the world than minors). As a result, although it *sounds* like the industry is doing its best to avoid advertising violent content to children, as the Federal Communications Commission points out, it's actually pretty hard for companies to *violate* this rule[8]. In other words, despite the existence of these industry guidelines, violent content is still advertised to children without violating these guidelines.

As another similarity, both the tobacco industry and the entertainment industry have devoted considerable resources to political lobbying and efforts aimed at denying the risks associated with their products. Both industries spend millions of dollars on lobbyists whose goal it is to convince politicians to adopt favorable attitudes toward their products[10,11]. In the case of the video game industry, this includes encouraging politicians to *oppose* a bill encouraging the National Academy of Sciences to study media violence effects[11], supposedly because funding research would "pressure" scientists into finding particular results[12].[c] As another example of the powerful influence of the digital entertainment industry, The Entertainment Software Association also sponsors the Video Game Voters Network, a group of more than 500,000 gamers opposing what they see as censorship, including "criminaliz[ing] the sale of certain games to minors"[13]. And, like the tobacco industry's *A Frank Statement to Cigarette Smokers*, the Entertainment Software Industry similarly denies and undermines the research on violent media, claiming, with a stunning degree of parallel, that[14]:

1. Numerous authorities have examined the scientific record and found that it does not establish any link between media content and real-life violence

2. Credible real-world evidence demonstrates the fallacy of linking games and violence

3. There is no scientific research that validates a link between computer and video games and violence[d]

---

[c] If this were the case, it leads us to wonder why anyone bothers to fund any science at all!

[d] As we point out in Question #7, one of the tactics of those who criticize media violence research is to make an extreme claim about media violence and *violent behavior*, rather than acknowledging that violent behavior is rare and that researchers typically focus on the link between media violence and *aggression*. It's telling that all three of the industry's statements refer to the link between media violence and "violence," not aggression.

Perhaps the biggest similarity between the tobacco industry and the media industry, however, is the fact that both industries try to convince their users that anyone who points out the risks associated with their products is trying to take away their freedoms. Many smokers, for example, saw their smoking as a matter of personal freedom, not a health issue[15]. In other words, they believed that researchers were trying to take away their choice to smoke. For players of violent games, the industry uses a similar framing: Researchers are trying to take away their right to free speech. Critics argue that media violence researchers are on a "moral crusade" to "ban" or censor video games and take away the artistic freedom of companies to make whatever games they want and the right of players to play the games they want[14]. As we point out in Question #3 and in Question #56, none of these claims are accurate: Most media violence researchers only want consumers to be able to make informed decisions about the products they're using. They want parents know about the risks before they expose their children to them. It would be silly to suggest that your doctor is on a crusade to put fast food out of business if she tells you that junk food is bad for you. And yet, you're expected to believe that media researchers are obsessed with banning or censoring media just because they point out that violent media have some risks associated with them.

Let's wrap this answer up: We can learn a lot about the media violence issue by comparing it to the issue of cigarette smoking. Although cigarettes put people at risk for far more devastating outcomes than violent video games do, it's nevertheless informative to find parallels in the way both industries have responded to legitimate scientific research. Both industries have a vested interest in keeping their user base, and so they advertise to those who are unlikely to question the research, deny the research altogether, and frame the research itself as an attack on personal liberty. Viewed in this context, it's clear that the "media violence debate," like the debate about cigarettes and lung cancer, isn't a scientific debate at all: It's a debate between science and commercial interests. Unfortunately, it's a debate that science is currently losing. In a study about news coverage of media violence research, it was found that, over time, the media has become increasingly inaccurate in the way it describes the research[16]. Media stories consistently underestimate the size of media violence effects and portray the topic as though researchers still aren't sure whether there's an effect at all[16] (despite the fact that, as we point out in Question #11, the debate was effectively settled decades ago). We hope, if you've read through the majority of this book, that you're starting to recognize the absurdity of this portrayal.

References

1. Moore, D. W. (1999, October 7). Nine of Ten Americans View Smoking as Harmful. *Gallup News Service*. Retrieved from http://www.gallup.com/poll/3553/nine-ten-americans-view-smoking-harmful.aspx

2. Doll, R. & Hill, A. B. (1950). Smoking and carcinoma of the lung; preliminary report. *British Medical Journal, 2*(4682), 739-748.
3. Doll, R., & Hill, A. B. (1954). The mortality of doctors in relation to their smoking habits: A preliminary report. *British Medical Journal, 328*(7455), 1529-1533.
4. Tobacco Industry Research Committee. (1954, January 4). *A Frank Statement to Cigarette Smokers*. Retrieved from http://archive.tobacco.org/Documents/dd/ddfrankstatement.html
5. Cummings, K. M., Morley, C. P. & Hyland, A. (2002). Failed promises of the cigarette industry and its effect on consumer misperceptions about the health risks of smoking. *Tobacco control, 11,* 110-117.
6. United States Department of Transportation, National Highway Traffic Safety Administration (NHTSA). (2015). *Traffic Safety Facts 2014 Data: Alcohol-Impaired Driving*. Washington, DC: NHTSA.
7. Cohen, J. B. (2000). Playing to win: Marketing and public policy at odds over Joe Camel. *Journal of Public Policy & Marketing, 19*(2), 155-167.
8. Federal Trade Commission. (2007). *Marketing Violent Entertainment to Children: A Fifth Follow-up Review of Industry Practices in the Motion Picture, Music Recording & Electronic Game Industries: A Report to Congress*. Retrieved from https://www.ftc.gov/sites/default/files/documents/reports/marketing-violent-entertainment-children-fifth-follow-review-industry-practices-motion-picture-music/070412marketingviolentechildren.pdf
9. Federal Trade Commission. (2009). *Marketing Violent Entertainment to Children: A Sixth Follow-up Review of Industry Practices in the Motion Picture, Music Recording & Electronic Game Industries: A Report to Congress*. Retrieved from https://www.ftc.gov/sites/default/files/documents/reports/marketing-violent-entertainment-children-sixth-follow-review-industry-practices-motion-picture-music/p994511violententertainment.pdf
10. Center for Responsible Politics. *Tobacco Industry Profile: Summary, 2010*. Retrieved from http://www.opensecrets.org/lobby/indusclient.php?id=a02&year=2010
11. Gamepolitics.com. *Report: ESA Spent $3.9 Million in 2013 Fighting Against State and Federal Anti-Videogame Legislation, Lobbying*. Retrieved from www.gamepolitics.com/2013/12/11/report-esa-spent-39-million-2013-fighting-against-state-and-federal-anti-videogame-legisl#.U3H8wOjapDs
12. Elson, M. & Ferguson, C. J. (2013). Gun violence and media effects: Challenges for science and public policy. *The British Journal of Psychiatry, 203*(5), 322-324.
13. Video Game Voters Network. (n.d.) *About VGVN*. Retrieved from http://videogamevoters.org/about

14. Entertainment Software Association. (2015). *Essential Facts about Games and Violence.* Retrieved from http://www.theesa.com/wp-content/uploads/2015/02/ESA_EF_GamesandViolence.pdf
15. Katz, J. E. (2005). Individual rights advocacy in tobacco control policies: An assessment and recommendation. *Tobacco Control, 14,* 31-37.
16. Bushman, B. J. & Anderson, C. A. (2001). Media violence and the American public: Scientific facts versus media misinformation. *American Psychologist, 56*(6/7), 477-489.

54 - Aren't violent media the only kind worth consuming?

The Short Answer:

No! There's a misconception among many that the most popular or best-rated media all include action-packed violence. Similarly, there's a misconception that games, movies, and television shows with pro-social messages or which lack violence must be either boring or targeted toward small children. In reality, there are *countless* examples of popular media that are both incredibly engaging and well-received by audiences, despite having little to no violent content in them.

The Long Answer:

The logic behind this question is best be illustrated by a classic episode of the television show *The Simpsons*. In the episode "Marge be not Proud," 10-year-old Bart Simpson is desperate to get his hands on the season's most popular, and incredibly violent, video game: *Bonestorm*. The popularity of *Bonestorm* is shown throughout the episode: Bart's friend Milhouse has a copy, the comic book store has rented out all of its copies, and Bart even watches a mother buy *two* copies for her children (so they wouldn't have to share.) In contrast, on Christmas morning, Bart receives the non-violent game *Lee Carvallo's Putting Challenge*. The humor in the scene comes from the fact that the game is comically boring. In fact, the idea that this non-violent game is boring and unpopular is reflected throughout the episode, though exchanges such as this one[1]:

Bart: May I please rent [*Bonestorm*], *please*?

Comic Book Guy: No you may not. I am all out. Though I do have a surprising abundance of *Lee Carvallo's Putting Challenge*.

We, the audience, laugh at the scene because we recognize that this is how we think about prosocial and non-violent media. We think of violent media as action-packed, cool, exciting, and popular. We think of non-violent media as boring, bland, and designed to appeal to young children. As a result, parents and gamers alike often assume that a choice between violent and non-violent media is a choice between something exciting and something boring.

We hope to show you that this conception is false in many ways. First let's tackle the myth that non-violent media can't be suspenseful or contain action. To be sure, violence is a simple and effective way to create excitement in the viewer or player. For evolutionary reasons, seeing scenes of violence *automatically* gets our hearts pumping and puts us on-edge.[2,3] But just because violence is a reliable way to get cheap thrills doesn't mean there aren't other, arguably better ways to get thrills out of an audience.[a] For example, scenes that feature fast-paced racing (e.g., car races)[4], competition (e.g., sporting events)[5], or danger (e.g., natural disasters)[6] all evoke just as much excitement in viewers. In these cases, the excitement comes from feeling a sense of attachment to the characters and a desire to see good things happen to them (or a desire to see them avoid bad things happening to them). To name just a few examples, films like *A Beautiful Mind, Armageddon, Apollo 13, The Truman Show,* and *Titanic,* are all highly engaging, suspenseful, financially successful, and critically-acclaimed films despite containing relatively little violence.[b] If nothing else, they show that excitement and suspense can be caused by things *other* than violent content.

It's also worth noting that people watch television or play video games for many reasons other than to be thrilled or excited. For example, players of computer games are often driven by many desires, including the desire to improve their skills and to achieve goals, the desire to interact with others and be part of a team, and the desire to immerse themselves in novel situations[7]. None of these motivations requires violent content. Indeed, designers have crafted incredibly popular games that cater to many of these drives with minimal violent content. For example, 4 of the top 10 bestselling computer games (including the bestselling computer game of all time) contain little to no violence[8]. *Minecraft,* the bestselling computer game of all time, primarily focuses on harvesting resources, crafting items for survival, and creating elaborate structures and devices. In *The Sims,* players simulate the day-to-day lives of their own fictional characters, including designing their homes, choosing their careers, managing their needs, and guiding their relationships. *Garry's Mod* is a physics sandbox that allows players to create games, movies, characters, and worlds of their own using many of the tools available to game developers. *RollerCoaster Tycoon 3* tasks the player with building and managing a theme park.

A look at popular television similarly reveals that people use screen media for far more than just excitement and thrills. The popularity of channels like the *Food Network, Discovery Channel, Comedy Network,* and *Science Channel*[9] all show that people are drawn to content that doesn't necessarily contain violence. They may watch shows about cooking or home repair to improve their own skills or to inspire their creativity. Documentaries and shows about science expand their

---

[a] Online film critics Jay Bauman and Mike Stoklasa of Red Letter Media correctly point out that you can easily get excitement out of a movie audience just by making a loud, unexpected noise. This gets the heart rate going, but few would consider this to be fulfilling or even good cinema.

[b] And, it should be pointed out, the tension in these films does *not* come primarily from the violence in them!

minds and inspire their curiosity about the world around us. Comedy shows provide us with light-hearted and clever entertainment to improve our mood or help just help us to unwind after a day at work. In short, whether we're talking about films, video games, or television, entertainment media fulfill a lot of different needs for people, not just the desire to be titillated by violence.

But even if it *were* true that all non-violent media were designed with education or prosocial benefits first and recreation second, we believe they could still be enjoyable. An excellent example of this is the television show *Mythbusters*, which many[c] have credited with fostering a lifelong interest in science and engineering.[10] The show teaches viewers about scientific principles and engineering in an engaging way that doesn't involve on-screen violence. We can see similar examples in computer games like *Portal 2*, a bestselling first-person, physics-based puzzle-solving game. The game's multiplayer mode encourages teamwork and cooperation, requiring the two players to work together to successfully navigate through the courses. And although the players *can* actively sabotage one another, doing so generally means failing to progress – which actually makes the game more boring. In this way, a game like *Portal 2* may have positive effects (e.g., encouraging critical thinking and spatial reasoning) without being boring or designed solely to appeal to little children.

As a final point, it's worth remembering that decisions about violent media content don't have to be all-or-nothing. Although there are plenty of examples of well-designed, engaging, and popular non-violent media available, few people would want to eschew all violent media. There's something to be said for the occasional guns-blazing action-thriller movie. In Question #49 we discuss this point at length, but for now we'll simply say that it's possible to choose media that, while containing some violence, doesn't glamorize violence or make violence its central focus. Choosing to cut back on violent media exposure doesn't mean *only* playing games or watching films with prosocial or educational messages. It might simply mean trying games or shows that focus on exploration or creation instead of killing and destruction. It could also mean watching television shows where intrigue, drama, or comedy are the selling points instead of body counts and blood.

To put it another way: Don't throw out the violent media you love or feel like you're being pressured to only watch shows for kids. Instead, consider introducing games like *Minecraft* or television shows like *Mythbusters* into your media diet. Because let's face it: We're probably all better off if we cut down on the amount of *Bonestorm* we play, but none of us wants to be stuck playing *Lee Carvallo's Putting Challenge* forever either!

---

[c] This includes one of the authors, Courtney, who was inspired to pursue science in university thanks to his love of Mythbusters in high school and as an undergraduate student.

References
1. Scully, M. (Writer), & Moore, S. D. (Director). (1995, December 17). Marge be not Proud [Television series episode]. In B. Oakley & J. Weinstein (Producers), *The Simpsons*. Woodland Hills, CA: Film Roman.
2. Ballard, M. E. & Wiest, J. R. (1996). Mortal Kombat™: The effects of violent videogame play on males' hostility and cardiovascular responding. *Journal of Applied Social Psychology, 26*(9), 717-730.
3. Doob, A. N. & Kirshenbaum, H. M. (1973). The effects on arousal of frustration and aggressive films. *Journal of Experimental Social Psychology, 9*, 57-64.
4. Fischer, P., Greitemeyer, T., Morton, T., Kastenmüller, A., Postmes, T., Frey, D., Kubitzki, J., & Odenwälder, J. (2009). The racing-game effect: Why do video racing games increase risk-taking inclinations? *Personality and Social Psychology Bulletin, 35*(10), 1395-1409.
5. Wann, D. L., Melnick, M. J., Russell, G. W., & Pease, D. G. (2001). *Sports fans: The psychology and social impact of spectators*. New York: Routledge.
6. Cantor, J. (2002). Fright reactions to mass media. In J. Bryant, D. Zillmann, & M. B. Oliver (Eds.) *Media Effects: Advances in Theory and Research*, pp. 287. Mahwah, NJ: Lawrence Erlbaum Associates.
7. Yee, N. (2006). Motivations for play in online games. *CyberPsychology & Behavior, 9*(6), 772-775.
8. List of best-selling PC games. (n.d.). In *Wikipedia*. Retrieved September 16, 2018 from https://en.wikipedia.org/wiki/List_of_best-selling_PC_games
9. Maglio, T. (2014, December 23). 50 top cable entertainment channels of 2014 – From USA to IFC. *The Wrap*. Retrieved from http://www.thewrap.com/from-usa-to-ifc-the-top-50-cable-entertainment-channels-of-2014/
10. Eredoctoraten voor Mythbusters. (2011, July 1). *Aandrijftechniek*. Retrieved from https://www.at-aandrijftechniek.nl/branche/eredoctoraten-voor-mythbusters/15691/

55 - What makes violent media so appealing to youth?

The Short Answer:

It's likely a combination of three things. First, violent media are often exciting and engaging, making them attention-getting and hard to ignore. Second, youth in particular like to test boundaries, including doing things that scare them. Violent media provide youth with a way to approach their own fear and disgust boundaries in a relatively safe way. It's a way to test and expand their control over their environment, and it provides a way to gain stature within their peer networks. Third, we live in a society that tends to glamorize violence (e.g., heroic soldiers, lovable action film stars), which may well add to the desirability of violent media.

The Long Answer:

As we point out in Question #54, it's hard to escape the feeling that violent things are "cool," while non-violent things are boring, childish, and lame. As a result, many parents find themselves dealing with the fact that their children are drawn to violent media like moths to a flame, despite their best efforts otherwise. This can be incredibly frustrating for parents, since the desirability of violent media to children only makes the task of keeping it out of their hands that much tougher. This leads to the present question: Why do children seem to be so darned attracted to the violent media we'd rather keep them away from?

Chances are, you already have a pretty good idea of at least one of the reasons. To demonstrate it, let's imagine that you've been asked to house-sit for a friend while they're away. As you tidy up, you notice something on the coffee table: A partially-open folder with the words "Confidential: Do Not Read" written on the front. Be honest – what's your *very first* impulse? If you're like most people, the first thing that comes to mind is an insatiable curiosity to know what's in the folder. To give you credit, you just might override that impulse and respect your friend's privacy. But, deep down, let's be honest: You were tempted to look in the folder, weren't you? Funnily enough, we probably wouldn't have thought about looking in the folder if it didn't tell us explicitly *not* to do it!

This phenomenon is known to psychologists as reactance[1]. In simple terms, we like feeling free and in control of our own behavior, and we'd like it to stay that way. When something comes along that tries to restrict our freedom, this bothers us. We react to such attempts to limit our freedom by reasserting our freedom. Even if we didn't *want* to do the behavior that's being restricted in the first place, the fact that something is restricting our freedom suddenly makes the behavior *far* more desirable. Why? Because doing that behavior allows us to reassert our freedom, to reassure ourselves – and others – that *we're* in control.

That's why we want to read the folder so badly: We're not going to let our behavior be determined by a stupid folder, are we? This is also where the so-called *boomerang effect*, or what people commonly call "reverse psychology," comes from: When you tell people *not* to do something, it paradoxically makes them more likely to do it.[a]

Now, let's apply the phenomenon of psychological reactance to children and adolescents, keeping in mind that adolescents are people who are in the process of trying to assert their independence from their parents and, as such, are especially high in psychological reactance to begin with[2]. Imagine a 16-year old sees an advertisement for a popular shooter video game or an upcoming horror movie. They may only have a passing interest in whatever the game or the film is about. Now imagine that you, as their parent, tell them "Don't even ask – you're not old enough for that yet." Based on our understanding of psychological reactance, we *know* that this phrase has just given the game or film a *lot* more value to the teenager, because it's no longer *just* a game or a film. Now it's "forbidden fruit,"[3] a symbol of the teenager's control over their own actions. Scientific studies confirm this idea: When told that a film is prohibited for someone their age, children are *far* more likely to want to watch it than if they're told it's appropriate for *all* ages[3]. This is also related to feelings of control and competence in youth. Youth love to be scared, but primarily in contexts in which they have some control and in which the danger isn't real. Violent media provides those sorts of opportunities for them. What's more, violent media use becomes a sort of badge of honor among one's peers. Who has (or hasn't) played the latest, greatest, bloodiest game? Among boys, at least, there's status to be gained from being able to "get away with it," and status to be lost from being the only one among your friends whose parents wouldn't let you play or watch it.

Reactance can explain much of the desirability of violent media for children. But let's discuss a few additional factors that may add to this desirability. For example: Violent movies and games are, almost by definition, exciting and even scary. It seems a bit strange to imagine a *boring* shootout or an uninteresting fist-fight (that's not to say that some are less interesting than others, of course). Couple this with the fact that violence is inherently exciting (it wouldn't be in our best interest, from an evolutionary standpoint, if we didn't pay attention when violence was going on around us) and with the fact that violent action films tend

---

[a] On the internet, this is famously known as the *Streisand Effect*, named after actress Barbara Streisand. By attempting to suppress photographs of her mansion from being shown on the internet, she inadvertently drew widespread attention to it. As news of her attempts to suppress the images spread, hundreds of thousands of people went out of their way to view the images, people who probably wouldn't have cared about Barbara Streisand's mansion if not for her insistence that the photographs not be posted online.

to have higher budgets than most other films[b] (and make up many of the most expensive films of all time).[4] The result is a film or video game that's slick, eye-catching, and attention-holding. When you put it this way, it makes sense why violence-filled media are so appealing for children and adolescents – their attention systems don't stand a chance against so much stimulation! This is especially true when you consider that the attentional "muscles" of youth are still weak.[5] Films and games with over-the-top action are the best-suited to hold their attention, with everything else seeming boring by comparison.

A final reason for the particularly attractive nature of violent media to children is the fact that they are raised in a culture that glamorizes violence. In news reports and documentaries, as well as in entertainment media, soldiers and police officers and violent characters are often held up as paragons of heroism and bravery. Acts of valor usually involve violent actions (e.g., killing a violent offender, attacking a group of enemy soldiers), and are the sorts of behaviors that earn people accolades and awards. In many instances, athletes and actors are often made famous for their aggression – whether it's *WWE* superstar John Cena or action film stars Arnold Schwarzenegger and The Rock. Kids often learn what society values by looking at the people who become famous and, just as important, the actions they took to get there. If wrestlers and action movie stars rise to fame and fortune by being fearless and attacking other people, that makes aggression and violence seem like a good thing. And when a child sees a film featuring their favorite action film star, or which portrays soldiers or police officers saving the day by going after the bad guys, it's hard to imagine how they can see aggression as anything *but* cool and desirable.

To summarize – violent media may be particularly attractive to youth both because of the misconception that non-violent media are undesirable and because violent media are often seen as (and designed to be) enticing. Being told that you're not allowed to view media violence may play a big role in its attractiveness to children, but other factors like their attention-grabbing nature and association with heroism and celebrity certainly don't make them *less* appealing.

References
1. Brehm, S. S. & Brehm, J. W. (1981). *Psychological Reactance: A Theory of Freedom and Control.* New York: Wiley.
2. Grandpre, J., Alvaro, E. M., Burgoon, M., Miller, C. H., & Hall, J. R. (2003). Adolescent reactance and anti-smoking campaigns: A theoretical approach. *Health Communication, 15*(3), 349-366.

---

[b] Much of which is devoted to stunts, explosions, and other eye-candy, many of which instinctively attract our attention – something called the *orientation response* in psychology.

3. Bushman, B. J. & Stack, A. D. (1996). Forbidden fruit versus tainted fruit: Effects of warning labels on attraction to television violence. *Journal of Experimental Psychology: Applied, 2*(3), 207-226.
4. List of most expensive films. (n.d.). In *Wikipedia.* Retrieved August 30, 2016 from https://en.wikipedia.org/wiki/List_of_most_expensive_films
5. Klenberg, L., Korkman, M., & Lahti-Nuuttila, P. (2001). Differential development of attention and executive functions in 3- to 12-year old Finnish children. *Developmental Neuropsychology, 20*(1), 407-428.

56 - What is your advice regarding public policy?

The Short Answer:

When it comes down to it, we – the authors – are scientists, not lawmakers or politicians. We provide information about how human brains learn and work (that is, data and scientific explanations) to help lawmakers, parents, and users of media make informed decisions. Research may tell us that violent media increase the user's risk of aggression, but as researchers it's not our place to tell people what they should do with this information. We believe that it's important to let people make their own decisions in an *informed* manner, fully aware of all the risks and benefits. The only suggestions we make focus on ensuring that people are given an honest and accurate picture about what the research on violent media says so that they can make good decisions for themselves. As researchers and consumers of media ourselves, we have no interest in trying to block or censor media for anyone. However, we *do* object to misrepresentations of science in the news media (including internet-based media) and even occasionally in poorly-reviewed scientific sources; such misrepresentations mislead parents and the general public and prevent them from making truly informed decisions.

The Long Answer:

In Question #3, we dispelled the misconception that media violence researchers are people who have a bone to pick with violent media. People erroneously assume that violent media researchers are on a crusade to rid the world of violent media, trying to get films, shows, or games censored. Likewise, people are largely misinformed about what the research on media violence actually says, something which is perfectly encompassed in Justice Antonin Scalia's opinion on the Supreme Court case Brown v. Entertainment Merchants Association[1]. The case involved a California law, sponsored by and voted on by politicians, which imposed fines on stores that were caught selling mature-rated video games to minors. The video game industry (e.g., the Entertainment Software Association and the Entertainment Merchant's Association) wanted to overturn this law on several grounds, most notably its violation of the right to free speech. As the case went on, one of this book's authors, Craig, was called upon as an expert witness to explain the state of media violence research to the court. The Supreme Court – a group of legal scholars, not scientists – did not consider the research findings to be strong enough to justify censorship[1]. Justice Scalia wrote:
"California relies primarily on the research of Dr. Craig Anderson and a few other research psychologists whose studies purport to show a connection between exposure to violent video games and harmful effects on children... They

383

do not prove that violent video games *cause* minors to *act* aggressively... They show at best some correlation between exposure to violent entertainment and miniscule real-world effects, such as children's feeling more aggressive or making louder noises in the few minutes after playing a violent game than after playing a nonviolent game."

For the moment, let's ignore Justice Scalia's gross misunderstanding and misrepresentation of the media violence literature (see Questions #11, #13, #15, and #16 for counterarguments to his points). After all, as we've mentioned, Supreme Court Justices are *not* scientists, and therefore lack the qualifications to critically assess the state of a field of research, just as psychologists are not experts in legal matters.

Instead, let's focus on the fact that Craig was called upon in the first place to speak about media violence research in a case about *free speech*. Whether or not scientists had found evidence of media violence effects is actually irrelevant: The question came down to whether or not video games are so different from other media to not have full first amendment rights. The court realized that games, like other media, are a form of speech and therefore have Constitutional protection. This case wasn't decided on the strength of the research evidence.

Nonetheless, because of this case, media violence researchers came to be associated with a "pro-censorship" position, because the state of California called upon Craig to explain the state of media violence research. It's an odd position, given that the law wasn't about censoring or banning games at all. It just said stores shouldn't sell violent games to children without parent approval.

To further demonstrate the way the "debate" has distorted public perception, websites and articles frequently refer to Craig as an "anti-violent video game professor"[2]. Interestingly enough, this is despite the fact that, when Craig was initially asked to sign the Amicus brief that argued for supporting the state of California's position, he declined, instead offering to work with Douglas to head up a group of media violence experts in writing a statement about the scientific evidence. This statement was included as an appendix in the Amicus brief, not in the brief itself. Nevertheless, due to the case, he was branded as an "anti-violent video game professor."[a]

We'll make our stance on this issue crystal clear to avoid any confusion or room for misinterpretation: Scientists are scientists, and lawmakers are lawmakers. The two jobs are very different. The job of a scientist is to learn truths about the world through systematic study. Scientists tell us what is accurate, what is false, and what is unknown about the world. A scientist can tell us that violent media increases consumers' risk for aggression and they can tell us that reducing violent media exposure reduces this risk. Scientists *cannot* (nor should they) be able to tell

---

[a] As Craig frequently notes, he was playing violent video games before some of his harshest critics were born.

us whether we need to pass laws or policies about violent media.[b] Politicians, public policy makers, and legal scholars are best-suited to the job of crafting laws.

True, scientists, like everyone, have their own beliefs and political opinions. That said, most would almost certainly agree that their scientific expertise doesn't qualify them to decide whether a law is constitutional or whether a bill should be passed. The same "stay in your own lane" policy should be true of lawyers, judges, and other non-scientists. That is, Justice Scalia should not have pretended to understand the research or acted as though he had the relevant knowledge and skill set to be able to weigh in on its validity. Instead, he (and the other majority judges) attacked the scientific field while ignoring the fact that virtually every major scientific body that has reviewed the research literature has concluded that media violence is a significant causal risk factor.

Think about it another way: Most of us would agree that medical doctors are among the most qualified people to study and determine whether eating junk food is bad for our health. But just because doctors find evidence that junk food is bad for our health doesn't mean that we should pass laws banning junk food. In fact, although doctors would probably recommend that we all eat less junk food, most would probably *oppose* laws banning the sale of junk food. And even if they did think such laws would be a good idea, we can all agree that it's not their job to pass laws. We entrust judges, politicians, and experts in public policy to make those decisions. And, in return, we don't expect judges to weigh in on what medical researchers have to say.

For these reasons, we're quite hesitant to make any policy recommendations about violent media. We're not legal scholars, nor are we public policy experts. We don't claim to know better than consumers or parents about what is an acceptable amount of risk for them or for their children. Like any other person, we have personal beliefs and preferences concerning the best ways to address media violence, but we have never publicly supported or opposed specific laws on this topic, precisely because we believe that scientific statements should be kept separate from our personal preferences regarding policy. So, instead of proposing laws, policies, or restrictions,[c] we believe it's more appropriate for us to summarize several important points about media violence and its implications. From there, we leave it up to consumers, parents, and lawmakers to decide for themselves what's appropriate for them.

Point #1: Most people probably agree that aggressive behavior – trying to harm another person – is an undesirable thing in most contexts, both for individuals

---

[b] Scientists *can* provide expert evidence on which policies are likely to have the intended effects and which are unlikely to do so, but U.S. lawmakers rarely seek such input.

[c] Which would almost *certainly* be taken out of context and used to "prove" that we're out to try to push an agenda!

and for society as a whole. Although it's sometimes necessary to use aggression, the world would be a better place if it had less harassment, bullying, hurtful gossip, and physical aggression.

Point #2: Violent media have been consistently shown to be a risk factor for aggression, regardless of whether the medium is television, films, or video games[3-13]. Critics may challenge how to interpret these effects (e.g., are they strong enough be of practical concern), or may take issue with the methods or measures used in particular studies. But ultimately, decades of research from hundreds of researchers around the world have converged on this conclusion, one that is consistent with what psychologists know about how human beings learn, store and access information, and how people respond to stimuli in our environment. Don't just take our word for it. Many of the top public health and scientific organizations have reviewed the evidence and concluded that media violence *cause* aggression in society. These organizations include the American Medical Association, the American Academy of Pediatrics, and the National Institutes of Health, among many others.

Point #3: People make decisions every day about how much risk they're willing to take: whether it's about serious risks, like deciding to smoke, drinking alcohol, riding a bicycle without a helmet, or engaging in risky sexual behavior, or about more mundane risks like driving, eating junk food, or sunbathing. Unless the costs to society as a whole are too high, we believe that these are decisions that adults should be free to make for themselves.

Point #4: When it comes to making decisions, most people would agree that they're better off making informed decisions rather than being ignorant about the consequences of their actions. If you're buying a house, you're better off knowing about the pros and cons of this house rather than blindly signing on the dotted line. Those who smoke or drink are better off knowing that these activities have risks associated with them rather than being blindsided by the consequences of these risks years later. As long as some people may decide, based on information about these activities, that the risks make the activity not worth it, it's important to make this information known to people.

Point #5: Freedom and autonomy are valuable and, all things equal, we'd prefer to not restrict them unless absolutely necessary. Ideally, we would prefer to give people the information they need to make informed decisions and let them choose for themselves, rather than censoring or prohibiting something – which is effectively making decisions for them. Even if you want to argue that it's for their own good, factors such as psychological reactance and the "boomerang effect" suggest that banning activities can be unwise (see Question #55).[d]

Point #6: We, as a society, have generally agreed that children are less able than adults to make informed decisions about their own behavior, especially when it comes to risky activities (e.g., drinking alcohol, smoking, driving cars). As such, we rely on parents (and only in rare occasions, the state) to make decisions about risky behaviors on behalf of children. It's important for people who are entrusted to make decisions for others to have access to *accurate* information about the risks involved so that they can make informed decisions. It's also important that they have the tools to put their decisions into action, such as better rating systems based on science and expertise, not on what a profit-driven industry decides is acceptable.

Although not every media researcher will agree with all of these points, as a set of guidelines we believe that these are defensible. None of these guidelines dictate what laws should or should not contain, nor do they state whether there *ought* to be laws at all. Instead, they recognize that violent media are a modest risk factor, just like many other risk factors we confront in our day-to-day lives. How you, as an individual, and we, as a society, choose to accept, reject, or reduce that risk is a non-scientific question. We humbly believe that when it comes to making these decisions, you're better off knowing that the risk exists rather than pretending – or being misled into believing – that it doesn't.

References
1. Brown, Governor of California, et al., v. Entertainment Merchant's Association et al., 564 U. S. 768 (2011, June 27).
2. Masnick, M. (2011). Supreme Court says anti-violent video game law violates the first amendment. *techdirt*. Retrieved from https://www.techdirt.com/articles/20110627/11000414873/supreme-court-says-anti-violent-video-game-law-violates-first-amendment.shtml
3. Anderson, C. A., Shibuya, A., Ihori, N., Swing, E. L., Bushman, B. J., Sakamoto, A., Rothstein, H. R., & Saleem, M. (2010). Violent video game effects on aggression, empathy, and prosocial behavior in Eastern and Western countries. *Psychological Bulletin, 136,* 151-173.
4. Andison, F. S. (1977). TV Violence and Viewer Aggression: A Cumulation of Study Results 1956-1976. *Public Opinion Quarterly, 41,* 314-331.

---

[d] If nothing else, the lessons of the prohibition era should be enough to convince people that banning something can have serious unintended consequences.

5. Hearold, S. (1986). A synthesis of 1043 effects of television on social behavior. In G. Comstock (Ed.), *Public Communication and Behavior, 1,* 65-133. New York: Academic Press.
6. Wood, W., Wong, F., & Cachere, J. (1991). Effects of media violence on viewers' aggression in unconstrained social interaction. *Psychological Bulletin, 109*(3), 371-383.
7. Hogben, M. (1998). Factors moderating the effect of television aggression on viewer behavior. *Communication Research, 25,* 220-247.
8. Savage, J., & Yancey, C. (2008). The effects of media violence exposure on criminal aggression: A meta-analysis. *Criminal Justice and Behavior, 35,* 772-791.
9. Paik, H., & Comstock, G. (1994). The effects of television violence on antisocial behavior: A meta-analysis. *Communication Research, 21*(4), 516-546.
10. Sherry, J. (2001). The effects of violent video games on aggression: A meta-analysis. *Human Communication Research, 27,* 409-431.
11. Ferguson, C. J. (2015). Do angry birds make for angry children? A meta-analysis of video game influences on children's and adolescents' aggression, mental health, prosocial behavior, and academic performance. *Perspectives on Psychological Science, 10*(5), 646-666.
12. Ferguson, C. J. (2007). Evidence for publication bias in video game violence effects literature: A meta-analytic review. *Aggression and Violent Behavior, 12,* 470-482.
13. Greitemeyer, T., & Mügge, D. O. (2014). Video games do affect social outcomes: A meta-analytic review of the effects of violent and prosocial video game play. *Personality and Social Psychology Bulletin, 40*(5), 578-589.

Conclusion

57 - What's the "take-home" message of this book?

The Short Answer:

Media violence effects are neither a monolithic doom nor non-existent. Among the general public, the issue has become polarized in an all-or-nothing fashion. We're told by the media industries that we either need to a) believe that violent media are turning children into killers and therefore demand that the government pass censorship laws, or b) believe that violent media have absolutely no effect on users and that anyone who says otherwise hates video games, TV, and movies and is doing biased science because they're fomenting a "moral panic" (a claim critics make with no evidence). What's worse, some people have tied their identities – and sometimes their careers – to this issue, making it impossible for either side to give any ground for fear of repercussions. If nothing else, this book is a call for a sensible, moderate stance: It's possible to acknowledge that violent media are a risk factor for undesirable behavior while still being allowed to consume it. It's possible to acknowledge that media violence studies (like all studies) have flaws without throwing out over six decades of research on the subject. It's possible for parents to make decisions about their children's media diet in ways that are neither recklessly permissive nor unreasonably restrictive. By avoiding both panic and denialism, we believe it's possible to have a rational and productive discussion about media violence.

The Long Answer:

For years, the violent media debate has been polarized. This polarization has served the violent media industries quite well because it prevents action by both consumers and politicians. Because of this polarization, discussion of media violence effects has become a ridiculous all-or-nothing affair. At the extremes, both sides are laughably improbable: One the one hand, violent media are claimed to turn normal well-adjusted children into mass killers. On the other hand, it is claimed that main-stream media violence researchers are conspiring to create a "moral panic" so that they can censor violent media, and that they somehow profit from doing so. Even worse, some people at both extremes have staked their personal identities and careers on the issue:

1. Parents fear that if they acknowledge that violent media effects exist, people might think they're horrible people for letting their children consume violent content.

2. Gamers deny media effects because they think scientists are attacking them personally, feel personally threatened by the possibility that their gaming history and habits have actually harmed themselves, and worry that people will try to ban or censor their favorite hobby.

3. The entertainment industry denies media effects for fear that acknowledging any adverse effects will threaten their sales or lead to laws restricting their products. Further, like gamers, they feel personally threatened by the thought that their products and life's work may actually harm consumers.

4. Lawyers and politicians have built their careers on one position in the media violence debate; adopting a moderate position might be seen as a sign of weakness or failure and discredit them altogether. Judges in the U.S. in particular are reluctant to rule in favor of any law that might later be overturned on the basis of free speech rights.

In other words, a lot of people have a lot to lose on this issue. This creates fear about what might happen if they were to take half a step back and adopt a moderate position on the issue.

Ultimately the issue of media violence effects is *not* a matter of public debate or opinion: It is, first and foremost, a scientific question. The data overall are clear: Violent media exposure is a risk factor for aggression. As we've discussed in Chapters 1 and 2, more than half a century of research converges on the conclusion that being exposed to violent media increases a person's risk for behaving aggressively. This conclusion is not the result of statistical fluke, an unusual study, or a weird measure causing these effects by coincidence. There *are* several important caveats in this conclusion, which critics of violent media are correct to point out. Violent media effects can be subtle, and they're certainly not the biggest known risk factor for inappropriate (and sometimes illegal) aggressive behavior (although they're also not the smallest). The effects of violent media are more likely to be seen in mundane, day-to-day forms of aggression rather than extreme violent or criminal behavior (although there is some evidence of significant effects on these as well). Violent media research, like any field of research, is not without its flaws and limitations (but the convergence of evidence across study types has done a good job of addressing these weaknesses).

It's possible to reconcile the "media violence effects exist" position with the "no they don't" position of critics without dismissing either one. Critics should acknowledge the fact that violent media effects are both consistent with other well-established psychological principles (e.g., learning, desensitization, cognitive priming) and that they've been well-supported by more than half a century of research from scientists across disciplines and from around the world. Proponents of violent media effects, on the other hand, would do well to listen to their critics to ensure that they continually improve upon existing methods while not losing sight of the modest size of these effects.

To put it another way, wouldn't it be nice to avoid throwing the baby out with the bathwater while *also* acknowledging that there's bathwater needing to be dealt with in the first place?

If the issue is a scientific one, what advice can we, as scientists, offer to lawmakers, parents, and gamers alike? The answer is simple, something we've done throughout this book: Treat "violent media exposure" the same way you treat "junk food." Most of us acknowledge that junk food is bad for us, and intuitively recognize that a person who eats too much junk food is at greater risk for undesirable health consequences than a person who only rarely eats junk food. As a culture, most of us can accept these principles, despite the fact that:

1. Most of us *do* eat junk food, probably more than we should.

2. There's no single "silver bullet" experiment definitively *proving* that eating junk food *causes* extremely poor outcomes, like death.

3. Other things besides junk food can cause poor health outcomes.

4. The effects of junk food on health are slow and subtle – We can't see the effects of a single snack cake or deep-fried candy bar on our health in real time.

For those of us who eat junk food, we know that we're doing so at our own risk. We don't have to deny that junk food is bad for us or accuse dieticians of having hidden agendas or hating junk food. We've decided for ourselves that the risk is small enough to for us to accept. Acknowledging these risks helps us recognize and tackle health-related issues in our society such like obesity and chronic heart disease while also avoiding draconian laws that forbid the sale of junk food.

One final comment on the junk food analogy: We should acknowledge that the harmful consequences of eating junk food are not borne solely by heavy (pun intended) consumers of such food. Their health issues (e.g., obesity, Type II diabetes…) cost society as well, most obviously in terms of health care costs, but also in lost wages and in a variety of less quantifiable ways. In other words, society at large *does* have a stake in the amount of junk food we collectively consume. Similarly, there are societal costs of high exposure to media violence. At present, those costs are not as easily calculated as the costs of obesity, but they certainly aren't zero. Whether they are large enough to warrant legal action is, as

392

we noted in Question #56, outside of our expertise, and so we offer no public policy advice for what we should do about it. But at very least, we can say that we're better off acknowledging that this cost exists, however big or small, rather than pretending that it doesn't.

In the end, we would like to see discussions about media violence change directions. We want to see it go from a shouting match with extreme positions to a discussion about what we can do to minimize this modest risk. We would like to move people away from extreme and impractical courses of action, like trying to cut funding to media violence research or trying to censor or ban violent games. And when it comes to parents and media consumers, we'd like to be able to offer moderate, practical solutions: Don't throw away your kid's violent games or feel like a bad person if you watch the occasional violent TV show. Instead, focus on the small, gradual changes you can introduce to improve your and your children's media diets by cutting back a bit on how *much* violent media is being consumed and consider less violent alternatives you might have otherwise overlooked.

It's about time we had a sensible discussion about media violence. And, if you've taken the time to read this book, we look forward to hearing your contribution to that conversation.

Made in the USA
Columbia, SC
20 May 2021

38136379R00222